THE U'
WIN

D1388063

WITHDRAWN FROM
THE LIBRARY

UNIVERSITY OF
WINCHESTER

KA 0362476 5

Frontier Feminist

Frontier Feminist

Clarina Howard Nichols and the Politics of Motherhood

Marilyn S. Blackwell and
Kristen T. Oertel

UNIVERSITY PRESS OF KANSAS

UNIVERSITY OF WINCHESTER
LIBRARY

© 2010 by the University Press of Kansas
All rights reserved

Published by the University Press of Kansas (Lawrence, Kansas 66045), which
was organized by the Kansas Board of Regents and is operated and funded by
Emporia State University, Fort Hays State University, Kansas State University,
Pittsburg State University, the University of Kansas, and Wichita State University

Library of Congress Cataloging-in-Publication Data

Blackwell, Marilyn S.
    Frontier feminist : Clarina Howard Nichols and the politics of motherhood /
Marilyn S. Blackwell and Kristen T. Oertel.
       p.   cm.
    Includes bibliographical references and index.
    ISBN 978-0-7006-1728-9 (cloth : acid-free paper)
    1. Nichols, C. I. H., Mrs. 2. Women social reformers—United States—Biography.
3. Feminists—United States—Biography. 4. Suffragists—United States—
Biography. 5. Women's rights—United States—History—19th century. 6. United
States—Territorial expansion—Social aspects. I. Oertel, Kristen Tegtmeier, 1969–
II. Title.
    HQ1413.N52B53 2010
    305.42092—dc22
    [B]   2010026288

British Library Cataloguing-in-Publication Data is available.

Printed in the United States of America

10 9 8 7 6 5 4 3 2 1

The paper used in this publication is recycled and contains 30 percent
postconsumer waste. It is acid free and meets the minimum requirements of
the American National Standard for Permanence of Paper for Printed Library
Materials Z39.48-1992.

UNIVERSITY OF WINCHESTER

03624765

For our children

CONTENTS

ACKNOWLEDGMENTS

One of the most gratifying aspects of collaboration is the sense of shared endeavor authors experience during years of painstaking research and lively conversation. Originating from different historical interests—in Vermont and in Kansas—our partnership arose out of the path Clarina Howard Nichols pursued across the nation and a common desire to write women into the historical memory of American political life. Beyond our joint authorship, this book is the product of a larger community of feminist scholars, state and local historians, and myriad archivists dedicated to recovering and preserving records of women's lives. It could not have been written without them, and we are grateful for their support and encouragement.

In common, we are most indebted to key individuals who identified Clarina Howard Nichols as an extraordinary woman and carefully preserved her words. Descendant Patricia Rabinovitz was responsible for collecting Nichols's private papers; Vermont historian Thomas D. Seymour Bassett assured that she would be included in *Notable American Women;* and most important, Joseph G. Gambone, former archivist at the Kansas State Historical Society, spent years retrieving and scrutinizing obscure newspapers before publishing her papers in *Kansas Historical Quarterly.* Without his detective work this book would have taken twice as long to complete. Librarians and archivists at both the Kansas State Historical Society in Topeka and the Grace Hudson Museum in Ukiah, California, deserve particular thanks for their help in guiding us through local collections and for permission to use photographic reproductions. We especially thank curator Karen Holmes, who carefully preserved Nichols's family artifacts and photos and generously offered her professional expertise and knowledge of descendants in Ukiah. Finally, we appreciate the valuable feedback from those who agreed to read part or all of the manuscript, including Diane Eickhoff, Carol Faulkner, Wendy Venet, and anonymous readers for the University Press of Kansas. Our separate thanks appear below.

———

Once I embarked on the trail of Clarina Howard Nichols I encountered a handful of people who have made this biography a truly collaborative effort. In addition to Kristen Oertel, no one was more helpful than Diane Eickhoff. From the day she phoned me nearly ten years ago, to the completion of her biography of Nichols, *Revolutionary Heart,* Diane has shown me what it means to share scholarly endeavor. She generously offered the fruits of her research, introduced me to local experts in Kansas, and acted as host, tour guide, and consultant. She referred me to descendants Juanita Johnson and Janice Parker, to whom I am grateful for early photographs of Nichols. Along with Diane's husband, Aaron Barnhart, who provided both technical assistance and cheerleading, she deserves my gratitude and respect.

Local historians and archivists are often key to finding the undiscovered sources that flesh out a life story. I am especially grateful to the late Tom Bassett, former curator of Special Collections at the University of Vermont, who saw merit in documenting women's history and Nichols's life before the advent of late twentieth-century feminist scholarship. An inspiration and mentor, he generously gave me his invaluable research notes covering two decades. In Tiz Garfield of Townshend, Vermont, I found an indefatigable researcher and generous host, who provided important photographs and steered me to local archives. She and members of the Townshend Historical Society recovered Nichols's memory locally and ensured she would be properly honored with a state historic marker. I am also indebted to John Carnahan of Brattleboro for his research assistance, his graciousness as a host and local sponsor, and his enthusiasm for my historical projects. In addition, Paul Carnahan, librarian at the Vermont Historical Society, offered leads and eagerly acquired a rare Nichols letter. Thanks also to Joan Marr, curator at the Historical Society of Windham County, who retrieved obscure local records from the depths of the society's archive; to the staff at the Schlesinger Library, Radcliffe Institute for Advanced Study; and to John Nichols of Wyandot Nation of Kansas Archives.

I am grateful to colleagues who listened patiently to stories about Nichols and willingly read unwieldy chapter drafts. Rebecca Davison, Woden Teach-out, Linda Gray, and Becky Noel asked probing questions and offered wise stylistic advice; Melanie Gustafson, Faye Dudden, and Thomas J. Mertz expanded my understanding of women in politics; members of the lively 2007 Summer Seminar on biography at the Schlesinger Library, especially Megan Marshall, encouraged me to convert this historical research into a character study. I am indebted to the late biographer Deborah Clifford, whose books inspired me and who lent both her expertise and her encouragement to my pursuit of an elusive subject.

Finally, my husband Edward, who has endured my preoccupation with Clarina and her religious imagination for nearly a decade, deserves credit for his patience and ever-ready support.

—Marilyn Schultz Blackwell

My first thanks must go to Lyn Blackwell for inviting me to join her in this project over five years ago. On the long road to publication, when my personal and professional life impeded our collective progress, she graciously adjusted our drafting schedule and shouldered the bulk of the workload, as I sat encumbered with crying babies, tenure interviews, and book deadlines. Her selfless and tireless work on the manuscript never ceased to amaze me, and her patient understanding of my life's many challenges repeatedly warmed my heart.

Lyn knew about my work on Nichols in part because Virgil Dean solicited me to write a short biographical essay for his anthology, *John Brown to Bob Dole: Movers and Shakers in Kansas History,* and I am grateful for Virgil's steadfast support of this full-length biography. Several colleagues—Kristen Brown Golden, Laura Franey, and members of the Millsaps WIP group— read parts of early drafts, and I thank them for their insightful comments and encouragement. Student Susan Hoerauf worked diligently on the bibliography, and the dean's office at Millsaps College awarded me release time for research and writing. I must also thank the teachers and childcare providers at the Privette School for providing kind and meaningful care for my children, and my Jackson neighbors for embodying the "it takes a village" mantra. Clarina had Eagleswood and her Townshend relatives; I had Privette, Millsaps, and my friends and neighbors.

Finally, I must express my deep gratitude to my husband, Bob, who embodies all the qualities of what Clarina called a "sympathizing friend," a co-equal partner in life and love.

—Kristen Tegtmeier Oertel

INTRODUCTION: REMEMBERING A "FORGOTTEN FEMINIST"

> I would like my picture to strike the reader as a womanly, motherly body.
> *C. I. H. Nichols, 1880*

Shortly before she died, Clarina Irene Howard Nichols hoped to capture the essence of her historical legacy with a portrait of herself as one of the pioneering mothers of the woman's rights movement. It was an image she had carefully cultivated during her career as a journalist and reformer. As a mother of four and defender of the home, she had spread a gospel of temperance, woman's rights, and free soil from Vermont to Kansas to California. Known as an "able writer and speaker" who could cite legal codes as well as "any judge or lawyer," she had secured "liberal laws" for women in Kansas. Her friend Susan B. Anthony sought desperately to procure such a motherly engraving of Nichols for the monumental *History of Woman Suffrage* and subsequently devoted an entire chapter to her memoir, noting that Nichols was "a large-hearted, brave, faithful woman, and her life speaks for itself."[1]

Indeed, Nichols's reminiscences, published only a few years before her death, ensured that the next generation of activists would not forget this pioneering feminist. Through the *History* and the efforts of memorialist Mary Tenney Gray, women in Kansas and worldwide could learn about Nichols's political adventures on the frontier. Gray, who witnessed Nichols's performance at the Kansas Constitutional Convention, pictured her for the International Council of Women as a "slender, middle-aged woman . . . of clear searching eyes and a high brow," sitting patiently with her knitting and "busy with pencil or pen" while plotting political change. Here was an authentic pioneer who had traveled "from her home three miles . . . daily, on horseback" and suffered the "scorching July days" to become "guardian of the laws for Kansas women."[2] In 1907 Clara Bewick Colby, editor of the *Woman's Tribune*, radicalized Nichols's motherly image by equating her with Charles Dickens's political revolutionary Madame Defarge, "who sat by the dreaded French tribunal working into her knitting the names of those who were the victims of the guillotine." Though Nichols was "serene where the Citizeness was violent, benign where she was . . . destructive," Nichols was "working into her stitches the rights of women," hoping to hold the "slippery politicians" to their promises by her silent presence. Like her fictional counterpart, Nichols was driven by righteous outrage at a political system created by powerful men, and she was determined to foment a democratic revolution, hiding her political skills in her knitting bag and under the veil of a mother's love.[3]

Yet by the late twentieth century, Nichols's name and reputation had receded in public memory. In the post-suffrage era, few accounts of the suffrage movement acknowledged Nichols's achievements. She initiated reforms in married women's legal rights in Vermont, and in Kansas she secured the first constitutional guarantee of school suffrage as well as property and custody rights. But these reforms were seen as only halfway measures on the long road to women's equality. Her maternalist rhetoric failed to resonate with most second-wave feminists, and her activities in Kansas were marginal in histories of the national movement focused on the eastern leadership. Considered by many historians to be a supportive but conservative—and therefore lesser—player in the antebellum movement, Nichols appeared briefly on stage as an effective speaker at national conventions and later resurfaced as a "veteran agitator" in Kansas.[4] Her profile was an exception to the prevailing interpretation of suffrage leaders like Lucy Stone and Lucretia Mott, who were radical abolitionists and defined the movement's ideology by linking it to the egalitarian rhetoric of the Revolutionary era; their talk of natural rights was far more potent for feminist scholars than Nichols's talk of mothers' rights.[5] Consequently, by the mid-1970s Kansas archivist Joseph Gambone, who edited her papers, noted a hole in the national story and dubbed Nichols the "Forgotten Feminist."[6]

If she fell between geographical and ideological cracks in histories of the national movement, Nichols did not completely disappear from local histories. Memorialists and local writers in Kansas and Vermont have periodically cast her as a singular and stalwart advocate for women, a foremother who blazed a trail of pre–Civil War activism. Biographers who highlighted her role in state history, however, offered a truncated version of either her Kansas or her Vermont career, without analyzing the totality of her experience.[7] Only in the past decade has Nichols's name reemerged in histories of women's antebellum political activities, suggesting the need for a reassessment of her contributions to the movement and to free-soil politics.[8] In addition, author Diane Eickhoff has reintroduced Nichols to the people of Kansas through her recent popular biography, *Revolutionary Heart,* which updates Nichols's feminist credentials as an inveterate storyteller who touched her audiences with a persistent and articulate voice for woman's rights.[9]

Although Nichols's profile has been on the rise in recent years, the significance of her achievements for the history of women's politics in the West is still not widely known. In this biography we have sought to connect the two major phases of her career and to assess her engagement in antebellum political culture. Nichols actively participated in two important interrelated developments in nineteenth-century American history: movements for social and political reform, and westward expansion. In creating a public voice and replanting her agenda on the frontier in Kansas, Nichols articulated the need to incorporate women into the national project of reforming and settling America. Part of a vanguard of activists who brought woman's rights to the West, her engagement in politics helps to refocus the history of the antebellum movement on the role suffragists played in the vigorous debates over slavery's extension and the impact of racial conflict on the ongoing struggle for women's legal and political rights.

Nichols's skill as a journalist carried her into the larger field of partisan politics, where she became an effective participant at a time when women were told to stay out of that "muddy pool." As editor of the *Windham County Democrat* in Brattleboro, Vermont, Nichols engaged in partisan debates in the 1840s, reincarnated herself as a reformer, and lobbied artfully for women's full citizenship by linking her plea for mothers' economic rights with suffrage. To that end, she developed a political style we call the *politics of motherhood.* "I want to have this power" to vote, she proclaimed, "because I am deprived of the power of protecting myself and my children. . . . I do not possess the power which ought to belong to me as a mother."[10] With knitting in hand, she fashioned a political identity out of the moral authority and respectability middle-class white women garnered in antebellum America. The hallmark of nineteenth-century womanhood, motherliness proved the selfless and feminine identity of political women and allowed them to successfully articulate public roles without being labeled a crowing hen or a "masculine brawler for rights."[11] Like a modern-day soccer mom presiding over the legislature,

Nichols ably negotiated the political gender divide, retaining her essential femininity and ethic of care while promoting a progressive political agenda.

Nichols was not the only woman of her day who constructed such an image, yet she was unusual in seeking to take advantage of the political opportunities available through westward migration. Her life span (1810–1885) nearly parallels the opening and apparent closing of the western American frontier.[12] When she left Brattleboro and a successful career in journalism and lecturing, Nichols launched her family on a now-familiar pathway across the nation in the mid-nineteenth century. As with so many settlers, she was motivated by the desire for economic opportunity and greater freedom, but she also viewed the West as a place where she could put her theories about temperance and woman's rights into practice. Territorial Kansas exposed her to a mixed-race community, ignited her abolitionist sympathies, and planted her in the middle of a quasi war over slavery and race.

In this chaos, Nichols harvested the fruits of her maternal image and made woman's rights seem both respectable and politically viable by effectively linking her claims to free-state politics. Having parlayed her moral authority into a role as a principled and formidable advocate for free soil, she used her reputation as a heroic defender of freedom in Kansas to harness her agenda to the bandwagon of progressive change in the territory. Both before and after the Civil War, woman suffrage became entwined with the myth of Kansas as a "martyred state" standing firmly for truth and justice against the advance of slavery across the nation.[13] Nichols's carefully crafted image dovetailed conveniently with the goals of free-state leaders and progressive Republicans, but women's full enfranchisement became embroiled in arguments over race and ultimately became a political liability rather than a party issue. Still, Nichols maintained her identity as one of the "mothers of Kansas," a moniker linked to the "strong-minded women" who bravely defended freedom in the territory. This was the persona she carried with her on her final journey to California, where she continued to tout the social value of motherhood as essential to the perfection of the nation.

In practicing this form of gender-based moral politics, Nichols coupled Yankee superiority with the zeal of a reformer eager to create an enlightened republicanism on the western landscape. The domestic and Christian values she touted were important signifiers of the moral benevolence and respectability women supposedly brought to an isolating and harsh environment, which also helped to ensure white settler dominance over Indian nations.[14]

As Nichols engaged in this so-called civilizing process, her womanly style of politics proved convincing to some free-state politicians. Genteel motherhood was emblematic of the stable social order they sought to implant in Kansas, and school suffrage appeared to be consistent with that goal.

Nichols's style of politics set a standard for other female activists who pursued a similar strategy in the second half of the nineteenth century, especially in Kansas, where they built upon her legacy.[15] Yet to say that her strategy was effective is not to imply that her experience in Kansas was typical of successful campaigns for enfranchisement in the West. The perception of white women as a benevolent and civilizing force on the frontier surfaced repeatedly in later debates over woman suffrage, but it apparently had less direct influence on outcomes than some historians originally assumed. The historical timing and the specific political context of these campaigns, including territorial status, unique party development, and class or racial concerns, had more impact on voter behavior than any single aspect of western culture.[16]

If Nichols's public career is recoverable, her private life is particularly elusive. She did not keep a diary, and most of her personal papers—sources that might have shed light on her inner thoughts and close relationships—were either lost or destroyed. Moreover, she purposely guarded her family life from public scrutiny and retained a self-conscious concern about her own legacy. Late in life, Nichols explained her nightmarish fears of unmasking to a Vermont historian: "Did you ever dream of finding yourself in respectable company denuded of your shoes and stockings, perhaps with your nightcap on your head; or that in dispersing you had unwittingly exchanged garments with a guest and were out of taste, or in—a fix?" Hoping to avoid an undressing, she appealed "as one sister may to another . . . against such a fate in your forthcoming History."[17] But she was also convinced of her importance, knowing her life was filled with "instructive and entertaining experiences" to inform "the thoughtful student of human nature!"[18] In the interest of bringing something of Nichols's character forward, we have mined her public writings for clues about her personal struggles, though much about her family life is simply unknowable. A consummate storyteller, she often used allegory, wit, and sarcasm to convey opinion, techniques that disguised her motives but also allowed her to create an identity as a public woman of integrity from her own authentic experience.

Our approach to biography has been informed by recent feminist scholarship highlighting the differences between male and female forms of expression and self-making and the connection between private and political behavior. Nichols used the prevailing language and cultural values of her world to assign meaning to her experience and to evaluate the impression she would make on others.[19] In antebellum New England, women were more likely to achieve a coherent self by actualizing ideal family roles. As daughters, wives, and mothers, they learned what was possible for a woman to accomplish in a lifetime, whether at home or within community. With few models of female political agency to follow, Nichols constructed a life of public activity intimately related to her private experience of marriage and motherhood. Secrecy about her past concealed the failure of her first marriage, which threatened her mothering capacity and her class standing.

These private experiences drove Nichols's reforming ethos and her critique of the marriage system as much as the collective ideologies that seeped into her consciousness, resulting in multiple contradictions. Evangelical Protestantism and the "cult of domesticity" were formative in shaping her belief in her responsibility to a Christian God, the sanctity of marriage, and her moral authority as a mother and member of the middle class in antebellum New England.[20] Yet she sought to escape the confines of home, secured a divorce, and eventually became a critic of church authorities. Hiding her personal grievances, Nichols struggled to overcome her vulnerability with a womanly and genteel persona while also advocating for legal and political rights that threatened to undermine the pillars on which she stood. Though she believed she was standing alone as a reformer, she continually sought the good opinion of others. Often righteous but rarely vengeful, she was diplomatic and patient with men, empathetic and gracious with women.

Nichols used the common cultural trope of "woman's sphere" to anchor herself and to glean public affirmation. The influence of middle-class white women on public opinion was largely rooted in this platform of private virtue and public benevolence. Sometimes referred to as *domestic feminism* and associated with Catherine Beecher and Sarah Josepha Hale, the standpoint opened a space for women's voices in civil society as the conscience of the nation.[21] Although Nichols and several other activists—notably Amelia Bloomer, Jane Grey Swisshelm, and Frances Dana Gage—exploited this form of female moral authority rhetorically, they surpassed Beecher and Hale, not only in their critiques of women's economic dependence within marriage but especially in their willingness to engage in reform politics.[22]

Nichols's pursuit of mothers' economic rights, rooted in her past experience, catapulted her beyond public benevolence into the woman's rights movement. Her claim was out of step with the discourse employed by leading antebellum feminists, if not with their chief demands. We have applied the term *feminist* to her generation of political activists because their grasp of female subordination and their goals aligned with movements to advance the status of women, even though the label was not employed until the early twentieth century. Linking their grievances to an American tradition of natural rights, they insisted that gender did not constitute a reason to deny women equal access to social, intellectual, economic, or political life. In lieu of patriarchy, they offered *co-equality*—meaning "simultaneously the same and different"—as an alternative system of gender relations in a liberal democracy and consciously avoided the rhetoric of female moral superiority in favor of an appeal to their natural rights to speak for their oppressed sisters.[23] More reluctant to abandon her essential femininity, Nichols spoke instead for helpless mothers and children and proffered her own version of co-equality. With her political identity rooted in the primacy of family relations, she recast motherhood as the basis of women's economic rights and full citizenship.

When Nichols brought her brand of women's politics to "Bleeding Kansas," she experienced a new freedom to express herself as politics invaded her household, melding personal and political life. After she witnessed electoral fraud, racially motivated violence, and the desperation of escaping slaves, universal rights became her mantra. Yet, like many New England reformers, she held romantic notions about homesteading on the frontier and shaping progressive laws in virgin territory that had little basis in reality.[24] Not only did pioneering involve more personal hardships than Nichols had anticipated, but the underbelly of her expansionist worldview was a general disregard for the displacement of Native American peoples and cultures. Even so, she adapted to dirt and privation without losing her political commitment and softened her ethnocentrism with womanly sympathy while leaving much of her anxiety about public exposure behind.

As a pioneering reformer, Clarina Howard Nichols created a feminine identity within the confines of her world that did more than compensate for her secret past. It fulfilled her intellectual needs, reflected her deepest values, and allowed her to pursue a public life devoted to reversing injustice. Hers was an individual struggle for the power to effect social change.

Frontier Legacies

I was born among soldiers of the revolution—both my grandfathers
having served in that war—who having fought the good fight of
American independence, packed their brides on horseback, with
feather bed strapped on behind, and . . . blazed tracks from Connecticut,
Massachusetts and Rhode Island to the green hills and fertile valleys
of the Green Mountain State.

C. I. H. Nichols, 1870

From the time she was a little girl, the stories of Clarina Howard's
grandfathers embedded an indelible image of frontier life in her
psyche. They entwined the lofty goals of the American Revolution with the struggle of pioneering, linking freedom and opportunity with migration and hardship. "When the aged grandsire took
the little ones on his knee, and telling the story of freedom's long
campaign of suffering and blood," she mused, he would sigh, "Ah
my children, you don't know what your liberty cost." Proud of her
heritage, Clarina typically evoked the image of her hardy, freedom-
loving New England forebears to connect her life and opinions to the
founding of the nation and a class of elite Americans. It was a tale
many families carried with them as they migrated across the United
States in the nineteenth century, facing unpredictable outcomes in
a quest for a better life than the one they left behind. Clarina was a
beneficiary of her grandparents' decisions to migrate to the Vermont
frontier, and as an adult she would repeat the pattern on the prairies
of Kansas, reaping similar praise for having "borne the hardships of
her pioneer life with a heroism that commands admiration."[1]

Though Clarina's grandparents served as models of Yankee perseverance—and would later inspire Clarina's sense of adventure—she was raised in a cozy Vermont village where she experienced few privations during childhood. With a combination of affection and religious discipline, Chapin and Birsha Howard began preparing their eldest daughter for womanhood at a young age. Ambitious parents, they envisioned a bright future for their eight children in the young American republic as they sought to convert the family's stake in Vermont land into commercial profits and community leadership. Such striving meant devising a program of moral and intellectual training that would equip their five daughters for the future with propitious marriage partners. To attract a husband of integrity and industry, a man with whom she could find mutual affection and sufficient economic support, Clarina would need the practical skills necessary to become a genteel housekeeper and devoted mother, the education and refinement to serve as a fit companion to her husband, and a sense of personal responsibility to fulfill her familial obligations. At first, this ethic of self-improvement would confine Clarina to dreaming of "domestic bliss" in a provincial home nearby, but eventually it would motivate her to seek a purposeful life and to follow her grandparents' lead in seeking opportunity and greater freedom in the expanding nation.[2]

At the time of Clarina's birth in January 1810, the western frontier beyond the Mississippi River was just opening to white settlement. It was a year after the birth of Abraham Lincoln and four months before that of Margaret Fuller, two intellectual giants who would help shape her generation. The Howards' little village of West Townshend was one of four hamlets in the town of Townshend in southeastern Vermont. Lying snugly along the eastern side of the Green Mountains and adjacent to a bend in the West River, it had developed rapidly in the 1790s around water power from a fast-running brook. Many of Clarina's Hayward (an earlier name for Howard) ancestors had staked out new homesteads in the area. Migrants from Massachusetts, including her grandparents, arrived during the American Revolution after walking an eighty-mile trail of marked trees from Worcester County. Most of these opportunists were young adults just starting families, the surplus population from southern New England who flooded into the beckoning borderland between New Hampshire and New York after the Seven Years' War. Despite rocky soil and uneven terrain, by 1810 Townshend had a population of 1,100. Still, it remained an isolated oasis in the forested hillsides of a relatively new state, split down the middle by the lofty Green Mountains.[3]

During Clarina's early childhood, her grandparents were part of the "old order of things." Townshend had "outgrown many of the primitive habits" of the pioneering generation and adopted "new-fangled notions," according to her. These ancestors linked Clarina to the struggle to survive in the wilderness and to secure land titles while heightening her appreciation of the trappings of settled society. It was not the amount of work but her grandmothers' domestic manners that signified the divide between pioneering and Clarina's comfortable existence in the village below their hillside farm. Stamped in her memory was the "childish enjoyment" of old customs, the way the older generation ate on a "pine plank" and served meals from a common bowl, in primitive fashion without plates or utensils. Visiting her grandmother was "like a play, or bit of romance," Clarina recalled, when she could partake of their "simple habits."[4]

When Levi and Bethiah Hayward risked their future by claiming lands on the precarious New Hampshire grants and supporting the patriot cause, the venture was far from romantic. Repeating family patterns of migration since the 1630s, Levi sought a way to make a living when his future in Mendon, Massachusetts, appeared dim. His father, Benjamin, a persistent religious dissenter, had succumbed to enough drunken behavior to destroy "a splendid property" and separate a family of sixteen children.[5] Levi and his brothers found an outlet for their youthful energies and discontent in resisting British authority in the mid-1770s and migrating to the northern frontier, where land was cheap yet marginally suitable for farming.[6] It seemed a better bet than staying in Mendon. Yet the venture held plenty of risk, for the land the Haywards began clearing in the hillside town of Townshend, a grant from New Hampshire, was also claimed by New York and part of the unresolved contest over land titles in the region between the Connecticut River and Lake Champlain. In between his trips north, Levi enlisted several times in the Massachusetts militia and married Bethiah Chapin. Meanwhile, the New Hampshire grantees set up their own political authority and proclaimed Vermont's independence from both neighboring colonies.[7] Casting their futures with these new Vermonters, the Hayward brothers melded the patriot cause with resistance to "Yorker land jobbers," and Levi joined the ranks of Townshend's Revolutionary heroes.[8]

It was her grandparents' willingness to take these political risks, along with their endurance, hard work, and frugality, that ensured a legacy for Clarina. Levi Hayward was a penniless migrant when he cleared land, planted wheat, built a log home, and began carrying his potash, wheat, and rye on horseback many miles to be exchanged for sugar, salt, gunpowder, livestock, and seeds. Eventually Levi, his sons, and the extended Hayward clan parlayed their original land rights into sufficient wealth and civic leadership to become one of the most prominent families in Townshend and neighboring Jamaica.[9] Clarina's maternal grandparents migrated shortly after the Haywards in the mid-1780s as part of the influx of newcomers following the Revolution. David Smith, who had served in the Revolutionary militia from Providence, Rhode Island, "was fond of practical joking," according to Clarina. She pictured her grandmother Mary Smith of Norwich, Connecticut, as "a sweet, plump little old woman, in white cap and checked copper-as-colored dress and white apron— setting her tea table." Their daughter Birsha was schooled in traditional housewifery—how to dry and prepare flax, tow, or wool for spinning and to weave cloth, labor that limited most women to only two everyday garments each. Seasonal tasks of boiling sap, sowing and weeding vegetables, curing beef, brewing cider, milking cows, and churning butter to supply the family table filled the remaining daylight hours. For a family scraping out an existence on a hillside farm, "children were regarded . . . as a source of wealth," and her grandparents "calculated on adding one to their number every two years, as much as they did on adding to their stock."[10] Whether they failed to produce enough—either goods or children—the Smiths eventually moved to nearby Newfane and then Londonderry to start anew. Their daughter Birsha stayed behind to marry Chapin Howard in 1809, a man who had the capacity to capitalize on his family's propitious stake in West Townshend.[11]

Born in 1785, Clarina's father, Chapin Howard, proved well positioned to participate in the region's rapid economic development. After Vermont entered the Union in 1791, the village of West Townshend flourished with mills and artisan shops, and Levi Howard, now perched on a hillside in a new frame house, began investing in local production.[12] Sited on the east-west post road from Brattleboro to Manchester, the hamlet developed more rapidly than Townshend village about five miles to the southeast, as its mills served families in nearby Jamaica as well. In 1805 Levi and his eldest son, Henry, invested in a tanning operation that later became Chapin's main source of wealth. Chapin managed and eventually bought the tannery and used his profits to purchase a blacksmith shop, which he operated during the 1820s, before buying a hotel in 1829.[13] Like other young artisan-entrepreneurs, who traded their products—leather, shoes, saddles, barrels, cloth, grain, lumber, and ironware—he participated in an incipient commercial market. But business was not without risks. In 1813 a devastating fire completely destroyed the tannery operation, which Chapin rebuilt on a grander scale. As long as the village grew, the local market for his output remained vibrant, and he served an expanded clientele as regional roads improved. "Frequent association with business and pleasure-seekers" from southern New England, according to Clarina, allowed the "inland village" to spawn a local clientele with more refined habits than their frontier predecessors.[14] Chapin's hotel, which accommodated travelers and served as a meeting place for local residents as well, was not only a wise investment and emblem of success but also evidence of his foresight in anticipating the needs of the growing village.

Indeed, West Townshend had attracted notable political and professional men, who created a vibrant intellectual climate in the neighborhood and provided models of social leadership for Chapin Howard. Prominent town fathers Paul Hazelton and General Samuel Fletcher lent their prestige to the hamlet and set standards of gentility that attracted visitors and other professionals to the neighborhood. Fletcher's son-in-law invested in various local enterprises, served in public offices, represented the town in the state legislature, spearheaded the local Baptist church, and promoted improvements in schools for his twelve children. Chapin Howard would follow his lead as the educated and professional men of the village organized associations for self-improvement and began a concerted effort to educate their children for leadership in the expanding economy. The local schoolhouse overflowed with over ninety scholars in the 1810s, and by the time Clarina was an adolescent, parents were eager to hire teachers for secondary schooling.[15]

Chapin and Birsha Howard supplied their share of children to this educational endeavor. According to a local nineteenth-century history, they had "a number of daughters and three sons, A. C. Howard, Ormando S. Howard and Bainbridge E. Howard." The eldest child—Clarina Irene—and her four sisters, Catherine, Mary, Laurinda, and Ellen, were not identified.[16] With her mother laboring in childbirth and burdened with infant care nearly every two years, Clarina was regularly called upon to "rock the baby" while Birsha washed clothes. She was a diligent and serious-minded mother who had little patience with the youthful spiritedness Clarina exhibited. At first the young family lived in a house attached to the tannery; Clarina recalled having moved to a new home just a few weeks before she witnessed its "smoking ruins" as a toddler. The Howards loaded "an ox-cart . . . with bureaus, chairs and bedding" and removed to a large frame house on the west end of the village, where she lived until she was eighteen.[17]

The Howards invested considerable energy in grooming their children for success, especially their promising daughter Clarina and their eldest son, Aurelius. She remembered her childhood as a time "rich in hope, love, [and] fun," which reflected Chapin and Birsha's devotion to parenting. Rather than pure "fun," the daily routine in the Howard household was more likely to be filled with lessons in the kind of housekeeping and economy that made the family's rising social status—and those pleasant hours—possible.[18] Endless rounds of common housework dominated Birsha's days, and as the family expanded she counted on her daughters' assistance to keep everyone fed and clothed. Moreover, assuring that her daughters were accomplished and thrifty housekeepers was a way to prepare them for marriage. In that regard, Birsha was as eager as her husband to demonstrate that they were no longer struggling farmers and to adorn their children with the trappings of refinement. She outfitted Clarina smartly in a "new short over-dress of red and blue domestic woolen plaid" when she was only three years old, but also economized using locally colored and pressed homespun that would later be turned to everyday use and handed down. The Howards' aspirations and their pride in their children are evident in a portrait of Clarina painted when she was about the same age. Tenderly holding a kitten and dressed in a soft white gown, she stares innocently from the canvas, as precious as any child of a New England gentleman. Though the format may have been generic, the existence of such a portrait reflects the Howards' middle-class aspirations for their daughter if not the effort required to achieve success. Investing their hopes in Clarina's future as a genteel mistress, they would balance discipline with kindliness, relieve her of hard physical labor, and monitor her moral development with care.[19]

Chapin's financial acumen and increasing wealth meant that the Howard daughters would develop different housekeeping skills from those their mother had learned while maintaining the industrious and frugal habits ingrained in their parents. As the family grew, Birsha employed domestic helpers, who washed, cleaned, and processed food, while her daughters concentrated on learning the more refined household tasks of a comfortable middle-class home. With access to ready-made cloth, they sewed shirts and dresses, knitted socks, and created ornamental décor, rather than spinning, weaving, and dying cloth. A skilled seamstress may have been imported to cut the more complex and fancier dress designs. This supplemental labor reduced

Clarina Irene Howard, age 3. An itinerant artist may have done this oil painting dated 1813. Courtesy of the Grace Hudson Museum and Sun House, City of Ukiah, California.

the tedium and time involved in producing garments, but still, economizing was essential because the Howards' rising standard of living required more elaborate clothing.[20] As Clarina adorned her dresses with delicate trimmings, she still turned old woolen skirts into warm petticoats. Birsha taught her to make oyster stew, delicate "sponge cake, jellies and blanc-mange," and to plant, cure, and pickle vegetables as well. Clarina's aptitude for knitting and sewing, which her mother found "ingenious," would prove particularly useful in the future. Decades later, she claimed she could fabricate "every article of men's or woman's apparel, save coats and shoes." By that time, these finer housekeeping skills signified what every well-bred woman should know in order to instruct her servants.[21]

Spared the most tedious domestic work, Clarina and her sisters enjoyed family circles around the fireplace, where they mixed household duties with plenty of laughter and lively conversation. They cut out pumpkin rings at harvest time and knitted stockings while relishing "the books, papers and animated discussions that filled" happy, playful evenings. One October eve, Clarina enlivened her cousin's ghost stories by secretly hiding a stash of acorns in the glowing fireplace embers and relished her sisters' screams as they exploded. When removed from Birsha's watchful eye, Clarina and her girlhood friends had time to romp in the woods and fields, gathering berries, singing songs, and playing childhood games, with "wild and joyous mirth."[22]

Clarina evoked fond memories of these days of "fun and frolic" and often touted her practical housekeeping skills, but it was her parents' interest in stimulating her intellect that distinguished her childhood years. Birsha, who was both "progressive and ambitious," according to Clarina, was anxious to send her eldest daughter to school and began teaching her to read and spell at an early age. When the local schoolmaster was boarding with the Howards, Birsha leapt at the chance to send three-year-old Clarina with him to the schoolhouse to get accustomed to the routine. A year later, beset with a toddler and another infant, Birsha persuaded a twelve-year-old neighbor to shepherd Clarina to school every day during the summer term, but her charge was still too active to sit for six hours at a time. Exhibiting little patience with laziness, Birsha was easily exasperated by any hint of dullness she found in her daughter, and on occasion she even resorted to whipping Clarina to get her to spell correctly. Eventually, Clarina would live up to her mother's ambitions as she "took to learning like a duck to water," but she clearly shouldered a high level of parental discipline and concern.[23] From Birsha's perspective, diligence in every task was important, and it was Clarina's duty not only to expand her mind but also to enhance her beauty to eventually attract a husband with the education and character to appreciate her fine accomplishments.

In the meantime, the crowded village schoolhouse in West Townshend supplied sufficient competition and intellectual stimulation for Clarina. During much of her childhood, the district enrolled between ninety and a hundred

Clarina's mother, Birsha Smith Howard, vignette from a daguerreotype taken in 1850. Courtesy of the Grace Hudson Museum and Sun House, City of Ukiah, California.

Clarina's father, Chapin Howard, vignette from a daguerreotype taken in 1850. Courtesy of the Grace Hudson Museum and Sun House, City of Ukiah, California.

students, although many attended irregularly depending upon their farm and household duties. Boys normally filled local classrooms during winter term from November to February; girls outnumbered them from May to August. Most of Clarina's schoolmasters were probably young men, but the district committee may have hired an occasional female teacher in summer term to save money. Crowded with the familiar faces of Clarina's siblings and cousins, the spare one-room school contained small benches, writing desks, and few books other than the Bible, but it provided Clarina with an opportunity to shine in the neighborhood. To her dismay, it went up in flames just before she turned nine, disrupting winter term before a somewhat larger and better equipped building could be erected. Clarina and her cousin Alphonso Taft were exactly the same age and received a comparable level of encouragement from their parents. Her uncle Peter Taft, who married her father's sister Sylvia, was the county land surveyor and a legal advisor. Son of a college-educated man and known as a "great reader," Peter had taught district school himself as a young man and probably supplied additional books to stimulate Clarina's imagination. The Tafts lived next to the old Howard homestead on what became known as Taft's Hill above the village, and as they promoted the intellectual advancement of their only child Alphonso, their interest in education set a standard for the Howard household as well.[24]

Beyond their intellectual ambitions for their children, both Peter Taft and Clarina's father provided her with models of leadership and public service. By all accounts Chapin Howard was a judicious and highly respected man who not only sought to ensure his family's financial security but also undertook his civic obligations seriously. Local voters obviously concurred in this assessment because over the years they elected Chapin to numerous town offices, including tax collector, petit juror, lister, highway surveyor, justice of the peace, and selectman. During Clarina's childhood and teenage years, he held at least one of these positions yearly, often trading roles with Peter Taft, who served in the state legislature during the 1820s and 1830s. Other men in their circle of friends in the village would appear regularly in town offices and were likely to be seen at the Howard home discussing local affairs or state politics with Chapin, who was elected to represent the town in the legislature in the mid-1830s.[25]

This coterie of men from West Townshend exposed the Howard children to the legal process and to the burdens of managing town affairs. As selectman, Chapin held the authority to direct public policy and set tax rates, but he also supervised road and building maintenance, set school district boundaries, and distributed poor relief. While serving as justice of the peace, he often mediated neighborhood disputes before they escalated into legal action and received complaints and petitions in his official capacity. Familiarity with Vermont law was essential for fulfilling his duties, and he probably consulted the statutes at his home or borrowed them occasionally from local lawyers or the town clerk. Earning a reputation for "integrity and ability," Chapin was hailed for his "courteous bearing, stability, uprightness . . . foresight and tact."[26]

If Clarina absorbed lessons in civic responsibility and legality from her father's activities, she retained the most vivid memories of his supervision of the poor. The Howards' doorstep became a regular stomping ground for men and women who sought alms. "On a hot Sabbath morning in June, 1821, a fat, dust-begrimed, sun-burned woman dropped into a chair beside the open door of my mother's cosy kitchen," Clarina recalled. With an infant in tow, the bedraggled migrant demanded that Chapin "take care of me and my baby." Though her predicament evoked his Christian sympathy and "regretful replies," Chapin felt bound by the local practice of minimizing town expense. In the absence of poor farms, local officials often held auctions for support of the indigent, who were housed by the lowest bidder. To avoid even this expense, they attempted to remove poor people from town if they could locate a legal residence elsewhere. Chapin's downtrodden visitor that June day was eventually carried thirty miles across state lines to New York. Clarina listened intently to these sad encounters, witnessing her father's kindly but firm responses, and in turn felt a young girl's sympathy for a mother and her baby without a comfortable home like hers. Later she would connect the experience to the legal rules that circumscribed their lives and her initial impulse to change them. Whereas her brothers, Aurelius and Ormando, eventually followed their father's example by serving in local offices and at the statehouse, Clarina would have to devise another pathway into the public sphere.[27]

Perhaps even more influential than the politics her father practiced was his religious sincerity and leadership in the Baptist church. Clarina's childhood coincided with a resurgence of religious evangelism in the region that shaped her understanding of her place in the world as much as her family's wealth. Beset by religious indifference during its founding, Townshend had seen Congregational ministers come and go; churches had been organized, disorganized, and reorganized in an era of "non spiritual discourse," as Clarina described

Former Baptist Church, West Towns-
hend, built in 1817. Clarina spent many
hours in this church from age 8 until she
married. Courtesy of the Townshend
Historical Society.

it. Chapin's father, Levi, had followed the family pattern of dissenting from the Congregational church and opted out of local religious taxes while his uncles helped organize a Baptist church in nearby Jamaica.[28] By 1796 Baptist believers had grown sufficiently in West Townshend to call meetings in the schoolhouse, and by 1810, the year Clarina was born, religious enthusiasm had resulted in the establishment of a separate church in the village.[29]

As Baptists, the Howards were part of a popular movement to ensure that Vermont retained a commitment to toleration and equal treatment of all believers. Baptists' insistence upon the independence and voluntary nature of each congregation had generated a tradition of dissent in New England, and by 1807 they had effectively demanded equity among all sects in Vermont, preventing the installation of an established church in the state. As the region became a hotbed of sectarian competition, Baptists were well positioned to supplant Congregationalists as the most respectable denomination in Townshend. In 1817 Chapin Howard, his brother, and other leading Baptists in West Townshend capitalized on this rising tide of religious fervor and their own interests in bolstering piety in the hamlet by building a new meetinghouse, which they shared with other smaller groups.[30] The spare white clapboard building with its spire pointing heavenward stood in the center of the village, a symbol of the leadership and dominance of Baptist believers.

Membership in the Baptist society not only confirmed the Howards' status in their community but also provided them with a moral framework that shaped their personal lives and public service. When Clarina was only eight years old, she was formally initiated into Baptist membership along with her parents. Her grandmother Bethiah Howard had led the family into the church society a few years earlier; one of her brothers, her sisters, her Aunt Sylvia Taft, her cousins, and other friends in the village followed. Membership required a demonstration of worthiness through a public profession of faith, and it is likely that Clarina performed this conversion ritual with other children her age. Full immersion in water at baptism symbolized their rebirth within God's community of believers. Although Clarina later admitted that the Baptists' Calvinist theology, involving belief in "predestination, justification, a vicarious atonement, the trinity and eternal punishment," was beyond her comprehension, sinning was clear enough. Lessons in upright behavior came regularly from the "pounding barrel" of her grandmother Howard's bosom as she preached against sin and "all uncleanness." As a result, Clarina developed a keen sense of guilt over her own misbehavior and learned to seek immediate forgiveness from those she loved. She was proud of her subsequent powers of self-control, recalling that she buried her anger and frustrations so well that she could thwart even diehard teasers.[31]

Yet Clarina's religious training went beyond gaining the "habit of self-control." She also learned that if she put her faith in God's grace, she could seek redemption by following Christ's teachings and thereby assure a "heaven here and eternal life." Her practical "living faith," as she called it, emphasizing the power of Christian love and obligations to adhere to the "golden rule" by loving others, would remain with her throughout life even though she would eventually discard other interpretations of Christian belief. This cosmology became the root of her sense of personal responsibility and self-regard. As a child, it meant controlling her own behavior and adhering to parental commands to achieve God's grace; as a young adult, it became "a longing desire to do good" in the world, the germ of a sense of mission that would profoundly shape her future.[32]

Religious activities permeated the Howard home, entwining the children in a shared faith. Beyond the hours she spent sitting quietly in the chilly meetinghouse, Clarina listened intently to her father's nightly prayers when the family gathered for "vesper hour" around the fireside. The stories she memorized from Scripture became embedded in her consciousness, where she harbored them for future use in writings and speeches filled with moral truths. Baptists prized the spirituality of all believers, afforded the laity important roles, and used the nomenclature "brother" and "sister" for fellow worshipers, allowing women and men to participate equally in society meetings if not in leadership. Elected deacon, Chapin assisted the minister and acted as clerk for the council of elders, who were responsible for disciplining church members for various forms of backsliding, including excessive drinking, swearing, theft, gossiping, lying, and religious indifference. Like other Baptists, Chapin believed in exercising "watchfulness" over his Christian brothers and sisters, both as a means to foster good in the world by helping other believers and to uphold his responsibility in the community. Though he modeled religious principles for his children, there is little evidence that he was a harsh disciplinarian within the family circle. Throughout her life Clarina revered her father's "kind concern" and regarded his faith as a beacon shining within her heart. "Clearly discerning the right," according to one local commentator, "he would mildly but firmly maintain it."[33] Nor did Chapin always operate his business affairs with strict religious principles. His village hotel still refreshed travelers with a swig of rum or hard cider though Baptists considered drink a sin. Clearly endorsing the egalitarian values inherent in the Baptist creed, Chapin attempted to treat his children with equal affection and support. At the same time his commitment to religious truth and social betterment would become one of his chief legacies to his daughter.

Clarina's mother and her Aunt Sylvia Taft, also known for strong religious convictions, provided her with models of female piety that complemented Chapin's leadership. Baptist elders—exclusively male—held elected positions, but women were hardly silent partners in the community of believers. Reverend Joseph Graves, "a rugged and forceful preacher," no doubt relied on their support as he orchestrated a revival in 1827, which resulted in the organization of a second Baptist society in Townshend Village, followed by a Sabbath school for adults and youths alike. Parents like the Howards who participated in this wave of evangelicalism were convinced that instilling piety in young people would ensure their future success and improve morals in the community.[34] A pattern of mothers shepherding their children and often their husbands into local church membership typified these religious awakenings along with educational and missionary activities that extended the Christian message of love and charity. Clarina probably joined her mother and aunt in meetings of the Townshend Female Missionary Society, which contributed clothing and goods to the state Baptist association, and she may have assisted in the Sabbath school as well.[35] Like many adolescents at the time, Clarina became anchored in Christian values through these institutions, while at home it was the daily "utterances of an old woman, an every day Christian," such as her grandmother, that impressed Clarina with enduring lessons in the strength of female piety and "uprighteousness." Church and family operated so symbiotically that she would find it difficult to separate the two in the future.[36]

For the Howards, situated on the rise in Townshend society, the moral and intellectual education of their children was as important as their material inheritance and signified their increasing gentility. Their sons needed land or an equivalent in cash to train for a profession, whereas their daughters' prospects were tied to their ability to attract promising husbands. Believing in equality among their children, Chapin and Birsha sought to provide dowries for each of their daughters, equal to that of their sons' inheritance, as a means to set up housekeeping. While Chapin invested in additional land, both locally and later in Pennsylvania and Michigan, to enhance his wealth and provide inheritances, Birsha concentrated on developing the domestic skills, genteel manners, and intellectual accomplishments of her five daughters to attract appropriate suitors.[37]

Clarina remembered learning about marriage customs and sexual attraction as early as age five or six. During a visit with her father, a young law student and the county deputy sheriff "amused themselves by bidding against each other for [her] favor." To avoid further teasing when she walked by their offices on the way to school, she sent her brother Aurelius ahead as a decoy before racing through the village hoping to escape their attention. Nonetheless, they often caught her, which precipitated screams and tears amid great "indignation." Eventually Clarina made peace with her flirtatious suitors and accepted a "supply of raisins," sealed with a "kiss of forgiveness" in return. Confiding in her mother that she "liked the lawyer best," she resolved to "be married right away and keep house in the 'spare chamber.'" To her dismay, she learned she must leave home and move to her new husband's house, an idea Clarina thoroughly rejected. The tale is laden with meaning, for her recollection of this childhood teasing was colored by her subsequent experience. Describing the episode as a form of persecution, she remembered foreswearing "matrimony *forever.*"[38] Later, she would discover the perils of sex appeal, the duplicitous behavior of a bad husband, crafty lawyers and sheriffs, and her ambiguous feelings about marriage would persist throughout a lifetime. The appeal of romantic attraction and domestic felicity with an affectionate partner was invariably marred by the confinement in a husband's house.

By the 1820s when Clarina was an adolescent, preparation for the role of wife and mother involved more than attention to appearance or housewifery. If a young woman was to avoid a life of endless domestic labor, she needed to acquire the knowledge and judgment necessary to accompany an educated and industrious man of good character and to become a wise mother for her children. Since the 1790s, writers and political theorists had circulated this ideal of womanhood, which historians have called Republican Motherhood, to promote better education for future citizens in the new nation. In the *Maternal Physician,* a widely circulated child-rearing manual, Mary Palmer Tyler of nearby Brattleboro outlined a program of child nurture emphasizing mothers' "duty, as *citizens*" to oversee their children's moral and intellectual development. To fulfill such a useful role in the nation and to develop the capacity for rational thought, American educators began urging parents to provide daughters with practical knowledge and ethical training rather than the kind of ornamental instruction deemed sufficient for an aristocratic lady of fashion. Moreover, such training would prepare them to teach occasionally before marriage, the only respectable occupation open to young women of the commercial class.[39]

Even as a young girl, Clarina apparently relished reading and writing, and her self-regard received a boost from the ease with which she acquired an education. Compared with her grandparents' pioneering era, the focus on children's schooling in West Townshend was far greater in the 1820s, and the Howards fully ascribed to the new educational ethos. In addition to time spent at the district school, Clarina recalled the pleasures of "writing at [old] Deacon S's," where his son and daughters who loved children, "'made much' of me." When she was twelve, her parents rewarded Clarina with a wooden laptop desk that encouraged her proclivity to write prose and poetry. Although they lacked formal secondary schooling themselves, the Howards' practice of regularly assembling the family around the hearth to read news and stories aloud from books, religious tracts, and local papers cultivated their children's intellectual appetites. Newspapers and almanacs were not only a means to expand the horizons of their world but also contained moral tales with lessons in good Christian behavior. Books and pamphlets were readily available from circulating libraries in the neighborhood, and there were several bookstores in the river town of Brattleboro, which had developed as a local print center ten miles away. Clarina fondly remembered the cozy scenes around the Howard hearth when the entire family listened eagerly to tales from the "home paper." The lively discussions that followed were "a feast of reason" at which she sensed that "her soul had eaten something."[40]

This form of intellectual stimulation sparked Clarina's desire to extend her formal schooling beyond district school. Later in life, she claimed that at age fourteen she had pleaded with her father for an education over a "setting out in the world," indicating she was mindful of the value of her intellect at an early age.[41] With no secondary schools in the neighborhood and eight children to educate, Chapin Howard faced a dilemma between his desire to monitor their development and provide equally for them, and the cost of secondary education. He was not alone in his drive to provide his children with more schooling, as the demands of an expanding commercial economy drew attention to the education of the next generation and secondary schools proliferated in the Connecticut River Valley. Yet at established academies, annual tuition, room, and board for his children would have cost Chapin between $100 and $140 per year per student, and the quality of cheaper home-based schools—especially for young women—varied widely. Clarina's generation of women would become as literate as their brothers, but it was still highly debatable whether they needed the same secondary education as young men. Literate women began operating small, select schools exclusively for girls in their homes to provide them with the kind of accomplishments—languages, drawing, music, and embroidery—that had distinguished genteel wives, but these were ephemeral and unlikely to provide the rigorous "classical" education Clarina sought.[42] While Clarina may have dreamed of attending an academy in the region, her father devised a more economical plan.

Instead of sending their children away, the leading men in West Townshend sponsored their own select school in the village beginning in 1826 to retain control over costs and educational quality. Existing records indicate that

Chapin paid tuition for his four eldest children—Clarina, her sister Catherine, and her brothers Aurelius and Ormando—at Timothy Cressy's school in fall 1828. The roster of over fifty scholars included an almost equal number of sons and daughters living in the hamlet or surrounding towns. Private select schools temporarily satisfied the demand for secondary school instruction in small rural villages while also providing college students like twenty-eight-year old Cressy with funds to pay his tuition at Amherst College. Clarina's cousin Alphonso Taft was college-bound as well and served as Cressy's assistant instructor in the program of studies. Heavily laced with religious content, the curriculum probably included philosophy, mathematics, literature, sciences, history, music, and classical languages. It was open to both sexes, but boys typically specialized in classical studies, philosophy, sciences, history, and mathematics while girls focused on literature, French, geography, music, and moral philosophy.[43]

Cressy's school provided the only formal secondary education Clarina received and was one of her few opportunities to exhibit her intellectual abilities as a young woman. With a strong ethical dimension, the school fostered self-improvement and self-examination as a means to human happiness. At the end of the term, the scholars displayed their achievements at a community exposition. The boys presented philosophical, religious, and political topics, including the importance of mathematics, a dialogue about presidential candidates Andrew Jackson and John Quincy Adams, and two sacred dramas, crowned by Alphonso Taft's valedictory oration, "Enterprise." Most of the girls addressed moral issues; Clarina's sister Catherine pondered "Love of Immortality," and others presented such topics as "Benevolence a source of personal happiness," "Moral influence of Novels," and "Reflection a source of improvement." Unlike either of her brothers, Clarina presented an original dissertation, and she addressed a contemporary debate. In "Comparative of a Scientific and an Ornamental Education to Females," she proffered her conclusions about the benefits of a rigorous curriculum for women compared with the traditional program of languages, music, geography, and textile arts available at small female academies. Unfortunately, her address no longer exists, but the seriousness with which she approached her studies suggests that eighteen-year-old Clarina already prized the life of the mind and advocated a curriculum that would prepare women for "higher and extended usefulness" over superficial talents of "dancing and musical performance."[44]

Given her wide reading, Clarina was obviously aware of recent debates over the quality of female education. By the late 1820s, educators Emma Willard and Catherine Beecher had opened female seminaries, where they hoped to replace the notion of ornamental education with a more academic program of study. Far from challenging gender roles, Willard argued that young women needed knowledge to raise their intellectual, moral, and physical capacities for their special usefulness as daughters, wives, and mothers to the world at large. As Clarina later explained, "the culture of the mind and heart" would enable women to exercise their moral influence over "man's higher and better nature." Willard and Beecher believed that single women should teach before marriage to fulfill their obligations to society, a practice that would also prepare them for their role as mothers. To that end, they advanced a modified program of study in natural sciences, philosophy, history, mathematics, and languages; Willard even required Latin, along with practical education that would fit women for teaching, domestic management, and, if necessary, self-support.[45]

Whether Clarina defended her composition at Cressy's Select School along these lines is unclear, but the treatise indicates her exposure to contemporary literary culture and suggests that her interest in education for women began at an early age. The intellectual capabilities of women became an increasingly debatable topic in literary circles. When promoters of education in West Townshend organized a local lyceum to sponsor lectures and debates in 1832, one of their first questions involved the "female mind" and whether it was as capable of "cultivation" as the male, a question they eventually resolved in the negative. Clarina's father and her two brothers participated in the debate, though their votes are not recorded. In either case, her parents and the strong neighborhood interest in schooling had certainly provided her with sufficient support to later claim an early "faith in my ability to achieve equal attainments with my brother man."[46] Indeed, Clarina's coeducational schooling and her ability to outshine her brothers and compete with her promising cousin Alphonso, who went on to Amherst and graduated from Yale, were the seeds of her lifelong willingness to prove her intellectual capacities by fully engaging in debates with men. Neither Aurelius, who became a land developer, nor Ormando, who took over the family farm, apparently went to college, either. Her father maintained his pursuit of better secondary education by helping to develop Leland Seminary in Townshend, where Clarina's younger siblings and eventually her children were educated.[47]

Rather than lack of opportunity, Clarina's health may have circumscribed her secondary schooling and potential for teaching. She explained years later that a "physical debility" turned her to "books and the study of human destiny" in place of the "severe discipline of a classical school." The onset of a lifelong struggle with periodic sciatica, which may have been the result of a curvature of her spine, caused pain in her back and probably radiated down her leg as well, making standing uncomfortable.[48] The condition was intermittently debilitating but did not prevent her from intellectual pursuits, perhaps under the guidance of her uncle Peter Taft or another local tutor. Her later writings indicate that she at least had a passing knowledge of a wide range of history and literature, from the moral philosophy of William Paley and Francis Wayland to English and American poetry and classical mythology. She no doubt anticipated teaching, for she recalled, "I had a longing desire to do good, but the teacher's desk was the only sphere that opened before me," and she may have tutored local children rather than endure hours of standing in a classroom.[49] Compared with the advanced schooling of her future colleagues in the woman's rights movement, however, Clarina's education was truncated. Although her intellectual curiosity abounded, she lacked the theoretical background, the practice in oratory and debate, and the social interaction among peers that launched other young women of her generation into public activism.[50]

Yet at age 18 Clarina was undoubtedly proud of her intellectual accomplishments and developed a passion for the "culture of the mind and heart" over what she considered frivolous activity or mundane household work. At the same time, she had learned to veil those achievements under a display of feminine modesty and a dutiful effort at "trying to look pretty."[51] She had grown to a stately five feet eight inches, much taller than most women of her day. Her potential as a future wife is evident in a miniature portrait on ivory that records her beauty and gentility. Though the painting is clearly stylized, it exhibits a young woman of refinement and reflects the Howards' eagerness to exhibit their elegant daughter as an emblem of their own success. With deep-set, piercing blue eyes, a high brow, clear skin, and long thin face, Clarina presents a cultured image uncharacteristic of the backcountry where she lived. Instead, she displays the clothing, jewelry, and sophistication as well as the pride of a woman of high station, clearly ready to attract the right kind of husband. At this age she may have been seduced by the attention given to her appearance and the necessity to display her feminine charms; years later she regretted that the vain quest for beauty had made her highly "sensitive to

Clarina Irene Howard, age 16. This
miniature on ivory was painted in 1826,
perhaps by Clarina's brother-in-law.
Courtesy of Janice Parker.

the sensation my face . . . creates" and insisted that intellect and virtue were the only sources of real attraction in women.[52]

Although Clarina would soon learn about the pitfalls of vanity, she had acquired other more enduring legacies from the Howard circle. "I commenced life with the most refined notions of woman's sphere," she later recalled, and indeed her parents had inculcated a distinct "pride of womanhood" in their daughter. In the late 1820s the bourgeois notion of woman's sphere, which elevated domesticity to a realm removed from productive labor, was hardly as defined as Clarina implied. Yet she understood her world in gendered terms, and the ideal framed her future responsibilities as a wife and mother. If her comfortable existence meant she expected to hire servants and was ill-prepared for a life of unrelenting toil, she also grew to maturity in a provincial backwater among a people who valued habits of economy and diligence and taught essential housekeeping skills. Far from pampered, Clarina gleaned a profound respect for established authority from the coupling of affection and discipline meted out in the Howard household. Chapin's commitment to his family's welfare, to fairness among his children, and to upright behavior set a standard for manly protection and kindness that she would look for in a husband. As she ventured out of the close-knit community in West Towns-hend onto new frontiers where men were on the make and women competed for their affection and respect, Clarina was confident that she possessed an equal chance at happiness. Schooled in the ways of a middle-class home, she believed she could reach womanly perfection and heavenly rewards through self-development, a form of striving that would drive her to action but would also leave her with a lifelong concern for social respectability.

The "Wrongs of Woman"

I would have written my life years ago from the beginning, but for the conviction that it would be like "the play of Hamlet with Hamlet left out," for the ten years of my life—from April '21 to March '43 [*sic*] which educated, disciplined and developed my conscious unity and obligation to humanity—could not be given to the public.

C. I. H. Nichols, 1884

On an April day in 1830, Clarina Irene Howard willingly left her father's kindly protection and married thirty-year-old Justin Carpenter of Guilford, Vermont. Ten years older, he was a college graduate with sufficient education and religious training to recommend him highly to her parents. It was the beginning of a decade that profoundly shaped her life, one that has been nearly lost to biographers because of Nichols's secrecy about her first husband and the absence of personal papers. At a time when the future happiness and economic security of a young woman of her social position depended almost exclusively on a successful marriage, her choice was important. As she and Justin pursued his ambitions on New York's western frontier and in the crowded streets of lower Manhattan, her naive belief in manly protection and fair treatment would be shattered. Reluctant to reveal the details of their adventures or the eventual failure of the marriage publicly, Clarina would harbor a deep-seated sense of disillusionment and resentment from the experience, which later informed and circumscribed her politics. But the story of the Carpenters' marriage, Clarina's efforts to ensure the well-being of their three children, and her ability to resurrect her self-regard can also be seen as a triumph over adversity, for it catapulted her into public activism and historical memory.

Little is known about Justin's courtship of Clarina. The couple may have met through Baptist connections, but it is more likely that Timothy Cressy, whom Justin knew at Amherst College, brought him to Townshend. Raised in one of the largest commercial towns in the state, Justin came from a family of patriots who followed the same pathway as Clarina's family—from southern New England to frontier Vermont—and located in Guilford about twenty miles southeast of Townshend. Renowned as a righteous defender of the infant state of Vermont, Justin's grandfather Benjamin Carpenter had served as lieutenant governor and a leader of Guilford's Baptist community. Though prominent, the Carpenters were not wealthy, and as the third son in a farm family of thirteen children, Justin was not likely to receive a legacy in land and needed to look elsewhere for opportunity.[1]

If Justin's family credentials qualified him as a suitor, he was also educated and had experienced the wave of evangelism sweeping the region. Raised in the Baptist Church, he and his younger brother Mark witnessed a series of religious revivals in Guilford during their adolescent years and were obviously encouraged to seek professional training as an alternative to farming because they both prepared themselves to enter Amherst College.[2] A Congregational school dedicated to educating poor but pious men for the ministry, Amherst offered classical and religious studies for young men with intellectual promise regardless of whether they intended to enter the ministry. The school had been operating precariously for five years in 1826 when the Carpenter brothers, then in their mid-twenties, were able to afford tuition and fees. At the time, Amherst's president, Heman Humphrey, an experienced evangelist and temperance advocate, presided over a teeming campus of more than 200 restless students so imbued with religious fervor that they set up their own government and attempted to monitor student discipline. For whatever reason, after three years Justin, Mark, and several other classmates transferred to Union College, a nonsectarian school in Schenectady, New York, from which they graduated in 1830. After college both Mark and classmate Timothy Cressy studied for the ministry at theological schools, but Justin chose not to follow their lead. With his new bride, he preferred to use his training as an educator and publisher on the western frontier.[3]

Justin Carpenter at age 30, portrait by artist Margaret Bogardus of New York, 1830.
Courtesy of the Cincinnati Art Museum. Gift of Mr. and Mrs. Charles Fleischmann III.

Clarina Howard's life changed dramatically when she agreed to marry Justin Carpenter at the age of twenty. Although the decision to marry was theoretically hers, for many young women it was fraught with a combination of great anticipation and impending doom. Justin no doubt wooed her with pious and earnest predictions about their future together, but his ambitions would remove her from the protection of a loving family and the close-knit community of West Townshend. She had thrived under her father's guidance, but would Justin provide the same level of emotional and financial support? Chapin Howard, who by 1830 had become one of the wealthiest men in West Townshend, provided Clarina a generous dowry of $1,500—a fine legacy with which to set up housekeeping, particularly for an ambitious man like Justin who had probably struggled to earn funds for his own education.[4] Without a separate premarital agreement, Justin would control this legacy as well as Clarina's earnings, and in turn, she would expect him to support and protect the family and pay her debts. Her domestic labor and child nurture would be essential to their welfare, but Justin held sole legal rights over children and common marital endeavors. These legal privileges would give Justin the upper hand, yet couples were customarily bound by a sense of mutuality within marriage; his marital privileges, including conjugal rights, would be softened with kindness if not affection.

Clarina's feelings for Justin flowered at a time when many young couples were encouraged to express themselves with authenticity but also warned about the excess of passion associated with romantic love. During courtship, a suitor needed assurance of a woman's virtue as well as evidence of her domestic economy while a woman sought honesty, industry, and sympathy in a suitor. Mutual respect and affection evolving during the course of marriage were supposed to provide the glue to hold this bargain together, but feelings of romantic love also colored contemporary images of the ideal partner.[5] Clarina displayed her romantic sensibility in youthful poetry, in which she dreamed about cultivating "rich bouquets of friendship" untainted by "interests" or "power" in a "garden of romance," an ethereal realm without grief or sorrows.[6] Sheltered in a rural village, she may have overlooked the pitfalls of romantic attraction, often portrayed in popular literature as a potential danger for both partners because of the vulnerability of young hearts unrestrained by practical judgment. "Beauty and accomplishments," Clarina later confessed, "address themselves to man's lower nature—his passions; and when age has robbed you of the one, and him of the other, you are left unloved and unlovely." A young woman smitten with passion was vulnerable to misjudging a suitor's character and becoming entrapped in a disastrous marriage, subject to a husband's duplicity and sexual excess.[7]

Romance aside, Clarina believed that marriage would allow her to develop her capacities as a woman and reach spiritual fulfillment. "In my whole soul

I felt that there *was* a position in which I might give expansion to my being," she recalled. "I became a wife and a mother, and felt that I had entered upon the most sacred relations of life."[8] By taking a partner for life, she anticipated becoming "companions in eternity" with her husband, two souls reaching heavenward in a life of religious devotion. Her Christian readings proclaimed marriage vows as sacred obligations, blessed by God and inviolable; partners strove together to achieve both "mutual joy" and salvation through sacrifice. Years later Clarina defended this concept of divine marriage based upon unselfish love, which mirrored the love of God: "Husbands love your wives even as Christ loved the church, and gave himself for it. . . . So ought men to love their wives as their own bodies." With two souls joined in open and frank communication, they could achieve the "grand object of [their] union." Assessing Justin as a man of piety, at least outwardly, Clarina believed he would accompany her on a life of usefulness that would fulfill her "longing desire to do good." During their courtship, she and Justin no doubt engaged in Christian conversation, conflating their feelings for God with their affection for each other. In a poem addressed to Justin in 1837, she mused about her commitment:

> To repose in thy truth from the cold hearted world
> To cheer with affection when sorrow unfurled
> To labour with thee heavenly treasures to win
> Were prospects that won me from kith & kin.[9]

This ideal of spiritual companionship filled Clarina with optimism as she embarked on her first venture among strangers on the frontier. Having witnessed the excitement of the westward movement during his year at Union College, Justin was eager to parlay his educational advantages into developing a school or literary journal to serve the growing population on New York's western boundary. With the opening of the Erie Canal between Albany and Buffalo in 1825, Schenectady had become a favorite gateway for canal traffic, and after arriving there by stage, the Carpenters bargained among other emigrants for the best fare on a packet boat for Buffalo. Dragged along by horses on the slow trip west, the packet was filled with a raucous collection of boatmen, hustlers, fancy-dressed travelers, and poor, bedraggled families with crying babies. As one passenger remarked, "I never witnessed so much immorality and vice, profanity and drinking in the same length of time before in my life. . . . Canal men are . . . a coarse and untaught set of vagabonds whose chief delight is to carouse and fight."[10] While the packet navigated through the locks at each bustling commercial village along the route, the Carpenters were free to explore the muddy streets, taverns, coffeehouses, and shops catering to the canal trade. It took seven or eight days to reach Brockport, a commercial village about twenty miles west of Rochester, where Justin's older brother Cyrus and his wife had landed. An upstart village of red brick buildings at a crossroads intersecting the canal, it housed a familiar array of boardinghouses, small shops, and processing plants that arose in the heart of the fertile Genesee Valley; grain and artisan products were shipped eastward opposite a wave of travelers heading westward. Brockport boasted between 700 and 800 residents when the Carpenters arrived. Like other transients and hustlers from New England seeking to take advantage of its commercial development, they probably rented rooms in one of the many boardinghouses in the village.[11]

With the help of his brother and fellow Baptists, Justin quickly established himself in the community. In partnership with J. M. Davis, a printer and bookstore owner, he launched Brockport Academy in a building leased from the new Baptist church, where they offered secondary schooling for young men and women and opened a circulating library. As teachers, Justin and Clarina guided students in creating literary works, which were published in an inexpensive bimonthly paper called *The Token and Student's Literary Repository*. They hoped to produce a "cheap and tasty" magazine for young people, including literature, poetry, and "Original Tales" to uplift "literary taste" in the new town.[12] Having either borrowed or purchased printing equipment, they anticipated recouping their investment with proceeds from the magazine; it was Clarina's first attempt at literary publication. These projects dovetailed nicely with the movement to improve education sweeping the Northeast, which energized earnest young men in Brockport to expand the scope of the schools. Self-improvement advocates organized a local lyceum, which met every Friday evening at the academy or the local hotel, and Justin joined in debates about social reform and the merits of school improvements. In addition to forming county educational associations, leaders anticipated establishing a nursery school, sponsored singing schools, and organized Sabbath schools in Brockport.[13] The effort was indicative of the kind of striving found in recently settled communities, where opportunists hoped to replicate the cultural institutions of New England.

UNIVERSITY OF WINCHESTER
LIBRARY

But in a matter of months, this frenzy of educational activity came to a halt for the Carpenters. The Baptists, who had supported Brockport Academy, redirected their attention to the development of a college in Brockport. Justin's partnership with Davis in the academy dissolved, reportedly by "mutual consent," and the Carpenters found themselves struggling to keep the fledgling school afloat in a competitive market for tuition-paying students.[14] Shortly thereafter, on March 8, 1831, Clarina gave birth to their first child, a daughter whom she named Birsha after her own mother. Suddenly Clarina's life became even more complicated as she juggled the demands of a newborn with the effort required to operate a school. Without her family nearby, she would have to learn how to manage the problems of feeding, swaddling, and medicating her baby with no help from her sisters or the comfort and advice her mother could provide.

Yet the Carpenters were not bereft of like-minded adventurers, especially among Baptists. As in other towns along the canal route, Brockport was on fire with religious fervor. Evangelist Charles Grandison Finney had sparked a sensation with his theatrical style of preaching in nearby Rochester in the fall of 1830. Membership in the town's Presbyterian and Baptist churches doubled after Finney's message of universal salvation spread throughout the town. Beginning in the mid-1820s, Finney had tapped into the yearnings of an earnest but mobile population in the region eager to shape community morals and tame youthful transients. Ripe for his fervent message that achieving God's grace was a matter of free will, they listened intently as he led converts to salvation by choosing to follow Christ's teachings. As Finney's revivals gained sway, not only in nearby towns like Brockport, but further west in Ohio and back east in Vermont and Connecticut, contemporary commentators proclaimed that the Millennium—the reign of Christianity—was at hand.[15]

The new creed encouraged followers to display their faith with evidence of upright behavior—no drinking, gambling, or backsliding—and to gather adherents to a Christian lifestyle in preparation for the Millennium. With renewed vigor, temperance advocates emerged as the leading edge of this evangelical movement and demanded total abstinence. Rochester's grocers and grog shops poured their liquor into the canal as a demonstration of their faith in the "good time coming."[16] In Brockport, the Carpenters joined the Young Gentlemen and Ladies Temperance Society, which boasted 214 members by January 1831. They included leading professionals like Thomas H. Hyatt, bookstore owner and publisher of the *Brockport Free Press*. Justin became a director and began recruiting new members. In a circular "To the Young Gen-tlemen and Ladies of Brockport and vicinity," the directors promoted tem-perance as the most patriotic of duties. "What! A nation boast of freedom," they questioned, "while slaves to intemperance? Madness!" Proclaiming that alcohol was an evil threatening the nation, they argued that temperate men were the true "patriots of the nineteenth century." It was not only young men whom they called to honor the nation. Attributing "the happiness and even the destiny of our nation" to the influence of women, they urged "young Ladies" to rescue those addicted to "the social glass and sparkling bowl" and shun the man "who touches, tastes, or handles, the fatal poison."[17] This ap-peal to women's patriotism echoed the rhetoric circulating at the time of the American Revolution when women who refused to drink British tea and buy British goods were revered as true patriots for their supporting roles. Clarina and other women were welcomed into the temperance society, though not as officers or directors.

The Carpenters met some of the most ambitious men of the new town among temperance advocates, who sought local leadership by creating a morally pure and educated elite. They solidified the association of temper-ance with American patriotism on July 4, 1831, by organizing a "Cold Wa-ter Celebration" as an alternative to the long-standing tradition of drinking and gaming on Independence Day. Justin helped supervise a procession of 250 "respectable citizens," who paraded up Main Street from the canal to the Presbyterian church. To replace the typical military display on such a day, the teetotalers substituted a hundred young women "neatly uniformed in snowy white" to represent the purity of the nation. After listening to the Declara-tion of Independence and poetic orations, converts to purity reconvened un-der tents to eat dinner and drink coffee, tea, and *pure, cold water.*" With righteous praise, Hyatt commended the celebrants who clearly had overcome "petty strifes" about the event and created a "pleasing and heart-cheering commemoration of our National Independence."[18]

For Clarina, commitment to temperance meant adherence to the values that had stabilized her world as a young woman. By displaying her private belief with like-minded teetotalers in a show of patriotism, she connected the religious and civic virtue of her New England girlhood with this new and unwieldy place. Temperance had become settled policy among Baptist believ-ers, who had shifted from a moderate to extreme position advising total absti-nence. A local temperance society was organized in Townshend, and Clarina would eventually join it.[19] The issue had not entered the realm of politics yet, but the reform was sweeping the Northeast. The Carpenters' activities in Brockport initiated Clarina's lifelong dedication to ridding society of social ills and would prove to be her first step on a pathway into politics. On the brink of a new life with her first baby, she clung to the optimism embedded in the evangelical movement that reforming oneself and urging others to do the same would usher in God's kingdom on earth.

Two years later, Clarina's hopes for the future were far less sanguine. By mid-1833, something had gone horribly wrong in the Carpenters' endeavors in Brockport and probably in their marriage as well. After their school ceased in July 1831, Justin began publishing the *Western Star, or Impartial Miscellany,* a four-page literary and religious newspaper. But the enterprise soon collapsed, probably because he failed to gain sufficient advertising and subscriptions or political backing to sustain it. In an era rife with financial risk and uncertainty in the publishing business, building a readership in a new and mobile community rested upon the reputation of the proprietor, the trust of his creditors, and political party support. Thomas Hyatt, editor of the *Brockport Free Press,* was a fierce competitor who may have wanted to eliminate a potential rival; or perhaps Justin generated a personal animosity with the fiery Hyatt. In either case, Hyatt ignored the existence of the *Star* until its demise in March 1832, when he ridiculed its presumptuous title with a short notice headlined, "Fallen * . . ." and ending, "Peace to its memory!" A year later Clarina described Brockport to her parents as a "scene of past sorrows, vexations & disappointments." The Carpenters' attempt at teaching had failed; Justin's various enterprises were unsuccessful, and Clarina expressed a longing for the warmth of home that intimated the coldness surely seeping into their relationship.[20]

For the next six years, the historical record on the Carpenters is nearly absent, but it is clear that Justin's erratic behavior contributed to his inability to make a living and to Clarina's increasing disillusionment with her husband. Fleeting references to having founded a "flourishing female boarding school," perhaps in Herkimer, New York, suggest that they may have settled briefly in another location close to the canal route, where she tried teaching again. But according to Clarina, Justin's "conduct . . . forced her to abandon it." Did he disrupt her classes? Alienate parents? Tarnish the family's reputation? Regardless of Justin's temperamental rashness, it was difficult for Clarina to manage her household and teach as well. Justin had obviously squandered at least part of her dowry in Brockport, and money for paid help was running out. Though their relationship was clearly unraveling, in the next three years she became pregnant twice, returning to Townshend each time for her confinement. Her son Chapin Howard was born in August 1834, and Aurelius Ormando arrived in November 1836. By that time the couple had been living in New York City, at least intermittently, for at least three years.[21]

It was in the urban den of lower Manhattan that the Carpenters' marriage disintegrated. The metropolis posed even greater dangers for getting a start in life than Brockport. For a time the couple rented rooms on Fulton Street, a place teeming with commercial activity, makeshift boardinghouses, and residential construction in the 1830s. Thousands of passengers arrived daily at the ferry and steamboat slips, including tradesmen selling wares, young clerks seeking apprenticeships, Irish and German immigrants looking for work, and young women destined for domestic service, sewing shops, or prostitution. No longer anchored by a network of relatives and religious associates who could testify to their fine character and social status, the Carpenters were at the mercy of a melee of strangers and confidence men ready to ensnare unsophisticated country bumpkins into gambling schemes and romantic liaisons in the city's narrow garbage-strewn streets. Justin may have felt liberated by the anonymity of city life, but he would also have to succeed on his own merits in a fiercely competitive newspaper world. The onset of the penny press—daily papers with titillating local stories—diminished his prospects even before a fire apparently destroyed his operation. He also studied or apprenticed in a law firm before depleting Clarina's remaining inheritance and leaving the family near poverty. The couple's troubles peaked during a period of financial speculation culminating in the Panic of 1837, which probably increased the pressure on Justin to repay his debts, but clearly he abrogated his legal obligation to support the family.[22]

Clarina never forgave Justin for his wanton behavior, labeling him the sole perpetrator of the injustice and disrespect she endured, not a victim of urban deceits. Years later, she provided a cryptic account of her early marriage experience in a column she penned under the name "Annie." In a highly stylized tale designed to defend her political activities at the time, she exposed the youthful trials of "Mrs. Nichols" to authenticate the value of women's labor and the domestic burdens under which they suffered. To earn money, she had "kept a boarding house for professional men and their wives. . . . To

Clarina Howard Carpenter, at age 22, two years after her marriage to Justin Carpenter. Courtesy of Janice Parker.

her boarders, she was only the intelligent mistress," but behind the scenes, she assumed the laborious duties of "cook" and "chambermaid, herself." She took in sewing and earned money doing "'French crimping' for a millinery establishment." Even if she was hosting a highly respectable clientele and designing exquisite hats, resorting to manual labor was degrading for a woman with Clarina's background and social expectations. Justin also damaged her pride by absconding with her earnings and perhaps even threatened to pawn her clothing, a scenario she later used for rhetorical purposes. Clarina told of a young mother she had met in the mid-1830s whose husband had "pawned the clothing which she had provided for herself and babes" just before her youngest child was born and subsequently "pursued her from place to place annoying her employers, collecting her wages by process of law, and taking possession of every garment not on her own or children's persons."[23]

Not the sympathizing friend and spiritual companion she had long anticipated, Justin proved to be a chameleon whose character she had misjudged. Clarina confirmed that drinking was not the problem; he may have gambled to satisfy debts or simply wasted their money on excess spending, investment schemes, or other women. Perhaps she would have forgiven him if he had not become a "dissolute & unfeeling husband," whose "legal executions & exactions" harassed her while she struggled to feed and clothe the children.[24] It was an experience familiar to other women of her class whose husbands failed as breadwinners. Begrudging their wives' needlework or teaching, they exercised legal rights over wives' earnings or other property while punishing them emotionally for their own failure to uphold prevailing standards of manhood. Even as the experience dispelled Clarina's youthful naïveté, it also fed her lifelong concern with women's earnings and her insistence upon the value of their economic contributions to the family.

With her dreams of marital bliss shattered, Clarina grieved over her fate and lost love in a poetry journal filled with sentimental and sorrowful pieces written from 1833 until 1839, some of which were designed for publication. In poems entitled "New England," "What Lady Loves a Rainy Day?" and "The Happy Wife and Mother," she found solace in nature, in a woman's "industry," and in her baby's smiles. But most of her poems are dominated by a sense of impending doom and "love despoiled." As her bond with Justin dissolved, she felt uncharacteristically hopeless and contemplated a "drear and dreaded future." Yet as late as 1837, she was still responsive to affection from Justin, despite his abuse. "'I love thee,' 'I love thee,' dear husband define,/ My heart cannot tell thee if found not in thine," she wrote. But only a few months later, she pined, "O hadst thou but treasured my love fond and free/ Thou couldst not have meted such measure to me." Feeling abandoned but still wrenched by the intensity of her attachment to Justin, she wept at night and moaned, "the sire of my babes can I ever forget?"[25]

The shame of revealing her predicament and Justin's disrespect even to her children, much less her family and friends, silenced Clarina for many months because it represented not only a social disgrace but also a quasi-moral failure on her part. It was proof that she had made a fatal mistake of judgment in assessing his character and lacked the moral influence to restrain his wayward behavior. Justin had published a column on "Female Influence" in the *Western Star* that extolled the capacity of a pious and educated woman to cultivate a man's "heart for sympathy and benevolence" and through him to ensure a virtuous republic. Clarina may have even penned the article herself. Unable now to fulfill that role or quell her own sense of guilt and swallow her pride, she later described herself as "bent & cowered, not knowing how but resolved to endure & give the world no sign." Separation appeared to be an unacceptable option at first, and she bolstered her resolve by concluding, "there are times when the burden seems too great to bear without help of sympathies;— Then is the time to be strong; to say to self, 'get thee behind me.'" Legally she had little recourse. If she threatened to leave, Justin could ruin her reputation by accusing her of adultery. As a married woman, she could not sue her husband for slander. Even more crushing was his legal right to remove the children. It was only after Justin exercised what she described as "a malevolent desire to wound her" and "stole her children" that Clarina's fears and her maternal sensibilities spurred her to action. Whether Justin abused her or the children physically is unclear, but he had certainly violated prevailing conjugal expectations. After alerting the Howards, who probably helped recover the children, she abandoned any hope of reconciliation and returned with them to her parents' home in mid-1839.[26]

Separation was a more common means of ending a failed marriage than divorce, but it plunged Clarina into an untenable situation without rights to her children or means of support. Although the divorce rate was slowly rising, divorce was difficult to obtain and ran counter to the Christian view of marriage as a sacred trust and lifelong commitment. Moreover, suing for divorce usually required proof of desertion or adultery, which was embarrassing to verify, opening the relationship to public scrutiny. Yet separation left Justin with sole guardianship of the children and control of Clarina's finances, including her future earnings, which his creditors could claim unless she obtained a legal separation from "bed and board," severing the economic tie. While distasteful, divorce was the only way to recoup her respectability through remarriage and to weaken Justin's paternal rights, for Clarina worried ceaselessly about his potential to harm the children. Vermont's divorce statute was one of the most liberal in the nation and provided for several legitimate pleas, including "intolerable severity," a way out for abused wives. The Vermont Supreme Court, which granted divorces, had interpreted the cruelty plea generously, particularly in cases of physical abuse, and even awarded compensation, but the plea was limited to causes originating in the state—a barrier for Clarina, whose marriage failed in New York. Not only that, but she had deserted her husband, making her vulnerable to any legal action he might initiate to prove her guilt.[27]

Even if Clarina was more downtrodden than angry at this point, her father was eager to disentangle her finances from the scoundrel. Chapin Howard was no doubt outraged by Justin's behavior and showed his love and compassion for his eldest daughter by receiving her back into the bosom of the family and defending her integrity. Complicating the issue was the fact that his second daughter, Catherine, had married Justin's brother Mark, now a respected Baptist minister. Remarkably the Carpenter family also supported Clarina in the marital dispute, disapproving of their own son and absolving her of accountability in public, which helped to assuage her guilt. Putting aside his religious convictions in favor of practical action, Chapin eventually decided that a divorce was in order, but first Vermont's divorce statutes needed amending to accommodate Clarina's situation. His stature as a selectman, former town representative, and experienced justice of the peace meant that Chapin was not only familiar with the statutes but also influential with lawmakers. They were mindful of the legal bind facing wives as the vicissitudes of the market economy and geographic mobility had caused increasing rates of marital desertion and abuse.

Even though dragging his daughter's marital failure into the political arena would involve public exposure, Chapin opted to use his political connections to release Clarina from Justin's claims and thereby gain legal sanction for her predicament. In 1840 Townshend's representative to the Vermont legislature initiated a bill to allow for divorce even if a couple's problems occurred outside of the state. Clarina supplied written testimony for the judiciary committee, causing her considerable angst as the details of her private life became public, but it helped convince legislators to enact a narrow exclusion in the law only for native Vermonters. The reform "opened a way of escape for me," Clarina recalled, and "let several other poor women escape also." More important, the experience became an indelible example of how legal rules shaped her life and how they could be changed through political action. Nonetheless, to prevent the state from becoming a magnet for divorce, legislators also instituted a three-year residency requirement. Clarina would not be free of Justin and able to remarry any time soon.[28]

For over two more years, Clarina remained in legal limbo, clearly wounded, filled with guilt about besmirching the stellar reputation of the Howard family, and still worried about her children's future. After submitting two petitions, she would finally procure a divorce on February 16, 1843, based on her claim that Justin had "treated her with cruelty, unkindness and intolerable severity."[29] The plea was designed to prove his wrongdoing and to establish a valid moral basis for her desertion and separation from him. Unfortunately, testimony in the case no longer exists, but Justin did not appear in court or contest the suit. According to Clarina, his father and brother testified to his deviant behavior on her behalf, which significantly bolstered her case and proved that community standards had been violated. They knew, she later claimed, that "I had never given him an unkind word & had supported my family from the first." In this way she absolved herself from any blame for the separation based upon her wifely obligations and strengthened her case for custody, an issue that remained unresolved although Justin made no effort to retrieve the children.[30]

Marital failure and its ramifications on her self-respect and sense of injustice became Clarina's most compelling explanation for her reform impulse. Throughout her life she sought to hide the past to protect her own reputation, to lessen damage to her children, and to relieve both her Howard and Carpenter relatives of further disgrace. Yet the experience also drove her to understand the law and to seek justice for wives trapped by similar predicaments. "My early marriage experience," she told Susan B. Anthony in a rare admission, "'set me apart,' consecrated, called me to the work." Her "dissolute" husband, his "legal executions & exactions," and her frustrations as a mother trying to support a family underlay her public career. "I *am* a walking storehouse of facts on the subject of woman's wrongs," she noted. "I know what a good husband is better than one who never tried a bad one." Neighbors and friends knew the details of her situation, making it "a clencher to my influence in the advocacy of rights," she explained. But she scrupulously avoided allusions to her "private experience in public channels," fearing the opprobrium often cast on a divorced woman.[31] Indeed, the experience of divorce set Clarina apart from most women in the mid-nineteenth century, even from her future colleagues in the woman's rights movement.

Legal dissolution of the marriage was only one aspect of the problem Clarina faced, as she sought to overcome the shame she experienced for having failed at a woman's highest calling. Separation had compromised her virtue, and divorce threatened her social standing. On January 24, 1840, she had turned thirty. Living in her parents' home, she was bringing new burdens—if not disgrace—upon her family, but she had no recourse other than to rely upon her father's understanding and financial support. She was nurturing three small children: Birsha, eight; Howard (who used his middle name), six; and Relie (short for Aurelius), four, and she needed her family's help with child-care. In an era when the stigma of divorce could condemn any woman to wearing a lifelong veil of dishonor, she was disillusioned with what life might offer, and her future was unclear. Not yet free to remarry, she faced a formi-dable legal ordeal and years of struggle ahead. How would she support her family? She could teach and write, but would she remain dependent upon her father's largesse for the rest of her life? She needed a new husband to protect both her financial future and her integrity as a genteel woman. How would she regain her self-respect, and what man would consider courting a divorced woman?

Clarina still maintained sufficient self-regard, intellectual curiosity, and faith in a benevolent God to avoid retreating into the kind of domestic inva-lidism that sometimes afflicted women in her situation. Instead, she began to transform her trials into a lesson for the future by translating her feel-ings and emotions into language that allowed her to understand her personal experience as part of the human condition. "As seekers of happiness," she mused, "we bring from the resources of our souls a proportionate share of forbearance and good humor in order to bring good from evil, otherwise we shall suffer the loss of our own self-possession."[32] Finding solace in God's love and a sense of purpose in her need to support her children, she sought ways to redeem herself by doing good works for others, whether it was within the Howard household or through community work.

For over three years, Clarina and her children remained at the stately home the Howards had purchased on the village green in Townshend. Chapin had become even more prominent as a local financier and leader in town affairs and could certainly accommodate her family, but there were now ten mouths to feed in the household.[33] Her anomalous position as a daughter but also a separated woman with the added burden of three young children weighed heavily on Clarina's conscience. She had been prized for both her beauty and intellect but had failed to fulfill her youthful promise, and now her younger siblings were thriving. Two of her sisters were married, and her brothers Aurelius and Ormando, who married in the early 1840s, were following ably in their father's footsteps. Aurelius traveled regularly to Michigan to monitor the family's investments and develop his own properties there. Her sister Catherine's situation as the wife of Mark Carpenter was perhaps the most difficult to bear, for Clarina's brother-in-law was a highly respected Baptist minister in Keene, New Hampshire, and a constant reminder that Clarina had married the wrong man.[34]

While her obligation to help support her children weighed heavily on her psyche, Clarina's physical health was also precarious, as sciatica had returned during her stressful marriage. Walking could precipitate shooting pains down her spine, buttocks, and/or legs, and standing for long periods of time or carrying heavy loads was out of the question. "Oh, how hard it was to do any extra work on my feet or lift or go up stairs," she later remarked about the condition. "These spinal troubles take the courage down below 0." Rest was the only known cure at the time. Shifting childcare and domestic responsibilities to others members of the Howard household no doubt increased the tension among family members. Clarina eased her mental angst about the everyday friction that commonly arose in such a family setting by preaching that "kindness rule in the domestic circle . . . for *God requires* it," she explained, "for *humanity's* sake."[35]

The prospect of teaching at Leland Seminary, or Townshend Academy as it was called locally, provided the most obvious option for Clarina to fulfill her obligations and help support her children. Established by leading Baptists in 1835, the school offered a classical program in Greek, Latin, and English as well as Spanish, French, and painting for tuition-paying students. A major contributor and trustee, Chapin intended his children to benefit from its operation. In 1840 Clarina became the instructor of the Ladies Department for at least one term, but sciatica may have limited her ability to withstand the rigors of the classroom on a regular basis. She taught English, languages, and painting, a common program for the female students along with music, and perhaps she tutored students privately. With her father's support, she could afford to write instead, and though less lucrative, writing at home could conceivably accommodate her physical limitations. Meanwhile, her daughter Birsha attended the academy, and the boys went to local district school until they were eligible for the primary department at the brick school.[36]

Chapin and Birsha Howard moved to this house, which still stands on the Village Green in Towns-
hend, in 1832. Two of Clarina's children were probably born here, where she lived for several years
after separating from Justin Carpenter. Courtesy of the Townshend Historical Society.

Despite her unhappy circumstances, motherhood filled Clarina with a sense of purpose and parental obligation that she undertook seriously. During her marriage, her children's welfare had dominated her daily existence as she sought to earn enough to feed and clothe them, and fulfilling her maternal role proved comforting. She found strength to endure a heartless husband in her babies' tender smiles, and she grew anxious when separated from them. "Ma loves little Birsha & wants her to be a good girl," she had written, expressing her motherly concern after having left her two-year-old daughter in her parents' care. During the late summer and fall of 1839 when she was living briefly with relatives in Meriden, Connecticut, she wrote letters and poetry to cheer her children and bolster her own spirits as well. Seven-year-old Birsha would "sit and weep" when her grandmother read Clarina's affectionate letters reassuring her daughter that she would be back soon. Feeling alone and unloved, Clarina turned to her children as compensation for her sorrowful existence.[37] After her separation, her feelings for them were heightened by her lingering fears that Justin could still exercise his parental rights. Would he try to use his leverage as a father to exercise his authority over her? Not until his death in 1848, probably from typhus in New York City, would that nightmare ultimately disappear. Yet she continued to fear that Justin's notoriety would tarnish her children's future prospects. "Far, far be the day when their innocent trust/Shall be grieved by the tale of thy treatment unjust," she resolved.[38] That was another reason to protect them under the umbrella of the upright Howards. Clarina would later convert the emotional intensity she invested in mothering into a viable political identity. Children were a divine gift, she insisted, the "medium through which the helplessness, the wants and the promise of humanity have appealed to the *woman*."[39]

It was partly her sense of maternal obligation that spurred Clarina to publish her writings. In 1840 she began submitting her poetry and short prose pieces to newspaper editors in nearby Brattleboro. Situated on the Connecticut River, the commercial town hosted a thriving publishing business and several newspapers, including the Whig-backed *Vermont Phoenix*, with the largest circulation, and its rival *Windham County Democrat*, which spouted Jacksonian rhetoric. While dependent upon political patronage for support, country weeklies fed the appetites of a rising number of middle-class readers eager for inexpensive literary material, and they became outlets for local writers as well. Editors William E. Ryther of the *Phoenix* and George W. Nichols of the *Democrat* often devoted the entire front page of a four-page folio to poetry and prose either clipped from other publications or submitted by local writers, interspersed with brief news items. The Howards were committed Whigs and no doubt subscribed to the *Phoenix*, but as avid readers, they may have taken both papers.[40]

It was in this context that Clarina Carpenter began developing her literary skills. Ryther featured several of her poems and short essays on the front page of the *Phoenix* in early 1840 with the byline "C. I. H. C." Until after the Civil War, anonymity was still a common practice for both male and female writers. For a woman writer to reveal her identity was unusual but acceptable as long as she presented content appropriate for her sex and avoided politics. For example, Clarina authored an ode to a dying widow who mourned for her patriot husband at the Battle of Lexington under her name, "C. I. H. Carpenter of Townshend."[41] Women's literary production had blossomed in the 1830s as they began to write and publish novels, stories, and advice about domestic topics. Editor Sarah J. Hale, who began to dictate literary style and fashion for American women in *Godey's Lady's Book*, epitomized the new role some women were assuming in publishing and literary production. Publishers were quick to expand the market by printing material women readers would enjoy, and newspapers became an inexpensive vehicle for distributing this literature. Clarina probably received no more than a few dollars for any of her pieces, but at least she gained the satisfaction of seeing her work in print.[42]

Clarina's early writings displayed a sentimentalism typically found in the regional literature of antebellum New England. She employed common stylistic conventions, producing an emotive style that allowed her to express her inner self and to preach a gospel of disinterested love and Christian sympathy.[43] Coupling romantic phraseology with reverence for God and his heavenly creation on earth, she used the trope of memory to write about domestic and historical topics. If the emotional content of her works, filled with sweetness, melancholy, and spiritual love, was commonplace in women's poetry, it also reflected the disappointment about her life and the sadness she was experiencing. In "My Faded Keepsakes," Clarina mused about a happier time:

> This tiny watch with its pewter back
> And earthen face so sadly crack'd,
> 'Twas my Grandmother's gift,—it softly ticks
> Sweet moments of childhood I would not forget,—
> Her loving smile and her tender care
> Are brightly twined in its chain of hair;—[44]

Her memorial poem entitled "For the Daughter of a Deceased Friend" expressed grief as well as hope for a Christian woman removed to "Heaven's all-sustaining power and love." Even while facing despair, Clarina's works reveal a deep underlying faith in a benevolent God as a bulwark against earthly trials. "With hopes and joys of heavenly worth," she affirmed, "the heart will not bow down to earth." Her prose provided readers with Christian principles for overcoming suffering with "the sunshine of a kind and well ordered spirit."[45]

Through this process, Clarina healed her emotional wounds and began to devise a way to reengage in the world. By spring 1840, she began interpreting her failed marriage as a character-building lesson and turned her anger into a source of vigor as she prepared for the ordeal of divorce. It is only when "disappointment curdles[s] the very springs of the soul," when "the canker of undervalued affection,—the chilling glance of selfish indifference blast[s] the confidence," that we "turn to glean from the past a lesson for present use—a surer foundation for the expected good of futurity," she concluded. No longer confident that she could achieve happiness through selfless devotion to domestic duty, she sought a rationale to redeem herself and recoup her reputation outside the home. "What but lacerated sympathies ever drew the retiring, affectionate woman, from her deep devotion to the unobstrusive joys of domestic life, to a theatre of public action?" she queried. Just as great business leaders were sometimes motivated in their endeavors by their failure to achieve personal happiness, so too broken-hearted women could be drawn by their depth of feeling to "thrilling resolves and heroic sacrifices" and into a public sphere of "universal benevolence."[46] This model of feminine self-sacrifice parlayed the virtue that supposedly characterized women's domestic and religious activities into an array of civic societies designed to improve the broader community.[47] Clarina had begun to engage in such activities in Brockport, believing benevolent work would fulfill her duty to God, but it could also help her overcome the shame associated with a failed marriage.

Concealing her past while devoting herself to doing good in the world would animate Clarina for much of her career. Rooted in the religious values that connected her to both her family and the Baptist community, her chosen identity was enhanced by the strength of the evangelical movement that had spread throughout the Connecticut River Valley, reaching into Townshend again in the late 1830s. Construction of a new Baptist church, which stood prominently across the Common from the Howard home and next to Leland Seminary, followed a revival in 1838 and boosted membership to nearly two hundred communicants. Under the guidance of Reverend William D. Upham, members initiated a Sabbath school and raised funds for foreign missions and ministers' education, and the Howard women no doubt helped support the church and these endeavors through organized fund-raising. Clarina, her uncle and aunt, Peter and Sylvia Taft, and several other Howard relatives joined the revitalized Townshend Temperance Society and pledged themselves to total abstinence and the promotion of temperance throughout the town.[48]

Clarina was filled with a desire to redeem herself locally through community work, but she was far less comfortable mingling in public and thus continued to put her energies into her writings. While she waited to proceed with her divorce, in the winter of 1841 she began working more closely with George Nichols of the *Windham County Democrat*. He was anxious to print a wide range of literary offerings and appreciated the sensibilities expressed in Clarina's writings. Though he informed her that he could not always print her pieces as quickly as she might hope given his numerous correspondents, he may have encouraged her to help him in his editorial work. She began annotating articles for him clipped from her readings and sending them as suggestions worthy of local publication, and in turn he sent her more papers and magazines to review. Politics aside, it was her gender that may have been an advantage to Nichols, for Clarina's perspective would provide insight into the tastes of mature female readers. With Whigs in power both nationally and at the state level, he needed to boost subscription income for his minority party paper. Recognizing her capacity to assist him, her "kindred feeling," and her heartfelt expression, George Nichols eventually sought to become more acquainted with the writer through a more intimate personal correspondence. From a purely professional relationship, their friendship flowered and intensified over the next two years. George's attentions helped restore Clarina's sense of self-worth and ease her anxieties about the future as she waited with anticipation for her divorce to be finalized in February 1843.[49]

A month later, Clarina Irene Howard Carpenter shed her past and married George Washington Nichols at the Howard home in Townshend with the blessing of her Baptist minister. Though it may seem surprising that she risked her future with a new marital bond, this time the bride and her family had plenty of evidence to testify to her new husband's trustworthiness. Both his character and career in the newspaper business were on record and verifiable in nearby Brattleboro. Born in Stowe in 1785, George was twenty-five years older than Clarina—the same age as her father—and he was clearly a father figure for her. With six surviving daughters, he knew about parental concerns and husbands' obligations. Like his new father-in-law, he had profited from the commercialization of Vermont's economy, and he had survived in the business of political journalism whereas Justin Carpenter had failed. At fifty-eight, however, Nichols had amassed little wealth; his career as an editor and publisher had benefited from fortuitous connections through his first marriage. Apprenticed to a printer in the Connecticut River town of Walpole, New Hampshire, Nichols had married Anne Fessenden, daughter of the town's Congregational minister and sister of the well-known writer Thomas Green Fessenden. The couple had moved across the river to Brattleboro when Nichols became foreman of the *Reporter*, a Federalist paper established by another brother-in-law. His subsequent employers, John C. Holbrook and Joseph

Fessenden, operated successful trade, papermaking, and print businesses in Brattleboro and were prominent members of the Congregational Church, as was Nichols. Benefiting from these connections to community leaders, he had purchased their National Republican paper, the *Messenger*, in 1826 and nine years later partnered with Ryther in the *Phoenix* as it developed a Whig following. But during a period of political upheaval, the partnership dissolved, and Nichols found a new home among local Democrats, from whom he purchased the *Windham County Democrat* in 1836.[50]

To complement his reputation as a worthy newspaperman who rose from lowly roots, during their two-year courtship George had displayed the kind of sympathy, affection, and spirituality that Clarina had anticipated in a husband. Only one letter survives from their premarital correspondence, providing clues to his character and feelings. Despite or perhaps because of his age, George treated her with profound respect and with a courtliness of manner characteristic of the romantic age. In print he could display fiery political rhetoric, but in person, he presented himself as a "diffident and reserved" man, anxious to curry favor with a woman of such literary talent. He admired Clarina's intellect, her frank but sympathetic expression, and her modesty; he needed both her companionship to quell his loneliness and her assistance in his business. With fond but sorrowful memories of his first wife, who apparently succumbed to an unknown but long-term mental illness before her death in 1830, George had suffered privately while reaffirming his faith in God. Though he belonged to the Congregational Society, he regretted having ignored his religious duties as a young man and had come to a new realization of his obligations to honor a "higher power." In Clarina he recognized the "voice of a kindred spirit" who spoke "in tones that make the heart vibrate with sensations that call up remembrances of other days." She expressed a sensibility and religious devotion he admired; reading between the lines of her prose, he found her suffering little different from his own "sorrow and bitterness." Like Clarina, he idealized a match in which two "hearts knit together in love and unison in this life" would leave the world for "a happiness that is to be *continued* and perfected in heaven."[51]

Beyond her need for mutuality, Clarina found in George an honorable gentleman who could resolve her greatest concerns about her reputation as a divorced woman and provide the opening to pursue her intellectual interests as well. A kindly man, George embodied the wisdom and security of an older generation with established careers. No more young, untested entrepreneurs for Clarina! Early in their correspondence, she displayed her own feminine modesty and tested the depth of his friendly interest in her by noting that she "possessed . . . few personal attractions." He reassured her that "personal beauty" only served to "excite the passions of youth" and held "no lasting influence upon the affections." Though she apparently rebuked him for "trespassing" on the "forbidden ground" of her unhappy circumstances, he consoled her as a "fellow sufferer," recognizing that her confidence and affections had been abused by the "brutal treatment [of] one who was legally and morally bound to defend and protect." Despite her experience of marital betrayal, Clarina continued to believe in a union of "mutual joy," in which two souls joined in open and frank communication would be sanctified in Heaven.[52] George was not only a sympathizing friend and kind father, but he would become a bulwark in the development of her literary and political work. Although her dowry had been spent during her first marriage, her father's wealth ensured that her children's education would not become a burden to George. She was no doubt anxious to have a home of her own, and her economic contributions to his business would help offset other expenses for her children.

Once again optimism characterized Clarina's state of mind as she anticipated her new life. With the help of a supportive family who took umbrage that their eldest daughter had been wronged, she had overcome her marital calamity. Steeled by her faith and her intellectual acumen, she resolved the problem of female dependence by entering marriage again. Given her options and need for self-fulfillment, it was a propitious choice. But the blow she had suffered to her pride and sense of fairness would continue to shape Clarina's self-image as a woman until she reached middle age. At a time when a successful marriage was the measure of a woman's ability to command respect, the experience had undermined her self-confidence and distanced her from other women. It was partly a result of the heights to which the Howards had propelled her that the fall was so mortifying. Having grown up to believe in affection as the basis of marriage, that she would partake in middle-class respectability, and that she was the intellectual equal of her male relatives and peers, Clarina Carpenter learned that these perceived realities were contingent and would not ensure her future. Justin's behavior had clearly wounded both her heart and her pride. Her lifelong effort to avoid publicity about these events, the eradication of any references to her first marriage or her life in New York City, and her quest for redemption from having failed at a divinely sanctioned union revealed the depth of her outrage. Now as Mrs. Nichols, she was prepared to go forward rather than back. With confidence that she had found an honorable man, she set about recouping her respectability and resuming her quest for a purposeful life.

3

Pathway to Politics

The conduct of a newspaper is arduous and wearing; but we must confess it is to us a pleasant business; . . . its rewards are not confined to dollars and cents; . . . It is a business which permits us to make our mark on the immortal spirit for good if we will—to mingle our sympathies with our kind—to cheer the despairing, to warn the headlong and speed the errand of mercy and the development of every human virtue.
  C. I. H. Nichols, 1846

In the 1840s the newspaper business was highly partisan, cut-throat, and risky, not the place for a woman who had envisioned a life devoted to "universal benevolence." Yet Clarina found a way to enact her dreams by partnering in her new husband's business. Beyond the affection and respect she craved, George Nichols offered a bounteous feast where she could satisfy her voracious appetite for literary pursuit and quench her thirst for doing good in the world. Seated comfortably in her new parlor surrounded by stacks of exchange papers and books, Clarina could indulge herself while editing her husband's paper. Her Christian sense of mission found a new outlet in the noble purpose of uplifting and educating readers with homespun advice and political commentary designed to improve their lives and the nation as well. But the work was not without its challenges. She faced the unfeminine task of promoting a partisan political agenda, a role few women undertook without considerable trepidation. Starting anonymously, it would take seven years before she was willing to reveal that Mrs. Nichols was wielding the editorial pen at the *Windham County Democrat.* By that time, she had fashioned a new identity as the "sensible and sarcastic Editress of the Democrat," who interrupted her domestic duties to offer her political opinions as only a benevolent woman could.[1]

Clarina's second marriage secured her future with a man of integrity and wisdom, even as it rejuvenated George's life and business with an earnest companion for his daughters. When Clarina moved into the Nichols home in Brattleboro at the age of thirty-three, she entered a household filled with young women, two of whom were close to her own age. George had eight children, but only his six daughters had survived to adulthood. The eldest, Eliza Ann, was still single and barely a month older than Clarina; Julia was two years younger. With a keen interest in education, George had sent his daughters to select schools in Brattleboro, and they were active in the community. Clarina's relationship with her new stepdaughters is unclear because they are nearly absent from the historical record, though she mentioned Eliza fondly in her later years. As long as she did not assert undo authority, she may have developed a sisterly relationship with Eliza and Julia, who mothered the younger girls, one of whom became mentally ill.[2]

Even while Clarina welcomed her stepdaughters' companionship, she was removed from the daily care of her Carpenter children. Twelve-year-old Birsha remained emotionally tied to her mother but apparently floated between Brattleboro and Townshend, where she finished her education at the Townshend Academy under her grandparents' supervision. Clarina also left her two sons, Howard and Relie, then ages eight and six, to be raised and educated in Townshend with their grandparents or uncles, where they probably earned their keep by working. Both boys eventually attended the academy, of which their grandfather was an active trustee and treasurer.[3] Less than a year after Clarina's marriage to George, the Nichols's household was once again alive with the cries and babblings of a baby boy when Clarina birthed her fourth and last child, George Bainbridge Nichols. With her older children in Townshend and a houseful of young women to help with both her baby's care and domestic duties, she was freer than many women of her era to devote time to writing and editorial work.

Unlike her temporary quarters in the upstart crossroads of Brockport over a decade earlier, Clarina's new home was nestled in a bustling commercial center only sixteen miles from Townshend. Cradled between low hills bordering the Green Mountains and the Connecticut River, Brattleboro had become a center of trade and local culture, linking residents to the fertile valley of

*George Washington Nichols with his
and Clarina's child, George Bainbridge
Nichols, born in 1844. Courtesy of the
Grace Hudson Museum and Sun House,
City of Ukiah, California.*

western Massachusetts to the south. With 2,300 residents, it was the center
of provincial exchange for southeastern Vermont and supported a flourishing
print business, small shops producing chairs and shoes, and wool and grain
processing mills; several bookshops, a bank, general stores, and apothecaries
lined its Main Street paralleling the river. Brattleboro's residents displayed
the "go-ahead principle," according to one booster, epitomizing "New England enterprise, industry, and thrift." Filled with transients, the village was
a day's journey from key transportation centers in the surrounding states and
hosted eleven daily stages with same-day service to Springfield and Boston,
Albany, and Montreal. The "stages came thundering up, . . . brim full of passengers, men, women and children—not to be mentioned, dogs, dandies or
monkeys outside and in" to be deposited in the provincial town, giving it a
cosmopolitan flare.[4]

Clarina arrived at a time when the village was recovering from economic
depression and on the brink of a new phase of development that expanded
its population and cultural diversity. By 1843 business was finally improving
after the financial Panic of 1837, which had depressed farm prices and economic development in the entire region. Local hotels swelled with transients,

and boardinghouses sprang up to accommodate young migrants from surrounding towns who sought work. Irish immigrants began filtering into the community during the 1840s, as men laid the railroad northward and young women filled the demand for domestic servants and chambermaids. The only black family in town ran a local barber shop. The Nichols's home on Green Street was only a ten-minute walk from the office of the *Democrat*, located in the second story of an old brick building opposite the Stage House. Heading north along Main Street, Clarina could encounter an array of local tradesmen, mechanics, and farmers peddling their goods, interspersed with fashionably dressed visitors who patronized local shops filled with dry goods, millinery, jewelry, and books. North of the commercial district, the Brattleboro Retreat, a state-sponsored private asylum, grew exponentially during Clarina's tenure in Brattleboro. Known for humane treatment of the mentally ill, it housed four hundred state patients by 1855 and employed many attendants and groundskeepers.[5]

Meanwhile, the opening of another kind of retreat for middle-class urbanites enriched the town's cultural life. After discovering pure springs along the brook running through the village, John Gray and Robert Wesselhoeft, a German doctor eager to practice hydropathy, opened a water-cure establishment in 1844 near the Nichols's home. It catered to hundreds of patrons seeking improved health and respite from the trials of city life. An offshoot of the flourishing health reform movement, the water-cure regimen was an attempt to counter the use of ineffective, harsh medical treatment and to purge the body of chronic disease by returning to the naturalness of bathing in pure cold water, walking in fresh air, eating a simple diet, and getting plenty of rest. Patients arrived with chronic coughs, asthma, back pain, and fatigue and were treated daily to hot blanket wraps alternating with cold-water showers and sitz baths. They plunged in the pure spring waters flowing down Brattleboro's hillside, walked well-trodden pathways meandering through the surrounding woods, drank cold spring water in lieu of alcohol and tobacco, and indulged in good conversation and entertainment. Almost overnight, Brattleboro became a summer resort, attracting health enthusiasts and intellectuals imbued with the romantic notion that a return to nature would restore both body and mind. By the late 1840s, as many as four hundred patients spilled out from the water-cure buildings during summer and fall to swell local hotels and boardinghouses, and a long line of fancy carriages with coachmen waiting for their owners commonly greeted Clarina on her walks. Visitors touting the

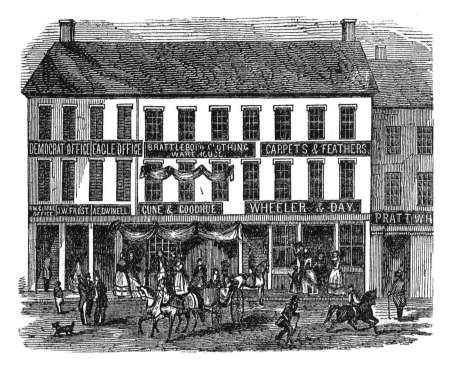

This woodcut from the Windham County Democrat, *September 2, 1850, shows the paper's office in the upper story of "Granite Row" in Brattleboro. Courtesy of Brattleboro Historical Society, Brattleboro, Vermont.*

village as "one of the most beautiful localities in the whole country" helped to spread its reputation as a healthful oasis, where "little rivers, creeks, rivulets and brooks, ravines, plains, terraces, rocks, [and] hillocks" complemented the mountain views. "It is strange to me that every one doesn't live in Brattleborough," exclaimed the writer Fanny Fern. "There is not an ugly walk or drive in the whole town." With the onset of railroad service in 1851, the village became even more accessible, attracting not only Boston's elite but also a regular contingent of southern visitors escaping the summer heat.[6]

Clarina Nichols thrived during this golden age in Brattleboro's economic and cultural development. She relished both the patronage and literary interests of the summer visitors, who brought a taste of urban culture to the community in the form of lectures and highbrow entertainment. There were writers, artists, musicians, and a number of reform-minded women, including the Beecher sisters, Catherine and Harriet, who treated their frail health with a holiday from their domestic duties and professional work. Mixing with local residents, these "distinguished strangers" added to the liveliness and diversity of the place, according to Clarina, offering a "rich treat" otherwise absent from a provincial village. She may have witnessed her first female lecturer when Mrs. Mary Gove, who was training in water-cure methods, gave a series of free lectures to the "Ladies of Brattleboro" on female anatomy and physiology. Providing women with knowledge about their bodies, Gove was in the vanguard of the women's movement to control their own health and sexuality. It is unknown if Clarina befriended Gove, who later remarried and became notorious as Mary Gove Nichols, exponent of free love, or if she knew the Beechers. But the Nicholses did open their home to summer boarders to take advantage of the tourist trade. In 1845 they hosted Henry Wadsworth Longfellow, his wife, and toddler Charley, who romped with little two-year-old George and filled the house with amusing talk and childish antics. Honored to converse with the Harvard professor, whose poetry she found both comforting and inspiring, Clarina offered to advertise his latest works in the *Democrat* after he sent her a copy of *Hyperion.*[7]

If many of these part-time residents were rejuvenating their physical health in Brattleboro, descendants of the town's Yankee pioneers were reshaping its moral and intellectual life through their religious and benevolent organizations. During the 1830s a wave of evangelists had revitalized the churchgoing community; Protestant sects, Sunday schools, women's benevolent societies, and temperance advocates flourished, much like they had in Brockport. Village leaders generally pursued a moderate approach to reform through moral suasion, and George Nichols partook in the effort to foster habits of personal responsibility through his paper and by publishing religious tracts to supplement Christian education; two of his daughters took the bold step of signing a legislative petition to prohibit local liquor licensing along with other Congregational women.[8] Eager to find her place among like-minded Christians, Clarina joined the society of local Baptists, a relatively new but energetic congregation imbued with the spirit of reform and seeking social leadership in the 1840s. The choice signified an enduring link to her Baptist roots and her family but also a degree of independence from her new husband and his association with Congregationalists. As a result, she was outside the circle of elite women and the benevolent associations they operated, but members of both sects were eager to promote a consistent set of religious and social values, which muted their sectarian differences. Under the leadership of Jacob Estey, an ambitious mechanic and superintendent of the Sunday school, the Baptist society eventually attracted many workers from Estey's rapidly expanding melodeon factory.[9] During Clarina's first summer in the village, Baptists rallied townspeople to join the Washingtonians, an organization of artisans committed to total abstinence from alcohol. They too were devoted to cold water and gathered young men and women to march up Main Street in a grand "Cold Water Army" with banners displaying their commitment to the "spirit of Temperance reform." Baptists and Congregationalists competed fiercely for these young recruits, yet they also cooperated in statewide temperance and Sunday school programs to promote social improvement. Teaching piety and morality at home, improving schools, organizing local lyceums for intellectual stimulation, and abstaining from alcohol were considered bulwarks against wayward behavior and the dangers lurking in a rapidly commercializing economy.[10]

Although both George and Clarina adhered to this evangelical viewpoint, George had become disenchanted with the network of local political leaders that had boosted his early career as a printer and publisher. As a National Republican he had employed a judicious approach to party politics in the *Brattleboro Messenger* while favoring protective tariffs and internal improvements for economic development, but the precarious business of journalism, dependent as it was on political patronage, barely tolerated a man in the middle. In 1834 when the National Republican Party fractured and disappeared under pressure from anti-Masons who dethroned local political leaders, so did Nichols's paper, despite his pleas for party unity and attempts to accommodate anti-Masonic principles.[11] Initially, he weathered the political upheaval by partnering with William E. Ryther in the *Vermont Phoenix* under the nascent Whig banner, but his relationship with the young and ambitious journalist— known for his liberal ideas, "native shrewdness," and "sharp wit"—floundered even before their political backers withdrew during the 1836 electoral campaign. Whether their differences were political or financial is unclear, but only five weeks after the paper was sold, Ryther repurchased it on his own with new Whig sponsors. Without income from a weekly paper, about $2 per subscription annually, Nichols could not survive as a printer on pamphlet and book publishing, and he sought an alternative home with the state's minority party.[12]

With the purchase of the *Windham County Democrat*, George Nichols inverted his political stance from advocate of business interests to champion of the "laboring classes."[13] In the early 1830s he had railed against Andrew Jackson's policies, yet by the end of the decade, he was rallying Democrats around "Old Hickory" as a symbol of the man of the people. A regular booster of American democracy, he extolled "our free institutions" and the rising consciousness of "free suffrage and equal rights" while promoting Democratic political issues, including support for state's rights, the dignity of workers, and opposition to high tariffs and corporate monopolies to restore sovereignty to the people. Nichols applied his belief in the "spirit of the gospel and the teachings of truth and justice" to the peoples' cause, denouncing Whigs who would legislate for the *"Rights of Property!!* And overlook the natural, indefeasible, inalienable *Rights of Persons!!"* His political rhetoric no doubt reflected ire at rival Ryther as well as at Whigs, who dominated the town and state after 1836 and national elections by 1840, leaving him without lucrative party patronage until 1844. Politics aside, however, both men published notices, advice, and sentimental tales designed to inform and improve the prospects of their middle-class readers. George's political diatribes did not prevent him from following a social code and offering a reform agenda similar to that of his political nemesis, calling young men to sober training, industry, and prudence; husbands to kindness and devotion; and wives to domesticity, benevolence, and amiability.[14]

It is unclear exactly when Clarina Nichols took full responsibility for editing her husband's newspaper. Upon marriage, she became his full-time assistant, chose most of the material inserted in the paper, and authored editorial comments anonymously. Though she later claimed to have penned all the editorials while working "under my husband's hat," George's style is apparent in a few of the scattered papers that still exist. At the end of the decade his health deteriorated markedly, and Clarina temporarily assumed both the editorial and the financial end of the business. When it became increasingly obvious to her readership that she was in the "editorial chair," she finally admitted that she had relieved her husband of his burdens only out of the practical "necessity for a mete help which first invited us to his side and made room for us in a 'public position.'" By 1850 she had earned a reputation for wielding a "sparkling pen" while attending to her "domestic duties" and all but shed her anonymity, but George's name remained on the masthead until 1853. In hindsight, she explained, "before I came out in my own name to give my sex a personal offering . . . I wished to make sure that I had secured the confidence of men in my ability to conduct their political paper! before I threw myself on their support in the matter of legal & social reforms."[15] At a time when her gender was an easy target for political opponents, anonymity neutralized the issue and allowed her to earn a respectable following in the press.

Few women edited partisan papers at the time, yet Clarina followed a practice that colonial wives and widows had pioneered by assisting with their husbands' publications. In the 1830s and 1840s, the number of published women writers and journalists increased dramatically, but most eschewed the male preserve of partisan politics altogether, confining their public voices to womanly religious, domestic, or educational topics. Those who advocated social change, such as moral reform, temperance, and antislavery, wrote anonymously or veiled their political opinions within fiction or appeals to Christian morality. As editor of the *National Anti-Slavery Standard* in the early 1840s, outspoken abolitionist Lydia Maria Child defended her public role as an economic necessity and coupled antislavery ideology with moralistic literary content, hoping to shift the fractured movement away from electoral politics.[16] With the exception of iconoclast Anne Royall, a fierce Whig partisan, female journalists who did embrace politics disguised their gender or used literary devices to assure readers that they still adhered to the unassuming, virtuous, and domestic traits normally expected of middle-class women. Democrat Jane Storm of the *United States Magazine and Democratic Review* and the *New York Sun,* for example, published her widely read columns under a pseudonym. Reformer Jane Grey Swisshelm, who established the antislavery *Pittsburgh Saturday Visiter* in 1847, publicly admitted her role but continually injected the high moral tone of a lady and principled reformer into her support for the Liberty and Free Soil parties, a model that Clarina would replicate.[17]

At the time of their marriage, however, George Nichols hardly anticipated that his new wife would join the ranks of the so-called Female Politicians whom Democrats often mocked. For a woman to openly engage in partisan rhetoric or behavior was to defy contemporary understandings of female virtue and to venture outside woman's sphere into the seamy world of political compromise and corruption. Yet American political parties had long accommodated the wives of prominent leaders who wielded female influence within political networks of the early republic. When parties began staging mass rallies to appeal to an expanded electorate in the 1840s, women emerged openly as partisans and organizers. Parading for candidates, Whig women appeared to validate the virtue and patriotism of the new party.[18] Democrats were quick to ridicule such behavior, using gender as a ripe political weapon, and George Nichols reprinted their rhetoric in the *Democrat*. By waving flags and singing "rowdy songs with tavern brawlers," female partisans were accused of joining the likes of Anne Royall and the utopian reformer Fanny Wright, notorious for irreligion, free love, and public appearances. "If there is one thing to make us proud of the party to which we belong," Democrats insisted, "it is, that the wives, mothers, sisters of our Democratic fellow citizens, have not thrown off their household duties to enact the politician."[19] As Clarina busily clipped and composed material for his paper, George Nichols may have considered her work largely literary, not partisan or even political. To avoid the rhetorical disadvantages of her sex on partisan issues, however, Clarina would have to remain anonymous and tow the party line. Alternatively, if she wanted to pursue reform and challenge the political establishment openly as a female editor, proving her moral virtue with a display of womanliness, benevolence, and nonpartisanship was essential.

In her new role, Mrs. Nichols used her skill as a journalist to negotiate the contradiction inherent in these two avenues into political discourse. She established her credentials as a party stalwart anonymously while also shifting the content and tone of the *Democrat* in subtle ways. As editor she sought to demonstrate both her gentility and her womanliness, particularly after her identity became apparent. With access to many partisan and reform papers, Nichols followed the example of other women writers who expressed the sentiments, decorum, and religiosity she admired as she developed the paper into a family newspaper with wide appeal. To that end, she reprinted literary sketches and advice that would attract middle-class readers: the "Pathology of a Lady of Fashion," "Take Care of the Pence," "A 'Love of a Bonnet,'" and "The Green Mountain Girls." These stories expressed a common set of provincial values Nichols had gleaned from her Baptist upraising, the importance of thrift, the practical value of women's domestic work, and disdain for pretentious behavior while striving for a better life.[20]

At first the format of the *Democrat* changed little, but its new editor provided commentary on a greater variety of material from exchange papers that began to influence her own ideas as well as the focus of the paper. Publishers typically benefited from agreements whereby they received free papers and clipped liberally from their colleagues. An increasing proportion of the articles Nichols printed addressed domestic topics and social relations of interest to other women. "Seated at our table surrounded by our exchanges," she mused, "we find ourself acted upon, our moods influenced by these silent chroniclers of ideas."[21] They included popular magazines and reform journals—*Columbian Magazine, Ladies National Magazine, Graham's Magazine, Christian Parlor Magazine*—and many regional newspapers. Her audience could delight in stories such as "The Poor Widow; or, Don't Grind the Poor," about a benevolent woman who resurrects a poor seamstress from poverty, and "Rug Raffles" by Fanny Forrester, lifted from *Columbian Magazine.* Beyond their reading value, Nichols also distributed these papers to local patrons, who supplied her in-kind with what she called "their harvests of fruits, vegetables, poultry, etc."[22]

Nichols acknowledged the influence of a wide range of readings but also began to recognize her ability to touch her patrons and to shape their ideas and values. When she reviewed the contents of these journals, she established her authority to dictate her readers' literary taste. The *Family Magazine,* a "special favorite," was balanced with the partisan and literary *Democratic Review,* which presented "a rich array of good solid reading." She assured her audience that her choices were infused with "high-toned moral feeling" and dedicated to truth, simplicity, and usefulness.[23] As she became more self-confident in her role as editor, Clarina cast herself as a missionary in the field of ideas, soothing the downtrodden and heartsick and steering her flock into good works. For readers "surrounded by difficulties and weighed down by many sorrows," she sought to provide a "paragraph speaking hope and courage." Expressing her satisfaction in sentimental terms, she remarked, "our heart leaps, with a tear-drop in the eye, to apply the balsam." For her more intellectual and philosophic readers, she enjoyed finding that "gem fresh from the mine of truth," a "precious morsel" that would provide them with "substantial food." Although Clarina recognized the need for nourishment among all age groups, above all, she hoped to guide young men and women who had little experience with the "realities of life." Fraught with temptations and unrealistic dreams, they needed "sweet lessons of truth and integrity" to ensure their "conjugal felicity and domestic usefulness." With her own experience in mind, she hoped to teach husbands that the golden rules of self-sacrifice, honesty, and mutual affection within marriage were just as valuable as "industry and economy." She warned young women about the dangers of passion and ostentation, advising them to cultivate "the intellect that can guide and the heart that can sustain" to secure a happy home and garner self-respect.[24]

Increasingly, she featured literature by women authors, who disseminated a standard of refined womanhood in stories about the trials women endured. "Lydia Darrah" portrayed the heroism of a spy during the American Revolution, and the "American Christian Citizen" glorified female patriotism and connected women to the national goal of freedom. "Woman's Mission," by Lydia Jane Pierson of the *Lancaster, Pennsylvania, Gazette,* replayed a sorry tale in which a beautiful, intellectual woman marries a soul mate who appreciates her at first before becoming a victim of gambling and alcohol; he is saved only through the prayers of his suffering wife.[25] The story resonated with Clarina's own experience, but it also conveyed a form of contemporary womanliness that permeated the literature she read and reprinted. The beautiful, educated, pious, and affectionate mother was often victimized by an unfeeling and depraved husband, but she also had the power to redeem him with her superior morality and capacity for forgiveness. Proud of women's productive work as well as their intellect and morality, Clarina extolled the "Green Mountain Girls," who learned from their mothers to make butter as well as read books and play music. It was a maternal ideal derived from her own childhood and one that laid the foundation for her future political engagement.[26]

If these lessons in everyday life cloaked in popular sentimental language temporarily fulfilled Clarina's desire to do good in the world, her polite commentary and womanly style became trademarks of her editorial work. Expressing the sympathy, benevolence, piety, and virtue expected from a woman of her class, she reestablished her own respectability and her credentials as an editor. Despite her anonymity, readers of the *Democrat* must have noticed its changing content and tone. A new column appeared in 1846 on the front page labeled "The Fire-Side," where she placed poetry and sentimental stories. As a symbol of domestic harmony, the title reflected the paper's focus on family readings that preached good behavior and good works derived from what she labeled "Bible philosophy." "Action is a better philosophy of the heart than feeling," she advised, "though to be efficient for others and blest to itself, it must be the result of feeling." As circulation widened, the Nicholses were able to afford new type, and they widened the columns, prompting compliments from other editors who admired the paper's "new dress." In collegial fashion, another Democratic editor praised the "neat and elegant" paper, which had "earned a most desirable reputation" for its "judicious and interesting" material. Circulation reached about 1,000 subscribers by 1850, making it less dependent upon the party for support.[27]

Even as Clarina reshaped the *Democrat* into a popular family newspaper, she engaged in partisan discourse. In this far more difficult task, she often couched her opinions in sarcasm and metaphors while repeatedly injecting moral imperatives and the value of nonpartisanship into the debate. As a Democratic editor, she found herself defending the rights of the common people against the rich and powerful, a party position consistent with her benevolent impulses to aid the hardworking poor. It was a refrain emanating from John O'Sullivan, editor of the *Democratic Review*. In their campaign to protect the people's interests, northern Democrats displayed a long-standing opposition to concentrations of power in the federal government and cabals of bankers and manufacturers. The Nicholses regularly advocated for lower tariffs and an independent treasury, and they opposed the interests of rich "monopolists" and "aristocrats" who exercised power at the "expense of the laboring classes." They often sparred with William Ryther, whom Clarina fondly labeled "our neighbor," over the tariff issue, indirectly criticizing his arguments while proclaiming her love of "frankness." During the 1844 election campaign, she belittled Ryther's defense of the tariff, noting that he had abandoned "his military tactics, for a display of sky-rockets and crackers; and finally bows himself off the stage mid a double line of exclamation points."[28] She relished these word battles yet regularly proclaimed the merits of nonpartisanship. After the Democratic victory she refused to "crow" and hoped to return to "good feeling and the memory of common interests" with her opponents. She concluded her column with a feminine-inspired sentiment to allay potential hostilities: "Wishing them joy over their newspaper, apples and nuts, around the domestic hearth, we bid them a cheerful good evening." Privately, of course, Clarina may have also hoped to endear herself with the Howard family, who were Whig in sympathy.[29]

Displaying her feminine sensibility served to moderate any hint of radicalism, but Clarina eagerly jumped onto the political bandwagon on issues that resonated with her benevolent concerns, especially when women were involved. In mid-1845 when the radical wing of northern Democrats, nicknamed "LocoFocos" by their opponents, focused on labor issues, she clipped articles about "Factory Labor," describing poor working conditions at the woolen mills in Lawrence, Massachusetts. She argued that high tariffs privileged manufacturers over mechanics and provided news of strikes in support of the ten-hour day. In "Song of the Shirt" she reprinted information about the poor wages and degrading working conditions women factory workers faced. Many of these "American born" women, a commentator remarked, had "once been in comfortable and even affluent circumstances, and have been reduced by the death or bankruptcy of husbands and relatives." These victims—poor widows, wives of ship's captains lost at sea, or those with sick or drunken husbands— were supporting children and elderly parents on their meager wages. Others faced the "agony of receiving home a fallen daughter or an outlawed son suddenly checked in his career of vice."[30] This expression of sympathy replayed a common theme bridging the partisan divide—that women needed protection from misfortune. While Whigs and Democrats disagreed about the solution to these problems, the portrayal of women as victims resonated with many voters, and it allowed Clarina to demonstrate her womanly concern while avoiding a radical stance that might alarm the business interests of Brattleboro.

Ignoring partisan differences on local and state issues, such as education and temperance, proved easier than on national ones. There was considerable momentum for education reform among local political leaders, who believed improving the schools was a key to keeping the town vibrant and its youth from joining the exodus to the city or the West. Young men needed preparation for employment in the commercial economy, and young women needed the skills to manage their domestic duties and teach their children. Following the lead of Massachusetts reformer Horace Mann, Whig leaders in Vermont adopted education reform as a campaign issue in 1844. By that time the common school movement, which included efforts to upgrade schoolhouses, curriculum, and teacher qualifications, had begun to awaken parents and school trustees to their roles in supervising district schools. The movement coincided with a dramatic increase in the employment of women as teachers, and Mann advised that young women needed improved training.[31] For Clarina and George Nichols, both of whom championed the value of education, the issue was vital to the "moral character" of the nation, overriding partisan concerns. Clarina advocated passionately for Vermont's education reform bill, which passed the following year; it instituted county and state school superintendents and upgraded teacher qualifications. Calling upon "Whigs, Democrats and Liberty men" to a "common field of labor," she urged the "friends of the youth—all who see in the 'wee ones' of our family circles, the future hope . . . of the nation," to support improvement in "our free institutions."[32]

In this way, she ignored partisan differences and displayed both her patriotism and motherly concern.

The same moralism prevailed in the Nicholses support for temperance as advocates pressed not only for total abstinence but also for state regulation of liquor sales. Hoping to educate and persuade her readers about the subject, Clarina continued to print news of temperance meetings and tales clipped from the temperance press. These sentimental allegories portrayed variations on a common theme: if allowed to drink, husbands would squander family income, desert their wives and children, and send them to the poorhouse, death resulting. In "The First Glass: A Tale of the Middle Walks of Life" and "The Drunkard's Wife," drunken and deserting husbands victimize women and children, threatening the stability of the home.[33] These stories, which proliferated out of the Washingtonian temperance movement, paralleled much of Clarina's own experience of marriage in its effects if not in the cause. The anti-alcohol campaign supplied her with a language to articulate the problems married women faced while upholding their prescribed domestic role, and to portray them as victims of unjust male behavior. The litany of male wrongs, which followed a storyline she had used in her own divorce proceedings to establish Justin's culpability, shifted the focus of the temperance movement from the unruly behavior of youths onto the reformation of drinking men and the protection of women and children.[34]

With a consensus in favor of temperance in Brattleboro and only minor divisions between the parties on the issue, Clarina Nichols took a stronger stand against liquor sales than her husband had previously exhibited. Both parties spouted temperance rhetoric, but they differed on the means of enforcement. Whereas Democrats generally promoted voluntary measures, Whigs advocated state regulation but initially resisted the radical demand for prohibition. After the Washingtonians swept through the region popularizing the movement with emotional appeals and attracting a working-class clientele, the momentum for regulation within both parties improved. With Whig leadership, the legislature passed a local option law in 1844, which prohibited liquor sales unless towns took positive action empowering county commissioners to grant local liquor licenses. Brattleboro voters opposed licensing and put the selectmen on notice to monitor local retail establishments, but other towns in the county continued to license sellers. Sentiment in Vermont's larger towns generally followed this pattern, but small rural communities resisted regulation.[35] With local partisan divisions muted, Clarina opposed licensing, printed

news urging total abstinence, and advocated election of "Temperance Commissioners" for the county.[36] In this way she upheld her religious convictions
and began her public commitment to prohibiting the sale of alcohol with its
damaging effects on the lives of women. As temperance became politicized in
the next decade, it ushered committed reformers like Clarina into the maelstrom of party politics.

Unlike local debates on temperance and education reform, national issues
of expansion and especially slavery forced George and Clarina Nichols to confront the partisanship at the heart of most newspapers. A sufficient display of
Democratic loyalty was essential to ensure national party patronage, which
meant taking stands on these weighty issues. Opposition to slavery had long
colored political discourse in Vermont, from legislative resolutions against the
spread of slavery in 1820, to widespread antislavery petition campaigns, to
vehement protestation against the congressional gag rule tabling those petitions. George Nichols had initially favored colonization to gradually end slavery and miscegenation by returning freed slaves to Africa. When abolitionism
rendered colonization untenable and antislavery became a dominant theme
in Vermont's electoral politics, he proclaimed slavery an evil, but he also expressed fears that abolition would release a deluge of "ignorant, stupid beings" upon the North and destroy the nation. A commonly held view of racial
hierarchy, the sentiment was expressed in the streets of Brattleboro when a
mob greeted a respected abolitionist speaker with a near riot in 1837.[37] After
becoming a Democrat, George either evaded a forthright position on slavery
or promoted a Unionist standpoint. Vermont Whigs took a stronger position
against slavery than their Democratic opponents, but their stance was too
moderate to satisfy abolitionists, who offered a Liberty Party ticket in 1841.
Opposed to slavery's extension and delighted at the thought that abolitionists
threatened to weaken the Whigs, whom he dubbed the "MONEY KINGS," George
Nichols showed a bit of political opportunism by printing the local Liberty
ticket in 1842, but he was not out of line with other Democratic editors in the
Connecticut River Valley, who equated the oppression of workers with that of
slaves and rallied around free speech in opposition to the gag rule.[38]

For Clarina, the notoriety of abolitionist women may have initially circumscribed her political rhetoric as much as her husband's partisan instincts. She
clearly believed slavery was immoral and against her belief that God prohibited one human being from owning another. Similar sentiments had driven
abolitionist women in the Northeast to organize societies in the late 1830s, to

petition state and national governments, and to garner public rebukes for attempting to lecture on the topic. Recognized as a moral force on the issue, especially in Massachusetts, a contingent of radical women had challenged the religious establishment and stood with William Lloyd Garrison to demand immediate emancipation. Baptists in Vermont had split over Garrison's radical stance, but it is unclear where Clarina's family stood on the issue. Their former minister, her uncle Peter Taft, and prominent lawyer Charles Phelps of West Townshend were involved in antislavery activities, and it is likely that the Howards were antislavery, but participation in Whig politics may have been enough to satisfy their moderate convictions. Whereas Garrisonian women remained outside the party system hoping to shape public opinion, Clarina was in the uncomfortable position of reconciling her humanitarian impulses with loyalty to a political party increasingly beholden to southern slave owners.[39]

As she assumed greater editorial control of the *Democrat*, Clarina Nichols struggled mightily to either defend her partisan views with moral principles or disclaim partisanship altogether. The annexation of Texas as a slave state and subsequent war with Mexico in 1846 entwined the two issues of slavery and expansion so tightly that northern Democrats found themselves seeking a way to maintain party unity as southerners stampeded to expand slave territory. Towing the party line in the 1844 electoral campaign, the Nicholses supported James Polk and annexation, but they also printed the local Liberty ticket again. They subsequently published articles from the *Democratic Review* to justify annexation on nationalist grounds without condoning slavery. Texas would provide an outlet for slave labor as it became increasingly untenable in older states, proclaimed New York's Democratic senator Silas Wright, and annexation would prevent the British from intervening and capturing the fruits of the cotton trade. Clarina took her cue from John O'Sullivan, the young editor of the *Review*, who grounded his expansionist views in a moral vision that appealed to her sense of mission. Coining the term "manifest destiny," O'Sullivan claimed that "Providence" had anointed Americans as the carriers of democratic values throughout the land. The following year, Clarina reiterated these sentiments by supporting Polk's policy to acquire the Oregon Territory, stressing negotiations with the British and a moderate claim to the 49th parallel, not the whole territory. Insisting that she held a "national rather than partisan" view, she claimed rightful possession of the region "to protect the whole area of freedom's domain" against the former oppressors.

Despite Vermonters' widespread disaffection with the ensuing Mexican War and the defection of leading Democrats in neighboring New Hampshire and New York on the issue, she upheld Polk's war and expansion policy, highlighted Mexican duplicity, and questioned the patriotism of Whig critics.[40]

Whether Clarina and George were in perfect agreement on foreign policy and how to negotiate the slavery issue is unclear, but for the moment they were willing to spout nationalist rhetoric in the service of party loyalty. Polk's election temporarily ensured financial backing for the paper, but political combat during the campaign disheartened Clarina. She fretted that "partisan zeal has been suffered to crowd individuals to unbecoming excesses" and instructed readers that "a cool temper" was the "best evidence of true moral courage." As the unpopular Mexican War subsequently heightened antislavery sentiment in the region, Clarina no doubt found her public stance personally uncomfortable. Her brother Aurelius, who would serve as a Whig legislator in 1846 and 1847, was steadfast in his opinions, she later remarked, implying a lack of sympathy with him. Meanwhile, her political opinions colored relations with the wider family network. A persuasive cousin with strong Whig sympathies wrote reminding her of their childhood friendship, praising the *Democrat,* and informing her about New York politics. "The bounds of slavery must be set, beyond which it shall not press," he insisted, hoping "Mr. Nichols" would take a stand against slave territory.[41]

As it turned out, the extended debate over slavery in the territories helped resolve her dilemma by providing the Nicholses with an opening to disassociate from a national party increasingly divided along sectional lines. As antislavery northerners questioned the war, a national debate emerged regarding the disposition of lands gained from Mexico. The Wilmot Proviso, a Democratic proposal to prohibit slavery in any new territory acquired as a result of the war, became a vehicle for antislavery Democrats to continue their expansionist rhetoric while opposing the extension of slavery. They feared the specter of a southern "Slave Power" that would privilege wealthy slaveholders over small homesteaders as the country expanded. Clarina's cousin informed her that northern Whigs were rallying around "a deep hostility to any further extension of the slave power" and would break away from their southern wing as well. He surmised that the Proviso could carry all the northern free states, hoping to sway the Nicholses in that direction. A month later, in September 1847, the *Democrat* was on record in favor of the Proviso, which reflected prevailing sentiment in the region and perhaps Clarina's influence with her husband. To placate party critics, George wrote a leading state Democratic leader affirming his support for the preservation of the Union above all and expressing his hope that slavery could be contained constitutionally within its present bounds. Even so, the Nicholses would eventually follow the pathway of the New York "Barnburners," who formed the Free Soil Party in 1848, backing Martin Van Buren for president rather than Democratic candidate Lewis Cass. Rival William Ryther was livid, charging the Nicholses with abandoning principle and displaying partisan motives to defeat the Whigs by siphoning off antislavery sympathizers.[42]

If Clarina's influence helped turn the *Democrat* into an organ of the Free Soil movement, the break also proved to be a turning point in her editorial career. Released from the constraints of Democratic Party discipline, she devised a backwoods housekeeper named Deborah Van Winkle to criticize the party and national policy while adhering to the moral principles she held dear. Modeled after the hardworking, sharp-tongued wife of Washington Irving's kindly but idle Rip Van Winkle, Deborah displayed the diligence and moral righteousness of Yankee women despite her lack of sophistication. As a congressional correspondent in Washington, Mrs. Van Winkle sat in the visitors' gallery with knitting in hand and unearthed legislators' betrayal of the people's interests. At first she was "dreadfully pestered" and even "dropped her stitches" as "some of the Southern members looked mighty comical at my knittin work, and one of them pointed me out to Mr. Adams and asked him if I wasn't one of the Abolition women that sent in their petition?— and another asked if I hadn't 'come on to petition Congress to stop the war right off, and whack them Mexicans till they'd stop fightin too?'" To distance herself from any such radicalism, she allowed John Quincy Adams to affirm her identity as "'a domestic manufactory come to Washington to represent home interests.'" Noting the "dreadful scarcity of home *virtues*" in the hall, Van Winkle warned voters, if they wanted to protect themselves they needed to elect "faithful representatives of the home virtues—*temperance, honesty, economy, industry, patience, perseverance and love.*" With the righteousness of a schoolmarm, she was ready to spank the lawmakers for pocketing government money and to put Senator John Calhoun in the corner for his unreasonable stance on "slavery and Mexican territory." But this "aint a party affair," Van Winkle noted, all the "crazy members" had wasted the people's money and time in "quarreling about 'em." "I had no idea," she complained, "that men, and well educated men too, could be so unmannerly and noisy."[43]

Van Winkle embodied Clarina's emerging sense of gender consciousness and her concept of women's purifying role in politics. As a virtuous and nonpartisan woman citizen, she criticized Democratic policy on slavery in the territories and southern leadership but also condemned the seamy game of partisan politics men played. Unable to express these feminine sensibilities effectively under her "husband's hat," Clarina devised the persona of Van Winkle to become a political player without betraying her womanliness. It was the beginning of her use of knitting to signal feminine industry and an ingenious ploy that she would resurrect periodically throughout her journalistic career to protect her identity while expressing her feminine outrage.

Even in this clever disguise, however, Nichols was subject to ridicule. Ryther of the *Vermont Phoenix* denied that Van Winkle was a respectable widow. She was an "imposter," he proclaimed, a toothless and "*pesky old maid*" who cavorted around town, with false teeth and wig, pretending to be half her age and displaying her sexual favors by dancing and kissing in public. Fear of this kind of challenge to her virtue led Clarina to keep Van Winkle alive and to retort that Ryther was a "pitiful coward" for his "attacks on an *old woman*."[44] Yet the female persona could too easily be dismissed as well. When the old widow responded indignantly to another Whig editor's criticism of Martin Van Buren, he discarded her remarks as "Van Winkle twaddle." "The *Democrat*, with all its 'granny Van Winkles' and 'Indignations' to back it," he scoffed, "may fire away about our remark touching that gentleman till doomsday, for all we care; it will neither harm nor frighten us."[45]

If womanly righteousness had its limitations as partisan strategy, it is clear that Clarina's columns forced rival editors to respond to her politics at a time when party loyalties were splintering. With "free soil, free labor, free trade, and free speech" as their motto, a new coalition of former Democrats, Liberty men, and antislavery Whigs was reshaping Vermont politics, diminishing traditional Whig dominance in the legislature, and causing a "political vacuum" in the state's power structure. In the 1848 presidential campaign, when the Nicholses openly supported the party's Free Soil faction, third-party candidate Van Buren garnered votes from 29 percent of the Vermont electorate, the highest in the nation, while the dominant Whigs ran Zachary Taylor, a slaveholder. It was a pattern repeated with varying scenarios throughout the Northeast as the battle over containing slavery weakened both major parties. For Clarina, the third-party option opened a way to inject her reforming zeal into politics as the parties remained in flux until the formation of the

Republican Party in 1854. Under the banner of the Free Democracy in 1849, she rallied free soilers, proclaiming that "*no northern Democrat will side with Northern or Southern Whigs in favor of slavery extension*," while lambasting Whigs for electing a slaveholder. The coalition soon frayed as Whigs accused Democrats of partisan manipulation, but all three parties in the state spouted antislavery rhetoric with moral overtones and supported containment of slavery.[46] Meanwhile, the near consensus against slavery provided Clarina with an opportunity to engage in political debate with a womanly nonpartisan flair. She could criticize the national Democratic Party on the immorality of supporting slavery while clinging to its equal rights principles and expansionist views. In the next few years, particularly after passage of the Fugitive Slave Law in 1850 and her identity became known, Mrs. Nichols would earn a reputation as an "Editress" with great influence in Free Soil politics.[47]

Building upon her success in partisan debate, Clarina Nichols launched her career as a reformer in the interest of her own sex. In her memoirs, she recalled that she had begun a "series of editorials" in early 1847 about the "injustice and miserable economy of the property disabilities of married women."[48] Unfortunately, none of these columns survive. She may have allowed the matronly Van Winkle to initiate her exposé of "wimin's wrongs," as she called it, waiting to assess readers' response before openly advocating such a provocative if nonpartisan issue. Her own experience of losing her inheritance to a wayward husband was enough to encourage her to speak out about women's disabilities under the common law. But understanding her personal experience as part of a systemic problem for all women only became clear from her identification with the female victims depicted in her wide reading—from abused mothers of drunken husbands to poor factory workers and struggling seamstresses. Even while she championed the role of wives and mothers as pillars of the family, her ability to recognize their individual interests separately from their husbands' represented a leap in her development and the beginning of a feminist consciousness.

Clarina may have been emboldened to become more outspoken by reading columns in the partisan *Democratic Review*, which detailed the inequities married women faced under the common law. Writing under a pseudonym in 1845, Jane Storm outlined a theoretical basis for reform in "The Legal Wrongs of Women." God assigned husbands and wives mutual obligations and equal interests in marriage, she asserted, but the law of property and child custody deprived women of their natural rights to children and control over earnings. She called upon women of talent to "come to the rescue of their sex from unrighteous bondage," echoing the pleas of abolitionist women to redress the wrongs perpetrated against oppressed slave mothers. In essays and reports about constitutional reform, editors of the *Review* highlighted the exclusion of women from full citizenship and praised the new constitution of Texas, which allowed married women the right to own real and personal property separate from their husbands.[49]

By the time Clarina began advocating such a change, reforming the law had been debated in legislative halls in the Northeast for ten years, not necessarily from a woman's rights perspective but to relieve debtors. In an effort to mitigate the negative effects of commercial and industrial expansion on families and to protect dependent wives from poverty, moderate reformers sought to shelter wives' inherited property, and family homesteads as well, from husbands' creditors. The cyclicality of the economy and increased mobility had disrupted families, leading to intermittent separations, and even divorce, exposing women's economic dependence. Because family wealth was no longer measured in land alone, wives' dowries, which typically consisted of household goods, clothing, and cash called "personalty," were relatively more valuable but also exposed to husbands' mismanagement. Clarina had experienced such problems when Justin depleted her inheritance, which probably aggravated his abusive behavior and doomed her marriage. The first married women's property acts passed in the 1840s were largely designed to salvage such a family by protecting wives' assets from creditors. Progressive legislators in New York were also eager to eliminate the discriminatory effects of equity courts, which adjudicated marital property of wealthy families; they intended to codify the law and in the process recognize wives' individual property rights. The controversial issue prompted widespread discussion in middle-class parlors, drawing women into the debate, and a scattering of women activists—including Polish-born Ernestine Rose and Elizabeth Cady Stanton in New York—became involved in lobbying state legislatures. A radical egalitarian, Rose had lectured widely and organized petition campaigns on the issue for nearly a decade, but even conservative women, such as Sarah Hale of *Godey's Lady's Book*, eventually lent support for married women's property reform.[50]

Clarina's columns in the *Democrat* followed a substantive if unsuccessful debate on the issue at New York's constitutional convention in the fall of 1846. Portraying wives as victims of an unjust system, she argued that a woman needed "legal protection in the accumulation and possession of means requisite to qualify and enable her to fill *'woman's sphere' as wife and mother.*"[51] Her rhetoric captured the essence of Jane Storm's argument while upholding the prevailing middle-class view of women's elevated role in the home, which appealed to the protective sentiments of Vermont's Whig legislators. Educating the public about "woman's wrongs" would become a trademark in Clarina Nichols's advocacy for women, long after other female activists had shifted their rhetorical stance to focus on universal rights. By persisting in her appeal to class-based protection, she expressed her benevolent standpoint and also avoided the seemingly radical stance of pressing for her own rights. Clearly, her husband and even some of her Howard relatives sympathized with her plea for justice for female victims of male abuse, a moral stance devoid of partisan implications.[52]

Indeed, Brattleboro attorney and Whig senator Larkin Mead proved sympathetic to this line of reasoning and introduced a reform bill in the Vermont legislature allowing separate estates for married women. With the support of Governor Horace Eaton, Mead and other Whig attorneys eventually secured passage of a more modest law that protected wives' inherited real property only from their husband's debts, affirmed joint ownership and mutual control over rents and sales deeds, and allowed wives to make wills. Cutting across party lines, the issue resonated with Democrats in the Vermont House eager to relieve debtors, and the resulting compromise protected family assets and mitigated wives' dependence without recognizing their individual interests through full separate ownership or control of earnings.[53] Although opponents expressed their concern that reform would threaten marriage relations by creating separate and conflicting interests, the majority ascribed to the view that women's natural propensity to do good should be guarded against the "cold-hearted avarice" of men.[54] Ironically, Clarina's conservative brother Aurelius was serving as Townshend's Whig representative at the time, but he was not present during the legislative vote, perhaps on purpose.[55] Her fellow journalists largely ignored the issue, but in a measure of local Whig support, opponent Ryther of the *Phoenix* praised the law as "an important advance in civilization." He gestured politely to Mrs. Nichols by recommending that lawmakers extend further protections against wives' income from being "squandered and dissipated" by husbands.[56] Her argument extolling women's devotion to family held sway and overrode partisan differences, but it did little to convince lawmakers that women needed individual economic rights.

Notwithstanding its limits, Vermont's 1847 property reform represented Clarina's first political success and bolstered her belief that female advocacy could reap just rewards. Unfortunately, she was the only woman in the state publicly advocating legal reform, and most women were unlikely to recognize the significance of the change at the time because it applied only to wives with inherited real estate, not to the penniless or to wage earners. But the right to determine control over their assets through wills was a significant advance, acknowledging a measure of legal individuality, if only after death. More inclusive reforms securing wives with greater control over their real and personal property were passed in New York and Pennsylvania in 1848, but neither withstood subsequent judicial scrutiny nor provided wives with a clear legal claim to their wages, one of Clarina's chief concerns. Nonetheless, she had begun the discussion about women's legal status in Vermont and would be remembered for having single-handedly initiated the woman's rights movement in the state.

By 1848 agitation for legal reform and the rise of women's antislavery activism had created a political climate that opened debate over every form of social hierarchy. Politicized by their exclusion from key abolitionist activities, radical women had begun to consider their own rights as well. Just as discussions of women's legal rights became widespread, murmurs about their political rights began to swirl around the margins of male political discourse, especially in New York. The link between legal and political rights had emerged starkly at the state's constitutional convention in 1846, when delegates engaged in a lengthy debate over liberalizing black suffrage, currently limited by steep property qualifications. While they considered married women's property rights, they also received a petition for suffrage from six women, who asserted their "equal, and civil and political rights with men." When New York lawmakers finally passed the married women's property reform in April 1848, Elizabeth Cady Stanton and other women took heart that women's public activism could produce results. By July Stanton was collaborating with radical Quaker women on a plan to call a convention in Seneca Falls to discuss a broad spectrum of issues surrounding women's status. The resulting "Declaration of Sentiments," modeled after the nation's founding document, asserted the individual rights and full citizenship of American women.

Neither Clarina Nichols nor most other politically active women were probably aware of the revolutionary implications of the document, which challenged women's inequality throughout society and included the controversial demand for enfranchisement. Nichols would not embrace suffrage publicly for several years, preferring at the moment to employ acceptable forms of womanly influence to persuade voters over questing for the ballot box. But she no doubt read about the Seneca Falls convention, as it was widely reported in the northeastern press and sparked an extensive debate about women's status in the polity.[57]

In the meantime, women's interest in equal property rights found a temporary political home within the Free Soil Party, where Nichols had staked her political future. Connections between advocates of free soil and woman's rights were strong in New York, facilitated by the leadership of Stanton, who maintained strong links with political antislavery through her husband, Henry. Many free soil men were wary of women's egalitarian claims but welcomed their moral stance on slavery, valued their influential role within the family, and advocated for expansion of their property rights. Among female journalists, both Clarina Nichols and Jane Grey Swisshelm appealed to this political constituency. Although Swisshelm had initiated her career as an abolitionist, not a partisan, both women were drawn into politics by a sense of mission to do God's work on earth; both were also tamed by a pragmatic and gradualist approach to effecting change through political action; and both believed in the effectiveness of female moral influence on the consciences of male voters.[58]

Consistent with this strategy, Nichols proceeded cautiously, educating readers about women's important role within the family, as she developed the feminist political philosophy that would undergird her future campaign for woman's rights. Reporting from "Van Winkledom" about her conversation with a "matronly lookin woman" she met on a journey to Boston, she described how the two knitted and conversed about "Wimin's rights" and, more to the point, "wimin's wrongs!" As "free-silers" and parents too, they "had got ideas in common." Vowing not "'to tell anything I don't bleeve as true as the gospels,'" she explained that the endless debate over the intellectual equality of the sexes was impossible to resolve by facts alone. Yet it could be shown based upon their God-given work. Whereas men could shirk their intellectual duties, "wimin must give character to and train the young immortal sperits," she insisted, "whether they chuse to or not, because they are *mothers*."

Claiming that "woman's sphere is God's sphere," she argued that the work of training the mind was as "intellectually important as man's." To disprove the argument that bodily strength and mathematical ability were evidence of male superiority, she noted that "God and the angels and glorified sperits hain't got no bodies, nor fisical powers at all."[59] Backed by the piety of a Christian woman, Nichols's version of Republican Motherhood linked women's reproductive function to their social roles and the political purpose of raising the next generation of citizens for the republic. Originating among political theorists and educators in the late eighteenth century, the connection justified educating the first generation of women in the new nation, suggesting that moral and competent mothers were essential to enlightened citizenship while simultaneously limiting their influence to domestic affairs.[60] Clarina Nichols appropriated the concept to proclaim gender equality while rooting her rationale in essential differences between the sexes that were deeply embedded in her consciousness and in the worldview of most of her readers. The folksy knitter Deborah Van Winkle became the embodiment of wise motherhood; she and her free soil companion linked women and their concerns to politics.

While she developed this motherly image in the press, Nichols was advocating for additional legal reforms that would protect women's individual financial interests. In 1849 Vermont legislators passed a homestead exemption law that protected the homes of debtors and their surviving widows from creditors up to $500, and a separate bill specified that wives could insure the lives of husbands or male relatives. Capitalizing on lawmakers' protective sentiments, Nichols began to address the limitations of dower provisions for childless widows. Under the common law, a widow retained dower rights to a third of the income from her husband's estate, but no control over the property, which descended to his heirs or to his male relatives if she had no children. Nichols ridiculed the law by questioning why the legislators had not required a brother or cousin to "marry the widow and raise up seed to him?" When the legislature responded by liberalizing dower laws, allowing childless widows to retain a husband's estate up to $1,000, she preened with success. "Heaven *bless* 'em," she crowed, "let the women of Vermont honor them for giving a *little* more of the husband's estate to his wife than to the rest of mankind, who hav'nt toiled for it, nor seen it swallow up their hope of bread and butter."[61] These political compromises paralleled reforms in other states during the late 1840s designed to preserve inherited property and avert widow's poverty, but

Vermont legislators failed to expand married women's rights to the property most women needed: personalty and earnings. By 1850 Nichols was publicly claiming that a wife needed more than simple protection; she needed the right to "acquire and hold property independent of her husband" during marriage, a claim to individual economic rights that would aid the poor as well as the rich, but one that also challenged the unity of marital bonds.[62]

Engagement in this legislative process, even as an outsider, strengthened Clarina's confidence in her persuasive powers and provided her with opportunities to sharpen her rhetorical skills. Her activism provoked the ire of attorney Joseph H. Barrett, editor of the *Middlebury Register* and leading Whig in the Vermont House. Barrett refuted her claims about the hardships women endured under the current system, arguing that few women were dissatisfied and few supported her cause. Her hard cases represented exceptions to the general condition of women, he insisted, and failed to present rational arguments at all. In reply to Mrs. Nichols's appeal for separate estates, he argued that the "individuality of interest" she proposed was a selfish claim that would destroy the "harmony and well-being" of marriage, reducing it to a business affair and belying its biblical roots. As Clarina had learned, the supposed mutuality of interests within marriage could prove false. "We can't see why a woman should work and not eat," she retorted, "her earnings turned into drunken wassail—squandered by her husband in haunts of vice and idleness!" To explicate the inequities of the legal system, she provided examples of the way the law treated wives versus husbands, widows versus widowers. Exasperated with her righteousness, Barrett concluded the debate by recommending that "Mrs. Democrat" should either recruit more converts or preach to the "unenslaved portion of her sex" about "remaining single."[63] Despite his refutations, the bachelor gave Nichols's claims serious attention; he printed her responses in his Whig paper, disseminating her complaints and proposed reforms widely.

Through her advocacy for legal reform, Clarina Nichols reinforced her belief in the ability of women to influence politics without transgressing gender boundaries and becoming embroiled in partisan debates. As she slowly shifted the content of the *Democrat* away from its partisan roots, she adopted a form of moral politics by supporting the nascent Free Soil movement, regulation of drinking, and redemption for "women's wrongs." In this way, she transformed her evangelical zeal into a weapon against social problems and established her right to influence public opinion as a moral arbiter seeking justice for victims of oppression. When sparring with Barrett, she coupled her sarcasm and wit with domestic metaphors that reminded her readers where her real duties lay. "He will forgive us that our domestic duties prevent us from serving up the whole of his reply in a single course," she mused, "but 'it will keep,' and that nothing may be wasted, we have just separated the 'sweet-bread' for a delicate fry, and lay aside the substantial roasters and soup knuckles for successive dishes." The more she extolled domesticity and mothers' God-given duties, the more she believed in the moral "necessity for woman's humane influence" in politics.[64] With the click of knitting needles she developed a nonpartisan, motherly persona, first as Deborah Van Winkle and subsequently as a lady "Editress," all the while engaged in supporting northern Democratic efforts to forge the Free Soil Party.

By 1850 Clarina Nichols was well known for her "sparkling pen" and her ability to "cross quills" with feminine grace and modesty and elicited praise even from her opposition. "We cannot part with Mrs. Nichols without expressing our admiration of the delightful manner in which she has dealt with us," one disputatious reader remarked; she writes "in such an agreeable, womanly way, and with such excellent and unpretending notions, that we always welcome her sprightly articles as a rare treat." Among reformers, Amelia Bloomer, editor of the *Lily*, noted Nichols's editorial work with a bit of feminine irony: "How she contrives to mind the babies, mend the stockings, and write leaders at the same time, is more than we can understand."[65] Indeed, Nichols had melded her sentimental religiosity seamlessly with witty political repartee. She could open a "Thanksgiving" column with a sermon about God's blessings and thanks for the chickens from Mrs. Van Winkle's "very best brood" and close it by chastising the Taylor Whigs for claiming to "be better free soilers than we."[66] Like a chameleon, she disguised her partisanship with female benevolence and domestic scenes to forge an identity that allowed her to play a part in American politics without appearing to wield manly power. As her self-confidence grew, she increasingly envisioned her role as an instrument of God's beneficence in the world. Wielding her "pen for the progress of the race toward a nobler and a purer life" was part of her duty to God and her mission as a Christian mother and a citizen of the republic. By bringing morality into politics she could help purify the nation and affirm her social status as an enlightened American. In this way, she reinvented herself into a viable political actor using the cultural constructs available to women of her class and intellectual capacity, regaining her self-respect in the process.[67]

If Clarina Nichols's professional work satisfied her need for purposeful activity, it also left her devoid of collegial social interaction and removed from her family in Townshend. Toiling largely alone in her work, apart from George's continuing encouragement, she lacked the network of female associates and relatives who typically bolstered reformers. With George's health in decline and her stepdaughters moved out of the house by 1850, nineteen-year-old Birsha was her closest female companion. In between Birsha's extended visits to Townshend, where she proudly claimed to be "a *little* representative of my mother," they spent hours sewing and reading together. Birsha was deeply attached to her mother and fond of her stepfather, yet she appears to have had little interest in her mother's editorial work. Clarina relied on her daughter to help manage the household, which included a young typesetter and a number of boarders during the summer months, while hiring local girls for the heaviest domestic work. Clarina rarely saw her parents, but Birsha kept her apprised of family news. As the *Democrat* evolved into a highly regarded family newspaper filled with moral content, and especially after the Nicholses joined the Free Soil movement, any partisan differences with the Howards probably diminished. Politics aside, Clarina's strong-minded mother praised George as "a dear, good man" and appreciated her daughter's continued involvement with the Baptist church. Moreover, to the extent that she maintained her reputation as a popular "lady editress" and refrained from radical abolitionism or woman's rights, she was a source of pride rather than shame for the Howards.[68]

In Brattleboro, Clarina was slowly reestablishing her respectability through her editorial diligence and a genteel self-presentation in the paper, rather than through community work. Despite a proclivity for congenial talk, she cultivated few social ties in Brattleboro outside the Baptist church. She blamed her work for cutting her off "from the usual social intercourse of villages and neighborhood," where mingling with women over sewing or a friendly cup of tea was a common practice. Advising a fellow editor "to remember that we have had to do with the stern realities of life, more than with its day-dreams and its fancies," she assured readers of her productivity and perhaps reminded local folks who knew about her history that she had overcome great odds. "We

UNIVERSITY OF WINCHESTER
LIBRARY

have had neither time nor heart to seek or be sought except with spade or hoe in hand, in the kitchen gardens, and fields whose cultivation promises harvest time, and their blossoming the ripe, rich fruit."[69] Laboring in the field of right ideas was Clarina's favorite pastime and her justification for worldly pleasure. But in the ensuing years as she ventured outside the region in search of solidarity with other committed reformers and new audiences, her underlying fear of public exposure among strangers would resurface to circumscribe her behavior and animate her political rhetoric as she strove for an acceptable form of public womanhood within a radical movement.

The Politics of Motherhood

As I would like, if noticed at all, to be noticed in connexion with my *lifework*—in which for some five years I labored in Vt. *first* and *alone*, against reproaches, ridicule, and the prejudices of many dear to me. . . . I feel sure [that] you will understand me and sympathize with what—as a woman—I must have suffered in my public advocacy of equality for woman, when "*pantaloons*" were threatened my advent at the Capitol, and prejudice every where cried "shame."

   C. I. H. Nichols, 1881

Looking back on her career in Vermont, Clarina portrayed the early 1850s as a period of emotional upheaval, a time when she stood "*first* and *alone*," bravely suffering ridicule for transgressing gender boundaries and public rebukes for her engagement in politics. The portrait reflected not only her "haunting fear" of public exposure but also her isolation from sympathetic reformers who could bolster her resolve. Ambitious and proud of her accomplishments as a journalist but still highly sensitive to public opinion, she faced a sea of male competitors in the newspaper business and felt geographically remote in Vermont's mountains. Her effort to bolster the fledgling Free Soil movement was difficult enough, but she was also the only regional voice on woman's rights. Her dilemma manifested itself in a sense of social deprivation and a yearning for the companionship of like-minded women. She had found a shelter in George's warm, cozy fireplace and a camouflage to shield herself from public scrutiny while she mapped out her "plan of work for humanity."[1] But the nesting and nurturing were over. Mrs. Nichols had emerged from her scarcely veiled anonymity and was eager if anxious to extend her influence beyond the comforts of her editorial chair.

Yet the road ahead was fraught with new challenges as Nichols sought to situate herself among reformers outside the political mainstream and to accompany them on the lecture platform. As much as she felt like a solitary voice, in fact, she was not alone in the Northeast, nor was she first. She was part of a movement—loosely organized at best—but a movement of outspoken women and men determined to change women's status in America. Nichols had no lack of determination, but she needed their mutual support and protection from potential critics whom she feared would inevitably seek to silence her voice, or worse, expose her divorce as proof that she and the movement were disreputable. As woman's rights leaders struggled for both philosophical and strategic direction, her somewhat idiosyncratic political philosophy and style would allow her to survive the rigors of associating with these radical activists and to maintain her composure in front of conservative audiences as well.[2] Centering on the natural rights of mothers, it would characterize much of her career as a public woman.

At first Nichols became acquainted with women who emboldened her "to do and dare for the cause of humanity" through the press. Just as newspaper exchange agreements helped to scatter the *Democrat* widely, so too they filled her parlor with new and radical voices with whom she communed weekly. "It is so like the dropping in of a friend to take tea and spend the evening," Nichols mused, "when our husband empties his capacious pockets and we find Mrs. Swisshelm, Mrs. Pierson and Mrs. Bloomer beside us, each with hearts full of stirring thoughts." To depoliticize these female journalists, she painted them into her parlor in a pleasing domestic scene. "We take our knitting— we always knit while we read, and can think so much better to the click of the needles . . . and, seated by the table, the cheerful beams of the solar lamp bringing in pleasing relief many an object associated with physical comfort and social enjoyment, from our pet flowers to the great arm-chair of the *invalid* husband—and who can say we lack anything?"[3]

Jane Grey Swisshelm, Lydia Jane Pierson, and Amelia Bloomer became "spiritual presences" who evoked Nichols's deepest sympathies, influencing her ideas and undergirding her ability to advocate change. Swisshelm edited the *Pittsburgh Saturday Visiter*, devoted primarily to antislavery and temperance; Bloomer of Seneca Falls, New York, focused on temperance in the *Lily*; and columnist Pierson of the *Lancaster, Pennsylvania, Gazette* promoted education and legal reform. Their diverse interests reflected the wide range of issues that channeled women into the woman's rights movement. Nichols gathered them around her fireside, ensuring that all would match her womanliness despite their radical notions. George, who was indeed recuperating from a serious illness, stood by admiring this new generation of "Lady Editors" as they usurped his columns. Although they were dubbed the "Petticoat Press" by some opponents, they garnered praise for their "clear and firm convictions," their "often strikingly original—nearly always novel" ideas, and their "womanly" expression. Meanwhile, the click of Nichols's knitting needles served to remind readers of their industry and true avocation as wives and mothers.[4]

By encouraging each other, these editors validated and extended their movement for reform while reassuring readers that they were refined and intelligent women. Pierson, who exuded feminine sensibility, blessed sister Bloomer as a "very lily herself; sweet, pure, and drooping with the dew of sympathy and pity for the unfortunate victims of intemperance." Bloomer coupled Nichols with others of "powerful intellect and great knowledge" and reprinted her columns, enhancing her reputation for outspokenness. She found it amusing that some men were sounding the alarm about this rebellion and "calling upon their clan to prepare to resist the army of women that are coming against them to battle."[5] The corps they hoped to inspire would come largely from a generation of educated middle-class women, mostly white but also free black, who had been involved in abolition, temperance, or moral or legal reform and were keenly aware of restrictions on women's participation in civil society. If they were not quite ready to voice equal rights claims, they believed in women's capacity to effect social improvement and recognized the injustice of a legal and political system that rendered them dependent on the generosity of men.[6] Bloomer was particularly effective in disseminating news and commentary about woman's rights, alerting her readers that women were seeking higher education and adequate wages, all of which whet Nichols's appetite to provide similar coverage in the *Democrat* and to participate in an ascendant movement that was barely visible in her own community.

If this congeniality and their womanly sympathy disguised the radical direction of their ideas, Nichols found it difficult to shed her own notions of proper female behavior as they sought to develop a common political agenda. To eliminate drunkenness, Swisshelm fearlessly urged the burning of grog shops while Bloomer railed against enabling legislation that licensed those

nefarious rum-shops and urged women to political action for their own protection. Shunning any thought of violence, Nichols queried instead, "'to vote
or not to vote,' is *that* the question?" Facetiously she pondered how men could
tempt women "to defy the tide of noisy politics and seize the ballot-box to
throw it at the rum-jug?" Still, she was wary about the "propriety of woman
voting." It was a real "stumbling-block," she later admitted; "the idea was
repelling." These sentiments were common to many women of her class, for
voting would require them to mingle with men at rowdy party caucuses held
in taverns and other local polling places where women were not welcome.[7]
Nichols still trusted that female influence could persuade men to emancipate
women from "legal and conventional subjection to wrongs," whereas Quaker
leader Lucretia Mott was advising activists not to "*ask* as favor, but demand as
right" and insisting "that every civil and ecclesiastical obstacle be removed."[8]

With her reputation at stake, Nichols moved cautiously toward a more radical public stance on enfranchisement because of its potential to compromise
feminine propriety. Elizabeth Cady Stanton, who had inserted the right in the
"Declaration of Sentiments" at Seneca Falls, may have alleviated some of
her concerns in a series of formative articles in the *Lily*. She denied that men
could legislate for women or even know the real interests of women because
men's interests were different, and she argued forcefully that women should
vote because they were equally endowed and accountable to God for their
natural rights and responsibilities. To counter fears about women mingling
in the "violence and vulgarity" associated with balloting, Stanton exclaimed
that "the mother surely should be there, to watch and guard her sons" and
thereby purify the process."[9] Both Nichols and Swisshelm agreed that "there
can be no impropriety simply in meeting [men] at the ballot box," the same
men they encountered at church every Sunday. Still, Nichols was circumspect
in her approach to the issue, often cloaking her commentaries in sarcasm or
allegory, even as she became attuned to the argument that single taxpaying
women had been denied representation in government. Six months later, reporting that property-owning women could vote in certain municipal elections
in Ontario, she quipped, "we think it would be well for Barnum to get some of
these voting women to exhibit around the country with Jenny." If entertainer
P. T. Barnum promoted their public appearances just as he did the Swedish
opera singer Jenny Lind, it would confirm the propriety of "women having
a voice in the objects which they are taxed to support."[10] Nichols's irony unearthed the contradiction between the willingness of Barnum's audiences to

gaze upon female entertainers and the horror critics expressed at the specter of women at the polls.

Claiming the right of suffrage was still controversial among politically active women, but most agreed that they deserved access to forums where they could educate the public about women's inequality. Broadly conceived, the "Declaration of Sentiments" demanded human happiness for American women as individual citizens on par with men and claimed that the political contract they made had deprived women of their "inalienable" and "sacred" rights as ordained by God. These natural rights and the recognized moral capacities of women provided the basis for a series of grievances against patriarchal society and a list of demands, including equal access to education, to the professions, to appropriate workplace opportunities, to property and marital rights, and to the elimination of the sexual double standard. To advance this expansive agenda, advocates needed to change public opinion about women's capacities to participate equally in society by writing and lecturing. Relying upon the supposed moral virtue of women, female abolitionists had argued repeatedly against their exclusion from conventions and lecture halls where they could wield their influence for good in the world and shape voter opinion. Now woman's rights activists issued the same complaint and sought to mount podiums as well.[11]

If Nichols was reluctant to advocate suffrage, she was equally queasy about the prospect of speaking in public on her own behalf. Controversy over women's public appearances had first erupted in 1828 with the lectures of notorious free thinker and equal rights advocate Fanny Wright, whom critics vilified as irreligious and sexually immoral. By 1850, abolitionists such as Angelina Grimké Weld, Lucretia Mott, Abby Kelley Foster, and Lucy Stone had overcome the objections of conservatives and established their right to address mixed audiences, at least on moral and educational issues.[12] Working together in religious and charitable associations, displaying sympathy for the downtrodden or even loyalty to country and party at political rallies, had allowed middle-class women to expand their influence in civil society, but advocating for their own rights was considered unwomanly because it belied the notion of female disinterest and benevolence.[13] When early woman's rights activists did appear in public, popular press coverage was often dominated by veiled or direct comment about their sexual roles and appearances rather than their ideas, challenging their reputations as virtuous women. Critics pilloried women on the platform as a troupe of Amazons in breeches and ridiculed male sympathizers as effeminate "she-males" wearing petticoats. Questioning a speaker's womanliness, her piety, or her sexual morality became a means to silence reformers who confronted the political and religious establishment.[14]

Initially, Nichols was content to wield her "sparkling pen" rather than subject herself to this form of public scrutiny, while she defended "female lecturers" against those who warned of "the degradation which a woman incurs by exhibiting herself in any capacity to the public gaze." Considering herself quite a "talker," she actually believed she could argue her principles more effectively in person than with "the limited power of the pen." Yet she shrank from the kind of ridicule that might question her femininity, embarrass her family, and undermine the movement. "I do not wish to make or have any allusion made to my private experience in public channels," she later told Susan B. Anthony. Ironically, the public activity that she believed necessary to overcome injustice to women threatened not only the cry "*pantaloons*" but also revelations about the sordid events that had driven her into the work. Locally her experience of marital abuse authenticated her reform work to some extent, but she feared that strangers could misconstrue her past and that as a formerly divorced woman her respectability had been compromised.[15]

It was only after she witnessed the bravery of other outspoken women and became convinced that their radical ideas were not so threatening after all that Nichols moved from genteel "lady Editress" to crusader for woman's rights. When reformers in Massachusetts issued a call to the first National Woman's Rights Convention, to be held in late October 1850 in Worcester, Massachusetts, it was a chance to fulfill what she increasingly viewed as "*the* object of my life." With George's health improving and her daughter in charge at home, she embarked on her first venture among reformers in company with Ann Elizabeth Brown of Brattleboro, a teacher and wife of liberal educator Addison Brown. To reach Worcester, the two women traveled by stage and rail; by mid-1851 the train arrived regularly in Brattleboro, making it even easier for Nichols to participate in the signature events of the early woman's rights movement.[16]

Widely publicized, the first convention attracted an estimated audience of a thousand people, who assembled in Brinley Hall in the heart of Worcester. The gathering included 268 formal members from eleven states. As Vermont's representative, Nichols earned a place on the nominating committee. The speakers were as impressive as the size of the audience, including well-known abolitionists William Lloyd Garrison and Frederick Douglass; health reformer Paulina Wright Davis, who had lectured widely on female anatomy and served as president of the convention; abolitionists Lucretia Mott, Lucy Stone, Abby Price, and Abby Kelley Foster; and progressive Boston Brahmins William H. Channing and Wendell Phillips. Constituting a significant minority, these men and others from the antislavery movement helped articulate a rational theory for women's advancement, lent their experience in organizing, and opened pathways into political and financial networks of support.[17]

The gathering at Worcester initiated the process of outlining a cohesive philosophical approach and set of strategic goals that would define the woman's rights movement at least until the Civil War. As President Paulina Davis remarked at the outset, this is an "epochal movement—the emancipation of a class, the redemption of half the world, and a conforming re-organization of all social, political, and industrial interests and institutions." The breadth of their reforming zeal meant that reaching a consensus would be difficult as speakers ranged widely in their viewpoints. Some appealed to natural law and universal human rights while others claimed equal protection under the law and access to the courts. To ground their demands in liberal political theory, they would have to demonstrate women's equality as rational beings capable of national citizenship. That meant somehow redefining the notion of Republican Motherhood without undermining their supposedly superior moral influence and claiming rights as individuals, not legal dependents. There was agreement that women's natural rights had been violated and that they were capable of self-government, but whether to emphasize political or legal theory and how best to persuade legislators and judges were by no means clear.[18]

If they were unable to completely resolve these questions, members of the convention did affirm women's natural rights as defined in Scripture. Explicating the biblical basis of women's equality was fundamental to establishing the validity of the woman's rights movement. Not only would it verify women's existence in the American theory of natural law and counter clerical admonitions, but adherence to Christian truths and a display of piety were crucial aspects of middle-class female identity and the basis of women's moral influence within civil society. Antoinette Brown of New York, who would soon become an ordained Congregational minister, "chained the attention of the audience" at Worcester with her logical arguments from the Bible. Equally persuasive were Abby Price, a Christian utopian reformer, and physician Harriot Hunt; both proclaimed women's "co-equality" by citing Gen. 1:27: "Male and female created he them and blessed them." This joint creation, they opined, was evidence that the sexes were equal and equally charged with moral obligations to fulfill God's will through their "co-sovereignty" on earth—an idea originating with elderly Quaker leader Lucretia Mott and theorist Elizabeth Wilson. Daughter of a Scotch Presbyterian minister and author of *A Scriptural View of Woman's Rights and Duties,* Wilson explicated the case for women's God-given rights in a letter to the convention, disclaiming the biblical sanction for husbands to rule over their wives. As active moral agents, men and women were responsible to humanity as "nursing fathers and nursing mothers," she asserted, claiming that male laws and social customs had artificially excluded women from politics and from fulfilling their duty to God.[19] Nichols was particularly impressed with the "trumpet tones" of Sojourner Truth, the only black woman to speak at the convention, who refuted ministers' claims to male privilege. "Whar did your Christ come from?" Truth asked. "From God and a woman. Man had nothing to do with him!" In the end, participants agreed to gather information, organize meetings, and educate the public in pursuit of a universal goal of achieving "woman's co-sovereignty with man."[20]

This concept reaffirmed Nichols's faith that the movement was compatible with her Christian beliefs and strengthened her political philosophy. Co-equality was the basis of her understanding of a mother's role in a divinely created universe where men and women held complementary obligations to God, a framework that incorporated women's difference within a common humanity striving for a better world. As abolitionists appealed to a higher law of God's creation to challenge the institution of slavery and the odious Fugitive Slave Law of 1850, woman's rights activists like Nichols invoked their own notion of God's law to argue against injustice. Although resistance from the established clergy had driven some women to seek more liberal sects or to leave the church altogether, their rebellion was rooted in the tradition of dissent practiced in the Protestant churches, and they remained committed to the morality found in early Scripture. This "religious lens" became the framework for constructing an ethical basis for equal rights claims for women through biblical exegesis.[21] Nichols differed from this group to the extent that she continued to cling to the religious authority of the Baptist community, with its connection to her family and local heritage, and in her rhetorical use of the concept of co-sovereignty. As the movement gained strength, nonsectarianism and appeals to universal rights would characterize its early phase while Nichols emphasized women's special roles as mothers instead.

Returning to Brattleboro after the Worcester convention, Nichols was exhilarated by her experience and emboldened to educate Vermont legislators more directly about legal reform. She now held an official role on the education committee of the national movement, which gave her confidence that she was not alone in marshalling her persuasive powers to change the law; she boldly sent fifty copies of a column about unjust inheritance laws to lawmakers. When this direct lobbying resulted in greater allocation of estates to widows, she gleefully proclaimed a "Glorious Progress of Woman's Rights in Vermont!" and noted that opponent Joseph Barrett would surely faint now that legislators had equipped the "widows 'for masculine pursuits.'"[22]

Nichols's pursuit of this practical legislative approach at home was fortified not only by her links to the national woman's rights movement but also by the millennial hopes she invested in its ultimate success. She assured Ohio activists that the reforms they sought would "emancipate and elevate the race, by opening to it the mother-fountains of humanity." Noting the "improved tone" of the press and the generosity of the Vermont legislature, she committed herself to "the good time coming" and recommended a strategy of presenting women's "responsibilities as growing out of God-created, fixed relations." Such an appeal to a higher law would be the "most powerful lever" to change "popular opinion" about unjust laws. Closing her letters to other organizers "yours for God and humanity," Nichols expressed a missionary zeal characteristic of the era's reformers. As an agent of God, she believed in her power to revolutionize politics and bring the nation closer to a heaven on earth.[23] To that end, she poured her zeal into making the *Democrat* an arm of the three main prongs of antebellum reform: temperance, antislavery, and woman's rights. When a reader questioned her status as editor in mid-1851, Nichols confessed, "So long as we can wield our pen for the progress of the race toward a nobler and purer life—so long as we have a soul that struggles for expression and draws strength from the exercise of its powers, in the conflict between right and wrong, between humanity and inhumanity—so long as we can, without compromising our duties as wife and mother, hold such a position, there is for us no 'pleasurable retiracy.'"[24]

By the time Nichols carried this commitment to Worcester again for the second two-day gathering of "Friends of Woman's Rights" in October 1851, she was incorporated into the leadership. As a vice president, she served along with Angelina Grimké Weld, William H. Channing, Samuel J. May, and Lucretia Mott and participated in developing key resolutions. During the past year, the movement had gained considerable recognition, and President Paulina Davis noted progress in married women's property laws and the opening of several medical and design schools to women. Widespread press coverage had been mixed, with praise coming from reformer Horace Greeley, editor of the *New York Tribune*, and ridicule from James Bennet of the *New York Herald*, who had characterized the 1850 event as a "motley mingling of socialists, abolitionists, and infidels."[25] There were also serious critiques, however, such as that from Horace Mann, a highly respected advocate of women's education, who declined to support the suffrage claim. The task at hand, Davis insisted, was to defend their reforms with greater philosophical clarity. To that end, they firmly linked woman's rights to human rights as defined in the Declaration of Independence and identified suffrage as the "corner-stone" of the movement to restore women to their rightful place in society. In response to critics, participants denied that women were either operating outside their proper sphere or were too preoccupied with important domestic and maternal duties to become full citizens.[26]

Nichols had arrived at the meeting with no prepared remarks, but she was clearly eager to speak extemporaneously and to make her debut as a lecturer in front of a congenial audience. Confident that she could "talk as I talk at home & elsewhere over my knitting," she was determined to have her say.[27] The crowd was even larger than forecast, with a cadre of reporters and curious observers eager for a glimpse of the radical women at the podium. After the assembled group moved to larger quarters in City Hall on the convention's second day, Nichols summoned her courage and rose to speak with the prodding of Wendell Phillips. No doubt privy to her lingering misgivings, he led her to the podium, urging, "You must speak now, Mrs. Nichols," she later recalled. With little to no experience of public address, she determined to use the womanly style of self-presentation that had become so effective in print and would provide the affirmation she needed. "I stand before you, a wife, a mother, a sister, a daughter;" Nichols explained, anchoring herself squarely within the family. Like the biblical Ruth, she stood as a gleaner, laboring in the garden of ideas, gathering stories and wisdom from her experience as a Christian woman.[28] Forty-one years old and taller than most women at five-foot-eight, Nichols was a "fine, majestic looking middle-aged lady," according to Horace Greeley. Dressed discreetly in a dark gown with heavy drapery folds and donning a silk bonnet to cover her brown ringlets, she was a seasoned

Clarina Howard Nichols portrait, c. late 1840s. This portrait, painted at a later date in Kansas, was produced from a daguerreotype. Courtesy of the Kansas State Historical Society.

matron, a model of female respectability and kindliness. More akin to Lucretia Mott than to the dynamic young orator Lucy Stone, she was confident that she could affect the sympathies of the audience with her "earnest womanly naturalness of speaking."[29]

The record of this speech is one of the few pieces of evidence revealing the power of Nichols's oratory and her facility with the spoken word. In a series of heartfelt tales sprinkled with biblical allusions and witty remarks, she touched the deepest sensibilities of the audience while revealing the legal injustices perpetrated on hardworking mothers, dependent wives, and widows. She informed them that she had been tutored in "the most refined notions" of womanhood yet was also "of mountain growth" and had witnessed farmers' wives and "women esteemed for every womanly virtue" laboring with or in place of their husbands, even clearing fields or rolling logs. "And what true-hearted woman would not do the same?" she exclaimed, showing the foolishness of designated "spheres." But "let me tell you a story," she implored, and then recounted the sorry tale of a poor industrious widow who had supported her husband's children by a former marriage and after his death found herself in poverty, robbed of the family estate by dower rules. "And now, my friends, how did the laws support and protect this poor widow?" Nichols queried. *"They set her up at auction, and struck her off to a man who had the heart to keep her at the cheapest rate!"* The plight of a drunkard's wife whose "brute" of a husband sold her clothing and absconded with her wages brought tears to the eyes of her listeners, but the cruelest arm of the law separated a divorced mother from her "only child, a son of tender age." Appealing to parents, she demanded, "Think of this, fathers, mothers! It is a sad thing to sever the marriage relation when it has become a curse—a demoralizing thing; but what is it to sever the relation between mother and child, . . . to commit the tender boy to the training of a drunken and licentious father?"[30] As testimony to the cruelty of patriarchy, these stories vibrated with Nichols's emotional delivery, but they also displayed her grasp of real-world conditions and legal rules, proving that women were deprived of a natural right to fulfill their Godly purpose. Indeed, they would have certified her as a truth teller, if anyone in the audience had known about her past.

Like a practiced raconteur, Nichols juxtaposed these stories with playful jokes about men's legal possession and sarcastic remarks about the contradictions and inequities of marital law. "Now, I do not understand the term helpmeet, as applied to woman, to imply all that has come to be regarded as within its signification," she explained. "I do not understand that we are at liberty to help men to the devil," a remark that elicited loud affirmation from the audience. "Our legislators tell us it is right to give the legal control of our earnings to the husband," she quipped, noting ironically that he must support us and pay our debts, and *"must have our earnings to do it with!"* While she indicted the legal system, she distanced herself from radicalism by citing honorable male authorities, affirming her love and respect for "manliness," and praying that legislators would behave like honorable gentlemen and release the *"'inalienable rights' of woman."* In the meantime, women needed practical education to prepare them to support families. "If my husband should be unfortunate, the sheriff can take his goods," she predicted, but, touching her forehead, she opined that "no creditor can attach the capital invested here."[31] As a successful journalist, she stood before a cheering audience as living proof of women's accomplishments while also proving that even a homespun, pious matron could participate in agitating the cause.

It was not only her pleasing style that distinguished Nichols's performance but also her emphasis on the maternal basis of women's natural rights. The alienation of a wife's right to property and earnings, she insisted, was the foundation of *"all her social and legal wrongs."* This claim to economic rights was a central tenet of the movement, but Nichols connected it specifically to motherhood to proffer her own interpretation of co-equality and lack of legal protection. Current law prevented mothers from fulfilling their natural God-given responsibilities, which are equal to those of men, she explained, because "next to God, woman is the creator of the race" and "God has endowed her with *equal powers* for their discharge." Extending mothers' sacred familial duties to their role in the nation, she asserted, "It is in behalf of our sons, the future men of the republic, as well as for our daughters, its future mothers[,] that we claim the full development of our energies by education, and legal protection in the control of all the issues and profits of ourselves, called *property.*" It was a theoretically virtuous rationale rooted in her experience, her faith, the family economy, and common law.[32]

In converting the devotion of mothers to family needs into a rights claim, Nichols was expanding Republican Motherhood beyond its contemporary application and also upsetting the balance of liberal political theory in which financial responsibility lay solely with fathers. Mothers' access to property and guardianship of children, she insisted, would serve the nation and protect the family more effectively than the common law of marital unity, which unjustly stripped women of the means to fulfill their equally important but different obligations.[33] A similar appeal to the natural rights of mothers surfaced in the arguments of radical French feminists Pauline Roland and Jeanne Deroin. In a sympathetic letter to the convention, the two socialists proclaimed their rights as "Mother[s] of Humanity" to full development and "true liberty" in the name of their children. Women's superior "love of humanity," they asserted, would ensure the ascension of the "kingdom of Equality and Justice" on earth.[34] Convinced that mothers had been robbed of the fruits of their labor, Nichols could easily have rallied around their maternal appeal while sidestepping their support for social revolution. Instead, she was promoting women's property rights and, as a corollary, women's access to practical education as a means to self-development and family preservation.

To many observers Nichols made a "profound impression" with her "mild, beaming countenance and the affectionate tones of her voice." Her address struck a chord with Paulina Davis, who recognized its powerful message even though she normally downplayed gender differences. "There was a touching, tender pathos in her stories which went home to the heart," Davis later recalled, "and many eyes, all unused to tears, were moistened as she described the agony of the mother robbed of her child by the law."[35] Though Nichols would continue to exploit the sentiment surrounding mother-child relations to press for woman's rights, her rhetoric was increasingly at odds with the egalitarian emphasis of the movement's leadership. A year later Lucretia Mott refuted Nichols's claim that motherhood endowed women with superior "moral susceptibilities," and she and Ernestine Rose continually affirmed the moral equality of the sexes. But these were minor points of relative emphasis, not grave disagreements. Nearly all movement participants recognized naturally appearing sexual differences and insisted that the world would be improved by bringing the "feminine element" to bear on the evils of society. Nichols's strength was in her knowledge of the law and its effects on women and in her ability to connect the movement to traditional notions of woman's sphere. Just as she overlooked theological debates, so too she was blind to the paradox in her stance—that in promoting women's special strengths she was theoretically undermining the claim to a male-defined equality of rights.[36]

Even so, Nichols was willing to expand woman's sphere, which encapsulated those differences, beyond its prevailing economic and political boundaries despite her apparent social conservatism. This point of view clearly set her apart from well-known domestic feminists such as Catherine Beecher and Sarah J. Hale, who promoted women's self-development to serve familial and social needs but feared that venturing into politics would sacrifice female virtue and destroy woman's moral influence to the detriment of society. By contrast, Nichols exploited the concept of woman's sphere much further in her quest to eliminate women's economic dependence on men and believed politics was a means to achieve that goal. She later denounced Hale, editor of *Godey's Lady's Book*, for asserting that female teachers should work for half the wages of men because they were single and not supporting families. Hale was wary of competing with men and thereby undermining male protection and support, which would "destroy all hope of [C]hristian progress," she claimed. Nichols ridiculed the notion that women could rely upon the "stronger sex" to take care of them even while she celebrated femininity to secure her goals, hoping to keep her virtue and status as lady intact.[37]

Her success at the Worcester convention marked a milestone in Nichols's career, enhancing her optimism that her desire to do good in the world would come to fruition in the advancement of woman's rights. As she explained to Susan B. Anthony a few months later, "I have the faith that moves *men,* & that, since it is *men* that are in our way, is better than faith that moves *mountains.*"[38] After the convention, Paulina Davis printed Nichols's speech in a pamphlet entitled "The Responsibilities of Woman" that gained an extended circulation because Lucy Stone later included it in a series of educational woman's rights tracts by such notables as Wendell Phillips, Theodore Parker, and British feminist Harriet Taylor Mill. Nichols's appeal to motherhood, though atypical, was part of a broader effort to awaken women to their social and political responsibilities and their natural rights to equal treatment. By the end of the century, similar claims to the rights of mothers would galvanize legions of women into the temperance and suffrage campaigns, but it would take much more than a discussion of women's God-given rights to change popular opinion in the 1850s. Moreover, as the movement progressed, it became clear that contention over strategies among advocates could be as serious a threat as the enemy without. Not only would they disagree about how to shape public opinion, but they also faced conflicting views about how to gain equality without sacrificing the protections, comforts, and respect they enjoyed. As Nichols faced these difficulties, she would rely upon her faith-based morality and her practical political experience as a guide to mold her place within the movement.

Even before her second trip to Worcester, heated controversy had emerged over the notorious bloomer costume, a harbinger of deeper trouble ahead. In spring 1851, Amelia Bloomer and Elizabeth Cady Stanton had boldly donned a shorter, simpler dress with ankle-length loose trousers underneath and de-fended the new freer, more healthful outfit in the *Lily*, where Bloomer dis-played herself decked out in the design that garnered her name. The dress reform movement arose from serious concerns about the constrictions of tight corsets and elaborate petticoats on women's freedom of action, and it dovetailed with a parallel desire among activists to assert control over their wardrobes. For female reformers, the dictates of fashion, which tied women to preconceived notions of beauty and adornment, undermined their efforts at independence of thought and action. The adoption of the so-called bloomers symbolized that the reformers had seized control over their public appear-ances and would no longer display themselves to please men or to secure social status.[39]

Yet the meaning of bloomers proved to be in the eye of the beholder. Rather than symbols of liberation, critics saw sexual transgression. As many male editors felt compelled to comment, either critically or otherwise, the controversy over women's proper attire embroiled Clarina Nichols in a di-lemma. Anxious to join her female colleagues, particularly the sympathetic Amelia Bloomer, yet fearful of public spectacle of any kind, Nichols squirmed for a middle ground that could anchor her political fortunes. While Bloomer responded to Jane Grey Swisshelm, who criticized the absurdities of high fashion but thought bloomers and their wearers ridiculous, Nichols praised the health and convenience of dress reform but declined to don the new cos-tume herself. Shortening her dresses, she feared, might "cut away . . . the in-fluence which we have or may win, to carry forward reforms vital to health and an improved morality." Alternatively, she would "fight for waists, short, loose, and without points," as well as lightened skirts.[40] Given her sensitiv-ity about her own appearance and her reputation for gentility, it was highly unlikely that she would have adopted the style, believing that no lady would don such an outfit and needing to maintain her class status to continue pro-moting reform. In the end, her objections proved prophetic, for Stanton and

Amelia Bloomer in an illustration from the Lily, *September 1851, showing the new bloomer attire. Courtesy of Baker-Berry Library, Dartmouth College, Hanover, New Hampshire.*

others eventually dropped the fashion after several years of harassment and ridicule. Rather than a form of rebellion, bloomers became a distraction, an excuse for critics to focus on appearances rather than on the substantive issues the reformers raised.

As the bloomer controversy raged, Nichols faced a more pressing challenge when movement leaders raised the question of liberalizing divorce laws. Elizabeth Cady Stanton took the lead in challenging the regulation of marriage, which she argued was a civil contract, not a divinely sanctified union, and therefore could be severed for reasonable cause. Marriage laws not only deprived women of their economic rights, the basis of citizenship, Stanton asserted, but their natural rights to children and their right to freedom from an abusive husband. As part of her involvement in the temperance movement, in January 1852 Stanton boldly proposed that wives should leave their drunken husbands and that drunkenness was a legitimate cause for divorce. To live with a man beset with alcohol who degraded his wife either through physical and sexual abuse or poverty was tantamount to "legalized prostitution," she proclaimed. Initially, Amelia Bloomer took a similar stand, arguing that a wife's higher duty to herself and to God required her to separate from the vice of drunkenness. It was a radical demand, causing havoc in the New York temperance movement, and by linking it with woman's rights, Stanton threatened to alienate the public completely.[41]

Though Nichols sympathized with Stanton's case against drunken husbands, she could hardly support Stanton's remedy. She believed marriage was a "holy tie" and that facilitating divorce was tantamount to engendering immorality. Clearly, the trauma of her own experience, with its accompanying humiliation and loss of respectability, prompted Nichols to disassociate herself from the notion of easy divorce, which could shatter her carefully crafted public image. Ironically, she still believed in companionate marriage and in reforming men through legislation, and she confidently offered alternative means to prevent marital abuse. Stanton had "lighted on a branch instead of taking the matter by the root," Nichols told Anthony, who had written asking her to attend a New York temperance meeting. Eradicating the sale of alcohol and securing wives with earnings, child custody, and "freedom of person" would "restrain men from sinful causes & leave the marriage relation to rest . . . in united sympathies, purposes and tastes," she explained. Whereas Nichols sought marital equity and feared weakening an institution enshrined in Christian belief, Stanton superimposed individual rights over the protections and social benefits derived from marriage. Nichols's position aligned her with a minority of feminists, including Antoinette Brown and Elizabeth Oakes Smith, along with reformers Horace Greeley and Wendell Phillips, who upheld the current institutionalization of marriage.[42]

The question of divorce, more than any other issue, bedeviled Nichols throughout her career. On the one hand, she believed that her personal experience, which she sometimes alluded to vaguely, would authenticate her reform work in the eyes of skeptics, but on the other, she coveted an untarnished reputation. Her adamant stance against divorce appeared to assuage her sense of defeat and guilt about having severed her own marital tie, an experience she felt compelled to conceal from the public. "Let women enjoy the same rights which men enjoy—of person & property & custody of children," she told Anthony privately, and they could "discharge their duties without going before a court & exposing details shocking to all their womanly instincts of delicacy." Yet despite having suffered this disgrace, Nichols was apparently blind to the fact that she had been released from her first husband's abuse because of her family's political connections and Vermont's liberal divorce statute. Most women were not so privileged, nor could they plead "intolerable severity," a cause unavailable in most states. Instead, Nichols clung to a feminine ideal—that a woman could "win man's higher and better nature" by cultivating her own "mind and heart," and if not, the law would reform men. In this way, she could redeem herself for having broken a sacred bond and protect other women from the humiliation she had experienced. After all, her marriage to George had met all her expectations, and marriage formed the basis of women's identity and their legal, economic, and sexual protection. Even some feminists feared that weakening those bonds could leave women unacceptably vulnerable to sexual exploitation, dishonor, and charges of irreligion. Nichols surmised quite rightly that the woman's movement would suffer a strategic blow from the clergy, who were adamantly opposed to divorce, if advocates attacked marriage directly, and she warned Anthony that woman's rights advocates were already being accused of "holding demoralizing sentiments" and deteriorating marriage relations.[43]

In this way Nichols began to carve out a practical political stance for herself, sidestepping theoretical inconsistencies to protect her reputation. Even as she remained in sympathy with the chief aims of the nascent woman's rights movement, she was unwilling to completely martyr herself or directly challenge religious authorities for the cause, and these personal reservations tended to circumscribe both her principles and her behavior. A number of activists—including Bloomer—initially followed Stanton's lead on divorce but later dropped the issue; Bloomer backtracked by suggesting that women simply separate from drunken husbands. Nichols maintained her opposing position, even writing a small pamphlet on the issue in early 1854, which may account for her reputation as a movement conservative.[44] Antoinette Brown, who became a minister, also urged the leadership to avoid this hotly contested marriage question, and like Nichols she continued to support an established church and emphasized gender differences in her rhetoric. By the time the divorce issue exploded at the national convention in 1860, when Stanton fought and lost a fierce debate over pro-divorce resolutions, other leaders deemed it politically unwise.[45] Nichols had recognized the political implications of this radical strategy, but by that time she had long since left the eastern movement and was politicking in Kansas.

Nichols disagreed with Stanton on divorce, yet both women believed in the effectiveness of political action, and Nichols was now ready to publicly endorse Stanton's call for the elective franchise. As her relationship with other woman's rights advocates deepened, Nichols's fears about impropriety at the ballot box diminished, as long as she could find a defense for voting consistent with her faith and feminine identity. At a convention in West Chester, Pennsylvania, in June 1852, suffragists sought to distinguish their demands from "the violence and intrigue, which are now frequently practised by party politicians." Nichols agreed, using the opportunity to proclaim that "the science of government . . . is of divine origin" and that participation in voting could hardly detract from "the true dignity of woman." Experiencing a new "freedom of spirit," she argued that voting was perfectly compatible with other mixed-sex activities formerly considered improper for women, such as voting in church and corporate elections and traveling on mixed-sex railroad cars and steamships. This rationale reflected her notion of a nonpartisan woman citizen, and she promptly argued in the *Democrat* that property-owning women ought to have the right to vote.[46]

The suffrage claim clearly aligned Nichols with other activists, who reiterated this theme at a contentious woman's rights convention in Syracuse in September 1852. Nichols was identified as one of the "distinguished women" present in the crowded hall, and as a highly regarded journalist with extensive knowledge of property law, she lent her expertise and respectability to the fledgling movement. Along with Lucy Stone, Nichols was "a favorite of the audience" for her heartfelt and earnest oratory; her resolution affirming the abstract principle that "the sexes are equally entitled by original claim to all the rights which cover *means* for discharge" of their God-given responsibilities was easily adopted. But serious debate emerged over immediate strategic concerns, including: Should they form a permanent organization? Should those who owned property launch a tax protest? Did they "discard the Bible or accept its authority"? Most participants rejected further organization and applauded the tax protest, but the latter question was tabled, even as Nichols publicly affirmed her adherence to the Gospel.[47]

Disagreements aside, Nichols did have the opportunity to meet Susan B. Anthony, who would become one of her most important links with the movement. Ten years younger than Nichols, Anthony was as committed to human perfectability and the notion that women's moral virtue should be turned to political purposes as Nichols, but she was far more self-directed and less concerned about the good opinion of others. Formulating her political consciousness out of her Quaker upraising and her experiences as a teacher and temperance advocate, she became a consummate political organizer. She

hoped to galvanize masses of women into the movement in New York and appreciated the persuasive powers of a woman like Nichols, who carried great
influence with the public as editor of a "good family paper." In turn, Nichols
recognized a kindred spirit in Anthony's commitment to human progress, to
temperance, and to women's economic rights.[48]

Back in Brattleboro with new ideas to fill her columns, Clarina Nichols resumed her roles as wife, mother, and editor. She believed that her special calling to do good in the world justified these absences from home. "We have no
fear of any true woman forsaking home duties to lecture on any subject," she
explained in the *Democrat*. "Those who feel called to do the latter, are the
very ones who most truly estimate and provide for the performance of the former."[49] As her relationship with George matured, he became a stalwart supporter and confidant, just the kind of "sympathizing friend" she had sought
in a husband, one who believed wholeheartedly in the notion that women had
a duty to reveal God's truths, which outweighed worldly considerations. "As
father said you two are one," their son George later wrote.[50] Their complementary and largely egalitarian roles on the paper, whereby George handled
business affairs and Clarina the editorial, mirrored their marital relations.

When it came to mothering, Clarina expected that her daughter, Birsha,
would act as surrogate, especially for eight-year-old George, belying her public devotion to maternal duty. In fact, it was Birsha and hired servants who
facilitated her editorial and reform work. Clarina never mentioned her children publicly, perhaps to segregate her private life from scrutiny. It is clear
she cared deeply about their future welfare and often considered their needs,
but her attention in the early 1850s was directed elsewhere. The Carpenter
boys, Howard and Relie, who were adolescents, found a substitute for maternal care at their grandparents' home and with extended family in Townshend.
In the summer of 1851, fourteen-year-old Relie moved to Brattleboro more
permanently and began a three-year apprenticeship in the printing trade under his stepfather's direction. He developed a fondness and concern for his
mother that lasted a lifetime, but there is little evidence that Clarina had a
close relationship with her other son, Howard, who remained in Townshend.[51]
Twenty-year-old Birsha was devoted to her mother, though she also enjoyed
her time with the Howard clan and sometimes resented returning to Brattleboro. Clarina appreciated her daughter's companionship and cared deeply
about her education, but that did not prevent her from expecting Birsha to

help with domestic management. Because parents typically required such duty from a daughter, the arrangement eased any lingering guilt Clarina harbored about neglecting her household. But during the summer and fall, when it was overflowing with boarders and her mother was at conventions, Birsha's responsibilities temporarily limited her freedom to pursue further education or a career of her own.[52]

At the same time, Nichols's heightened gender consciousness directed her attention to the plight of poor women and to the servants in her own household. The equal rights principles embedded in Democratic Party rhetoric had sensitized her to the social and economic status of working-class women, and now her abiding empathy for the poor led her to contemplate greater social justice for them. Expressing considerable affection and concern for her Irish servant named Peggy, she urged readers of the *Lily* "to treat your own sex as sisters" within your own homes. Why not invite the kitchen servant, who bears your domestic burdens, to your table and fireside readings along with the young male apprentice, she queried. Noting that Peggy held a mutual interest in home and would soon be mothering young "freemen" herself, it would be the "first step in righting the wrongs of woman."[53] Whether Nichols actually ran a democratic household herself is unclear, but in addition to this kind of advice she educated her middle-class readers with reports about the horrible working conditions of urban factory workers and her observations of institutional treatment for the poor. After visiting the Delaware County Poor House in Pennsylvania, Nichols condemned the practice of housing poor, unhealthy women and children in the same building with the insane. Yet she extolled the efficiency and womanly deportment of the institution's matron to prove that women were empathetic and competent at administrative work.[54]

While exhibiting her feminine sensibility in this way, Nichols raised awareness about the plight of poor women and earned a reputation for benevolence. She became so well known as a reformer attuned to the difficulties of women's lives that local women began soliciting Nichols's help with their problems, and in turn, they provided her with more firsthand knowledge to illustrate the wrongs inflicted upon women. "Many a time has the sorrow of an almost stranger been poured into my soul like a blister diverting the pain from my own underlying & hidden griefs," she told Anthony. "I am the attorney to whom the suffering ones send their facts & urge 'a vigorous prosecution of the warfare.'"[55] These experiences bolstered her commitment to overturn

Clarina's children by Justin Carpenter (clockwise from the top): Birsha Clarina, 22; Chapin Howard, 19; and Aurelius "Relie" Ormando, 17, in 1853, a year before Clarina and her two sons left for Kansas. Courtesy of the Grace Hudson Museum and Sun House, City of Ukiah, California.

women's economic dependence within marriage, which she believed was the root of women's poverty.

In one of her most innovative examinations of the local legal system, Nichols revealed the unequal status of poor women under the laws of settlement, which tied a married woman to her husband's legal residence. Vermont's poor relief system was particularly brutal if a man without a settlement in town deserted or failed to support his wife, and she was thereby subject to removal to his official residence by the overseer of the poor. Nichols exposed the problem by describing how a penniless woman had even been shipped out of her birthplace to her "worthless" husband's former residence. To prevent this gross inhumanity, women needed legal rights to their earnings to keep them out of the hands of "drunken" husbands, she asserted. Barring that, Nichols proposed a more efficient remedy, that "instead of *Town* paupers, we have only *State* paupers" funded through a state tax.[56] Support at home would have been more humane than other contemporary efforts to centralize poor relief, which involved housing the poor in county workhouses and teaching good habits and morals. Rather than lazy, Nichols believed workers on relief were unfortunate victims of economic cycles, and the state owed these "producers of wealth" support. Her concept of social provision predated the twentieth-century welfare state by half a century, yet it was rooted in a similar vision of a compassionate state protecting women and children from male abuses and mitigating their economic dependence on men.[57]

Nichols's analysis of political economy surpassed that of most benevolent women of her day and led her to advance the argument that self-support was crucial to women's freedom, regardless of prevailing gender roles. Indeed, she ridiculed the notion that performing work reserved for men would rob women of their femininity, that they could become "unsexed—and enriched by a comfortable salary." In a sarcastic allegory, entitled "The Birds," Nichols observed that Mr. and Mrs. Robin had inverted the rules of domestic relations by allowing Mrs. Robin to help build the nest, even though it belonged to her husband, and by putting Mr. Robin "to nursing and feeding the young ones." She admonished Mrs. Robin for letting her "husband stay at home and take care of the little birdies" while she was "away, flitting in the sunshine and singing in public. . . . To be sure, God has given you wings, and an appetite and a bill for picking up your living in the fields; but then you are a mother bird and should not use these gifts—it is a shame and a scandal to your sex!" Legislators were unlikely to change the rules, she advised, so "sing and dress your feathers and let "*him* hunt worms;—it's dirty, masculine business; and sitting in the trees is so nice and lady like!"[58] A mother bird confined to her nest, unable to find food for her own babies, was just as absurd as wives and mothers robbed of the fruits of their labor by an unjust legal system.

As Nichols became increasingly zealous about woman's rights, she also strengthened her voice in the Free Soil movement and the liberal side of the Democratic Party. Having broken with the party in 1848, after Van Buren's unsuccessful bid for the presidency, the Nicholses realigned themselves loosely with the Democracy the following year, joining an influential wing known as the "Free Democracy." They promoted free-labor ideology, including no slavery in the territories, free homesteads, and access to education for self-improvement. Delighted with her principled position between the established parties, Nichols chortled over the Whigs' "nervous tremors" and praised the "perfectly harmonious, and unanimous" nomination of a "Freesoiler" for governor who would warm the hearts of every Whig and Democrat.[59] In this context and bolstered by her associations with radical abolitionists at woman's rights conventions, Nichols unfurled her antislavery sentiments. She exhorted "every Democrat" to act in the "cause of truth and justice" and to "remember that 'God speeds the right' as surely as he opposes the wrong." Passage of the Fugitive Slave Act as part of the Compromise of 1850 had ignited a furor of northern indignation against the Whig administration and precipitated state legislation designed to protect fugitives. The law obligated northerners to participate in the return of runaways, and Nichols railed against a rule allowing authorities to capture "freemen on our free soil." She admonished Vermont Whigs for condoning the "unrighteous" enforcement of the hated law and noted that she intended to "pick up the stitches dropped by the 'True Anti-Slavery party' one at a time."[60]

Nichols's moralism affirmed both her womanly virtue and apparent non-partisanship, even while she used it for political ends by supporting the liberal wing of the party. "*Principle* should be the ground of action," she insisted, "*expediency* should be rebuked and we expect it will be so in the rout of whiggery." Yet in an ironic twist, she invoked a higher law to condemn Whigs. "The conflict between democracy and whiggery is with us, at least, a conflict between the advocates of God's law and man's law," she revealed, placing Democrats on the side of divine justice, and recommended the party's candidates as "the friends of freedom, and respecters of human rights." At

the same time, she straddled local party positions on temperance by supporting a Whig for county commissioner and arguing that Whigs had regularly
elected Democrats in the past. A year later when the Free Democracy revolted
against the major party's nomination of Franklin Pierce in the 1852 campaign, Nichols concluded that both national parties had pledged themselves
on the slavery question "to what they know is impossible, not to say God-
defying." Nichols superimposed a veil of morality over the Free Soil movement, helping to elevate it above the partisanship practiced by either Whigs
or Democrats with her womanly rhetoric. Local Whigs were quick to note the
absurdity of coupling Democrats with "God and Democracy" and critiqued
her partisan inconsistency on temperance as well. Indeed, political maneuver-
ing had cost Free Democrats considerable credibility in the state, and they
were vulnerable to charges of political opportunism.[61]

Yet the debate over slavery allowed Nichols to participate more fully in
partisan politics without compromising her gender. Unlike woman's rights,
which put her perilously close to notorious radicals, antislavery rhetoric
strengthened the appeal of the *Windham County Democrat* for many northern readers and actually camouflaged Nichols's promotion of partisan goals.
"While so many of the Presses of our land are the slaves of Party prejudices,
bigotry, oppressive institutions and anti-[C]hristian laws," one reader com-
mented, "it is quite refreshing and encouraging to find a journal that speaks
out fearlessly for good morals and the highest interest of humanity." With
a reputation for boldness "in favor of freedom and righteousness" and her
ability to express the spirit of reform with "light and love," Nichols reached
a pinnacle in her journalistic career. Noting the widespread influence of her
political commentaries reprinted in various journals, Frederick Douglass, who
ran an antislavery paper in Rochester, New York, admired the "great force
and high intellectual order" found in the *Democrat*.[62] Nichols's antislavery
sentiment was largely driven by a righteous outrage against injustice and
sympathy for enslaved mothers robbed of both their children and their labor,
without practical consideration of its implications for racial equality, at least
at this point in her life. Equally worthy in the eyes of God, slaves needed protection and liberation from cruelty.

If Nichols's righteous voice bolstered the Free Soil movement, it also set her
strategically apart from most radical abolitionists, many of whom eschewed
electoral politics. Following the lead of William Lloyd Garrison, who refused
to participate in a government whose constitution condoned slavery, many

female abolitionists, with the notable exception of Stanton and Swisshelm, considered party politics not only unwomanly but also unconscionable. As they demanded suffrage, however, they struggled mightily to reconcile voting and office holding with the belief that partisan politics was inevitably corrupting and unfeminine.[63] Antoinette Brown eventually resolved the contradiction by arguing that women's political engagement would purify politics and further human progress, and she resolved to become a "practical politician" by supporting principled men like political abolitionist Gerrit Smith, who ran for Congress. Nichols did the same, insisting upon nonpartisanship and touting moral principle to reconcile her activities with feminine propriety and with the stance of radical feminists. She may have even hoped to lobby Democrats about the Fugitive Slave Law when she attended the Democratic Convention in Baltimore in 1852. But engaging with the party of slaveholders was too close for some of her feminist colleagues, who precipitated rumors that the *Democrat* would endorse the party's candidate, Franklin Pierce, for president. Nichols promptly denied the accusation, affirming her distance from the national party and its proslavery agenda. It was not just the Democracy that worried woman's rights leaders; they maintained their distance from electoral politics completely that fall by refusing to endorse the Liberty Party—the only political organization that had countenanced their movement. Disheartened by party corruption, they hoped to purify politics when women got the vote, as did Nichols, but in the meantime, she continued to use the *Democrat* as an organ of "freedom and righteousness" rather than party.[64]

Keeping both political avenues open had its benefits because Nichols was able to capitalize on her connection to electoral politics to advance her agenda for women. Known as the "champion of woman's rights" in Vermont, she felt energized by the respect she had received as a righteous voice for the Free Soil movement, from her success at public speaking, and from local allies as well. She had found a kindred spirit in Ann Elizabeth Brown's husband, Addison. As school superintendent, he had promoted training and fair wages for female teachers, and she had collaborated with him in organizing a local fund-raiser for the celebrated Hungarian revolutionary Louis Kossuth. In fact, she had earned praise for speaking in favor of Kossuth's democratic cause at the New Year's Eve event and believed that the momentum for change was in her favor. "I feel more & more mischievous!" she exclaimed to Susan Anthony. In a bold move, Nichols decided to initiate a petition pleading for the right to vote in school meetings, which Brown submitted to the Vermont Legislature in October 1852.[65]

Petitioning the legislature was not a radical act in itself, but at the time Nichols was singular in her appeal for woman's rights in Vermont. Local women had sent petitions to the assembly against slavery and in favor of prohibition in the late 1830s, setting a precedent in the state; elsewhere, in New York, Ohio, and Massachusetts, activists were petitioning for full suffrage. Surprisingly, there had been little to no discussion of school suffrage per se among leading reformers. Nichols may have been inspired by talk of a tax protest at the recent convention and by physician Harriot Hunt's refusal to pay her school tax in Boston. In a widely reported letter to the city tax collector, Hunt, who was single and a taxpayer, had displayed outrage at her exclusion from municipal and school elections; she refused to pay her taxes and condemned the gender inequities in the public school system. Nichols was aware that taxpaying women in Ontario could vote on school issues, and she may have known that a few women in Kentucky and Ohio had asserted such a right as well.[66]

With these examples to follow, she designed her appeal to capitalize on the political situation in Vermont. Knowing she would need support from Whigs, Nichols hoped to exploit their commitment to school reform and temperance as well as their sympathy for protecting married women's property rights. In a remarkably brave move, she went door-to-door to gather over 200 signatures from supporters in Brattleboro; according to Nichols, they included "the most substantial business men, . . . the staunchest conservatives, and tax-paying widows" as well as men of every political party. Addison Brown, who probably canvassed with her, had worked with Whigs on school reform, and the editor of Brattleboro's newest Whig newspaper, the *Semi-Weekly Eagle*, was devoted to raising parents' awareness of their responsibility to attend school meetings and monitor school affairs.[67] With a rising number of female teachers in the schoolhouse and mothers as acknowledged educators of the young, Nichols believed she could argue for their rightful place in school meetings.

The petition epitomized Nichols's strategy of attaching her claims for equality to women's maternal role and to their essential nature. Contending that voting would simply extend women's acknowledged expertise in education, she predicted that their involvement would result in "the elevation of the race." With wry sarcasm, she noted that "the fathers and bachelors of the State" had hardly perfected the schools.[68] In this way, she hoped to offset objections to the prospect of women's public activity by exalting their potential for effecting social improvement. Local school elections were largely nonpartisan, and women could participate without tarnishing their supposedly superior morality by becoming entangled in party politics. Stressing women's parental responsibilities and her concept of marital equity, she requested a repeal of "all those laws which distinguish between the paternal and maternal relation." Nichols would present a similar argument the following year in a petition for equal custody for mothers, hoping to parlay the consensus about their supervision over children into political and legal rights.[69]

Notwithstanding its slim prospect of success, Nichols mustered considerable political influence to promote the petition despite its risks. In anticipation that her former antagonist, Joseph Barrett, a powerful Whig and chairman of the House Education Committee, would greet her proposal with ridicule, she enlisted support from Daniel P. Thompson, editor of Montpelier's Free Soil paper, *Green Mountain Freeman*. Thompson encouraged her to address the legislature herself, an idea that turned a relatively anonymous petition into a far bolder form of lobbying. To stand before a welcoming audience, as she had done at the Worcester convention, was hardly the same as entreating an assembly of male politicians, where no woman had tread. With Thompson's encouragement, Governor Fairbanks, a sympathetic Whig and supporter of free soil, endorsed her appearance, but representatives still debated the merits of such an innovation. According to Nichols, Barrett was the only legislator who refused to accommodate a woman in the statehouse, and rumors abounded that he would present her with a suit of male clothes. Eventually he agreed, exclaiming, "if the lady wants to make herself ridiculous, let her come and make herself as ridiculous as possible and as soon as possible, but I don't believe in this scramble for the breeches!"[70]

Nichols described the unnerving event in considerable detail in her memoir, signaling its significance in her mind and her sensitivity to public appearance. Despite fears about compromising her womanhood and the reaction of her relatives, she attributed her decision to George, who insisted, "there should be no reproach for the performance of duty."[71] After traveling to Montpelier, a small interior village still struggling for status as the capital, she was escorted by Thompson to the imposing granite statehouse on a Friday evening in late October. Facing a sea of male faces from the Speaker's Desk, she recalled an "intense anxiety" about her ability to avert ridicule, excessive trembling, and a near fainting spell. She anticipated opposition on woman's rights, for there had been some joking in the House about the "sundry females" of Brattleboro, but in fact there was considerable sympathy for her political positions on temperance, education reform, and antislavery among Whigs. As the editor of the *Semi-Weekly Eagle* remarked, "the appearance of such a *hero* in such a field . . . must be calculated to fill the hearts of all opponents with consternation."[72] Whigs maintained a five-seat majority in the Vermont House, but they were deeply divided over what was called the Maine Law, a proposal to prohibit liquor sales and to authorize confiscation from vendors, which Nichols supported. She no doubt drew the strongest sympathies from the minority, Free Soil, and Free Democrat members, who also favored the Maine Law and generally sympathized with her claims for woman's rights—at least their property rights—while old-line Democrats and conservative Whigs barely tolerated her appearance.

According to press accounts, Nichols spoke for an hour and a half, using only skeleton notes. The only record of her address appeared in several Free Soil papers after she submitted a summary for publication. She may have omitted her usual assortment of sorry tales about female hardship for the printed version, but the text reveals a strikingly different style from the one she employed at Worcester. Knowing the Whig majority was attuned to married women's property rights but skeptical of her capacity for rational argument, she began by highlighting "woman's legal wrongs" and their effect on the welfare of families, rather than school suffrage. She believed she could not demand suffrage "before convicting men of legal robbery, through woman's inability to defend herself."[73]

While she focused on family needs and strove to appear feminine, she also wanted to show that she could think like a man, to pose as a genteel mother who also understood political economy. By providing women with separate rights to property and earnings, she explained, legislators would be protecting the community against pauperism, facilitating the transfer of family wealth to daughters, and upholding the freedom of all property owners to save or squander their resources in a capitalist economy. Invoking legislators' sense of justice, their masculine obligations, and their concern about social order, she asserted that "many a man, in spite of the legal injection into his veins of his wife's means of subsistence, has proved *dead* to all the claims of family." According to the editor of the *Burlington Courier*, Nichols concluded that a mother also needed "an equal voice with the father, in the education and guardianship of children," which she supported with facts and judicial comments. This was the only reference to her pending petition for school suffrage.[74] Before exiting the hall, however, Nichols took aim at Joseph Barrett.

Even though she had "earned" the dress she wore, she noted indignantly, her husband owned it, not because he wanted to, but because of a law passed by "bachelors and other women's husbands." Moreover, she challenged lawmakers' manly sense of honor for tolerating Barrett's taunts while having "legislated our skirts into their possession." Despite her inner anxieties, Nichols was a proud woman who relied upon a display of gentility to affirm her class status; rather than suffer ridicule, she would claim the respect due to a woman of refinement.[75]

Nichols remembered that her performance generated foot-stomping applause and that Thompson proclaimed it "a complete triumph," but it would take more than a successful performance to convert the protective sentiments of lawmakers into real political change. Keeping families out of poverty and protecting the so-called weaker sex from "cold hearted avarice" were not the same as sharing power with women in school meetings. Yet apparently Nichols had changed the hearts of a few women of Montpelier, whom Thompson had installed in the gallery, and they exclaimed, "'We did not know before what woman's rights were, Mrs. Nichols, but we are for Woman's Rights,'" she later recalled. The remark no doubt reflected the novelty of her plea in Vermont as well as her need for affirmation from potentially scornful women. In the end, Barrett's committee speedily dismissed her petition, which he claimed would only result in women "mingling in noisy and excited debates" ill suited to their natures. But in a testament to her support among political allies, Free Democrats introduced a new bill providing separate estates for married women. It failed to gain sufficient attention from the assembly, which became engulfed in an angry debate over the Maine Law under Barrett's leadership.[76]

Nichols waited anxiously for comments from the press, but she hardly needed to worry. Only a few editors noted her address, and those who did esteemed her earnest presentation, compared her favorably as a "sensible, practical" exponent unlike the "ultra and absurd" reformers, and acknowledged that women's natural usefulness and proclivity for goodness needed protection against improvident husbands. According to Nichols, even Barrett admitted that "in spite of her efforts Mrs. Nichols could not unsex herself." The summary of her remarks gained wide circulation in Horace Greeley's *New York Tribune*, even while Nichols assured local editors of her modesty and denied any interest in the "personal exhibition of myself in public places."[77] But for the moment, turmoil over the Maine Law had upstaged her efforts. Ironically, on that issue she agreed with Barrett, who brokered a legislative compromise that would enact the controversial measure only if confirmed by a popular referendum.

With renewed energy for politics, Nichols temporarily shelved her woman's rights claims, launched into a campaign to promote the Maine Law in the *Democrat*, and gave local lectures hoping to use her feminine influence on voters. In her pragmatic way, she rejoiced that lawmakers had strengthened prohibition and proceeded to ally with her Whig opponents by urging votes for the referendum. Since passage of statewide "no-license" in 1850, she had supported the election of local officials with impeccable temperance credentials, hoping to strengthen enforcement. Most of the state's Democratic editors opposed the Maine Law on constitutional grounds, and even some Whigs had lost their fervor about the issue. Nichols complained that editors in Windham County had "taken to the fence," insisting it was time that women, the "greatest sufferers" from liquor consumption, should be heard. Her lectures no doubt gave voice to those sufferings. When the referendum passed by a slim majority, Nichols rejoiced, although the legislation was amended the following year to mollify critics. Enforcement remained weak, and she continued to harp on blatant violations of the law with tales of drunken travelers and lax county agents.[78] With her strong support for this Whig issue, Nichols once again exhibited the kind of principled, nonpartisan stance that affirmed her womanliness. Meanwhile, her readers knew that she was fully capable of fierce partisan rhetoric when it suited her reform agenda.

These swings in the political pendulum failed to shake Nichols's optimism that women ought to and could shape public policy. Despite the interdiction against women's involvement in political affairs, by the close of 1852 Nichols could point to minor achievements in reforming property laws and considerable respect from fellow editors as an able political player who wielded her righteous pen in partisan debates. She had also overcome her fears of public speaking, having gained a "cordial recognition" from lawmakers. Her venture onto the podium had brought her "no reproach, no ridicule from any quarter," including her relatives, apparently. Driven by an inordinate need to maintain her reputation as a genteel but sensible woman, Nichols reconciled these political activities with that goal by anchoring herself within woman's sphere, and she confidently defended her efforts to secure home and happiness for other women in the *Democrat*:

"It isn't a *woman's* vocation to write politics; her sphere is at home," says one and another, and we always say *amen*. "Astonished" are you, gentle reader! And did you think that Mrs. Nichols "meddles with politics" because she finds their details congenial with her tastes, or for any reason but that politics *meddle* with the happiness of home and its most sacred relations, with *woman* and all that is dearest to the affections and hopes of a true woman! If you dreamed that politics have any hold upon our sympathies not strictly belonging to their power over the *homes* of the land for weal or woe—any claim upon our time and efforts not identified with our own home interests, you have done us grievous wrong, dear reader, and we pray you just listen to a brief chapter of state policy which was forced upon our notice, a few days since, and say if women, as the "guardian angels" of the "*sanctity* of home" and the "inviolableness of the home relations," have not a call to *write* politics, to *talk* politics.[79]

Nichols had a long history of presenting herself in this fashion, but ironically for the last two years she had spent little time on her own home relations and considerable energy breaking down the concept of "woman's sphere" by expanding it beyond its normal confines.

5

Lady Orator

I assured my audiences, that I had not come to talk to them of
"Woman's Rights," that indeed I did not find that women had any
rights . . . but to "suffer and be still; to die and give no sign." But I had
come to them to speak of *man's rights* and *woman's needs*.
    C. I. H. Nichols, 1881

After her successful performance at the Vermont statehouse, Clarina
Nichols's spirit soared with the conviction that she could "*talk* politics," but her anxieties about actually standing alone in front of an
audience continued to shape her political style. The year 1853 marked
a watershed for the woman's rights movement as it became entwined
with state temperance campaigns and gained increasing national
press coverage. Talk of woman's rights was everywhere, and Nichols kept readers of the *Democrat* informed about the progress of the
movement. As activists frequented the lecture circuit, they became
notorious as the country's "strong-minded women" for their claims
to the public sphere. While Nichols insisted upon the womanliness
of her colleagues, her journalistic profile as a sensible proponent protected her from critics bent on sensationalizing their radicalism, and
it proved useful in heralding her speaking engagements as well. The
editor of the *Whig Sentinel* of Manheim, Pennsylvania, lauded her
"mighty pen" and proclaimed that her arguments for women's advancement were "too true and reasonable to be contradicted honestly
by the veriest 'woman-tyrant.'"[1] Still, finding a balance between her
commitment to the movement and her new friends without incur-
ring public embarrassment would prove difficult. Moreover, Clarina's

desire to be out and about wielding political influence and communing with other activists was pitted against her responsibilities as a breadwinner, wife, and mother, not to mention her loyalties to her Baptist heritage and the Howard family.

Torn between her need for public affirmation and her association with radicals, Clarina defended the propriety of her colleagues who were forging a place for women in the lecture hall, even in front of rural audiences unaccustomed to female display. "How I used to tumble & my heart sink under the personal scrutiny of a curious audience!" she later recalled after having faced such a challenge herself. She admired the nerve of women like Abby Kelley Foster, Sallie Holley, and Lucy Stone, who had become professional antislavery lecturers and were known in the region as dynamic speakers, attracting large crowds. Aware that Stone had won praise for her heartfelt oratory and feminine appearance, Nichols had asked for her help in the campaign for school suffrage. When Stone eventually appeared in Brattleboro in January 1853, the legislature had already adjourned, but she gave two lectures at the Baptist Church on "Woman—Her Rights and Duties," which were apparently well received. With her popularity rising, Stone delivered successful speeches on woman's rights at Metropolitan Hall in New York City, but she was highly controversial among conservative clergymen. They continued to resist this invasion of women on their traditional turf, especially those like Stone who provoked their ire by criticizing their stand on slavery. When Stone returned to Brattleboro later in the year to deliver a powerful abolitionist lecture, she not only condemned slaveholders and all three political parties but also the established churches. Hoping to quell local criticism, Nichols defended Stone's "Christian truth and faithfulness" against charges that she was an infidel and recommended abolitionist Sallie Holley on the same grounds.[2]

Nichols perceived quite rightly that the local clergy could become a significant obstacle, and she was determined to counter their criticism with a display of her own piety and femininity. After successfully refuting one minister in the *Democrat,* her circulation soared. Local people were "indignant with his lecture," she told Susan Anthony, and even strangers had responded to her rebuttal with the "warmest commendation."[3] During the winter of 1853, when Nichols spoke frequently at churches and lyceums in the small towns of Vermont and northern Massachusetts, she invariably encountered ministers and their wives. These intimate settings provided a comfortable forum to practice her skills, and the novelty of a female speaker appealed to local promoters. She was "not a 'ranting fanatic,'" according to one advertiser, but "eminently a sensible and judicious '*female woman*'" and "able editress," who argued with "reason and common sense." At lyceums, where both adults and their youthful recruits debated social and political issues, she was invited to argue about the question, "Ought Women to have equal rights with Men?" Nichols later claimed that she orchestrated these events by allowing a conservative clergyman to open the debate, after which she would regale the audience with a recitation of woman's wrongs sanctioned by biblical authority. With hindsight, she gloated about the approbation she received from timid women and the mortification or begrudging endorsement she elicited from obdurate clerics. Indeed, press accounts of her appearances indicate a generally warm reception to her womanly performances. In neighboring Guilford, she was lauded for "her earnestness and tenderness of appeal" and her "fine extempore style, graceful and eloquent manner, interspersed with lively illustrations." Whether her audiences were simply respectful of her gentility or she was overcoming latent prejudices, the experience boosted her self-confidence, and she informed Anthony that "great things have triumphed for woman among us." This affirmation coupled with her mission to overcome injustice drove Nichols to become a lecturer as much or more than the fees she could garner.[4]

If Nichols rendered the woman's rights movement more respectable with her plea to protect mothers, in challenging the assertions of local ministers she was drawing a fine line between her continuing support of the Baptist church and the conservatism of some of its clerics. Though she denied the biblical subordination of wives to their husbands, she retained her membership in the church and remained committed to religious truth, freely displaying her piety and knowledge of Scripture. Baptist ministers strongly supported temperance, but their views on other reform issues and the fitness of women for public activity ranged widely. Brattleboro's Baptist church hosted Lucy Stone's lectures, indicating an endorsement of her right to speak, but talk of woman's rights was rarely condoned because it contradicted the established interpretation of the Bible. Under the cover of anonymity, Nichols exposed the absurdity of another Baptist cleric in the *Democrat;* he argued that economic rights would cause women to earn too much and become independent, and men would have trouble finding wives. In response Nichols joked that women voters would banish liquor, and with it "men's liberty to drink, and the liberty of women and children to suffer from intemperate husbands and fathers."[5] Such a sarcastic critique probably did little to undermine church authority, but it is evidence that Nichols was beginning to separate the religious establishment from her abiding Christian faith.

In the meantime, she made her voice heard while keeping her political opponents at bay with a womanly performance. Some observers conceded that she was clearly different from radicals Fanny Wright and Abby Kelley Foster, proving that she had at least overcome the barriers against public speaking, even if her message proved unpersuasive. The editor of Burlington's *Free Press*, a staunch Whig, marveled at Nichols's lecturing style. Expecting to "see a 'strong-minded' woman, and to hear a 'strong-minded' lecture," he was disappointed; Mrs. Nichols was a "*woman,* lacking in none of the sensibilities proper to her sex, modest, religious, a little *outré* but not fanatical or absurd." Indeed, he concluded:

> She is not the person we feared to meet, nor was her lecture the tissue of wild abstractions we expected to hear. It was hardly a lecture at all . . . it was rather a pleasant, somewhat rambling talk on an interesting subject, in very much the same tone and manner that a mother would use in addressing her children—sometimes with smiles, and occasionally with tears, which latter coming apparently from a kind heart, were received with respect by her audience. On the whole, we were greatly pleased with the fair Editress.[6]

Notwithstanding his admiration, he offered little support for either additional property rights or woman suffrage. The hardships Nichols detailed were rare, he insisted, and women were not in favor of suffrage; they would simply vote with their husbands anyway.

Nichols's experiences traveling by rail and stagecoach to these events also supplied her with colorful material to enhance her repertoire of stories about women's disabilities under the law. On a trip to Templeton, Massachusetts, she was seated comfortably with her knitting in the "Ladies Saloon" when two men, an "old grandfather" and the "High Sheriff," burst into the railcar looking for two little girls who were huddled next to their mother. When they attempted to seize the children, the woman cried out, "Don't father, don't take away my children; they are *my* children, father; they *are* my children!" After he grabbed the four-year-old, "crying in his arms," Nichols "sprang to her feet" to intercede and to enlighten the sympathizing and "indignant" passengers with a "Woman's Rights lecture" about the "kidnappers." They were exercising the father's custodial rights and claimed the mother had "stolen" her own children. How could that be, Nichols remarked; it was "almost equal to a man's stealing himself!" Persuaded that the mother had a "right to her babes," the group protected the younger child from the "child robbers," who left the train at the next stop in Massachusetts. In the meantime, Nichols boldly informed the Vermont sheriff, who appeared sorrowful at exercising his duty, that he had no jurisdiction in another state. Eventually she took the two-year-old under her care while another man on board helped the mother recover the abducted child with assistance from officials in Massachusetts, where only a father, not a grandfather, could exercise custodial rights. After word of the incident spread, Nichols was credited with helping to rescue the hapless children, for which she received kudos and gifts of yarn to "keep me in knitting-work while preaching woman's rights on the railroad."[7]

Whereas her convictions drove Nichols into action in this case, she also exploited the family crisis for its emotional appeal without revealing all the details. The mother had apparently filed for divorce on the grounds of abuse and in the meantime had secreted the children away from their grandfather's home, where he was caring for them legally during a separation. The dramatic railcar abduction held special meaning for Nichols because her former husband had threatened the safety of her own children and her capacity as a mother; it also resonated with public sentiment at a time when northerners were sensitized to kidnapping of runaways and free blacks under the notorious Fugitive Slave Law. Nichols used the story repeatedly to elicit sympathy for women as victims of unfeeling men, and to display mothers' private sorrows to an unsuspecting public. As an illustration of the horrors of custodial law, it proved an effective vehicle to display her womanly instincts and to advocate for "a mother's right to the care and custody of her helpless little ones!"[8]

Even while she portrayed herself as a public protector of mothers and children, to some extent Clarina had forsaken the company of her own children and extended family to pursue her lecturing career. To be sure, the Carpenter children were nearly all adults by 1853, but nine-year-old George still needed her attention and schooling while her husband was aging rapidly. Should she send her son to Brattleboro Academy and trust Birsha to supervise, or to Townshend Academy, where the Carpenters had been educated under the Howards' supervision? Neither seemed appropriate given Clarina's distance from her family in Townshend and the appealing world she had discovered among reformers. Although Clarina believed her female relatives were in

sympathy with her cause, especially her younger sister Ellen Cobb, the Howard men were apparently skeptical. There is no direct evidence of what her
father thought, but some of her male relatives were scornful of her work
and often told her so by insisting that she could have developed a lucrative
business if only she would forget abolition and woman's rights. Her brother
Aurelius was "trained in less liberal times," Clarina recalled, and "tenacious
in his opinions." Her political differences with family and friends no doubt
contributed to a sense of isolation from them, a compensating longing for the
company of like-minded women, and perhaps a hope for an alternative life for
George and Birsha.[9]

Otherwise, it is hard to imagine why Clarina decided to send both children
away to boarding school at the home of famous abolitionists Theodore and
Angelina Grimké Weld in New Jersey at the same time she increased her lecturing activities. Was she seeking an education for her children that she had
missed, to expose them to principles and people she admired rather than conservatives in local schools, or did she harbor a dream that they would follow in
her footsteps? In any case, Birsha would replace Clarina's maternal oversight,
keeping George from becoming too homesick, and her husband could manage
alone during her absences, especially now that Relie was assisting him with
typesetting. Moreover, at twenty-two, Birsha needed to find either a direction in life or a husband, hopefully both, and the Welds' school would provide her with an opportunity that Clarina had merely dreamed about in her
own youth. Paying for boarding school was an unusual choice for a normally
thrifty woman like Clarina, who prided herself on home nurture, but it also
indicated her eagerness to embrace the reform community, her genuine concern for directing her children's development, and her assessment that local
institutions were inadequate to prepare them for the kind of purposeful life
she admired.

Nichols probably met Angelina Grimké Weld at the conventions in Worcester or heard about the Welds' school from other reformers at meetings in 1852.
Renowned abolitionists, they had retreated from active reform work and operated a small family boarding school on a fifty-acre farm bordering the Pas-
saic River in Belleville, New Jersey, where they had lived with their three
children and Angelina's sister Sarah Grimké since 1840. The Grimké sisters
had rocked established authorities in the late 1830s by challenging the biblical interpretation of women's subordination and promoting the education and
full participation of women in American society. To enhance their income

and their children's learning, the family offered schooling to about twenty children of other reformers, including two of Elizabeth Cady Stanton's sons and those of abolitionists James G. Birney and Gerrit Smith. The Welds were part of a network of religious liberals in the abolition movement, thoroughly Christian but devoted to free inquiry, and Nichols ascribed to their ideals for practical and equal education of the sexes, which integrated schooling with their life on the farm. Theodore Weld, who had captivated audiences as an abolitionist orator, had largely abandoned speaking but proved to be a patient and beloved teacher who respected the capacity for learning in every child.[10]

Confident the Welds would provide her son with a fine education, Nichols also hoped they would inspire her daughter with their idealism. George and Birsha spent two winters at Belleville, where they learned and played among the Welds and their associates. While she mothered George, Birsha may have also monitored or tutored the younger children, perhaps in exchange for lower tuition at a time when Angelina and Sarah felt overwhelmed with school duties. George liked his new friends and regaled his parents with their outdoor activities, which seemed to interest him far more than grammar and composition. He missed his "Dear little black pussy cat," but Birsha reassured her mother that he was not homesick despite the fact that he would "cry for half an hour if forgotten." Neither as intellectual nor as sensitive as her mother, Birsha possessed a sunny disposition and adapted easily to the school routine. The Welds' kindly management style created an atmosphere conducive to learning, and Birsha relished their company and her capacity to please them with accounts of her mother's travels and lecturing. Notwithstanding her own interest in abolition or woman's rights, she was a link between her mother and progressive reformers, helping to solidify Nichols's relationship with a group she longed to join.[11]

Indeed, Nichols was so pleased with the arrangement that Birsha and George followed the Welds when they moved the school to Raritan Bay Union, a planned community in Perth Amboy, New Jersey. Reincorporated as Eagleswood School in 1854, it was dedicated to coeducation, open to black students, and designed to integrate intellectual and practical training. Under the leadership of Quaker abolitionists Marcus and Rebecca Spring, the Raritan Bay Union, situated on a secluded estate of 268 acres on the shores of Raritan Bay, was not as radical as most utopian communities of the 1840s. It was intended to provide a mix of communal social life and practical education under the guidance of Christian principles and capitalist economic and social relationships. Along with more than fifty other boarders, Birsha and George were housed in a partially finished but stately dormitory and offered an exhausting schedule of activities, including art, theater, and gymnastics, as well as practical lessons in such topics as bookkeeping and dressmaking. Eagleswood became a center of abolitionist and liberal inquiry, and as such it attracted intellectuals and artists from New York and Boston, including Elizabeth Peabody, who experimented with a kindergarten program, and William Henry Channing, who taught occasional classes. George had more difficulty adapting to the larger school than Birsha and missed the fact that he did not "have any cows to drive," but Clarina could still hope they would benefit from the feast of talent and ideas swirling around the progressive school.[12]

Back in Vermont her reputation as a speaker was enhancing Nichols's value to the woman's rights movement and cementing her connections with other reformers. Yet finding a role compatible with her public image remained challenging. While she spoke to local audiences in New England, Susan Anthony drew her into the temperance movement in New York during 1853. Anthony had energized the movement with a statewide effort to promote the Maine Law and gather local women into the cause the year before. But the effort to politicize more conservative women and the entanglement of woman's rights with temperance was fraught with controversy. Leaders of the New York State Temperance Society, leery of women's influence and their proclivity to slip seamlessly into woman's rights advocacy, had refused to allow their equal participation, which sparked the formation of a woman's temperance society under the leadership of Stanton, Anthony, and Bloomer, among others. When Stanton pressed her radical proposals on divorce for drunkenness, the women's group fractured over the issue. Always the strategist, Anthony recruited Lucy Stone and Nichols, aware that they held differing opinions on divorce, to speak at a women's temperance convention in Rochester along with other radical prohibition supporters. Nichols was welcomed on the platform as a distinguished speaker because of her ardent effort to pass the Maine Law in Vermont, and Anthony valued her "sprightly" presentation style. She denounced easy divorce as "the sin for which all mankind suffered—divorce from the law of God," but apparently the audience was more impressed with Stone's dynamic delivery. When Nichols began advocating for women's legal control of children and their self-support, there were rumblings in the back of the hall, presumably against her drift into woman's rights, and she left the speakers' platform, claiming fatigue. The next day, she soothed the audience with a sorry tale about an abused wife whose hard-earned home was attached by rumsellers but who still protested against filing for divorce.[13]

Caught between radicals like Stanton and Stone and temperance advocates uncomfortable with woman's rights, Nichols continued to identify with feminists who were totally committed to the cause, but she also needed to affirm her respectability and religiosity. A month later she admitted privately to Anthony that she was "miserable" and believed she had been "badly shown off" in the press, but she did not blame Susan. Her appreciation for Susan's commitment and her affection for her younger new friend had only blossomed. "Please remember it is *Susan B. Anthony* whom I prize in you & *nobody else,*" Clarina wrote, marking the beginning of an enduring relationship between the two women.[14] Years later, she explained that she had "longed to live by women" like Susan, "whose whole souls were in the work, instead of their leisure time & unused scraps of heart!" This was the sentiment that sent her children away for a costly education with just such reformers and one that frequently allowed Clarina to overlook minor differences with her colleagues. She not only wanted to be with them, she wanted to be as dedicated and forthright as they were. She developed a close sympathy with Anthony because Susan was principled and collegial with her. "It seems to me that we two more than any I know, live in this woman move[ment] because we see in it the divine development of humanity as a whole," she later wrote her friend.[15] For her part, Anthony admired Nichols's performances and the appeal of her domestic politics, but at the time she found greater strength in the courageous stance taken by Stanton and Stone, both of whom patiently endured ridicule with fearless determination. Even while Nichols strove to emulate their nobility, she also developed sisterly relations with Hannah Darlington of Kennett Square, Pennsylvania, another Quaker and temperance advocate. Darlington was amazed at how Nichols could send her dear children away or neglect her husband while she lectured and politely warned her about too much "plodding" around the hinterlands.[16]

If their ability to withstand criticism varied, solidarity among these feminists increased as controversy within the temperance movement reached a peak at a series of conventions in New York City in September 1853. The stage had been set in May, when organizers of the World Temperance Convention refused to allow Anthony a place on the business committee and excluded women delegates altogether in an effort to disassociate themselves from radical feminists. In a dramatic display of resistance similar to that of abolitionists, the woman's rights advocates and their male allies exited the temperance meeting and organized an alternative gathering. The subsequent Whole World's Temperance Convention, held in September and designed to welcome everyone regardless of sex, class, race, or sect, overshadowed the competing men's meeting. A mammoth affair, at which temperance songsters regaled audiences of two and three thousand, the conference was part of a major campaign to pass the Maine Law in New York. Visitors from Canada, Britain, Germany, and Belgium lent an international flavor to the event and elevated temperance as a worldwide movement comparable to antislavery. Thomas Wentworth Higginson, a Unitarian minister and abolitionist who had led the rebellion, presided while Horace Greeley of the *New York Tribune* headed the business committee and authored numerous resolutions. Determined to play an equal role in the proceedings, many of Nichols's colleagues peopled the officer list and felt compelled to address the audience.[17]

Arriving in the crowded city in September with great anticipation, Clarina was a far different woman from the downtrodden wife and desperate mother who had left it fifteen years earlier. Memories of her formative experiences on Fulton Street must have seemed a distant nightmare as she mingled with fellow reformers and throngs of tourists drawn into the city for the World's Fair. Conventions on abolition and woman's rights were scheduled to follow the temperance conventions, all strategically planned to coincide with the fair. Nearly everyone wanted to visit the exhibits under the dome of the spectacular Crystal Palace, an iron-and-glass building displaying American inventions and technological prowess along with impressive works of art from many nations. These attractions, such as the popular veiled statues of Christ and the Apostles, enhanced the appeal and significance of the conventions and the likelihood of crowded audiences.

When Nichols joined the assembled temperance advocates at Metropolitan Hall, the momentum for change was palpable as the reformers' triple-headed agenda attracted national media attention. Appointed a vice president representing Vermont, she was well known for successfully advocating the Maine Law, and now she had found a collegial forum to spout her views on prohibition on a national stage. In the evening she would appear as an honored guest and speaker at a "Great Vegetarian Banquet" for 500 advocates of prohibition, many of whom ascribed to Sylvester Graham's dietary program designed to improve health, reduce bodily cravings, and curb sexual desire. Clearly sympathetic with the movement, Clarina had adopted a modified vegetarianism at home and pressed a meatless diet on her children. For a woman accustomed to rural simplicity and unfamiliar with a thoroughly cosmopolitan audience, to dine on a platform with notable reformers—Horace Greeley, Lucy Stone, Amelia Bloomer, Susan Anthony—and to speak to the assembled dignitaries was both exhilarating and frightening. Characteristically, she asked reporters "to take no notes of her speech."[18]

The roster of speeches at the Whole World's Temperance Convention was calculated to showcase women and their ability to participate equally with men in the movement. Antoinette Brown, soon to be ordained as a Congregational minister, was triumphant as she announced, "Here is Woman invited to speak into the great ear-trumpet of the world." Some male reformers welcomed women on egalitarian grounds, but others sought their influence because they could bring "a moral element into politics," in effect replacing the conservative ministers who had shunned them. Yet women like Lucy Stone could deliver more radicalism than they anticipated. In a diatribe on the effects of alcohol abuse on the family, Stone concluded that drunkenness on the part of either husband or wife was grounds for divorce. Such a law would not only relieve victims but also act as a deterrent, threatening men's marital rights. Her extraordinary daring in introducing the contentious issue at a temperance convention was characteristic of Stone. Unlike Nichols, she defined herself as an outsider willing to challenge any institutional authority and maintained a self-regard independent of the good opinion of others. When Horace Greeley, whose support for woman's rights proved limited, politely disagreed with her, she shouldered the public rebuke courageously.[19]

If Stone appealed to the radical element in the audience, Nichols curried favor with its most respectable members by touching their emotions and displaying her piety without shocking their social standards. Instead, she displayed her outspokenness by exhorting Christians to political action. Tapping all three of the convention themes, she defended women's role in the temperance movement, the necessity of the Maine Law, and the formidable role the churches could play by enforcing total abstinence and exposing the horrors of the liquor trade. Women were the greatest sufferers from alcohol abuse, she explained, "bound hand and foot" through legal dependence on men, who could "take the babes from our bosoms." To prove that men, who had attempted all manner of social improvements, could not operate alone, Nichols regaled the audience with a travel tale about encountering a father who "fancied" he could feed his baby with "a pocket full of cakes." The world would become "dyspeptic," she joked, if the child were not "restored to the mother-fountain of humanity, and [allowed] to drink the milk of human kindness that God has stored in the breast of woman." When it came to the duty of Christians, she praised the clergy for supporting the Maine Law, but she also admonished them for failing to do more than sermonize and demanded that they hold parishioners to account for their votes. "God himself," she exhorted, sanctions "political acts as Christian duty." Making no distinction between the church and its individual members, Nichols explained her own commitment to the Baptist Church, God's "high and holy purpose," and the necessity for discipline "against every man who votes against the Maine Law." With a nod to religious liberals, who prized the freedom to follow their own consciences unfettered by clerical authority, Nichols apologized for appearing "ultra." Yet in fact she was only following a common practice among Baptists, including her own father, who regularly disciplined each other to save communicants from their own sins. The plea, mixing the sacred and the secular, was a measure of the way her religious inheritance informed her politics.[20]

Participants at the temperance convention congratulated themselves on two days of heartwarming speeches and relative unanimity, an experience that was not to be repeated as they reassembled to discuss woman's rights. Negative media coverage about controversies at the temperance and antislavery conventions in the *New York Herald*, *Times*, and *Express* amplified the antics of outside agitators and alerted the public to yet another spectacle as the women convened. By charging only $.25 admission for each of six sessions, organizers had hoped to provide easy access for women, but instead they attracted crowds of two to three thousand people, including both educated professionals and lower-class "rowdies" opposed to the cause. Stately but mild-mannered Lucretia Mott, who had hoped to focus on achieving coequality, allowed speakers to range widely and provided opponents access to the platform. Serious disruption threatened during the first evening as shouts and hisses interrupted Polish-born Ernestine Rose. Widely known for her atheism and advocacy of human rights, she ignited abuse from loud and ill-mannered men, and the session closed when an opponent jumped on the platform demanding to hear three reasons why women should vote.[21]

The next morning, refreshed and invigorated from the previous day's tumult, Nichols responded by proclaiming her need for self-protection as a citizen and a mother. "Women should have the right to vote" to control their "own moral, intellectual, and social interests," she insisted. "I want to have this power because I do not possess the power which ought to belong to me as a mother." If the protection of children was not reason enough, enfranchisement would ensure that "the best measures for the good of the community would be carried." Nichols laid her case before the immense audience of nearly three thousand people using a familiar array of anecdotes about poor wives and widows deprived of their property. She made her views on political economy and the importance of mothers clear by upbraiding one of her characters for scoffing at his wife, who failed to do anything but raise nine children:

> Nine. Nine children to attend to!—nine children cared for!—and she could do nothing more, the wife of this most reasonable man. Now, which is of more importance to the community, the property which that reasonable husband made, or the nine children whom that mother brought, with affectionate and tender toil, through the perils of infancy and youth, until they were men and women? Which was of more importance to this land—the property which the father of George Washington amassed, or the George Washington whom a noble mother gave to his country?[22]

If Nichols evoked these national heroes to claim citizenship for mothers, by contrast physician Harriot Hunt evoked her Revolutionary heritage to demand individual rights as a citizen, asserting that as a single woman she owned taxable property but had no representation in the government. A stream of famous reformers who defended women's need for equal citizenship with their favorite rationales ensued, occasionally interrupted by opponents who contested their demands by citing Scripture. But as the day progressed and the evening session opened, ruffians in the balcony began heckling, targeting women with racial or ethnic slurs, and disrupting their presentations. Sojourner Truth, the only African-American woman speaker, and German-speaking Matilda Anneke were greeted with shouting, stomping, and calls to "go to bed" and "shut up." By that time, mass confusion reigned despite Wendell Phillips's effort to maintain order. Mott surrendered her gavel, and Ernestine Rose called for the police to intervene and clear the hall.[23]

The spectacle of the "Mob Convention," as it was later dubbed, marked a new stage in the woman's rights movement. Media attention elevated it to national status, and advocates exploited the opportunity to defend their free speech rights. Antoinette Brown became a hero for her brave but unsuccessful attempt to address the men's temperance association and for her performance leading a religious service for 5,000 in Metropolitan Hall. The abrogation of free speech and volley of insults at the meeting and from unsympathetic reporters thoroughly established activists as victims of injustice and dishonor; as Greeley predicted, the backlash largely strengthened the movement. Nichols expressed her indignation by defending the proceedings with evidence that honorable gentlemen had wholeheartedly supported the cause. Yet the disruption also confirmed her latent fears that she was dangerously close to becoming a pariah and that her reputation could be shattered at any moment. By contrast, other feminists were emboldened and determined to exploit the publicity by launching petition campaigns in New York, Massachusetts, Ohio, and Pennsylvania. Stanton and Anthony broke away from more conservative evangelical women in the New York temperance movement by redirecting their efforts into a legislative petition drive for full legal and political equality.[24] Nichols kept her options open by supporting their efforts and also maintaining her contacts with the temperance society. She was sufficiently removed from them to remain an outsider, and her determination not to hold grudges proved to be a strength as these new strategies divided politically active women. She admired Stanton's intellect and her bravery, praising her as "able and true" in her dedication to the "emancipation of woman," but she could not abide a similar public presence for herself, preferring instead to cling to established social and institutional structures to attain the same goals.[25]

Nichols's performance in New York had enhanced her national reputation as a persuasive and womanly lecturer for prohibition, even though the reform had become hopelessly entangled with woman's rights. Impressed by her performances in the city, Whig leader Horace Greeley recommended Nichols as an able spokeswoman to Sherman M. Booth of Wisconsin, who had attended the conventions and was recruiting women lecturers to promote passage of the state's upcoming referendum on the Maine Law. An outspoken abolitionist and former Liberty Party leader, Booth edited the *Milwaukee Daily Free Democrat,* one of the earliest radical papers in the state. He was determined to convert the Free Soil movement into a major force for abolitionism nationwide, but he also defended prohibition in the interest of women and children and publicly condoned women's political activism. Using his wily political skills, he hoped to capture the votes of Wisconsin Whigs by linking prohibition to his antislavery goals. He welcomed the gentility and novelty that women like Clarina Nichols brought to the temperance movement because they attracted curious audiences and their supposedly pure motives and womanly deportment elevated the campaign above personal ambition or partisanship. Billed as the greatest sufferers of alcohol abuse, women could touch the hearts of small-town farmers and artisans, thereby producing a rural groundswell of temperance support to offset the urban Democratic majority in Wisconsin, which rested firmly on the votes of German and Irish immigrants.[26]

Booth's proposal captivated Nichols's sense of adventure. She envisioned an opportunity to extend her political reach and practice her lecturing skills under the wing of a righteous abolitionist with congenial political views, but only as long as she could reconcile the trip with contemporary propriety. Booth was a practical, if tactless and unpredictable, politician with bushy black hair and a shaggy beard, but he carried a shady personal reputation. The prospect of traveling on an expense-paid adventure to the far West plus earning $25 a week drew Nichols like a magnet away from the melee in the East, but she needed a better chaperone than Booth. He assured her that the Wisconsin Temperance League would sanction the endeavor, and she convinced George that the trip was part of her duty to the cause and a rare and otherwise unaffordable opportunity to see the West. The deal was cinched when Dr. Lydia F. Fowler also agreed to the venture, which Nichols believed would confirm that she was not hankering "for a space to cut loose from the marital 'buttons' and go out into the world alone!" Fowler, a New York physician and temperance advocate, and her husband, Lorenzo, practiced phrenology, the analysis of brain size and shape to determine mental capacities for self-improvement. Lydia was living proof that a woman held equal capacity for self-development with men, having lectured widely on anatomy and physiology, and she promised Booth a separate series of lectures on the devastating physical effects of alcohol.[27]

Clarina would remember her adventures in Wisconsin as one of the highlights of her career as a reformer, a triumph of high moral tone and womanly presentation over the remnants of prejudice against female speakers. In fact, she devoted 20 percent of her memoir to the six-week trip, signaling its impact on her life course. She left from New York only two weeks after the "Mob Convention" and arrived without incident in Milwaukee after a five-day trip by rail and steamer across Lake Erie and Lake Michigan, an excursion that Nichols recounted vividly in the *Democrat*. Agog at the newly constructed suspension bridge at Niagara and smug in her commodious upper-deck stateroom with Mrs. Fowler, Nichols assured eastern readers that the work of a reformer was both enlightening and genteel as they arrived in Milwaukee just in time for an "early tea."[28] Much to Booth's apparent dismay, the temperance league refused to engage Nichols after all, but turning the group's disapproval of women speakers into a political tool, he persuaded a newly organized women's temperance society to vindicate his plan. After hearing admirable addresses from Nichols and Fowler about the benevolent nature of their work, the society sponsored the women agents to canvass the state. Nichols and Fowler traveled approximately 900 miles, chaperoned by Booth and his wife, Mary, partly by rail but mostly by carriage, and spoke to crowds in over forty towns, sometimes twice a day. Booth promoted the lecture circuit in the *Daily Free Democrat* and reported that the perfect "order, decorum and propriety" of their engagements and the "magic spell of their eloquent appeals" converted large welcoming audiences; a recalcitrant tavern keeper even opened his ballroom for them.[29]

Yet not all audiences greeted this spectacle of high-toned womanly temperance talk with approbation. To conservative temperance men, who sponsored a competing male lecturer, Booth's tour was a political stunt, a means to wrest control of the temperance movement from the state's orthodox clergy and to camouflage his political goals. Members of the temperance league agitated local communities to boycott the speakers and slandered the operation as a "Barnum speculation" designed to enrich Booth's pocket. While a new People's Temperance Association, open to anyone without regard to "party, sex, or denomination," galvanized ample audiences, orthodox church leaders either refused to open their doors or tried to thwart their presentations. In Waukesha, a temperance stronghold, Nichols waited for hours while a minister and deacon extended the business meeting and substituted a male speaker in the evening to forestall her lecture before preaching against the "infidelity of these Temperance lecturers." Booth used the "clerical onslaught" to champion the people's right to hear refined women speak.[30]

For her part, Clarina resurrected details of the incident in her memoir to exemplify how her missionary zeal in "service to a common humanity" vindicated her right to speak for women against long-standing tradition. Opposition from conservative ministers far from her home turf furnished her with opportunities to display her womanly deportment, her finesse, and her rhetorical skills without having to challenge her local religious establishment. She described curious and doubtful men and women from miles around Waukesha who became indignant at the minister's tactics and demanded to hear her lecture. After negotiating her way to the podium, she claimed to have conquered both the audience and her opponents with apt quotations from Proverbs, pleading "the cause of the poor and needy." When the minister publicly endorsed her a week later and sent her an apology, Nichols was triumphant, having proved to local women that she could speak for them even in front of the most conservative religious leaders. Casting herself as a moral crusader for poor women and children wronged by male privilege, not a radical for woman's rights, she assured her audiences that she would "speak of man's rights and woman's needs." Opponents were blinded by prejudice, grateful for enlightenment, and full of remorse, exclaiming, "'Mrs. Nichols has made me ashamed of myself—ashamed of my sex!'" she recalled righteously. Repeated in town after town, these affirmations that women had suffered injustice confirmed that Nichols had been wronged herself years ago, if not from the same cause, and that with her effort "God's rule of love and duty" would prevail.[31]

If the campaign gratified Nichols's sense of justice and her ambitions, it ultimately failed to boost Sherman Booth's political agenda. He sought to unite temperance and Free Soil advocates behind legislative candidates under the umbrella of an anticorruption People's ticket. The importation of nonpartisan women speakers into the state and the temperance tour had been part of his effort to build an independent party, attract former Whigs, and break the Democratic stranglehold on Wisconsin politics. He calculated that as a moral issue the Maine Law and the purity of the women would remove the taint of politics from the campaign. Nichols rejoiced in the potential of a temperance and Free Soil combination, noting that the party had support from the Whig ex-governor. The Democratic *Milwaukee Morning News* tried to undermine the tactic by associating it with woman's rights and suggesting that "strong-minded women" were infiltrating the state and acting like politicians by "taking the stump." Indeed, Wisconsin's temperance women had put lawmakers on notice "that *the Women are COMING* " and sponsored another woman speaker from Illinois, while Amelia Bloomer also regaled audiences in her bloomer outfit. Notwithstanding complaints about their presence, by the time Nichols and Fowler reached Madison, where they spoke in the statehouse, Booth was elated by the way his strategy seemed to have transformed public sentiment and anticipated he could secure legislative seats for the "right sort of men" as well.[32] In fact, Nichols and Fowler were doing his political stumping. He exhibited these highly respectable eastern women to rescue Wisconsin from sin, German and Irish immigrants, and the Democratic Party. In the end, they were gratified that the tour helped produce a popular vote for prohibition, but the People's Party failed miserably in the effort to defeat Democratic candidates, who took office and refused to enact such a law. Meanwhile, Booth resumed his antislavery agenda, calling for a mass protest against the "Slave Power," and famously went to prison a few months later for rescuing runaway Joshua Glover from jail, in a challenge to the hated Fugitive Slave Law.[33]

Notwithstanding Booth's ability to exploit the virtue and nonpartisanship of women lecturers, Nichols left Wisconsin with a sense of personal accomplishment and a dream for the future. With a romantic notion of western development, she described Wisconsin as a garden of Eden, a "'home to come to.'" The trip had sparked her imagination about what could be accomplished in a place fertilized with free soil sentiment and primed for liberal legislation. Wisconsin's "broad prairies" and "gallant lakes" were interspersed with fertile fields of grain and neat brick houses, she explained to eastern readers, domesticating its frontier image. But most of all, it was the "noble humanity" and "responsive souls" of the people that endeared her to the state. Wives and widows were "better protected" in Wisconsin than in the "old States," Nichols noted, because its enlightened lawmakers had already secured them with married women's rights to real and personal property. Harboring this notion of their progressive views, for months she dreamed of settling in Madison, a capital city surrounded by lakes, filled with tree-lined streets and "tasteful residences," and with a substantial "noble brick" Baptist church in construction. If only she could purchase one of these house lots within reach of the statehouse, she would be able to "look after the interest of the women and children of the state."[34] This vision of a settled, orderly community in the West—not the spare, isolated, and often dangerous existence of pioneer tales—coupled with the freedom to pursue her mission for humanity animated Clarina's imagination. In Wisconsin perhaps she could escape the frustrations and criticism she faced at home and fulfill her calling as one of God's chosen agents.

Nichols was not the only activist who had become energized by the upsurge of interest in woman's rights and its convergence with temperance campaigns in the West. Women in Michigan and Ohio were exercising their moral authority for political ends by appearing boldly at polling places to convince anti-temperance men to change their votes; the angry women of Ohio and Indiana marched in the streets, barged into liquor shops, and dumped out all the liquor. Along with Wisconsin, Amelia Bloomer toured Ohio, Michigan, and Indiana, where she galvanized women against the liquor trade. After selling the *Lily* to Mary Birdsall, who furthered the cause from Richmond, Indiana, the Bloomers moved to Council Bluffs, Iowa. But it was not just temperance that was alighting western communities. Lucy Stone delivered speeches in Ohio, Michigan, Illinois, and Ottawa, Canada, and even brought woman's rights to the Upper South in Kentucky, Missouri, Indiana, and West Virginia. Frances Gage, a journalist from Ohio known as "Aunt Fanny," had moved to St. Louis, and kept eastern readers abreast of women's activities in the West. Eagerly tracking news from the region, Nichols was pleased to report that Indiana's Baptist Society was planning a nonsectarian Western Female University, the first evidence of "sympathy with our churches."[35] This small vanguard of woman's rights activists saw potential in the aura of freedom connected to western settlements, where they believed women ought to take their rightful place in society unencumbered by patriarchal legal and political structures and social conventions. Driven by belief in progressive change, they often overlooked the loneliness and privations that normally beset pioneering women and were equally blind to the effects of western expansion on Native American populations.

If Clarina had felt torn between her duty to her family and her work for humanity, she was even more restless after returning from her venture in Wisconsin. Instead of resuming her editorial work, she resolved to make a living through lecturing while harboring her western dreams. Her reputation as "one of the most entertaining, effective and instructive speakers" on temperance—a "grand reasoner" and "fine story teller"—had spread beyond New England. George could no longer operate the *Democrat* in her absence, and with Vermont politics in disarray, they ceased publication. Clarina secured engagements to speak on both temperance and woman's rights in an increasingly wide geographical circle around Brattleboro, extending to eastern New York and to Boston and Providence, Rhode Island, where she booked a series with Lucy Stone, Ernestine Rose, and Antoinette Brown. According to Hannah Darlington, Clarina was no longer "tame," and temporarily at least, not alone. Presenting herself as a conventional mother concerned about the welfare of her children, she felt comfortable and likeable within her own distinctive political identity. "If there is any door worth knocking at, in your vicinity, I will be happy to enter & do good service," she boldly wrote a patron. Through her associations with other reformers Nichols had expanded her work for women from legal to political reform; she had overcome her anxiety about speaking to mixed audiences; she had conquered her fear of "Clerical vetos" without losing her faith; and she had learned to suppress her irritation at insults. Her victories over the clergy were particularly poignant moments, giving Nichols a great sense of accomplishment, especially when she received "warm greetings" from "intelligent men & women."[36]

Just as Clarina reached this pinnacle in her speaking career, her father, who had been so instrumental in her youthful development, interrupted the trajectory of her reform work. In the spring of 1854, sixty-nine-year-old Chapin Howard became fatally ill. Clarina abandoned her lectures and spent several weeks at her father's bedside nursing him and feeling nostalgic about the loss of family ties. The hours she spent comforting her "dear father" who suffered while still in "his strong manhood" left her with an indelible and painful memory.[37] Chapin's legacy to his daughter was far greater than the money she would eventually receive from his estate. He had guided her early girlhood with a firm but just hand; he had modeled the piety and principles of fairness that shaped her life and animated her career; and he had provided the financial, legal, and spiritual support she needed during her marital calamity. She would remember him fondly for the rest of her life.

Her father's death meant that Clarina would forgo the national woman's rights convention in 1854, and the break from political work gave her time to reassess her future prospects. If the movement to secure woman's rights was becoming respectable in her motherly hands, it had made only meager progress in Vermont. She had tried to muster interest in a petition campaign for a mother's right to guardianship, but it had failed to materialize. In Brattleboro she had become notorious for keeping "the whole community in a fuss about woman's rights and temperance," which threatened to compromise her family's good name. Repeatedly, she had heard the refrain that her measures would be contrary to the "Scripture injunction of obedience . . . to husbands." Neither her encounters with ministers nor her opponents' use of biblical logic seemed to shake Nichols's attachment to the Baptist Church or her faith in her God-ordained mission, yet these confrontations tried the stamina of a woman who prized the good opinion of others. The thought of leaving "conservative old Vermont" for a new state in the beckoning West where she could escape these pressures and find a more open-minded populace offered a promising future, not only for herself but also for her two sons who had reached adulthood. At the same time, a national furor had begun to erupt over the specter of slavery in western territories, redirecting her righteous pursuit of justice into saving the "victims of the Slave Power."[38]

6

"This New Oasis of Freedom"

I could accomplish more for woman . . . and with less effort, in the
new State of Kansas, than I could in conservative old Vermont, whose
prejudices were so much stronger than its convictions. . . . I went to work
for a Government of "equality, liberty, fraternity," in the State to be.
C. I. H. Nichols, 1881

Perhaps it was a twist of fate that the Kansas-Nebraska Act, which
opened up a vast region west of the Mississippi for white settlement,
passed Congress in May 1854, only two weeks after Chapin Howard's
death. In the midst of her grief, Clarina Nichols fretted over Senator
Stephen Douglas's Nebraska Bill, which unleashed one of the bit-
terest debates over slavery the nation had ever seen. Now that local
settlers would decide whether Kansas would become free or slave territory, Clarina put aside her dream of migrating to Wisconsin and
instead chose to participate in a great experiment in popular democracy, one that held the potential for advancing woman's rights and
providing opportunities for her sons. With the death of her father
and of the *Democrat*, Clarina's emotional and financial ties to "conservative old Vermont" had loosened, setting the stage for her departure to Kansas in October 1854.[1]

The territory provided the perfect laboratory in which Nichols
could hone her evolving political style; she was sure she had found
a "people whose character and whose destiny are to turn the scales
of westering power for the *right*, for the *true*." Like others opposed
to slavery, she sought to ensure free labor in Kansas, but she also anticipated that it would be easier to design a new legal and political

system favorable to women in the fluid political environment in the West than to struggle endlessly for "repeal of unjust laws in an old State." There were other woman's rights leaders who recognized this potential for progress in the West, but Nichols was the only one who purposely chose to activate her philosophy on the Kansas prairie. The state's first governor, Charles Robinson, would later remark, "She was the personification & incarnation of the cause in Kansas," a cause that for Clarina meant expanding the horizon of freedom for women as well as for blacks.[2]

But the Kansas experiment was fraught with immense political and personal uncertainties. While promoting this "new oasis of freedom," as she called it, Clarina and her family would face a degree of privation and physical toil they had scarcely known in the East. They risked their health and a good part of her inheritance struggling to make a home and a livelihood on a frontier suffused with violence. The experience of living in a highly mobile and insecure community, swarming with new kinds of people—from the backwoodsmen of Ohio and Indiana to mixed-race Indians and free or fleeing blacks—would deepen Clarina's understanding of the political and personal risks of attacking slavery.

If Clarina found some solace in her father's death, it was that her inheritance helped finance her family's adventures in the West. At ages eighteen and twenty, her sons Relie and Howard Carpenter were as eager to reach Kansas to find cheap land or other work opportunities as their mother was to further her political agenda. Relie had learned the printer's trade from his stepfather but lacked the necessary capital to invest in a newspaper or some other business; Howard was engaged to a young woman from Keene, New Hampshire, and ready to start his own farm. George Nichols's health had improved modestly, and he and Clarina hoped that the milder climate in Kansas would prove beneficial. Unlike many westward-moving families, however, it was Clarina, not George, who led this adventure. She and her sons made the initial trip to investigate the possibilities in Kansas while George remained in Brattleboro until the following year. George Jr. and Birsha were still safely ensconced at the progressive Eagleswood School in New Jersey when Clarina and her older sons embarked upon a kind of utopian experiment of their own.[3]

It is doubtful whether the family would have made such a rash decision without anticipating the support of like-minded sojourners, who were spurred by passage of the Kansas-Nebraska Act. During much of the winter and spring of 1854, northern antislavery advocates had expressed their fury as Congress debated Senator Douglas's proposal to divide Nebraska Territory into two states under the principle of popular sovereignty, which left the question of slavery to the determination of local voters. The bill abrogated the old Missouri Compromise of 1820, which prohibited slavery in the unorganized section of the Louisiana Purchase north of Missouri's southern border. As the "Nebraska infamy" ignited northern sentiment, Douglas's larger goals of developing a northern transcontinental railroad route fell prey to a deep sectional divide among Democrats. Northern antislavery Democrats propagated a slave power theory, insisting that southern leaders had conspired to subvert the Constitution in favor of chattel labor. Once passed, the Kansas-Nebraska Act also proved fatal to remnants of the Whig Party and signaled the organization of the Republican Party around the core belief that free soil in the territories would ensure economic independence and social mobility for all wage earners.[4] More significant for the Nichols family, it ignited a contest between northern free soil settlers and proslavery Missourians to determine whether slavery would take root in Kansas soil.

Even before the legislation passed, Massachusetts legislator Eli Thayer sought to engage in the race to settle Kansas. With Boston industrialist Amos A. Lawrence and Dr. Thomas H. Webb of Providence, he organized the Massachusetts Emigrant Aid Company, a joint-stock company founded to support northern emigration to guarantee that Kansas became a free state.[5] For Thayer the company was a business proposition as much as a vehicle to further political goals. No friend of the abolitionists, he believed profits from early land speculation would fill the company's coffers while he enhanced his political prospects by promoting free soil. His actions electrified proslavery Missourians who envisioned an invasion of abolitionists in the territory they believed should rightly become a slave state. As proslavery men spilled across the border into Kansas, ready to defend the institution of slavery, Thayer's association, reincorporated as the New England Emigrant Aid Company (NEEAC), and other northern emigration groups sponsored hundreds of settlers to counter what they saw as the slave power's growing influence in the expanding West. By enacting popular sovereignty in Kansas, Congress had ensured that slavery and land possession would be entwined in the settlement of the territory, distilling the national political struggle over slavery into one place.[6]

Determined to win this contest, NEEAC's organizers hoped "to plant a free State in Kansas, to the lasting advantage of the country," a mission that inspired

Clarina Nichols. NEEAC offered to provide logistical support and financial assistance to the emigrants during the course of their journey west, and it was these advantages, said Nichols, "which turned my steps this [Kansas] way." She was also drawn by the company's explicit designs to transplant New England "civilization" to the West. Organizers planned to rapidly populate the Kansas Territory with settler-citizens who would prohibit slavery and "[use] at once those social influences which radiate from the church, the school, and the press, in the organization and development of a community."[7] By investing in land, mills, schools, and churches, some of these Yankees hoped to reap profits while others viewed the project as a charitable venture. NEEAC and groups such as the American Missionary Association and the American Home Mission Society, which sponsored emigration from New York and Ohio, were imbued with the same "religious-humanitarian impulse" and overt Free Soil political goals that filled Nichols with high hopes for the project. Like their ancestors who colonized New England with the purpose of building a "city upon a hill," NEEAC's leaders touted the project as a means to people the Kansas plains with the sons and "Daughters of Massachusetts" who would extend "the area of freedom by creating new free states, a cordon of the sons of liberty to the Gulf of Mexico."[8]

Nichols stood ready to enact NEEAC's somewhat utopian plans, and she augmented the company's goals with her own strong convictions about slavery. Like many other Free Soil advocates, her ire at national legislation protecting slavery had grown exponentially and erupted with the Nebraska proposal. Passage of the Fugitive Slave Law, the publication of Harriet Beecher Stowe's *Uncle Tom's Cabin,* and several high-profile runaway slave cases had ignited northern antislavery sentiments. Nichols sent a scathing critique of Senator Douglas's "Nebraska Bill" to Sherman Booth for the *Milwaukee Daily Free Democrat* and roundly supported Booth for helping to rescue the captured slave Joshua Glover from prison, proclaiming that the "Slave-drivers and kidnappers do violence to human souls and human flesh." Increasingly, she linked her righteous defense of the enslaved with the status of white women. "Well may woman feel herself in bonds, as bound with the poor enslaved humanity," she wrote Lucy Stone in June 1854, and concluded that "this aristocracy governed nation" was to blame for their degradation. Thus, news that Nichols would go to Kansas led editors to remark that her departure would surely help stem the tide of slavery in the West. Amelia Bloomer proclaimed, "If the wives of all the men who settle in Kansas are like her in this particular,

UNIVERSITY OF WINCHESTER
LIBRARY

slavery will never gain a foothold on that soil." Similarly, the editor of the *Worcester (Massachusetts) Daily Transcript* claimed that Nichols would "keep out the slave holders, if any one can."[9]

Imbued with high expectations, Nichols and her sons joined the fourth group to embark on the eleven-day trip to Kansas. They traveled to Boston, where they joined approximately 120 other emigrants at the Western Rail Road Depot on October 17, 1854. Memories of her original move west likely resurfaced as Clarina watched the New York landscape zoom by at a markedly faster pace than she had experienced almost twenty-five years earlier while floating on the Erie Canal. Since that first failed venture on the frontier, she had transformed herself from a hopeful but naïve twenty-year-old bride into an accomplished journalist and public speaker. The train picked up more than a hundred more earnest travelers as it chugged its way toward Detroit, where NEEAC's agent Charles H. Branscomb met the group and shepherded the families to Chicago and then St. Louis, the gateway of the West. On board the *Sam Cloon*, they slowly steamed their way up the Missouri River to Kansas City. Finally, shedding all modern modes of transportation, they hired horses and wagons for the overland trek to their final destination in Kansas.

Although NEEAC's leaders promised to protect the party from "fraud & delay by providing food & shelter at the lowest price," the company failed to match the expectations of many emigrants, most of whom were unaccustomed to crowded third-class accommodations. Fellow traveler George O. Willard complained that NEEAC had failed to provide rooms in Chicago and that many in the party slept inside the congested and cold railcars because hotel rooms were unavailable in the bustling city. Furthermore, he grumbled, during the trip from St. Louis to Kansas City, the emigrants were packed like cattle into the hold of the *Sam Cloon*, where Willard and about seventy-five other travelers were forced to sleep on the floor of the "miserable old boat." Relie Carpenter reported the problem to Brattleboro papers, explaining that the accommodations were very unsatisfactory for such a large party, and some emigrants were so disheartened that they turned back even before reaching the territory.[10]

Nichols, in contrast, brushed off these inconveniences and regaled northern readers with a triumphant arrival in Kansas. She mentioned the dire warnings from Missourians about starvation in new settlements but reported that they all proved false. After the forty-mile journey to Lawrence, instead of starvation she found "the most beautiful and magnificent scene" she had ever imagined. Here was an "embryo city" with a "noble" elevation at its center, framed by the conjunction of two broad, deep rivers. Surrounded by a "splendid line of forest" and the empty prairie, Nichols viewed Kansas as a blank slate on which she and other settlers could draw the outlines of real change. Indeed, the prairies were not exactly empty because much of the land still belonged to the Delaware Indians. But like many other emigrants from the East, Nichols saw only open land and opportunity. She acknowledged that the Delaware still held a tract in reserve across the river but noted that it would soon be open for settlement. In the meantime a tent or a sod house, which Relie compared unfavorably with those of poor Irish railroad workers, would provide shelter from winter winds but little comfort. For meals, the family sat "a la Turque" around a large box for a table and dipped their knives and forks into a common cooking pot.[11]

Nichols's reports about life in the territory became fodder for eastern Free Soil editors eager to salvage Kansas from the hands of slaveholders, and Clarina became known as an enthusiastic promoter of the free-state cause. Writing to the Boston *Evening Transcript*, she downplayed the inconveniences of crowded railcars and Spartan living conditions and applauded the high caliber of her fellow emigrants: "I assume the responsibility of saying, we are a company of workers; toil and privation are not strange to us; *they cling to us if we stay*. . . . In reference to the general character of the emigrants, I can say [that] . . . I am pleased with the intelligence and spirit which they evince. Freedom's host in the free States, may rely on them at their chosen post of duty."[12] There was no doubt that pioneer life required "toil and privation," but Nichols was confident that Yankee determination and intelligence would transform the West into the kind of hardworking, egalitarian society she envisioned. If they had any "starch of aristocracy in their dickies or their stomachs, it was all shaken out before they arrived," she insisted. As for the nascent settlement in Lawrence, it was already blessed with a rudimentary church under a thatched tent, and Nichols's faith in the high moral purpose of the fledgling town bolstered her resolve under the stress of pioneer existence.[13]

In her role as publicist, Nichols insisted that these lofty moral goals would never be accomplished without women, the "good angels for Kanzas." With close to 230 members, the fourth NEEAC party was the largest that fall and included thirty women and forty-five young children. Nichols described their presence with delight, as they were "laughing, crying, tumbling" all around her. She insisted that the "mothers who have gathered up their treasures" for the long journey were essential to establishing successful free-state communities. Recognizing, as did other pioneers, that women played a key role in settling the free West, Nichols argued that all the male emigrants who brought wives with them, except for a couple of rare cases, stayed in the territory, building cabins and establishing the foundations of a stable community. "Men who have wives and children with them," she reported, "keep up good spirits." In addition to providing crucial emotional support and practical skills such as cooking and sewing, women would also encourage important social habits like diligence and temperance. She noted proudly that property owners in the city of Lawrence were already prohibited from dealing in "intoxicating drinks" and asserted that the "*women* are 'strong-minded,'" which would "be no objection to a woman, among the pioneers to Kanzas."[14]

Nichols was thoroughly familiar with the moniker "strong-minded," as it had been used to critique female lecturers in the East who stretched the limits of femininity by expressing their forthright opinions on temperance, antislavery, or woman's rights in public. In Kansas she immediately linked it to all the freedom-loving women in the territory, where the term took on a new more positive meaning. Unlike most pioneering women, a significant number of those who migrated with the emigrant aid parties embraced a moral purpose that helped them endure the lack of home comforts and female companionship normally associated with western migration. They were ready to go beyond contemporary gender boundaries to engage in civic life and defend their homes in conjunction with like-minded men to create a free society. Conjointly, their expansive female influence could be employed to check the disorder typically associated with male-dominated frontier regions. Sara Tappan Robinson, wife of NEEAC leader Charles Robinson, noted the scarcity of conveniences in early Kansas but rationalized her situation, noting that "most of us have come to this far-away land, with a mission in our hearts, a mission to the dark-browed race." Margaret Wood, who moved to Kansas from Ohio with her husband, Sam Wood, asserted that "woman's sphere is wherever there is a wrong to make right. . . . It is here to guard our beautiful embryo State from the invasion of wrong, oppression, [and] intemperance." This kind of strong-mindedness became associated with the female side of the free-state movement, and in turn the involvement of supposedly virtuous women enhanced the legitimacy of the cause.[15]

Nichols expressed free-state womanhood when she proclaimed that "'woman's sphere' here is out of doors," not only breaking sod, splitting logs, and performing many other traditionally male tasks but also shaping opinion and institutions outside their homes. She had long promoted a modified idea of separate spheres, one that incorporated the work of provincial housewives while championing women's moral influence in the community. This notion gained particular resonance for the free-state movement in Kansas, where the practical need for women's participation enhanced their moral clout and validated the movement in the eyes of northern supporters. With benevolent intent, Nichols and other free-state women envisioned "a social order within which domestic virtues and family life could flourish" within a free state.[16] Whether free-state leaders would ascribe to Nichols's full political agenda was unclear upon her arrival. But many of NEEAC's male migrants were willing to accede a significant role to women, which opened opportunities for her to test their receptiveness to woman's rights.

Although Nichols remembered lecturing even on her first trip up the Missouri River to Kansas City, it is more likely that her politicking began shortly after she arrived in the territory. As her covered wagon rolled into Lawrence on October 28 and stopped in front of the NEEAC office, she recalled that the men inside had been "hotly discussing women's rights." Proponents wished their critics could hear Antoinette Brown or Susan B. Anthony, and another cried for "Mrs. Nichols" just before she appeared at the doorstep, which caused an eruption of "triumphant cheering." Though they pleaded with her to lecture that evening, Charles Robinson, a NEEAC agent, delayed her appearance until the next day, when he hoped she could dedicate the new church building. Whether Nichols embellished this welcoming party for readers is unclear, but the story does indicate that her reputation as a speaker had proceeded her.[17]

As Robinson suggested, Nichols gave a woman's rights lecture at the dedication of the makeshift church, and she recounted the scene for Sherman M. Booth of the *Milwaukee Daily Free Democrat:* "Now let me give a picture of this Meeting-House . . . adding with pride that I had the honor of dedicating it to the equal rights of woman, in the first audience that ever congregated within its walls." Her listeners sat "'*a la Turk*'" among "bundles of prairie hay" and were scattered haphazardly "till no aisle remained between the desk and entrance." Nichols stood behind a desk "constructed of two tool-chests, piled one on the other, and lighted by two glass lanthorns" that lit up their eager faces. It was such "a novel scene," she remarked, that "I enjoyed it as I have seldom done a lecture occasion."[18] Indeed, a mixed audience lounging about on the floor of a tent for a woman's rights lecture would have shocked the Victorian gender conventions of New England, but perhaps it was understandable for Booth's Wisconsin readers, who were more accustomed to the exigencies of frontier life. That a well-known advocate of woman's rights was performing a church dedication ceremony was perhaps even more astounding. The positive reception Nichols received in Lawrence reinforced her belief that she had found a place where women could speak their strong minds and not be censured.[19]

As she romanticized the scene in Lawrence for northern readers, Nichols chronicled the frontier adventure, noting how it inverted traditional gender relationships. The NEEAC emigrants lived in makeshift tents constructed of small timber, hay, and cotton cloth fortified with sod, and they slept on beds of prairie hay. From the common cooking area, Nichols observed "the domestic scene" admiringly as the cooks, "about as many of them men as women," struggled to keep their precious morsels out of the fire and in the unstable kettles. While adjusting to these rudimentary living conditions, Clarina abandoned her vegetarian diet and ate whatever food, including meat, she and her sons could scrounge from traders. Attributing her own adaptability to her grandparents' pioneering legacy, she connected Kansas to the stories she had heard during girlhood and to her New England ancestry. "But *that* was all *head* knowledge," she noted, "for it was received second hand, and did not reach the heart like pioneer experience in these blessed days of 'Emigrant Aid' Companies, when the misery is sweetened by plenty of company."[20] Whatever the change or challenge, Nichols dismissed the harsh realities of daily life for her readers, in part because she was joined in this venture by like-minded, committed pioneers, but also because she hoped to lure more emigrants into the project of creating a free Kansas.

Meanwhile, Howard and Relie were gripped with the reality of finding work and land in a town that was quickly becoming a hotbed of conflict between NEEAC settlers and Missourians. The best tracts in Lawrence had already been divided and sold to members of the first two emigrant parties, and earlier proslavery claimants were still contesting titles, sometimes tearing down tents and intimidating occupants in the process. The Missouri "squatter sovereigns," as they called themselves, had formed vigilante organizations to prevent northerners from settling and linked their land claims to the right to legalize slavery in Kansas. Moreover, New Englanders were also jostling for settlement rights with migrants from Ohio, Illinois, Tennessee, and Indiana, many of whom were intent upon a state free of slavery but free of blacks as well, and they often treated NEEAC settlers with disdain. Relie expressed frustration with the political situation, and he bemoaned the endless conflicts among settlers in Lawrence. "With a soil and climate like this," he noted, "one could be contented to till the soil and sit under his own vine and fig-tree, and not meddle with politics in the least." Because of these political tensions, Relie and his brother, Howard, would have to venture to other nascent settlements in the surrounding region, miles from the NEEAC group in Lawrence, to secure uncontested and affordable land.[21]

The debate over Kansas placed Nichols in the center of both the local struggle with Missourians and a national political debate over the tactics northerners and southerners used to control who voted in the territory. Indeed, NEEAC became a lightning rod for the southern critique of radical abolitionism, and Nichols injected her feminine perspective into a partisan debate driven by the sectional rift. Democrat Benjamin F. Stringfellow, a proslavery Missourian and secretary of the Platte County Self-defensive Association, called for the tarring and feathering of Eli Thayer and the removal of any and all settlers financed by the "Northern Emigrant Aid Societies." The prairies of Kansas could not be profitably farmed without slave labor, Stringfellow asserted; northern men were poor farmers, "could not live in the prairies," and were returning quickly to New England. He also charged abolitionists with intent to destroy slavery in his home state of Missouri as well as in the nation.[22]

With characteristic indignation, Nichols responded to Stringfellow directly, vehemently resisting the accusation that the colony was failing because New Englanders were lousy pioneers. Calling Stringfellow simply "ignorant of the character of the emigrants," she noted that they came from hearty stock whose fathers had "subdued the heavy-timbered and rocky lands of New England" and whose contemporaries had already successfully settled prairie states like Iowa and Wisconsin. According to Nichols, what New Englanders lacked was not ability, but wives. A wife was a necessity, "a preliminary step to success in pioneer life," she insisted, and men could not set up housekeeping to defend their claims without women. She condemned Stringfellow's slaveholding and defined women's role in the settlement process by citing Scripture: in the Garden of Eden, "God said, 'It is not good for man to be alone; I will make a help-*meet* for him' and this was a *wife* not a 'slave.'"[23]

Nichols's focus on the importance of settling the West with industrious, companionate families expressed the gender ideals embedded in Free Soil ideology, which the new Republican Party would adopt in its platform in 1856. Formulating its appeal around free labor, the nascent party embraced the active roles of northern women in the family and society in opposition to the degradation that slavery imposed on both black and white women. Nichols's highly politicized journalism fed Republicans with authentic testimony from Kansas that validated their moral purpose and women's role in territorial expansion. Their campaign slogan in 1856, "Free soil, free men, free hearts and free homes," expressed Nichols's vision, which she believed was an infinitely more effective and more Christian basis for settling Kansas than with slaveholders and their chattel.[24]

Nichols linked this ideal to the electoral system by attacking the undemocratic tactics Missourians practiced in the territory's first election. She led a chorus of outraged voices that critiqued popular sovereignty, a policy that had made a mockery of democracy during the November 1854 election for territorial representatives. While perched high on a hilltop in Lawrence, she witnessed dozens of "wagons and horses bearing Missourians to Kansas ballot-boxes." These illegal voters, 80 percent of the electorate, "came armed and equipped, (as the *law* ALLOWS) with whisky by the barrel to aid them in the exercise of 'that *noblest* privilege of the freeman, the elective franchise!'" To Nichols, the majority of proslavery men were nothing but drunken brutes who abused the "privilege" of voting by stuffing ballot boxes, intimidating judges, and depriving true free-state settlers of their rights. By connecting liquor and slavery to antidemocratic practices, she showed how these evils would deprive Americans of their liberties. Stringfellow upheld the election results, asserting that there were four times as many proslavery men living in Kansas as freesoilers, and expressed the sentiments of Missourians' who were simply "defending their own homes," their right to migrate with slaves, and the liberties embodied in "the Union itself."[25]

It must have frustrated Clarina to leave the territory in the midst of these heated debates, but like some of the men, she was not prepared to stay for the winter and had anticipated a trip home to collect the rest of her family before returning to stake out a permanent claim. Once back in Brattleboro, Clarina organized her household goods and arranged for eleven-year-old George to return home from New Jersey. She continued to promote Kansas in the press to reassure northern readers that the free-state project would succeed and even lectured locally about the precarious situation in the territory.[26] The return trip to Kansas would include Clarina's husband, her son George, and her son

Howard's fiancée, Sarah Jones. Birsha, who was twenty-four, chose to remain at Eagleswood, probably as an assistant teacher.

Leaving Boston on March 20, 1855, the Nichols family joined another NEEAC party that left the city with about 170 emigrants, including nineteen others from Vermont. William Hutchinson, a fellow journalist from Randolph, Vermont, his wife, Helen, and their two young daughters joined the company. This fortuitous meeting would prove beneficial for Clarina, as both William and Helen would later become important allies in her reform work. Led by Deacon John T. Farwell, the party suffered few privations until St. Louis, where they boarded the *Kate Swinney*, captained by a member of the locally renowned Chouteau family. While they inched up the Missouri River, spending more time stuck on sandbars than steaming toward Kansas, the passengers were subjected to the schemes of "miserable men—a few drunk nearly all the time," pickpockets, and gamblers, who wreaked havoc on innocent travelers. Not wanting to miss an opportunity, Nichols took advantage of their leisure to give two lectures on board, which shocked a young minister but converted his wife into "an outspoken advocate of woman's rights," according to her.[27]

The long river trek and a rousing wagon ride were minor inconveniences compared with the political turmoil the family encountered upon their arrival in Lawrence. The settlement had just recovered from another invasion of Missourians who had crossed the border a few days earlier to vote for the first territorial legislators. Once again Nichols was outraged at the ridiculous process and was quick to condemn the "low-lived, drunken and reckless" crowd of "rowdy 'sovereigns'" who voted illegally. The Missourians had endangered free-state settlers with threats to shoot, hang, or lynch them; Nichols predicted that they would have perpetrated robbery and manslaughter if their sober leaders had not "tapped the whiskey barrels and spilt the liquor to keep 'popular sovereignty' from becoming dangerous to its own advocates." In a self-proclaimed victory, these "border ruffians," as they were labeled, had elected a proslavery legislature. Nichols dismissed their victory with confidence that the newly appointed governor, Andrew Reeder, would reject the "bogus legislature" despite his connection to the Democratic administration.[28] Reeder later disallowed a portion of the ballots in some districts and called for a revote, but the election was a harbinger of the way territorial politics could lead quickly to violence. Regardless of the deteriorating political situation, Nichols trusted the integrity of the free-state project. As she walked down muddy Massachusetts Street admiring the rise of New England–style wooden framed buildings, she remained confident that more young couples like her newly married son Howard and his bride Sarah would populate the territory and ensure that freedom prevailed.

But like other free-state settlers, the family's success was contingent on finding suitable land. Leaving the protection of Lawrence, Clarina and her family "*set off behind a pair of mules!*" for Osawatomie, about 40 miles southeast, where they reunited with her husband George and Relie after "footing" the last 13 miles. They spent the night with the new postmaster at a hamlet called Lane, and it was there that the family eventually laid claim to 160 acres. East of present-day Baldwin City in Douglas County, Lane was 6 miles from the Ottawa Indian Reservation and 16 from Lawrence, but it was still isolated and sparsely populated with a mix of Missourians, "westerners," and local Indians. Relie reported enthusiastically about the abundance of natural resources and wildlife in the area, noting that the soil in Kansas "was richer than any garden in Vermont" and that the claims were surrounded by "the best wooded land in the country." The region was suitable for settlement, but transportation was expensive and basic provisions—such as flour, pork, and seed potatoes—were scarce. "Do not expect to eat oysters and go to a ball," Relie cautioned; you must "live on mush and molasses for a week, and sleep on a log for a fortnight," which apparently they did. Even as she welcomed a few more Yankees, Clarina warned that it was difficult to acquire land unless the "people like you," and everywhere the "land sharks" were hoarding claims, hoping to sell at outrageous prices.[29]

After locating their claim, the family spent several days with John Tecumseh "Tauy" Jones, a prosperous Ottawa Indian and local interpreter, before striking out to construct their own one-room log cabin and to begin spring planting. Crowded into a 15-foot by 18-foot abode with mud walls and a thatched roof, the Nichols family ate dinner on "the lids of tree trunks," and Clarina fought daily with endless dust and debris; to visit the closest neighbors 2 miles away, she mounted behind George on his "large bay." To assure her readers that the "lady editress" could endure these primitive conditions, she joked about the situation, remarking how the lack of rooms "simplifies housekeeping wonderfully. The *chamber work* is soon done, *parlors* soon dusted, (whew! How the wind does blow in the dust!) and the table is soon cleared (not a morsel is allowed to be left, for we have no dishes for extra bits)." The frontier scene was a graphic illustration of the great sacrifices this

Sketch of early Lawrence, Kansas, c. 1854–1855, by J. C. Reid, reprinted in Richard Cordley, A History of Lawrence, Kansas *(Lawrence, Kans.: E. F. Caldwell, 1895).*

"true woman" and her family endured in the cause of freedom, yet their daily existence remained grim.[30]

Exhausted by the pioneer regimen, Nichols barely managed to maintain her eastern correspondence. "I have written with little of order in the arrangements of topics, and much awkwardness of expression," she apologized, "but I plead extreme fatigue and feel confident that if your readers could have followed us in our efforts to get here . . . and our labors since to put our house in living shape—they would only wonder that I could think of trying my fingers to pen at all." With the eastern thirst for news of the experiment in Kansas unquenchable, Nichols had apparently agreed to supply material to Samuel Woodward, editor of the *New Hampshire American News* in Keene. A free soil Democrat and avid promoter of temperance, Woodward found a like-minded political journalist in Nichols, who joined a number of other correspondents advocating the free-state cause. By June she had recovered from the initial shock of homesteading and was reporting about the beauties of the prairie, the fine spring weather, the green shoots in her garden, and the availability of good timber stands for the deluge of "Yankees" arriving in the region. Notwithstanding her bleak life in a remote one-room cabin and frequent interruptions in mail delivery, which deprived her of political news, Nichols remained enthusiastic about the free-state movement. In addition to her positive letters for Woodward, she communicated with editors John Speer of the

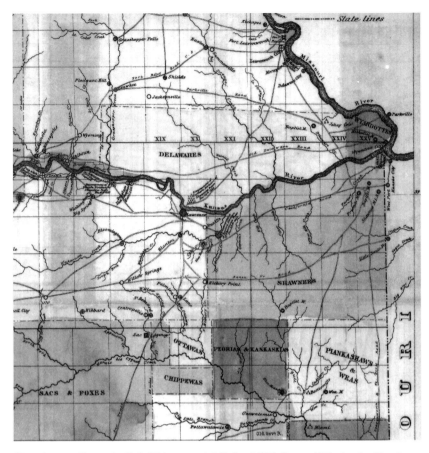

Map of eastern Kansas, by E. B. Whitman and A. D. Searl (J. B. Jewett, 1856), showing Douglas County and Lane. Lawrence is along the Kansas River close to the center of the map, and Lane is south of Lawrence and south of the Santa Fe Road, which runs east and west. Courtesy of Special Collections and University Archives, Wichita State University Libraries.

Lawrence Kansas Tribune and George W. Brown of the *Herald of Freedom*, the organ of NEEAC in the territory.[31]

Nichols's offerings, like those of Methodist Julia Louisa Lovejoy, testified to the virtue and nobility of the emigrants in a way that only female writers could convey. A New Hampshire native, Lovejoy sent graphic reports to the *Concord Independent Democrat* filled with missionary and abolitionist zeal. Her Kansas was a virtual Eden where peaceable, hardworking emigrants struggled against drunken Missourians prone to violence. Both women tended to shroud the project in moral uplift, but Lovejoy's messianic language expressed her horror at the human cost of slavery in vivid terms. After witnessing a slave woman unloading a cart full of manure, she wailed, "O slavery, thou unsexing demon, how art thou cursed of God and humanity!" Nichols maintained faith in the political process, at least in print, and was far more sanguine about the future, whereas Lovejoy predicted that "Kanzas is the great battlefield where a mighty conflict is to be waged with the monster slavery, and he will be routed and slain. Amen and Amen."[32]

Regardless of their concern for black slaves, women like Lovejoy and Nichols generally paid little heed to the rights (or lack thereof) of Native Americans. Though proslavery and free-state settlers were at odds when it came to policies regarding slavery, they often found common ground in regard to what they called the Indian "problem." Both proslavery and free-state settlers trampled on Indian rights and exhibited blatant racism when interacting with the local tribes, particularly the Osage, Kaw, and Kickapoo.[33] Local agents for the Bureau of Indian Affairs observed countless illegal land claims by both southern and northern settlers, as whites encroached upon Indian reserves and ignored treaties that outlawed such practices. Indicative of common stereotypes, one free-state settler referred to a local tribe as a bunch of the "wildest looking Indians" he had ever seen, and he disregarded their rights because the "indolent" and "lazy" Indians lacked the intelligence and benefits of white civilization to guide their behavior.[34]

Nichols failed to challenge these racist characterizations, and a number of Indians received her derision and disapproval. She once described the Kaw Indians as "the lowest and most degraded tribe in the territory, who are beggars and thieves, but otherwise harmless." Many missionaries and even other reformers held similar derogatory views. Amelia Bloomer, who migrated to Iowa in 1855, found the local Indians in Council Bluffs "disagreeable visitors" and described them as "thieves and beggars" who were "filthy and disgusting." Beyond the obvious racism that even reform-minded whites possessed, Nichols's opinion of the local tribes was based in part on their degree of conversion to Christianity and on their adoption of white middle-class values, all measures of their ability to adapt to the enlightened civilization she envisioned in Kansas. She claimed that the Kaws' "faith [was] unchanged since the time when Pope wrote of the 'poor Indian'" and was dismayed by a Kaw's grave laden with provisions, including the deceased's dog and pony. Though she was perhaps more empathetic than some of her contemporaries, Nichols believed that those who embraced Christian civilization, as exemplified by her New England heritage, were qualified not only for God's grace but also for civil and political rights.[35]

Indeed, Nichols appreciated Indians like John "Tauy" Jones, a mixed-race Ottawa who was adapting readily to white ways. The radical abolitionist John Brown referred to Jones as a "highly civilized, intelligent, & most exemplary Christian Indian."[36] Much to Nichols's delight, Jones and his white wife, Jane, had provided shelter for her family upon their arrival in Lane, and the couple sold essential provisions to the region's settlers. Jones, who served as a liaison between the local Ottawa tribe and government agents, showed his adaptability by lobbying for a treaty providing the Ottawa with capital to begin free-labor farming. "If ever the Ottawas were convinced of the importance of going to work for a livelihood, now is the time," he urged, hoping the tribe would "emerge from ignorance to learning, from laziness to industry, from degradation to elevation, from poverty to wealth and from darkness to light." Nichols respected Jones's intelligence and diligence along with that of other Ottawa neighbors who worked to plant "free-labor gardens" in the region in the face of political turmoil.[37]

By early summer, with her garden growing and George's fine cattle grazing, Clarina was hopeful about prospects for both farming and freedom in the territory. The family had been able to hire an extra hand to ease the workload, the area began filling up rapidly with other white settlers, and though neighbors were still distant, they were even getting along well with Missourians. "Time is allowing opportunities for a better acquaintance between us and our pro-slavery opponents than furnished at the ballot box," she reported. Confident about resolving their differences, she predicted that "neighborhood intercourse will allay most of the bitterness which false prejudices engendered."[38]

But Clarina's optimism soon faded as she confronted threats to the family's health and the political climate deteriorated. After George was injured in June and confined to bed rest, he was unable to work and needed her nursing care. To make matters worse, in early August a hickory rail struck George Jr. in the head, causing a severe concussion and inflammation of his brain and skull. George Jr. recovered, but his seventy-year-old father did not. His condition worsened after he contracted a cold and probably pneumonia, and on August 29, Clarina became a widow. George's death left her without the partner who had stood by her for twelve years, a man thoroughly committed to her ideal of egalitarian marriage. Though his health had been fragile for years, George had been a source of strength and inspiration, a "sympathizing friend" and a kind father and stepfather. Moreover, he had rescued Clarina from the ignominy of divorce, helped restore her respectability, fostered her political career, and bolstered her courage to speak out publicly against injustice. Now she would bury him on the Kansas prairie, a silent martyr to the cause she held dear. Birsha wrote her mother from Townshend and lamented, "Oh! How I long to see you dearest, and how I regret and blame myself that I was not by to comfort you in this last deepest trial of your heart!" But the "boys will be drawn closer to you," she reassured, "twill be one tie added to the many which already bound them to you, but mother I covet that place in your heart. I would always be your comfort as in days gone by."[39]

Her daughter's sympathies notwithstanding, Clarina had little time to weep that summer. Howard had been running a low-grade fever that spawned a two-month bout with ague, a form of malaria; the hired man contracted a "'chill fever'"; and Relie lay prostrate for ten days with the same infection. With help from a neighbor's son, she kept the household running, but her mental stamina and nursing skills were at a premium; survival was a testament to her strength of character under the worst of pioneer conditions. To compound the family's problems, ague raged throughout the territory, and there were reports of cholera in other settlements. By summer's end, Clarina had fallen ill herself, and she relied on Relie to nurse her tenderly back to health.[40]

While sickness and death punctuated Nichols's personal life, mounting sectional tensions characterized politics in Kansas. Conditions in Lawrence had worsened after proslavery Missourians proclaimed victory in territorial elections, threatening to hang free-state editors and shoot the governor. With a sense of impending doom, NEEAC leader Charles Robinson vowed to repudiate the elected legislature and wrote Eli Thayer pleading for 200 Sharps rifles to defend against the Missourians who would destroy Lawrence "root and branch." On July 4, Robinson rallied free-state supporters at a gala celebration a mile from town, insisting that they had come to "found a new State, and to plant anew the institutions of our patriotic ancestors," not to submit to a "foreign power" or an armed rabble "maddened with whisky." Are we "Subjects, slaves of Missouri!" Robinson cried. Nichols would have been heartened to hear him and to see Mrs. Levi Gates boldly exhorting the crowd to create a "new Declaration of Independence" for Kansas and to "move firmly and fearlessly in the path of truth and right principle." Yet not all free-state men agreed on how to respond to the threat to their rights from proslavery Missourians, and some were just as anxious to exclude free blacks from the territory as slavery. Meeting repeatedly in Lawrence during the summer, they sought consensus about whether to recognize the authority of the "bogus legislature" or form a government of their own. Meanwhile, the legislature replaced its only free-state representatives with proslavery men and wrote a set of onerous laws upholding slavery and prohibiting antislavery activity.[41]

Nichols longed to be a part of these momentous political deliberations, but distance, family duty, and ill health separated her from the active process of state-making. While nursing George before his death, her aggravation mounted, and she vocalized her complaints by resurrecting her "'old wife' character," Deborah Van Winkle, in a letter to the *Herald of Freedom*. "Nobody out here knows anything about *wimin's* rights," Deborah bemoaned, even though her Yankee friends had brought their freedom-loving ways to Kansas. "Our old Revolutionary mothers . . . had pretty much sich rights as we wimin of Kansas have—the right to bake johnny-cakes and help the men folks build log cabins, and fight for 'em." Driving cattle and cutting wood are "feminine employments," she charged bitterly, "they'd *make* ammunition of us" if they could. Linking free white women to their enslaved sisters, she lambasted slavery as the cause of female degradation. "The women of Kansas feels that slavery threatens *their* rights when it would parade a degraded, beastly womanhood, to be trampled beneath the contempt of their husbands, sons and brothers. *Our* rights will never be won and secured while slavery tramples upon our black sisters." In an even greater insult, she suggested that the chivalrous men of Missouri, who had protected wives and widows with limited legal rights, were more trustworthy than Yankees. With such a charge, Nichols sought to shame free-state leaders for having ignored women and demeaned both black slaves and their own wives with heavy work while they fussed about their own rights and armed themselves for battle. Feeling overburdened and bereft of ladyhood on the prairie, Nichols expressed her own class-based frustrations, but she was also a rare voice willing to publicly expose the degraded position of black women.[42]

Stationed in what seemed like a remote outpost, Nichols would have been surprised if any free-state men were listening to her sharp critique of slavery, much less her feminist concerns. Indeed, it was not her plea for woman's rights but her assumption that all Missourians were proslavery that prompted a response from a correspondent posing as "Back Woodsman." He objected to her insinuation that New Englanders had imported free-state ideals to the territory. The "free State voters who hail from Missouri, are as firmly devoted to their principles" as any Yankees, he retorted; they migrated to escape the "tyrannies and oppression of slavery" and had not changed their political views on the subject. But do not equate free-state Missourians with abolitionists, he cautioned; we are not "as humane as some profess to be, for we claim no relationship to the African, and shall not recognize them as brothers until their sable skins become white, and they comb their hair straight." Just as "Back Woodsman" exposed Van Winkle's Yankee biases, so too his overt racism and disdain for abolitionists revealed the sharp division among free-state men, some of whom hoped to rid the territory of abolitionists as well as blacks. Frustrated by these political divisions and talk of black exclusion, a correspondent under the byline "Rueben Rustic," who professed to write in "aunt Debby's" place, defended the integrity of abolitionists. Inspired by his mother's style, Relie Carpenter probably wrote this satire in conjunction with her. It exposed the racism of some free-state men and invoked the principles of the nation's founders to argue that *"total exclusion of the African race"* was "anti-republican."[43]

Several weeks after George Nichols's death, Van Winkle responded politely to "Back Woodsman," expressing her humanitarian values in religious terms. She exhorted the Missourian to glean political principles from God's "Bible platform" and cast blacks' curly hair and whites' straight hair as God-given traits. She advocated for a social and political platform that embraced a "universal brotherhood" with no distinctions other than moral ones, concluding her sermon with a rhetorical missive on the afterlife: "I take it for granted, nabor, that you recognize the African as included among the subjects of gospel salvation, and travelers to the same eternal home.—If so . . . ain't it wise to make up your mind to recognize them as brothers here. It won't look well there or be quite heavenly, to pout and talk about skins and hair, as title deeds to a heavenly relationship—will it nabor?" Just as Nichols's Christian evangelism determined her classification of local Indians, so too it framed her belief in racial equality. Bidding a neighborly farewell, Van Winkle "remain[ed] yours truly for black and white, Missourians and Yankees." But "Back Woodsman" had the last word; a month later, he reassured her, "When we all get to Heaven we'll all be white," so stop "quarrelin' about the niggers" and "let's make Kansas a free white State."[44]

The telling interchange not only displayed Nichols's continuing appetite for politics and her growing radicalism but also the way divisions over slavery and the future status of blacks dominated political discourse in the territory, eclipsing woman's rights. In a letter to President Franklin Pierce, the newly appointed Governor Wilson Shannon described the increasing anxiety felt by local settlers in the fall of 1855: "Affairs in this Territory are daily assuming a shape of real danger to the peace and good order of society. . . . It is in vain to conceal the fact, we are standing on a volcano, the upheavings and agitations beneath we feel, and no one can tell the hour when an eruption may take place." Just 5 miles from the Nichols's home, free-state men defended their claims in Palmyra against Missourians who attempted to destroy the town. After putting aside their differences and launching the Free State Party at Big Springs, free-state men denied the legitimacy of the territorial legislature and met at Topeka in late October to write their own constitution in preparation for statehood. Charles Robinson, one of the few free-state men willing to countenance woman's rights, apparently invited Nichols to speak to the assembled body, but she was still mourning her husband and too weak from illness to appear in public. She must have been gladdened, however, to learn that seven delegates supported enfranchising blacks and a few of those bravely endorsed the radical notion of woman suffrage.[45]

By November, the political conflict turned violent when Missourian Franklin M. Coleman murdered Ohioan Charles W. Dow, presumably over a land dispute. Proslavery and antislavery settlers immediately took sides over the issue, and the fallout from the incident earned the misnomer "The Wakarusa War," after a river near Lawrence.[46] As local militias formed on both sides of the political divide, free-state women joined the men in defending their rights to the territory. When proslavery forces threatened to invade Lawrence, free-state women gathered at Charles and Sara Robinson's home to make cartridges for rifles, and some were rumored to actually practice shooting. Lois Brown, whose husband edited the *Herald of Freedom*, and Margaret Wood smuggled kegs of gunpowder underneath their petticoats to cross enemy lines and supply free-state men with ammunition. Longing to participate, Relie Carpenter helped defend Lawrence, and Nichols wrote the Committee of Safety devoting her son to the cause. He was ready to "shed his blood and die in defence [*sic*] of it," she claimed, suggesting that she would come herself if she could. "So noble & patriotic a deed as the offering of a son on the Altar of Freedom," proclaimed an eastern editor, was surely an inspiration for other "acts of patriotism & virtue."[47]

Indeed, even while mourning, Nichols rebounded with indefatigable optimism knowing that free-state men were prepared to defend their principles. "The sick are all recovering and cheerfulness reigns," she reported. "Sharp's rifles are in all our cabins, and Kansas' freedom sworn upon all our domestic altars."[48] Although most abolitionists were opposed to violence, Robinson and others had been quick to recognize the need for defensive weapons. The escalation of conflict in Kansas converted many settlers, including Nichols, from pacifism to a belief in the utility of violence as a means of self-defense. Even Quakers, such as Susan B. Anthony's youngest brother, Merritt, abandoned their religious scruples, joined the free-state militias, and fought in several skirmishes against proslavery men.[49]

With her sons and her heart committed to Kansas, Nichols left the political maelstrom and returned to Vermont in late December, ostensibly to settle George's estate. She had not yet spent a winter in the territory, but she intended to return as soon as possible. "My home is in Kansas, and come weal or come woe, there is a tie to her soil and her struggling people which I cannot undo, and would not if I could," she proclaimed. Converting her first-hand knowledge into propaganda for the Free Soil cause would preoccupy her for over a year before she could return. To bolster free-state emigrants, she noted that "the weather is cold, [but] not so the free hearts that are . . . swelling with ominous indignation towards the perpetrators of the dark deeds . . . of the Missourians and their government aiders and abettors."[50] In a Special Message to Congress in January 1856, President Franklin Pierce encouraged proslavery emigration to the territory and essentially charged the free-state leaders with treason for resisting the laws created by the territorial legislature. A month later, he threatened federal support for the local militias if the free-state men refused to disperse or if they perpetuated any "insurrectionary" behavior.[51]

But admonitions from President Pierce could not dampen Nichols's optimism, and she responded to his threats by citing the courage and strength of her fellow free-state emigrants, especially the women:

> Kansas may well glory in her aspirants for martyrdom. Her 'strong minded' women will be content to run bullets, transfer ammunition, and inspire their husbands and sons with hope, faith and courage, until public offices of honor and trust are redolent of domestic peace and quiet before

they ask a share in their responsibilities. Yes, woman, self-denying now as in the past, is forgetting herself and her wrongs in the great national wrong that threatens to deprive the manhood of the nation of the right and the power to protect the altars and the hearths consecrated to God and humanity.

Nichols's political rhetoric was designed to legitimize the arming of free-state leaders with the support of peace-loving women. With selflessness, women in Kansas would table the struggle for woman's rights in favor of the battle for free-state rights, a shift that reflected a change in Clarina's own consciousness. The wrongs against Kansas were equal to those against women, but Nichols prioritized their need for male protection, a predicament that would also check women's activism during the Civil War.[52]

Notwithstanding her distance from the conflict or the fragility of the Topeka government, Nichols was not about to let the free-state men write a set of laws without her legal advice. She was ensconced comfortably in Townshend, dependent once again on her family, and as a widow, she was reminded of the legal issues that had catapulted her into politics. No matter how benevolent, men controlled her financial affairs: the Howards held the mortgage on George's house, her brother Aurelius was executor of his estate, and the legal system denied her an equal share in the estate despite her contributions from writing, boardinghouse fees, and lecturing that had supported it.[53] These disabilities informed her letters to George W. Brown, editor of the *Herald of Freedom* in Lawrence, in which she educated free-state men about women's legal status while also sustaining their effort to save Kansas from slavery. Under the leadership of Charles Robinson, who was elected governor, the free-state legislature was preparing to write laws under the Topeka Constitution, a document that recognized married women's property and custody rights but ignored women's "*political* rights," much to Nichols's dismay.[54]

In an appeal to the "warm-hearted, honest yeomanry" of Kansas, Nichols prompted free-state men to honor both women and blacks by creating a "progressive civilization" in Kansas. To overcome their vast differences, free-state men had disassociated themselves from abolitionists and initially voted to exclude free blacks from the territory. Nichols warned against such a provision, suggesting in her accommodating fashion that it would undermine the free-state movement. "That Kansas will legislate with the intent to protect her *'white male'* citizens in the enjoyment of equal rights, is a conceded point," she mused with sarcasm. "But the black males and white females, what will she do for them? The latter will be allowed to live in the State because—happy circumstance—the *free* "white males" can't get along comfortably without them! But will the area of their freedom be extended?" Nichols appealed to free-state leaders' class and racial instincts by challenging them to uphold the standards of "noble manhood," restore black rights, and release the "'inalienable' rights of woman" for the good of humanity. To her nineteenth-century readers, that "woman" was white.[55]

Nichols further admonished Kansas lawmakers not to enact the "legal wrongs" that still restricted married women's freedom in the East. To their credit, the free-state men had written a constitution directing the first assembly to provide married women with separate property rights and equal custody, but Nichols knew this was a vague directive and no guarantee of the kind of legislation she preferred. Illinois, Iowa, and even Missouri provided women with more liberal provisions than many northeastern states, she noted, while explaining that mothers needed equal rights to inheritance and homestead exemptions plus "joint rights of guardianship." Beyond rights to real property, Nichols explained that in many parts of the country married women still lacked full rights to personal property—in some cases even their own clothing—and to their own earnings. In her characteristic style, she asserted mothers' natural rights to labor for their children and charged legislators with upholding their manly role to protect them. "Legislate for the mothers, legislate for your wives as you legislate for yourselves," she entreated, noting that otherwise they would surely create a state full of paupers. She even dared to note with some exaggeration that Kentucky, a slave state, allowed "women (the educators of the race,) to vote in district school meetings." Citing lessons from Scripture to prove women's equality, she asserted that women were "God-endowed with self-dependence" and exhorted men to make "it *true* political Gospel" in Kansas.[56]

Even as Nichols practiced the politics of motherhood through the press, violence escalated in Kansas, temporarily cutting off her access to legislators. Proslavery forces stepped up their threats to destroy Lawrence, captured and detained Governor Robinson and other leaders, and culminated their actions with an attack on May 21, 1856. During the "Sack of Lawrence," key antislavery monuments like the Free State Hotel and the office of the *Herald of Freedom* were destroyed, and the press itself was thrown into the river. Publisher George Brown wrote to Eli Thayer and pleaded with him for assistance:

"Our triumph is the triumph of liberty every where. Our enslavement is the death knell of freedom in this republic—throughout the world."[57] The attack on Lawrence was soon followed by violence in Congress when South Carolina Representative Preston Brooks caned Massachusetts Senator Charles Sumner on the Senate floor on May 22, 1856. Sumner had just delivered an indictment of southern practices in Kansas in his speech "The Crime against Kansas" and suffered retaliation for his inferences that southerners were "raping" the virgin soil of Kansas. If these events cast free-state men as victims of the slave power, sympathy for their plight would soon become clouded. Abolitionist John Brown and his sons, who had emigrated to the territory, responded to both events by striking a blow against proslavery forces. Brown led a party of men, including four of his sons, who proceeded to murder five proslavery men near Pottawatomie Creek, adjacent to Osawatomie. The murders were clearly ill placed, as none of the victims were directly involved in the Sack of Lawrence, but the "Pottawatomie Massacre," as it was called, catapulted Kansas into civil war and the center of a national debate over abolitionist violence that would forever mark it as "Bleeding Kansas."

The dispatches from the territory and inaction from Congress stunned Nichols, and her desire to fight the slave power overwhelmed her comfortable existence in the East. On the day Lawrence burned, she was safely visiting with relatives and friends in Elmira, New York, but the suffering in Kansas compounded her ardor. "The white freeman and his wife and little ones are bound in the same bundle with the slave," she wrote, recognizing along with other free-state settlers that slavery endangered not only the lives of blacks but her own family as well. Proslavery men with reinforcements from Missouri were attempting to drive out unprotected free-state settlers by force. In June her worst fears were realized when she learned that Relie had been wounded at what would eventually be known as the Battle of Black Jack. He had joined John Brown's small company then stationed near Lane to defend against retaliatory proslavery forces who were burning and pillaging in pursuit of Brown. When Brown's men advanced against a larger force of Missourians, Relie's crack shots downed enough horses to prevent their retreat and force a surrender. During the skirmish he was slightly wounded in the face and shot in the chest, but luckily the bullet exited his shoulder. Immediately after the battle, free-state women gathered to nurse and feed the wounded while men guarded an encampment of prisoners nearby.[58]

Overwhelmed with newfound energy and concern, Nichols wrote Samuel

Woodward, now editor of the *New Hampshire Sentinel,* eager to display her proof of the crimes against Kansas: "But my pen has lain in rest, that I might lift up my voice against the crying wrongs of the people of Kansas—my adopted home. If I had needed mementoes to inspire me for the duty, such a one now lies before me—a *bullet* taken from the shoulder of my son, A. O. Carpenter. . . . I thank Heaven, that I have sons ready to live or die for the rights, for which their great Grandfathers fought and sacrificed treasure." Lawlessness persisted into the fall, making it too dangerous and difficult for her to return to Kansas. Proslavery militia blockaded the Missouri River in an attempt to starve free-state settlers of supplies, and Nichols poured out her frustrations with the Pierce administration for failing to protect innocent citizens. "My whole soul revolts from the supposition that the freeborn daughters of the North, must look on and see their sons disarmed and enslaved by the complicity of a traitorous government," she wailed. President Pierce had shown his true colors by supporting the proslavery militia in the territory, and she brazenly rallied women to call for his impeachment. "It is high time that the *women* of the North, prove themselves indeed 'strong-minded,' and worthy to be the wives and mothers and sisters of *freemen* and by protesting, and demanding the *impeachment* of the tyrant." Shaming all those who would condone such outrages in Kansas, she concluded, "we [shall] be made to acknowledge as a people that in consenting to the enslavement of the blacks, we were pleading guilty to the *sin* and the penalty of oppression."[59]

Nichols's verbal attacks on President Pierce and the proslavery arm of the federal government in Kansas raised her partisan rhetoric to an unprecedented level at a time when the Republican Party was recruiting voters for the 1856 election. Support for suffering families in Kansas provided party leaders with the cause they needed to gain sympathetic followers in the East, and they readily adopted free Kansas as the central tenet of the 1856 presidential campaign. Their nominee, John C. Frémont, was a dashing western adventurer and army officer who had married the politically savvy Jessie Benton, daughter of Missouri's pro-Unionist Senator Thomas H. Benton. Party leaders celebrated his life story and "Our Jessie" as well, which thoroughly incorporated the role of the first lady into political campaigning. Republicans portrayed Jessie as both a beautiful prize and a principled, politically astute wife committed to antislavery, signaling their tacit support for women's engagement in politics, at least as wives.[60]

While the couple represented the kind of enlightened family that would populate western territories if Republicans triumphed, party leaders also welcomed the voices of a chorus of women who championed free Kansas. Accounts from the territory carried the authenticity and moral power needed to repudiate the political experiment of popular sovereignty, and Nichols applied the same rhetorical pleas she had used to expose the wrongs of woman to the suffering in Kansas. To right the wrongs committed by proslavery politicians, the federal government needed to protect free-state settlers, who would replace the disorder in Kansas with free labor and the home values associated with middle-class women. Writing from Lawrence, Julia Louisa Lovejoy characterized the violence as a "war of extermination" by lawless savages and equated freedom in Kansas with a holy cause as she converted her religious morality to Republican propaganda. Uncomfortable with politics, however, Lovejoy refused to be associated with "these gadders abroad—these women-lecturers who are continually at the old theme, 'woman's rights.'" Instead, she exhorted her sex to remain within their sphere and "exert their individual and associate influence over their husbands and brothers in favor of freedom and Frémont."[61]

A number of other women supplied Republicans with propaganda but also stopped short of direct political participation. While her husband was imprisoned by proslavery forces, Sara Robinson wrote a timely history of the territory designed to bolster the free-state cause just before the election. Equally cogent were the works of more famous women writers, including Harriet Beecher Stowe, who reignited northern public opinion around antislavery sentiment with her new novel *Dred*, and radical abolitionist Lydia Maria Child. In a serialized story, "The Kansas Emigrants," Child bolstered Frémont's campaign by chronicling the sufferings of a fictional family in Kansas and modeled her chief protagonist, Kate Bradford, after women in the territory who were defending their homes and establishing free-state institutions. These literary works tacitly endorsed the Republican Party's effort to end slavery and in the process validated women's political voice.[62]

With the situation in Kansas worsening daily, Nichols was not content to simply write about politics. As a seasoned speaker with a son wounded in battle, she had the skills and motivation to assist the Republican effort even more directly. During the fall of 1856, violence escalated, putting her farm in Lane and her sons' lives in imminent danger; proslavery Missourians marched on Osawatomie, killed one of John Brown's sons, burned the town to the ground, and destroyed John "Tauy" Jones's farm nearby. The Free State Party solicited help from northeastern states, and local committees throughout Vermont, including Brattleboro, began raising money to supply territorial emigrants with aid and arms. Eager to participate, Nichols was just the sort of "lady lecturer" who could speak with authenticity about Kansas for the Republican Party. After Horace Greeley, editor of the *New York Tribune,* enlisted her help, she lectured extensively on the "Wrongs of Kansas," first in Connecticut and Pennsylvania, and finally in New York. The party paid her for five lectures a week at $10 each, money she sent immediately to her sons in the "Free State army of Kansas." Nichols relished the opportunity to influence voters directly, and remarked: "If old Penn. is to be carried by only a few votes & I could change the votes of that few to Fremont, nothing would induce me to leave the field I am now in."[63]

In the meantime, Thaddeus Hyatt, head of the National Kansas Committee, an association devoted to gathering and distributing aid for free-state settlers, solicited Nichols to organize New York women to help the cause. The blockade of the Missouri River and lawlessness had interrupted supplies and food, threatening free-state settlers' survival. Nichols recommended that Susan Anthony, who had family members in Kansas, join her on the lecture circuit, but Anthony maintained her single-minded focus on women's advancement and declined the invitation. Expressing her deep concern, she wrote Nichols, "Poor bleeding Kansas—how the soul sickens. All free State men & women will be crushed out, ere the North will awake." Meanwhile, Nichols's political lecturing was a smashing success. "I have not found a house that would hold (standing) all the people who came to hear me on Kansas," she reported with enthusiasm. "The people are awake."[64]

Nichols remembered that these "semi-political labors," as she called them, were "often racy" because voters were keenly interested in the topic and female lecturers were still controversial, especially at political party meetings. While nominally she spoke for Kansas, Republican organizers had conveniently melded party events with the cause and exploited her novelty as a woman speaker. In a Democratic stronghold in Pennsylvania, they falsely advertised her lecture about Kansas to attract a crowd but supplied male speakers instead to avoid controversy. In Sinclairville, New York, a minister barred her from the pulpit, shouting angrily, "It's my pulpit, and if you speak in this house to-night you speak from this platform!" With her signature composure,

Nichols resorted to a poorly lighted side platform and before leaving elicited an apology from the minister for his "ungentlemanly language." Her ladylike presentation and her authenticity on Kansas outweighed the potential impropriety of her presence for the audience. Yet she could not stop the editors of the *New York Daily News* and *Express,* who, perhaps intentionally, confused her with Mary Gove Nichols, a self-proclaimed advocate of free love, and implied that Frémont and Free Love had joined hands. Greeley defended her respectability, claiming that Mrs. Nichols from Kansas had not "said one word about Frémont or the Presidential election." In fact, Nichols was performing political work normally reserved for men and had veered well outside woman's sphere, albeit under the guise of a mother of Kansas.[65]

Notwithstanding Greeley's denial or her discomfort with partisanship, Republicans reaped the benefits of Nichols's lectures and the moral influence of women during the 1856 campaign. She was not the only woman who contested the supposedly unfeminine nature of politics by displaying a party affiliation in public. Republicans placed women strategically in front of voters to associate their benevolence with campaign goals. Women in Wisconsin, Indiana, and Ohio participated actively in political rallies and stood on parade floats in virtual representations of "Bleeding Kansas." The women in Chicago, Boston, and New York who organized to raise money and supplies for destitute free-state settlers in Kansas thereby supported the party's goals and symbolized its high moral purpose. At a gathering of women in New York City, where she joined Thaddeus Hyatt and Charles Robinson on the platform, Nichols waved the bullet taken from her son's shoulder and issued a maternal plea for contributions:

> Are you mothers? Let me speak to you for the mothers of Kansas. I am one of them. My sons are among the sufferers and the defenders of that ill-fated Territory; their blood has baptized the soil which they yet live to weep over, to love, and to defend. I ask of you, mothers of New York, but a tithe of the sacrifices and devotion of the mothers of Kansas. Their "jewels," more precious than silver, or gold, or houses and lands, are already laid a sacrifice upon the altar. Can you withhold from them the bread that shall win to you the blessing of those ready to perish?

Republican editors frequently praised the actions of these Ladies Aid Societies, which helped relieve the suffering caused by "Missouri vermin" and other agents of the Democratic Party. Appealing to women as nurturers of the human race, Nichols queried, "Will you send out the lifeboat to save these sinking, struggling victims of foul oppression?"[66]

The lifeboat quickly filled up with supplies after Greeley printed Nichols's appeal in the *New York Tribune*. Stationed with friends in Elmira, she continued to lecture nearly every night throughout the upstate region about the "Wrongs of Kansas" long after the election was over. Barrels of clothing and supplies earmarked for sufferers left the Northeast for the territory, only to be waylaid by corrupt handlers who insulted needy settlers despite Hyatt's efforts to allocate goods fairly. Relie waited in Lawrence for three days for a distribution box before becoming angry and mortified by mistreatment as a poor beggar. Knowing he was Nichols's son, Hyatt resorted to giving Relie $20 to supply the family's needs at the local store, but others were not as fortunate.[67]

Confident that her work was crucial to saving not only her family but Kansas as well, Nichols had subordinated her woman's rights agenda to the free-state cause, a core tenet of the Republican Party. At the time of the National Woman's Rights Convention in New York City, she was lecturing upstate and did not attend. Even so, members endorsed "Mrs. C. I. H. Nichols, of Kansas" as one of seven vice presidents, an honor that expressed her new identity. She had engaged more fully with Republicans than most other female reformers and had faith in their pledge to end slavery, but Lucy Stone, among others, distrusted party politicians and cautioned activists not to be fooled by Republican men who would solicit women's help just to rule over them. Although Frémont lost the election, Republicans did not lose faith in their platform, nor did Nichols become discouraged about politics and the free-state movement, even after the proslavery president, James Buchanan, took office in 1857.[68]

By March of that year, Clarina was eager to return to Kansas despite the uncertainties about its future. Federal troops had opened the Missouri River and quelled the worst violence, but lawlessness still reigned in some counties. After the peacemaking efforts of the latest territorial governor, John W. Geary, eroded and he resigned, the territorial conflict remained in limbo as settlers awaited further action on the part of the proslavery legislature. Widespread publicity about Kansas during the presidential campaign, however, had swelled the ranks of potential emigrants from the Northeast and helped boost prospects for the state's future in Clarina's mind. She knew the difficulties of pioneering, but she had risked part of her inheritance, her family's welfare, and her reputation as a champion of freedom in Kansas. With a keen desire to reunite with her sons and a renewed sense of her political effectiveness, she was determined to join the wave of settlers who embarked for the territory and to resume her mission to secure rights for women in the new state.

7

Strong-Minded Woman

The *women* are "strong-minded." And by the way, "strong-mindedness"
will be no objection to a woman, among the pioneers to Kanzas.
C. I. H. Nichols, 1854

Clarina Nichols remembered her third trip to Lawrence, "the Mecca
of the Free State pilgrims," as a joyful experience. With "fresh recruits from the east" comprised of "intelligent and happily expect-
ant" emigrants, she traveled with Birsha and George up the Missouri
River and transferred to the *Lightfoot,* a small steamboat retrofitted
to carry passengers from the new "paper city" of Wyandotte up the
Kansas River to the free-state stronghold. But the river was barely
navigable in the spring of 1857, and the steamer's smokestacks col-
lided abruptly with a low-leaning tree, causing the unsuspecting passengers to quickly seek cover from the branches crashing all around.
The tumult subsided, and Nichols recalled that an "unpretending
little woman admonish[ed] us (women) 'not to act like fools,'" just
as a youthful, dreamy-eyed abolitionist emerged from under a table
exclaiming, "Let us be men! Our women are turned to men and our
men are all women!" Several other men subsequently crept out from
under the table, red-faced and embarrassed from their "womanly"
hiding place. Delighted by such gender-bending behavior so characteristic of the West in her mind, Nichols recounted how the passengers socialized and danced during the delay before they proceeded to
a hearty welcome in Lawrence.[1]

Indeed, Nichols was sanguine that the strong-minded women of
Kansas and the free-state men who welcomed their presence would

not only secure freedom for blacks but also provide the support she needed to resume her campaign for woman's rights. A number of free-state women had actively defended their homes in 1856 and voiced their opinions about the shape of local institutions in the territory, and this was the kind of "strong-mindedness" that resonated with free-state politicians in Kansas, not the radicalism often associated with woman's rights. Yet the bravery and endurance free-state women had displayed in the nascent state provided a politically viable basis for Nichols to urge lawmakers to include woman's rights, as well as those of blacks, when they crafted a state constitution. "What new pledges of humanity shall eternal justice win from the Legislators of Kansas?" she had asked, pressing for the twin prongs of race and sex equality.[2] As a mother of sons who had fought against slavery in the territory and lectured for Republicans in the East, Nichols spoke with an authority rooted in experience that was virtually unmatched among antebellum reformers, and she was determined to capitalize on these political assets. Moreover, her family's well-being rested on the success of the Free State Party, which continued to jockey for power against proslavery counterparts. There was considerable reason to be hopeful, but racial politics also loomed menacingly on the horizon, dominating the political terrain and threatening to impede her mission.

Clarina's optimism about Kansas was matched by her desire to reunite her family. Unlike the desperate days in Lane, she would enjoy Birsha's help and constant companionship in setting up a household along with the labor that thirteen-year-old George could provide. Her son Howard; his wife, Sarah; and Relie had all remained in the territory during her absence. While Relie was recovering from injuries after the Battle of Black Jack, he had met eighteen-year-old Helen McCowen, who had helped nurse the wounded. The daughter of committed abolitionists, she had been educated at secondary schools and emigrated with her family from Indiana in 1855. Soon Relie and Helen were courting, and they married in Prairie City on Christmas Day 1856.[3] Clarina was no doubt eager to meet her new daughter-in-law and to embrace Howard and Sarah's baby boy, her first grandchild.

But neither the free-state "Mecca" at Lawrence nor her former homestead in Lane would become Clarina's final destination. Instead, she settled the family in the new and propitious town of Quindaro, perched on the bluffs overlooking the west bank of the Missouri River, about 10 miles northwest of Kansas City, Missouri. Organized in the fall of 1856, Quindaro was a free-state project instigated by Charles Robinson and widely advertised in the East. The other thriving ports on the Kansas side of the Missouri River—Leavenworth and Atchison—were dominated by proslavery advocates, which prevented free-state immigrants from landing comfortably and from investing in prime riverside property. The landing at Quindaro was one of the best on the river, but the terrain was less than ideal. To reach the town site, visitors faced a steep climb up a craggy hillside ascending from the waterfront up to Main Street, which ran parallel to the river.[4]

Disregarding this obvious pitfall, Quindaro's promoters had laid out town lots in January, just a few months before Clarina arrived. Originally part of the Wyandot Indian Reserve, the land had been divided into allotments for tribal members who chose to become citizens in 1855. Abelard Guthrie, a former land registrar from Ohio who had married a Wyandot woman, helped negotiate an agreement with tribal members to sell him and Charles Robinson the town site. They named the town after Guthrie's wife, Nancy Quindaro Brown, and according to Guthrie, they "were wholly indebted to her exertions and influence with the Indians for every foot of land on which the town is built." Guthrie worked closely with Robinson and other settlers to develop the town, and NEEAC invested heavily in the site by buying lots and sponsoring commercial development in anticipation of making it a railroad hub to feed travelers into Kansas. The leaders anticipated great profits, and Guthrie predicted that Quindaro would be "the great city of the West."[5]

The town's prospects were equally compelling for Clarina, who envisioned her future in a neat little cottage in a bustling river town much like Brattleboro, where she could read the newspapers and books that fed her intellectual appetite and commune with like-minded reformers. Her only regret was that Relie and Helen had decided to join Helen's parents and cast their western nets even wider toward California. Helen's brother had sent glowing reports about California, urging the family repeatedly to migrate, and Helen was eager to leave Kansas and the danger of marauding "border ruffians" and "rattlesnakes . . . as thick as the leaves of the trees." Relie was perhaps closest to his mother in his sense of adventure, his interest in journalism, and certainly his willingness to act on his political views. Yet the appeal of California was overwhelming given the uncertainties in Kansas. Clarina would miss her brave and ardent son, but with her heart and soul dedicated to Kansas she was too preoccupied with her new venture to bemoan his leaving for long. By the time the extended McCowen family headed for the Santa Fe Trail in May in a wagon train, she was thoroughly wedded to Quindaro.[6]

Unlike the stark existence Clarina experienced on the prairie, life in

Abelard Guthrie, cofounder of the town of Quindaro, which was named after his wife, Nancy Quindaro Brown, a member of the Wyandot tribe of Indians. Courtesy of the Kansas State Historical Society.

Quindaro seemed to spring up "like mushrooms in a spring rain." A hotel, shops, and offices quickly lined the town's Main Street and enhanced the value of Clarina's lots, and the ferry to Parkville across the Missouri provided access to commercial markets. Her son Howard had learned carpentry, formed a partnership with a fellow tradesman, and found ready work building stores and homes. Clarina "watched the progress of [the] masons day after day, as if they were building a tower by which we might scale Heaven." By June they were calling for more mortar for her "'home, sweet home.'" With Howard's family next door, Clarina, Birsha, and George grew much of their own food, milked a cow, raised chickens, and began planting fruit trees. In a year's time, Quindaro would host a hundred frame and stone houses, two hotels, plus a number of dry goods shops, grocers, blacksmiths, and offices filled with lawyers, doctors, and realtors. One observer exclaimed that Quindaro had experienced "a species of town-building madness."[7]

Witnessing such rapid commercial growth was an exhilarating and sometimes frustrating experience, but Clarina embraced the civic life and multiethnic community she found in Quindaro. Its free-state leaders dominated town affairs and sought to recreate the cultural institutions—schools, churches, libraries, and lyceums—that graced New England in this western seat of freedom. But Quindaro was not New England. In addition to Abelard Guthrie and Nancy Quindaro Brown, the town hosted a number of large Wyandot families who retained considerable land and commanded respect for their efforts at assimilation. Committed Christians and full citizens, they also maintained a tribal identity, and as such were granted equal civil status with the newcomers. Clarina noted appreciatively that the federal government had granted land to each individual Wyandot, including married women, who held land "in their own right," thus affording them more legal equality than white women. The Wyandots dwarfed Quindaro's free black population, but the town quickly gained a reputation as an antislavery stronghold; by 1860 thirty blacks lived in the small town, along with a trickle of fugitive slaves who took refuge in the area on their way to Iowa and Canada.[8]

Quindaro's leading men accommodated these ethnic differences to some extent as they organized churches and schools, but not as thoroughly as Clarina would have liked. Ministers, both Congregational and Methodist, began preaching in the schoolhouse, and the Methodists welcomed Quindaro's Wyandot families by providing services with an interpreter on alternate Sundays. With little concern for sectarian differences, Clarina probably attended Congregational services. Though she had transferred her Baptist membership to the Ottawa Mission Church, she was content to listen to any spokesman as long as he spread the Christian morality she held dear. When the town's new settlers deliberated over schools, they were unconcerned about Wyandot children because tribal leaders ran their own schools. But to Clarina's dismay, they decided initially to exclude black children from the public school, following a rule passed by the proslavery territorial legislature. While they argued whether or how to educate black children, Birsha became the first school mistress.[9]

At the same time, Clarina directed her energies into collaborating with editor John M. Walden on the *Quindaro Chindowan*, a free-state paper first published on May 13, 1857. An ardent Republican from Ohio, Walden was only twenty-six years old and a far less experienced journalist than the well-known Mrs. Nichols, but he had been recruited by town leaders to tout free Kansas in the East and boasted plans to circulate the *Chindowan* throughout the territory as well. He adopted the town's Wyandot identity for the paper's exotic title, though he had little interest in the Wyandots. "Chindowan is a

Wyandott [*sic*] word, meaning Leader," the ambitious Walden explained, and "'Quindaro' is also a Wyandott [*sic*] word that some interpret by the adage 'In union there is strength.'" Convinced that free-state men had been deprived of the rights to self-government, Walden was wholeheartedly committed to the Republican policy of developing the West with "homes only of Free Men and Free Women." But he distanced himself from abolitionism and assured his readers that the U.S. Constitution protected slavery where it existed.[10]

As associate editor, Nichols graced the paper with a feminine touch and used it as a medium to express her moral philosophy and her views about politics, slavery, intemperance, and human rights. Introducing herself under a "sun-bonnet," she pledged to "speak for what we regard as truth and right" and advised readers that "we must, one and all, labor to promote intelligence and virtue in our neighborhood relations, and loving freedom, lay broad and deep its foundations in the great social heart." To be "morally free," she asserted, we must "*know* what is right or true in principle, and *live* it." With her pen, she scattered biblical truths to express her womanly piety, but her politically charged columns were hardly evangelical. Instead, Nichols echoed the rhetoric of the Revolutionary era as she argued that universal and practical education was the key to eradicating ignorance and nurturing a virtuous and productive republic. It was a lesson she hoped to instill in her neighbors who had refused to apply the principle to freed blacks by segregating the town's school system. "Equal legislation and general education" were the "two arms of a wise political economy," she argued, claiming that slave masters had ignored this truth by "monopolizing education." Slaveholders not only deprived slaves but also free blacks and poor whites alike of knowledge, the bedrock of freedom and industry.[11]

Coupling these weighty issues with commentary about the political situation in Kansas, Nichols promoted the free-state cause. She informed eastern readers that "domestic comfort" had returned to the territory thanks to their charity, and everyone was "'up and doing'" while waiting for the political stalemate to end. So "Why Don't the Free State Men Vote?" she queried, in an effort to justify the free-state boycott of the upcoming election for delegates to another constitutional convention. Proslavery advocates intended to write their own constitution at Lecompton in June 1857 and apply for statehood, but they restricted voter registration to minimize the free-state turnout. Quite simply, free staters could not vote because they were unlawfully excluded from the democratic process by a bogus territorial legislature backed by a corrupt federal government, Nichols argued. To help shore up the free-state movement, she urged instead that free-state leaders resume their work on an alternative government.[12]

This explicitly partisan editorial notwithstanding, Nichols adhered to her customary mode of avoiding direct political engagement while espousing the Yankee values that she believed would ensure free institutions in Kansas. Adopting the role of a public watchdog, she eagerly sought to maintain sanitation and good order in the frontier town; under the cover of Deborah Van Winkle, she admonished the "men folks" of Quindaro to rid the streets of a dead horse, which had befouled the "sweet air," and warned them directly to preserve the shade trees from the excesses of the woodman's axe.[13] With a bright, "Good Morning, sister housekeepers!" she advised wives and mothers to shoulder their duties with Christian forbearance and bolstered their efforts by investing Monday morning "washing-day" with spiritual meaning. Scrubbing "soiled linen and mud-tracked floors" was a task confirming their true Christian character. The "kitchen" cabinet was as important as the "National Cabinet," she proclaimed, because it provided the bodily comfort necessary for amiability and self-possession. Both "avocations . . . must be prosecuted with grateful reference to God, and a tender consideration for all the human interests involved, or we, as individuals, fail of that Christian discipline, without which we can neither worship God, nor properly respect ourselves."[14] Underlying her cheerful veneer lay a town cluttered with felled trees, rubbish, and piles of dirty laundry. It would take unremitting daily labor plus a woman's eye for cleanliness to turn Quindaro into the seat of progressive civilization she had envisioned.

Embedded within these pieties was Nichols's belief that free labor—for both women and men—was the basis of independence, self-regard, and human progress. "Wherever the worker worships through his toil, both himself and his calling are elevated," she argued. Her praise for labor was not only part of her Baptist upbringing but also reminiscent of Democratic Party rhetoric of the 1840s, and now it matched the sectional ideology Republican men like Walden espoused. They hailed the free white laborers who "built schoolhouses, churches, and villages; put up manufacturing establishments; constructed railroads; and developed the free states in every way."[15] Nichols had an eye for the ways women featured in this process. Only through free labor for all—men and women, white and black—and by serving this godly purpose could the domestic and political sphere thrive. The fruits of free labor were evident in New England, she noted, where the spread of knowledge and "the power of productive industry, of self-support and an honorable independence" had "overcome the disadvantages of soil and climate." By contrast, in the southern states, society had stagnated from a lack of development and progress because labor was "degraded in the fettered limbs of the slave." Every southerner, black and white, suffered from a lack of free institutions.[16]

Nichols's free-labor ideology was both a political stance and a practical prescription for pioneers in Kansas Territory, where the common need to labor blurred gender, class, and even racial differences: "It is labor digs deep the foundations; it is labor weaves the social web, and makes it possible and desirable to gather men in towns and cities, and schools and churches," she insisted. Frontier conditions encouraged mutual dependence, a positive phenomenon in her mind, because it nurtured "humane consideration" among new inhabitants. Kansas provided the ideal environment in which to build a free labor society, a place where settlers could open up the "rich veins of human brotherhood" and unite in a common vision of equality and freedom.[17]

If this egalitarian vision did not exactly exist in Quindaro, Clarina sought to put her philosophy into action as best she could. Birsha, imbued with antislavery principles from her years at Eagleswood, was eager to teach black children, who had been excluded from the public schools, and together they opened an integrated school in their home. Birsha could have taught three times as many students and earned four times the money if she had excluded "the colored children," Clarina explained to a friend, but "tho it looks like starving for our principles, . . . we will wait till we *have* starved before we abandon them."[18] Equal access to education was a tool for racial uplift in Clarina's mind, a means to redress the degradations of slavery and effect social improvement. She and Birsha were not alone in acting on these benevolent sentiments; the Congregational minister's wife also provided private lessons for black children, and eventually the townsmen funded a separate school for the children of freed people. Still bitter about their segregationist attitudes, Clarina fumed privately and mocked the widespread fear that mixing black and white students would result in racial amalgamation: "'White wom[en] would be marrying [colored] men' says one 'gentleman'—you pay my sex a compliment sir in advising that they would form a legal relation—an improvement certainly upon the present illegal amalgamation of white men with the degraded dependent slave woman!'"[19]

Just as Nichols took action based upon her beliefs in equal education, so too she sought to rid Quindaro of that "deadliest foe to all"—intemperance. Residents had been warned that the town company would not countenance "rummeries," and after a number of alert women detected a hidden stash of whiskey, the company solicited Nichols's help. She acted swiftly to gather twenty-eight women, who signed a petition appealing to the men to take "speedy and efficient measures" to eradicate the "vile demon" that was "degrading manhood" and would thereby destroy their homes.[20] Women in Lawrence had set a precedent for temperance activism in 1856, when Helen Hutchinson, with whom Nichols had emigrated in 1855, and about ten other women wielded axes and hammers to destroy the casks and bottles of liquor found in a Lawrence tavern.[21] In Quindaro, Nichols's petition spurred men to organize a temperance meeting, at which they formed a three-man vigilance committee to attack the problem. The following day, they investigated the "doggeries" and overturned barrels of whiskey at three establishments, while also making it clear that neither ale nor beer was destroyed.

Nichols clearly instigated and secretly condoned this destruction of property, but she was also quick to assure readers of the *Chindowan* that the women of Quindaro had no part in violence. "They have my warmest sympathy in their determined opposition to rum-selling and rum-drinking," she affirmed. "Personally I could not take part in any violent measures for the suppression of the liquor traffic. But looking into my own heart I must confess that for women, whose husbands, sons or brothers are being destroyed, *and destroying others*, through the influence of liquor dens,—for such women in the madness of despair, to go hatchet in hand against them, seems eminently womanly."[22] In this way, she maintained her own gentility while arguing that unruly women were acting in self-defense and assuming their God-given role as "guardians of home and mothers of the race." It was a common rhetorical device for contemporary domestic feminists, who argued that women who ventured into the public sphere rested on a firm morality. "It is as unwomanly as it is unmanly to suffer wrongs to exist which we have power to prevent," Nichols concluded. Three months later, temperance men organized the Quindaro Temperance League, which secured a short-lived prohibition on liquor sales, though eventually the town relied upon high license fees to police the liquor traffic.[23]

Nichols was heartened by their commitment, and for the first time in her life she thrived on the company of local activists. Filled with a constant stream of youthful newcomers and transients, Quindaro was alive with causes. Not everyone supported progressive ideas, but NEEAC's financial backing allowed its followers and other like-minded men to hold the balance of local power. They also fostered a vibrant intellectual community, formed a library association, and created the Quindaro Literary Society. Modeled after the lyceums of New England, the literary society was committed to the intellectual and moral development of the community and to open debate on all subjects. Nichols and her children Howard and Birsha served as officers, and it was within this group that Nichols hoped to germinate interest in woman's rights. Early in its existence, members debated a question she no doubt proposed: "That under the present organization of society, Woman is deprived of many rights to which she is entitled by Justice and by Nature." Curiously, Howard argued in the negative. Whether he opposed his mother's politics or was just playing devil's advocate is unclear, but in either case the debate was inconclusive and the issue remained open for further discussion.[24]

Indeed, with a few notable exceptions, Republican men were generally wary of woman's rights, which may explain why Nichols severed her relationship with John Walden after only three months. A week before the literary society debate on the issue, Nichols politely resigned her post at the *Chindowan*, noting that her conditions of employment had not been met but wishing the editor well. She may not have been paid, but it is also possible that she and Walden parted company over woman's rights. The topic had been absent from her *Chindowan* articles, but she had apparently hoped to devote a whole page to women's issues, including their rights. Walden filled the paper with free-state politics, interspersed with announcements of local meetings and advertisements. He was a keen advocate of temperance and perfectly willing to report that Nichols lectured "on her favorite subject, the rights of Woman," at the library the following January, but he did not believe women belonged on the podium and was unwilling to engage the topic in his paper. Whether she recognized it at the time, Nichols's differences with Walden were a harbinger of the problems she would face with other Republicans. Walden was far more concerned with defending free white labor than entertaining rights for either women or blacks.[25]

The literary society, in contrast, proved to be a haven for Quindaro's progressive reformers, especially abolitionists. The group published its own literary journal, the *Cradle of Progress*, which according to one historian Nichols edited, but unfortunately no issues have survived. The society met regularly "to enjoy the wit and wisdom of its weekly journal" at a house west of the town center that was soon dubbed "Uncle Tom's Cabin." Years later Nichols explained that it was not only the "intellectual center" of Quindaro but also "dedicated to emancipation without proclamation," a convenient station on the mythical Underground Railroad. Samuel C. Smith was in charge of providing safe passage for fugitives through Quindaro, according to abolitionist Samuel F. Tappan of Lawrence. He noted in private correspondence as early as January 1858 that the "Rail Road" was in "full blast." Easily accessible from Missouri, Quindaro soon became known as an "Abolitionist Hole" across the river in Westport, though John Walden vehemently denied that anyone in town would "entice away slaves, [or] knowingly harbor fugitives." The conspirators may have used a deserted mill below the village landing, where the "hoot of a domesticated owl, brought a farmer and his boat from the opposite shore." From there, according to Nichols, "Uncle Tom's boys" enacted "some exciting escapes from Quindaro to the interior, by day and by night."[26]

Just as sympathetic abolitionists became increasingly ready to assist fugitives, so too Missouri slaves took advantage of the porous border. Nichols claimed that "of the many slaves who took the train of freedom there" only one was captured and returned to Missouri. One slave who fled from near Parkville after learning that his master intended to sell him to the deep South arrived in Quindaro carrying a pair of broken iron manacles, which "Uncle Tom's boys" filed off from his still-confined foot; Nichols took the manacles and eventually carried them back to Vermont, where she intended to donate them to the Vermont Historical Society.[27] Coupled with her son's bullet, these slave manacles were concrete evidence that both whites and blacks suffered under slavery's presence in Kansas Territory.

Conspiring with abolitionists to harbor fugitives transformed Nichols's antislavery sentiments from abstract moral principle into radical action and a firmer commitment to racial justice. Like others changed by their experiences in Kansas, the respectable Mrs. Nichols had willingly condoned violence in the cause of human rights; now she had broken the law to uphold her principles. Through her actions and private correspondence, she openly expressed her opposition to exclusion of free blacks from the territory and advocated for integrated schools, measures that split free-state men as they assumed control of the territory. "My blood boils at the efforts to drive out the col[ore]d freemen & exclude from educational advantages," she wrote a colleague. Yet this commitment was increasingly at odds with the racism embedded in the Republican Party she had supported so fervently. "[I] sympathize with you perfectly in the sentiments you express about laboring for the colored people," her friend responded. "I wish the Republican party were more thoroughly Anti-Slavery."[28] Garrisonian abolitionists had continued to shun partisanship for this reason, and Nichols would soon face a conflict between her commitment to racial justice and her desire to practice politics in Kansas.

Even as Nichols's concern about the future status of blacks mounted, she could take heart that the political situation in the territory finally seemed to favor the free-state settlers, opening the way for her to resume her advocacy for women. By the fall of 1857, free-state emigrants far outnumbered their Missouri rivals; and after the new territorial governor, Robert J. Walker, promised to ensure fairness at the ballot box, free-state men had decided to vote and end their two-year boycott of elections in October. Walker's rejection of thousands of disputed votes gave free-state men a majority in the territorial legislature; they affirmed the free-state Topeka Constitution at its session in December and began planning for a new convention in Leavenworth. Meanwhile, pro-slavery men pressed Congress to approve the Lecompton Constitution, which they had submitted still hoping to create a slave state and undermine the free-state majority. Although President Buchanan and dozens of southern congressmen supported Lecompton, unexpected allies like Governor Walker and even Senator Stephen Douglas voiced their opposition to admitting Kansas under the flawed document, which had not been properly submitted to the people for ratification. When Lecompton, a national symbol of the debate over slavery, was defeated in local elections in January 1858, free-state men appeared to have gained a sufficient victory against the Buchanan administration and its southern allies in Congress.[29]

Nichols was confident that free-state homes were no longer threatened by "the aggressions of the slave power," but the shape of the new government was in limbo. Now that free-state politicians appeared to have secured their political rights, would they accommodate the rights of blacks and women? The question of woman's rights was a minor issue as they sought to control the territory and gain legitimacy from the federal government. Moreover, the separate property and custody rights for married women in the Topeka Constitution seemed adequate. Yet as Nichols noted, those rights were not clearly defined, leaving the vital question of whether a woman would have possession of her earnings to the whims of the legislature. Ironically, the language of the Lecompton Constitution was more explicit; it guaranteed married women's rights to separate real and personal property, thereby protecting family property from creditors and wives' inheritance in slaves.[30]

Nichols was not the only woman in Kansas who hoped to broaden the definition of political rights to include women and blacks. Under the leadership of the Wattles family, a group of radical abolitionists in Linn County organized the Moneka Woman's Rights Association (MWRA) in early 1858. Brothers Augustus and John Wattles, along with their wives, Susan and Esther, had emigrated from Ohio and eventually settled two adjoining claims near Moneka in the southeastern border region, where violence persisted. Their homes served as local Underground Railroad stations, and they harbored dozens of free-state militia men, including the notorious James Montgomery and John Brown. While protecting eleven fugitive slaves on their way to Iowa, Brown was impressed by the Wattles's kindness, later calling them "Angels of mercy" who "ministered to the wants of myself; & of my poor sons; both in sickness & in health."[31]

Well known for their radicalism and their work with fugitive slaves, the Wattles family quickly gained attention in the territory for their commitment to woman's rights as well. In fact, like other radicals in Kansas, they converted their reform impulse into political engagement because the territory provided the possibilities to effect real change. John had given speeches on woman's rights in the Northeast and in Ohio before moving to Kansas, and it was after one of his lectures in Moneka on February 2, 1858, that the MWRA was founded by twenty-five women and seventeen men.[32] In line with the Declaration of Sentiments of 1848, the MWRA's constitution outlined their grievances against a society that deprived women of human rights despite the fact that women shouldered the "responsibility of shaping the destiny of the race," and proclaimed a goal "to secure to woman her natural rights and to advance her educational interests." At the first meeting, members resolved to promote temperance by hiring women as lecturers and to insert prohibition in the territory's new constitution. Even more radical, however, was their resolve that "Kansas cannot be truly free while the words 'white' or 'male' are found within the limits of her constitution." To educate the public, they planned to secure woman's rights tracts from the editor of the *Lily* and to circulate them within the territory. Soon Moneka became "celebrated for its peculiar political character," a place where the "ladies wear 'pants' and talk of their 'rights,'" while the men supported violent abolitionism.[33]

One of the MWRA's first actions was to petition the Leavenworth

John O. Wattles, an abolitionist and organizer
of the Moneka Woman's Rights Association.
Courtesy of the Kansas State Historical Society.

Constitutional Convention, which met in April 1858. Members of the organization urged the delegates to "frame the organic law of the State of Kansas for the *citizens* without any invidious distinctions," encompassing both race and gender equality. They submitted a second petition seeking equal rights for wives within marriage—including separate property rights, equal access to marital property, and equal treatment of widows in property ownership and child custody.[34] They were not bold enough to plead for rights in person, but they planned to publicize their petitions in the Lawrence and Topeka papers. Augustus Wattles, who had become involved in free-state politics in 1855, may have alerted his contacts in Lawrence about the effort because Samuel Tappan, secretary of the Leavenworth Convention, expected the women "with a petition, for a recognition of their rights." But when they failed to appear, he used their absence to conclude that they lacked conviction about voting and "make but little effort to secure the right to do so." Susan Wattles later explained that it was not conviction but experience in public speaking and writing that they lacked. Since her arrival in the territory, Wattles had read the *Lily* and worked diligently to get new subscribers and influence anyone she could on the topic, but they were "strangers to the work."[35]

If the women of the MWRA were politically inexperienced, there were free-state men at the Leavenworth Convention who were willing to promote their cause. Abolitionist Samuel N. Wood boldly introduced a motion to eliminate "male" from the franchise clause. The delegates agreed to delete "white" (pending the outcome of a popular referendum on "universal" suffrage) and to open the common schools to every child, but they were not ready to enfranchise women. In a final effort, Wood offered gender neutrality instead by inserting "he or she" in place of "he" throughout the document, in effect eliminating all "invidious distinctions" per the MWRA's petition. When another delegate argued that "his mother, sister and wife should have the same right at the ballot box, that had been extended to Negroes and Indians," it was clear that sex and race were linked. Twenty men, a significant minority, voted for the provision, but extending suffrage clearly threatened free-state unity and failed to pass.[36] In the end, the delegates did expand and clarify married women's property and custody rights. But the Leavenworth document reflected the sentiments of the radical wing of the free-state movement, not the popular will, and failed to gain legitimacy. As free-state men fractured into partisan positions, those who favored black exclusion gravitated toward the Democratic Party. Meanwhile, Sam Wood, who remained a staunch supporter of woman's rights, helped ensure that married women's property rights, including their earnings, were inserted in the territorial statutes in 1859. Supporters of the issue had obtained the appropriate wording from Lucy Stone.[37]

Indeed, while Nichols and these allies were spreading woman's rights in the West, they clearly rested on the backbone of the movement in the East, where activists continued to press state legislatures for suffrage and married women's property rights. After marrying Henry Blackwell in 1855, Lucy Stone was even more determined to overturn discriminatory coverture laws: "Now that I occupy a legal position in which I can not even draw in my own name the money I have earned . . . or make any contract, but am rated with fools, minors and madmen . . . do you think that, in the grip of such pincers, I am likely to grow amiss?" Elizabeth Cady Stanton echoed her sentiments: "A man in marrying gives up no right; but a woman, every right, even the most sacred of all—the right to her own person."[38] By the mid-1850s Massachusetts and New York had passed new laws providing married women with limited property rights, and Nichols hailed the change: "Formerly, married women were spoken of by the legal fraternity . . . as 'legally dead.' . . . But under more recent laws, restoring to them certain independent property rights, 'dead' women have been resuscitated in hopeful numbers."[39] Stanton, Anthony, and Stone concentrated their efforts on righting these married wrongs during the late 1850s, in part because they believed that gaining married women's prop-erty rights could be a stepping-stone to full suffrage. In mid-1859 they circu-lated memorials to state legislatures demanding full rights and elimination of the word *male* from state constitutions.[40] Meanwhile, in some new western states—Texas, California, and Oregon—women's property rights were out-lined in the constitutions, an indication that lawmakers in frontier areas rec-ognized women's role in western development.[41]

Nichols was hopeful that she could build upon this national progress, and craving the support of like-minded reformers, she contacted Susan Wattles as soon as she heard about the MWRA. Familiar with her reputation, the Wat-tleses were confident that Nichols could provide the expertise they lacked and also assured her that the "good and intelligent men in this neighborhood are about as zealous in the cause as the women are." This was the beginning of a regular and fruitful correspondence between the two women, but it was not until the following spring that the organization hired Nichols to pursue their goals at yet another constitutional convention to be held in Wyandotte City near her home. After the final defeat of the Lecompton Constitution, the 1859 territorial legislature had not only repealed slavery and enacted liberal property rights provisions for women but also prohibited sales of liquor to a drunken man "against the known wishes of his wife." When the free-state majority succeeded in calling for the Wyandotte Convention, Nichols wrote Wattles immediately, requesting vital support and outlining her strategy: "I am ready to act at the Con[vention]; speaking before Committee or the Con[vention] if allowed to do so, and can 'lobby' outside." But she also felt she needed "to be authorized by petitioners—by my own sex especially" to not appear self-interested. "It is vital to the full influence of a womanly presen-tation of the subjects before the Conven[tion] that your agent, whoever she be, shall not seem to put herself forward uncalled," she explained. "My age, my past history and action endorse my suitableness personally." Nichols knew better than to demand rights, but instead she would "make a forcible showing of the wrongs" women suffered.[42]

Nichols was confident in her persuasive and diplomatic skills, but the pre-cise method of presenting the petitions to the convention caused her much consternation, especially because she knew racial politics could inhibit her success. She longed to "plead for equal rights to *all*," particularly for black rights to education, but her pragmatism and primary commitment to woman's rights ultimately prevailed. Assuaging her guilt about this difficult choice, she wrote Wattles: "In reference to any allusion in our petition to the enfranchise-ment of the colored—I am forced to the conclusion that it would mar our effort and do no good to them. I am persuaded that the enfranchisement of woman involves their enfranchisement and the sooner we get our hands into the ballot box the sooner will their freedom come."[43] Acutely aware that "the colored question here hampers us in a measure," she wanted to keep woman's rights "aloof from the political wrangles." Despite these potential difficulties, support from MWRA fortified Nichols in a way she had never experienced before. "It does my soul good to think of you as feeling with me & bound in spirit with the oppressed," she wrote Wattles.[44]

Nichols's strategy reflected her assessment of the political climate in the territory. Both Republicans and Democrats formally organized in anticipation of the convention and jockeyed for power using racist rhetoric to articulate their partisan differences. Republicans included radical free-state men as well as moderates who only sought to ensure "Free Labor and Free Homesteads." Even radical Sam Wood was urging Republicans not to endorse black suffrage at this point because it could hinder their primary goal of gaining admission to the Union. Many free-state men associated their Democratic opponents with the infamous "Bogus laws" and tyranny of the proslavery Buchanan ad-ministration, and some even labeled them "Africans" or the black Democracy for condoning slavery. In turn, Democrats appealed to white voters by demon-izing the "Black Republicans," all of whom they claimed would vote for "ne-gro suffrage, negro equality, and a mingling of negro children" with whites. To attach woman's rights with black rights in this racial divide would have been political suicide, especially after the influential Horace Greeley came to Kansas and advised his fellow Republicans to limit suffrage to white males, which infuriated Nichols.[45]

But rabid free-stater George Brown of the *Herald of Freedom* decided to use woman's rights to provoke the Republican leadership, whom he believed had forsaken the idealism of the original Free State Party. Three days before the convention opened, he challenged them to recognize the inconsistency of enfranchising foreigners and placing women "on the same political basis with the negro." Using these racist arguments, he urged Republicans "to contend for the civil freedom of the thousands of white women in Kansas" or the Democrats would take up the cause. Indeed, as Nichols surmised, adherence to womanly nonpartisanship would serve her well in this political climate. "The Dems are as much on our side, so far as I know, as the Rep.[ublicans]," she told Wattles. "My sympathies and word are with the latter, but I appeal to all parties for woman's rights."[46]

Even so, Nichols needed to reconcile her agenda with the partisan goals of the dominant Republican Party if she was to achieve any progress for women. Admission to the Union was likely to preclude full suffrage rights for women, but Nichols believed she could secure school suffrage and that married women's property rights would be sustained. Consulting with several male allies and Susan Anthony, she devised a complex strategy to present petitions for woman suffrage and force opponents to compromise by supporting a statewide referendum on the issue after admission to the Union was secured. "This will carry the whole question of extended suffrage to the people and we gain time to work for *universal* suffrage," she wrote Anthony. On the outside chance that women *could* get full suffrage rights in the constitution, "the col[ored] suffrage will be settled also & adversely—Our only hope for the free blacks, is to keep their rights an open question till the election of a Legislature under the New Con[stitutio]n."[47]

As a result, Nichols crafted a petition in conjunction with the women of the MWRA that ignored the race question and only protested "against any constitutional monopoly or pre-eminence of rights, based on sex." It was a pragmatic strategy reflecting her political experience and in keeping with her ability to adapt to the shifting political climate of territorial Kansas. Her petition emphasized women's "common interest" with men, appealing to the need of all citizens for protection of "*life, liberty, property* and *intelligent* culture." She reminded lawmakers that women had undertaken "greater and more complicated responsibilities" and therefore they needed "all the legal and constitutional guarantees" of any citizen secured by "equal political rights."[48] Nichols would hardly have ventured such a radical plea a decade earlier. Even though she still embedded mothers' responsibilities in her appeal, she no longer emphasized female difference. Instead, the egalitarian language reflected a broader understanding of the parallels between gender and racial inequalities in America and her maturity as an equal rights activist.

Nichols's shifting consciousness, however, did not mean she would abandon her motherly political style. With her petition in hand, she began a preconvention effort to gather signatures by traveling to key towns where she knew men who would assist in the canvass. Both Nichols and Augustus Wattles wrote Wendell Phillips, treasurer of the newly endowed Francis Jackson Woman's Rights Fund, for money to cover her expenses, and Phillips eventually

Clarina Howard Nichols, portrait, c. 1854. Courtesy of the Grace Hudson Museum and Sun House, City of Ukiah, California.

funneled $200 for the Kansas movement via Susan Anthony's younger brother, Daniel Read Anthony of Leavenworth. Although he was skeptical about the prospects for woman's rights and told Susan that it "costs too much to have conventions in Kansas & people have too much else to occupy their minds," Susan eventually prevailed upon her brother, and Nichols received vital funds for the constitutional campaign.[49]

With little time left before the convention, Nichols was not only chief strategist but the sole female canvasser in the field as she sought public support and signatures in womanly fashion. She gave speeches on "the Legal and Political Claims of Woman as the guardian of the Home and the Educator of the Race" in Topeka, Leavenworth, and Lawrence and traversed the rough and dusty roads of the new territory by stagecoach without male accompaniment. She told Anthony, "There is no man to go with me & I don't want one. The work can be better done by calling to my aid the noble men of each place I visit & I know many such." Charles Robinson was one such supporter, and he circulated a petition locally, but Nichols recognized that the men and women who lived in frontier Kansas had responsibilities to fulfill during the growing season—crops to tend and animals to feed—and reminded Anthony, "We have to work differently here."[50]

Even though Nichols attracted "overflowing" and "attentive" audiences, she received a mixed response in Republican papers. The moderate editors of the *Topeka Tribune* admired her skill and acknowledged that she spoke "with easy manners and a remarkably clear mind, and applied her arguments and logic . . . with as much force and weight as the nature of her position would admit."[51] But they argued strenuously against Nichols's demand for marital equity and were clearly unglued by the specter of finding women "'out-about-town' laboring in the political vineyard" and going to the polls. Others offered humorous taunts, such as trading places with these "strong-minded" women for a year. As she gained publicity from these comments, Nichols secured the signatures of 588 women and men to her petition, including that of her son Howard. Abelard Guthrie somewhat reluctantly signed after informing her that he "reserved the right to attach a proviso to the effect that they (women) renounce the privileges and immunities now exclusively enjoyed by them and perform all the duties appertaining to male citizens." Guthrie's sarcasm, however, could not mask the significance of his support, which he augmented by loaning Nichols a pony so she could ride to Wyandotte for the convention the next day.[52]

Despite backing from a few of the territory's most influential men, Nichols faced an uphill battle when she arrived in Wyandotte City. Delegates at the convention graciously agreed to give her a reporter's seat in the hall, but it was unclear whether she would be allowed to speak. Not only were men unaccustomed to the presence of women in political forums, but as she knew all too well, "any 'unwomanly obtrusiveness' of manners" on her part would have resulted in ridicule, damaging the movement and her reputation. This was the "'big 'fraid,'" Nichols recalled, but she had other reasons for feeling out of place. Most of the fifty-two delegates who clamored into the top floor of the unfinished two-story hall were in their twenties and thirties; she was forty-nine. Some sported white linen suits and appeared "spic and span and handsome" in their Panama hats, whereas Nichols was primly attired in a plain black dress like that of a New England Quaker. Sitting on a daily basis next to Methodist chaplain Werter R. Davis and Lucy B. Armstrong, widow of Wyandot Indian leader John Armstrong, Nichols maintained a motherly watch over the convention, clicking her knitting needles alternately with her pen.[53] She suffered from the oppressive July heat and accompanying stench of tobacco spit and complained to Susan Wattles that it was "exceedingly warm to be 'dressed' all day." But the heat did not impede her ability to maintain a feminine decorum, and with a few ribbons woven through her "silver-gray curls," she exuded a "frisky appearance somewhat inconsistent with her years," according to one observer.[54]

A womanly, nonpartisan presentation, however, could not disguise the fact that Nichols was an abolitionist, a "strong-minded" woman with Republican friends. She was likely to receive a chilly reception from many of the delegates, and she knew that "button-holing" on the floor of the convention was simply out of the question. But as she told Susan Anthony, she made contacts with many men—"directly or indirectly as seems most politic"—inside and outside the hall. Republicans outnumbered Democrats two to one, but most were relatively new to politics and feared the partisan repercussions of publicly sympathizing with her cause. She relied extensively on the influence and initiatives of fellow Vermonter William Hutchinson, chairman of the Bill of Rights committee, and abolitionists John Ritchie and John Wattles, who introduced her to the convention. Eventually she could claim "12 men, *thorough reformers*" on her side, and they proved crucial to her lobbying effort.[55]

Nichols carefully cultivated these relationships during recesses and in the evenings at Lucy Armstrong's "hospitable tea-table . . . [which] offered abundant womanly opportunity for conference and discussion with delegates." An adopted Wyandot, Armstrong was well known for her tireless efforts to secure her land rights in former Wyandot property, and her repeated defense of other tribes' land rights put her in contact with numerous government officials.[56] Armstrong's boardinghouse, where Nichols stayed, was a convenient gathering place for delegates and other politicians. Nichols recalled smugly the day Democratic Governor Samuel Medary queried, "But Mrs. Nichols, you would not have women go down into the muddy pool of politics?" In reply she quipped, "Governor, I admit that you know best how muddy that pool is, but you remember . . . how the angel had to go in and trouble the waters before the sick could be healed." With their superior moral power, nonpartisan women were just the agents to clean up the "muddy pool" of politics. Although Medary declined to sign her petition, he treated Nichols with respect and welcomed her presence at the convention.[57]

At the outset, Nichols's planning and lobbying efforts appeared to be working. When Hutchinson introduced her petition on the first day of the proceedings, instead of tabling it, delegates referred it to two committees. To avoid a sure death in committee, he immediately requested a vote allowing Nichols to address the whole convention on behalf of the women of Kansas, and behind the scenes she interviewed nearly every delegate seeking their consent.

The lengthy debate that ensued was an indication of the esteem she garnered and the seriousness with which they were willing to consider the issue. John Ritchie reminded the young delegates that they had received their "first and best impressions" from their mothers and urged them to put aside their partisanship "when the mothers speak" and not "to stop our ears." Ritchie's argument prevailed, and Nichols delivered her address two days later in the convention hall after hours. Though the Democrats spent the evening at the circus, the *New York Evening Post* reported that her audience was "large, promiscuous, and quite attentive and respectful." Yet the paper's correspondent was otherwise unimpressed with Nichols's "distorted and illiberal" views. She was obviously a "decent person for a reformer," he remarked, and posited that "proper culture and direction would undoubtedly have rendered her a worthy and useful member of society." For her part, Nichols informed Wattles that the convention's "reception of my pleas was hearty and spontaneously sympathized."[58] Indeed, compared with the treatment of her colleagues in the East during the past decade, the respect Nichols received and the absence of ridicule in the hall at Wyandotte was remarkable.

Throughout the debates on her proposals, the delegates expressed their appreciation for the womanly influence in civic life that Mrs. Nichols seemed to embody. Even before her evening address, they passed her school provision. It required the legislature to make "no distinction between the rights of males and females" in the "formation and regulation of schools." Nichols had persuaded Solon O. Thacher of Lawrence to shepherd the provision through his committee and defend it. That Kansas schools should be coeducational was generally conceded, but opponents seriously questioned whether women should or even wanted to vote, hold office, and supervise school finances. Thacher deflected these concerns by stressing the importance of "female influence, as it radiates from the fireside" into the schools, and the head of the Education Committee, who also consulted Nichols, stressed the "efficiency and energy" with which women would manage the school system. Both men dismissed its connection to the elective franchise as insignificant. After the measure passed with a vote of 22 to 19, Nichols was brimming with optimism and reassured Wattles that "we will get other advantages—all helping the final success."[59]

When delegates considered her broader proposal to eliminate "distinctions based on difference of sex," however, their proclivity to honor women's special roles was used adversely. Samuel A. Kingman, a thirty-eight-year-old lawyer and Republican originally from Massachusetts, was her chief adversary.

As chair of the Judiciary Committee, he argued convincingly that indeed women's responsibilities were so great that as a consequence they should be "relieved" of any political duties. Moreover, he asserted that legislation guaranteeing women's property rights had "protected" all their "natural" rights, precluding any need for merely political rights. Thus he undermined Nichols's second proposal to insert "taxation & representation shall be inseparable" as a basis for enfranchising women. Even so, Kingman's argument assumed that women's equal rights to property and custody would be guaranteed, and the delegates unanimously agreed a few days later to include the liberal provisions originally defined in the Leavenworth Constitution. Nichols was elated with the clause providing "equal control of our children during their minority," which she often referred to as mothers' rights to babies, a weapon against the discriminatory rulings of probate judges.[60] This commitment blinded her to the way Kingman had revealed the downside of promoting mothers' rights; it enhanced women's differences from men, not their equality.

A keen desire to protect struggling families on the Kansas frontier and to ensure future emigration to the state animated the majority of delegates, not necessarily a commitment to woman's equal rights. That sentiment also led them to include wives in a provision exempting homesteads from forced sale without joint consent. Republican William Griffith, a farmer originally from Indiana, argued for inclusion of the "voice of the wife" as a means to "protect the poor, the weak, the orphan children and the destitute mother of the family." Even Kingman, who later became chief justice of the state Supreme Court, was an enthusiastic promoter of this family-friendly provision. Indeed, the economic benefit of advancing women's legal rights was an important aspect of the rising status of women throughout the West.[61]

Legal acknowledgement of women's familial roles was enough to bolster Nichols, who wrote Anthony exclaiming, "We are accomplishing something practical besides creating a public sentiment perfectly irresistible by politicians." A correspondent for the *Philadelphia Evening Bulletin* agreed with her upbeat assessment and attributed much to her influence on the convention. The positive response to her petitions was "an indication of a great change in the public mind, and a growing interest upon the subject [of woman's rights]." Nichols also received affirmation from local residents who petitioned the convention for use of the hall for another lecture, which brought out an "overflowing house."[62] The editor of the *New York Times* expressed amazement that Nichols had infiltrated a working political body so effectively. The "strong-minded females" of Kansas, he noted with hyperbole, "have deliberately assaulted the new Constitutional Convention" and "demand[ed] . . . a full and free recognition of their female human rights." He praised the "gallant gentlemen" of Kansas who graciously permitted her to invade their space and who treated her with a respect absent from eastern legislative arenas.[63] Nichols's genteel, motherly presence appealed to the delegates; to honor her was to affirm their gentlemanliness and to display the civility of this two-year-old frontier city to the nation.

It seemed like the tide would turn in favor of women in Kansas, but racial fears complicated Nichols's efforts. Discussion of black rights was everywhere; it arose "in the convention, outside of the bar, in the streets, hotels, boarding houses and even in the fashionable parlours of our Wyandotte friends," according to one delegate. Race overshadowed partisan bickering over gerrymandered electoral districts, the boundary with Nebraska, and the site of the future capitol. Democrats promoted the exclusion of free blacks, the validity of the Fugitive Slave Law, whites-only schools, and white suffrage, knowing that moderate Republicans would support some forms of racial exclusion. By the third week, Nichols reported to Susan Wattles that the convention was "in a 'mess'" and delegates were struggling to determine exactly how to define the word *white*. Democrats claimed that having a "preponderance" of white blood, loosely defined as "more than half," would suffice. In this way, they courted the votes of "civilized" Indians, who were currently enfranchised under territorial rules. Republicans resisted the effort to define whiteness, but only three Republicans voted to delete "white" completely from the franchise clause.[64] Nichols lamented to Anthony: "The poor colored man and the Indian have been cut off by 'white' the con[vention] ruling that all are white in whom the *white blood preponderates!*" She worried that the "negro-hating" people would manipulate this definition to exclude anyone with black blood but held out hope that Indians could eventually qualify.[65]

As the delegates wrangled over black rights, editors fueled the partisan divide with racist rhetoric. George Brown of the *Herald of Freedom* warned Republicans to "let poor Sambo alone" or risk a quick demise. He reasserted the principles of the free-state movement to disabuse readers of the notion that any free-state men were "Negro lovers," exclaiming: "Now, we beg leave to say, that a tender regard for *Sambo* does NOT lie at the bottom of this great movement. On the contrary, it is based up on the idea of the *best interests of the* FREE WHITE LABORERS *of the nation*. Let *Sambo* stay where he is." Diverting attention from black rights, he asserted that the "[negro question] is a white man's question, the question of the right of free white laborers to the soil of the Territories. It is not to be crushed or retarded by shouting '*Sambo*' at us. . . . We object to *Sambo*. We don't want him about."[66]

Determined not to expand the franchise to blacks, Republicans were hardly ready to consider women as voters despite subsequent efforts to reintroduce Nichols's proposals. Hutchinson inserted a clause in the bill of rights to eliminate "any constitutional distinctions on account of sect or sex," linking the issue with religious freedom; another delegate proposed her third option, a popular vote on woman suffrage after authorization from the legislature. But both measures were handily defeated. In the end, freedom and education for blacks were upheld by large majorities, but they refused to expand the franchise to either blacks or women. Although fears that these radical measures would impede statehood were probably well founded, Nichols may have surmised that admission to the Union was a convenient pretext for maintaining a monopoly on power. In her memoir she blamed Kingman and others in the legal profession who "played upon the old harmonicon, 'organic law,' and 'the harmony of the statutes'" to defeat her proposals.[67]

Despite Kingman's effective opposition, the acquisition of school suffrage was a milestone in the history of woman's rights. Nichols knew it was sufficiently vague to be manipulated by opponents, but no state in the Union had enacted a constitutional guarantee of partial suffrage for women, nor would similar provisions be passed until the late 1870s and 1880s, rendering Kansas a progressive reputation on woman's rights. Eastern activists who had besieged state legislatures with unsuccessful petitions for full equality failed to see the merit in school suffrage. They were intent upon arguing the case from a human rights perspective, which appeared more potent at the time, with little reference to women's special capabilities. Nichols's political experience and her personal commitment to the natural rights of mothers convinced her to follow a different strategy and present a specific, if limited, proposal that appealed to the sentiments of enough politicians in Kansas to be successful. Sam Wood announced in his new paper, the *Kansas Press*, that the convention had "adopted a resolution extending the right of suffrage, to females in all matters connected with schools," hoping voters would applaud the new measure in its broadest terms.[68]

Yet even Wood was otherwise silent on the merits of the school clause or exactly what it meant. During the convention, delegates debated whether it guaranteed coeducation in universities as well as common schools, and it was unclear which elections were included or if women could hold school offices. Thoroughly disgusted with Republican hypocrisy, George Brown concluded that the school suffrage measure was an "adroit dodge" of the issue and accused the "white *man's* party" of ignoring the "civil rights of women just as completely as they have those of the negro." He continued to complain that the new constitution enfranchised ignorant foreigners but not civilized Indians and intelligent women.[69]

Brown's defense of woman's rights, even as it rested on white privilege, was rare during the six-week-long ratification campaign. In the ensuing partisan battle, racial diatribes once again overshadowed Nichols's cause. In fact, race was so salient that voters may have attached little significance to the provisions relating to women. Democrats refused to sign the Wyandotte constitution and fought against ratification, knowing it would leave Republicans in control of Kansas. Republican leaders disclaimed any interest in blacks and either ignored or downplayed woman's rights because a connection to either would undermine their appeals to white male voters. The influential James Lane claimed the school clause only implied coeducation. A Republican correspondent to the *Freedom's Champion* reassured readers that it only enhanced female influence by arguing that mothers would have "watchful care over the School Fund and the administration of the School Department.—Mothers! wives! advise your husbands and sons to vote for the Constitution." Popular confusion was reflected in the comments of another advocate who praised the document but trivialized its innovations. It was "full of 'all the latest fashions' in politics," he noted, including the homestead exemption and woman's rights. "Everybody but the 'negro' is carefully looked after," he explained.[70]

Not so, proclaimed "Cora," the anonymous author of a long and highly ironic poem, who asserted that "*woman's* clatter" had been thoroughly squashed by the powerful men who ran the convention and controlled every other aspect of their lives. Preferring the wife who would "wield the ladle, and rock the cradle" and obey her "lord and master" rather than plead for rights, "Cora" parodied the suffrage debate:

Women and *niggers* are facts and *figgers*,
　'Tis plain as two and two!
But—they've *rights enough! a quantum suff*,
　We must really keep them under;

Nor let petticoats *go in* for votes,
    For so they'd "*steal our thunder.*" . . .
She's for *our* pleasure, [a very good measure
    In the plan of the creation!]
And a little longer, as we are the stronger,
    She'll keep her *present* station! . . .
And the grave convention with trifling mention
    Laid *that* thing *under* the table!"[71]

Even in this biting indictment of white male privilege, there was little serious debate about woman's rights.

While the party avoided the issue, perhaps wisely, Republican men were eager to ratify the constitution and sought help from eastern leaders and from Nichols, who could allay public prejudice in her nonpartisan womanly way. In a parallel effort, the Wattleses wrote Anthony, Stone, Wendell Phillips, and Thomas Higginson, seeking more funds to cover Clarina's expenses and to "establish her in the future with a press."[72] She was already pursuing a plan hatched with the MWRA to spread the woman's rights gospel, and she worked separately from the party pursuing her own goals while also campaigning for the Wyandotte constitution. Traveling widely to a number of towns, she delivered lectures and sought out women who could write and speak about woman's rights. She reported "fine audiences at Osawatomie, Prairie City, Baldwin City and Bloomington," although her reception in Lecompton, not surprisingly, was less than hearty. Riding by stage over dusty roads and sometimes facing hostile audiences, Nichols maintained her distance from partisanship, appealing to men of both parties.[73]

After canvassing for weeks, it must have felt like a homecoming to arrive in Moneka for the first statewide woman's rights convention on September 7. Nichols finally had a chance to embrace the Wattles family, who had provided the vital moral support and organization she needed. To the Moneka audience Nichols was a hero, the only woman in the territory brave enough to plead for woman's rights before a hall filled with male politicians. According to John Wattles, her speech before the well-attended convention was "most thrilling and convincing" and contained "more real *gospel* in it than often falls to the lot of mortals to hear." Afterwards the group passed a series of resolutions affirming that their advocacy of woman's rights stemmed from the "great God of Nature" and committed themselves to achieving universal "*human* rights." They pledged to honor marriage and as citizens of Kansas "to secure to woman her rights and equality with man in the security of a home and the means to make that home a place of comfort and happiness." Nichols had finally reached the zenith of her career with a leading role among supporters who affirmed the co-equality of men and women without fear that gender differences limited their equality in any way. When the Wyandotte constitution was ratified on October 4 by a 2-to-1 margin, she could count as accomplishments the "Universities and higher institutions of learning opened to our girls as pupils and professors.—A vote in Common School affairs; equal rights in our babies & our separate property & earnings & equal division of prop[erty]." Although much of the groundwork for this progress had been laid by radical free-state men, for Nichols it was a singular achievement.[74]

If the constitutional struggle launched Mrs. Nichols as a political player in Kansas Territory, her visibility as a feminist and abolitionist could prove problematic in its immediate aftermath. Her personal commitment to spreading woman's rights and ensuring that the constitutional guarantees were implemented was curtailed as the border region erupted with renewed anti-abolition furor. When she traveled across the river to Westport, Missouri, to lecture in the fall of 1859, rather than receiving accolades from an admiring audience, Nichols found herself sequestered with the hostess of her boardinghouse because a "'dozen rude boys,'" aroused by news of John Brown's raid on Harper's Ferry, threatened to denounce any "known Abolitionist."[75] The failed raid and subsequent execution of Brown, notorious for violence in Kansas, ignited southern fears while turning him into a Christian martyr for abolitionists. Meanwhile, fellow abolitionist Daniel Anthony was indicted by a federal grand jury for kidnapping fugitive slave Peter "Charley" Fisher from a Leavenworth jail and sending him to Nebraska on the Underground Railroad.[76] Nichols's own work with fugitives and her reputation as a defender of free Kansas were enough to link her with violent abolitionism, which now smacked of murder and treason.

Back in Quindaro, Clarina's connections with abolitionists both complicated and facilitated her work for women. Her personal life became embroiled in politics again when she befriended and sheltered Lydia Peck, a desperate and abused mother from New England who had arrived at Quindaro's hotel, seeking the whereabouts of her two young daughters. About two years earlier her husband, Horatio Peck—using the alias James Diamond—and the girls had turned up in Quindaro after Lydia had initiated divorce proceedings in an attempt to gain custody and financial independence. Once he learned of Lydia's presence, Horatio warned against any legal action, claiming he would take the girls across the border to Missouri and prosecute Clarina for "harboring" Lydia. Friends and neighbors advised capturing the girls, who were living in squalor with their ill-tempered father.[77]

But in a bold move designed to serve her political ends, Clarina offered instead to plead Lydia's petition for divorce and custody with territorial legislators, hoping to gain firmer legal backing for seizing the children. Republican lawmakers had passed a liberal divorce statute in 1859, providing for numerous causes including drunkenness. With the courts not yet operational, the legislature was still granting divorces, and Nichols hoped to parlay her prowess at lobbying into a custody decree for Lydia. She had steered clear of the dicey issue of divorce in Kansas, but with a liberal law in place she could easily defend mothers' rights to their children and advocate for more secure guardianship rights without appearing to promote divorce reform.[78]

Nichols arrived in Lawrence for the legislative session armed with the Peck case, ready to demonstrate a mother's need for equal guardianship rights, and a petition to codify such a measure. Using her political connections to gain a hearing before the Judiciary Committee, she appeared with Helen Hutchinson, William's wife, to enlighten the lawmakers about the Peck case and the entire scope of "woman's legal wrongs." In the ensuing days, Nichols gathered sufficient testimony to prove Horatio's abuse and Lydia's victimization, and after private negotiations with his lawyer and lobbyist, she succeeded in procuring a bill of divorce with custody for Lydia signed by the governor.[79]

These legislative proceedings notwithstanding, Nichols and her friends in Quindaro still needed to wrest Lydia's children from their father. While Horatio was in temporary custody and the children were staying with neighbors, a "little band of . . . rescuers" recovered the girls and sped the family out of town using the well-worn secret pathways of the Underground Railroad network. After his release Peck looked in vain for his children, enlisting the help of proslavery officials from Wyandotte; Nichols delighted in fooling the sheriff and his deputies, who scoured the town in search of the children for three days. While she and her abolitionist friends preoccupied the posse with false clues, Lydia Peck and her daughters were traveling back to safe harbor in Maine.[80]

Nichols's own arrest shortly thereafter was just as politically useful. Along with eight others, including her son Howard and daughter-in-law, Nichols was arrested in her home and charged with "kidnapping" the Peck children.

Even before the case was heard, she began enlightening the public about the injustice of her arrest under the pen name "Quindaro" in the *Lawrence Republican,* whose editor was more than happy to oblige. Embellishing the tale to enhance Lydia Peck's maternal role, she provided her readers with a theatrically cast and serialized drama; she sought to evoke sympathy for the victims of male abuse and their benevolent rescuers and to indict local Democratic officials. Six months after her arrest, a grand jury eventually dismissed the case, but not without providing Nichols an opportunity to exploit its political overtones.[81]

The Peck case was a perfect illustration of the legal wrongs that Nichols had detailed to her audiences for much of her political career, and it became one of her favorite tales in a repertoire of female triumphs over injustice. It conveyed her deepest personal and political concerns, the reason she championed mothers' rights, and the skills she employed to assist both women and former slaves. Although she continued to avoid divorce as a women's issue, in pleading for Lydia Peck, Nichols was reliving her own experience and publicly condoning divorce, at least for abused women, as an essential woman's right.[82]

Long before Lydia Peck arrived at her doorstep, Nichols had intended to lobby members of the territorial legislature for full equality. "We must besiege the State Legislature in earnest," she had written Susan and Esther Wattles. Just as predicted, the governor publicly denied that the constitution guaranteed school suffrage for women, affirming only that it provided "equal rights as *pupils!*" Confident that she could defend every argument presented, Nichols wanted to prove by example that women were capable of voting because they could "cope with men in their sophistries as in their logical deductions." She prepared and circulated two petitions, one urging legislators "to frame the laws of the State of Kansas . . . to fully establish the legal equality of Women with Men," citing their constitutional rights to property and custody as a basis, and another requesting a state referendum on a constitutional amendment for woman's suffrage.[83]

But when Nichols arrived in Lawrence, eager to save Lydia Peck, she submitted only a petition for equal custody, banking on her success with the politics of motherhood. It was not the first time she had compromised her goals or politicized the issue of child custody. Back in 1853 she had urged Vermont women to circulate a similar petition and beseech their representatives while she was absent in Wisconsin.[84] Fathers' absolute legal rights to their children had begun to erode by the mid-nineteenth century as judges used their discretion to recognize mothers' connection to child welfare in an era of increasing rates of separation and divorce. Yet no state had enacted equal custody. In fact, lawmakers in Kansas had recently affirmed the paternal rights of fathers as "natural guardians" of minor children, leaving mothers to face legal proceedings and court fees to prove their worthiness and their husbands' incapacity.[85] Having experienced this situation herself, Nichols sought to replace judges' discretion with a statute for equal guardianship, which she believed would codify the custody provision in the new constitution. Her ardent plea for Lydia Peck before the Judiciary Committee garnered the sympathies of friendly Republican legislators in the interests of all mothers.

In this forum, Nichols's reputation proved to be an asset. Showing their respect for one of the "strong-minded" mothers of Kansas, Republicans legitimized her presence by giving her a seat in the hall as a reporter and even awarded her a clerkship in the "Enrolling" department to help cover her expenses in Lawrence. "Blessed providence!" Nichols proclaimed; "Three dollars per day in scrip at 75c enabled me to stay and engineer the case."[86] And of course, the wages also helped fund her lobbying efforts.

To that end, she appeared daily with Miss Grant, a supporter perhaps from Quindaro or nearby, to press for equal custody, leaving the other petitions in abeyance. Besieged with divorce petitions, the legislators focused on revising the divorce statute rather than addressing the custody issue separately. In a session characterized by Republican merrymaking and apple throwing, they granted a record number of divorces (forty-three), rewrote the statute liberalizing procedures, and affirmed the authority of district courts. Given her former opposition to easy divorce, Nichols must have been astounded and also frustrated. The new law provided alimony for mothers during separations like that of the Pecks, but instead of granting equal guardianship, it supplanted parental rights with court authority, leaving custody to judges' discretion again. This was not an adequate remedy. "We do indeed need 'Old women' on the judge's bench for men are heartless, the best of them in office," she had explained years earlier. Whereas women's activism in New York that year resulted in a statute confirming joint guardianship, equal "rights to babies" was not encoded in Kansas until 1868.[87]

Notwithstanding the respect Nichols garnered from members of the Judiciary Committee, she became a target for Democrats seeking to undermine her credibility and Republican dominance. "The everlasting Mrs. Nichols and her yoke-mate, Miss Grant, are on hand for the purpose of participating in the affairs of State," quipped Democrat George Chase of the *Atchison Union*. Eager to discredit both her and the Republicans, he equated these "strong minded women" with "masculine women," who were "not satisfied with their physical condition" and bemoaned that they had "resigned their knitting work, and take upon themselves the business of legislation" in an effort to "attain man's estate." But he queried whether the legislation they sought could "repeal an ordinance of Nature." Always ready with a rejoinder in these newspaper wars, Nichols sent a copy of his remarks to the *Lawrence Republican* and asked Chase to send her copies of his paper; if he included sufficient yarn as well, she would "keep him stockinged until superseded in our labor of benevolence by some less aspiring knitting machine."[88]

This clever retort belied Nichols's resentment at the public insult and only served to animate Chase. He politely accepted her offer, extolling knitting work, but he persisted in his taunts by suggesting that the advent of machines had destroyed relations between the sexes, and that women should return to the traditional work of spinning and weaving. "Instead of teaching by example *home* virtues, . . . we see mothers trotting after politicians and conventions and dabbling in state affairs," he remarked. Nichols responded almost viscerally in a remarkable column that appeared on the front page of *Freedom's Champion*, whose editor was a leading Republican eager to challenge Chase at any opportunity. Under the byline "Annie," who lauded the advent of machines that relieved women from drudgery, Nichols used her own experience to defend her political activism, revealing the story of her first marriage in the process. It was no accident that she penned this tale at the same time she was pleading for Lydia Peck and equal custody; it appeared the day after lawmakers approved Peck's divorce, two days before completing the revised statute.[89]

"Annie" posed as "a plain, matter-of-fact, domestic little body," an obedient housekeeper and foil to the "'strong-minded woman.'" She was clearly scornful of female lecturers but mindful of "Mrs. Nichols's" capabilities. Despite her considerable household skills and devotion to her husband, "Annie" argued that the exhaustive labor of making cloth—even with the help of *"free white"* servants—would leave women no time for development of their intellects or to learn "lessons of virtue and goodness" that would make them fit marital companions. She peppered her long-winded account with sarcastic quips at "Mr. *Union*," as she rolled out her arguments for the benefits of technological advances—sawmills, railroads, sewing machines—that had lightened "*man's* labors" as well as woman's. But she saved the most poignant argument for the end, when she recounted "something about the character and history" of "Mrs. Nichols," hoping that the lady would pardon her for "drawing aside the veil from the sanctity of home and private grief."[90] By exposing her dark days as a milliner and boardinghouse keeper and her husband's treachery in "stealing" her children, Nichols outlined the injustice at the root of her activism, hoping to grab readers' sympathy and to silence George Chase. It was the first and last time she alluded in public to her personal history to justify her politics, but it was indicative of the level of maturity she had reached. In the end, Chase retreated, and Nichols continued her work at the legislature, able to claim victory in this contest of words and a divorce decree for Lydia Peck.

The incident marked a watershed in Nichols's transformation from benevolent reformer to fearless political activist, even in the face of these temporary setbacks. Though Clarina would never breach the bounds of womanliness, she was no longer afraid that her past would damage her reputation, dissolve her self-regard, or confine her activism. The social networks of progressive idealists she found in Kansas and the polite treatment she received in political forums bolstered her self-confidence and tore down the social stigmas that had circumscribed her public performance. Proud of her accomplishments, she had opened one door to the ballot box and secured equal property and custody rights within marriage. No other woman in the country could boast such constitutional guarantees. Few people at the time recognized school suffrage as a significant step on the pathway to full citizenship, and eastern activists, unwilling to tie their claims to women's familial roles, did not immediately follow her cue. Yet at the end of the century Elizabeth Cady Stanton praised Nichols for "her conversations with the young men of the State," which "made the idea of woman suffrage seem practicable" to lawmakers. On the long road to women's enfranchisement, Nichols had linked the radical notion to the brave mothers of Kansas and middle-class respectability. Recognizing that the battle was far from over, she believed it was an "entering wedge" in a series of progressive changes. Little did she know, however, that historic events would soon derail her reform efforts, as Kansans faced a devastating drought and the sectional conflict spread beyond the territory to the whole nation.[91]

The Price of Patriotism

8

The national life is in peril, and woman is constitutionally disabled from rushing to her country's rescue. Robbery and arson invade her home; and though man is powerless to protect, she may not save it by appeals to the ballot-box.

C. I. H. Nichols, 1863

A few months before the election of Abraham Lincoln, Republican rival Senator William H. Seward of New York visited Lawrence to rally the spirits of party stalwarts around the recent history of Kansas Territory. On September 26, 1860, he anointed the free-state men and women of Kansas as national heroes who had bravely defended "Human Freedom" without resorting to undue violence. "When I look at field after field, and cabin after cabin, and church after church, and school house after school house, where but six years ago was the unbroken range . . . ," Seward remarked, "I am prepared . . . to declare, and do declare, you people of Kansas to be the most intelligent, the bravest and most virtuous people of the United States."[1]

Seward's political rhetoric reflected the special place Kansas held in the minds of Republicans and confirmed the mission of free-state emigrants like Clarina Nichols, who had yoked their futures to the vision of a new life in the West. Kansans had overcome more hardships than many other pioneers, had succeeded in preserving their own freedom by barricading slavery from the territory, and had anticipated making a good living while planting progressive institutions on the prairie. Little did Nichols know that the violence and racial politics of Kansas would soon be magnified on a national scale and that the people of Kansas, who held a keen sense of the territory's role in precipitating the war, would remain embroiled in an ongoing struggle with Missouri's proslavery faction.

Nichols's perennial optimism about the future would be sorely tested during the next ten years. The upheaval caused by the Civil War not only disrupted the trajectory of the woman's rights movement but also threatened the future of Kansas, the viability of Nichols's home in Quindaro, and the lives of women and children she sought to rescue from the ill effects of patriarchy and slavery. At the peak of her career, she had firmly established her political identity as an accomplished lecturer—a strong-minded but loving mother who respected both marriage and genteel manhood—but the work had only just begun. Notwithstanding Nichols's ultimate goal of full suffrage, lawmakers still had not implemented the provisions of the new constitution with appropriate legislation. But a local drought and the advent of war interrupted Nichols's agenda, reduced her access to politics, and forced her to make hard choices between her loyalty to the cause of woman, to sustaining Kansas, and to the Union.

Nichols's appearance at the 1859 legislature had bolstered her prospects for future lobbying, and her desire to continue to shape public opinion was undaunted despite the difficulties she faced. The Wattles family had finally sent her a hundred dollars to continue her lectures and gather signatures on petitions to ensure women's legal equality within marriage in anticipation of the next year's session. Traveling by stage or hired wagon over dusty roads to Johnson and Shawnee counties, she claimed a few converts before worries about money and conditions at home curtailed her activism. Her son Howard, who lived next door with his wife and two babies, had fallen thirty feet from a building while working as a carpenter two years earlier.[2] Clarina had used a chunk of her savings to pay off his creditors to secure his home, and she had been worried about money ever since as the economic depression that had begun in the fall of 1857 began to affect Quindaro. No longer able to afford permanent hired help, she had turned to housekeeping herself while Birsha continued to teach school and George handled milking, tending the chickens, and cutting wood. She even decided to boost her income by taking in a "gentleman boarder," who proved helpful around the house, but she also needed a woman with domestic skills while she was away and a new dress for public appearances. To add to her miseries, her housekeeper Susannah, whom she hoped to hire temporarily as a substitute during the legislative session, had been snatched by Missouri "wretches."[3] Proslavery men just across the border continued to exercise their prerogative to kidnap former slaves and send them down the Missouri River for the reward money. Susannah's capture was a perfect example of the way politics not only interfered with domestic arrangements but more seriously threatened the freedom of local blacks. Unfortunately, neither Clarina nor the local papers recorded Susannah's ultimate fate, but her departure was troubling on both practical and ideological levels.

Even so, Nichols's personal problems were dwarfed by those of some of her neighbors. Quindaro had lost its favored position as a free-state port, and it was slowly losing population to other more prosperous river towns. Many of the institutions and businesses that had appeared so promising just a few years earlier were either defunct or bankrupt, and settlers were suffering from excessive land speculation. Over 600 residents still remained in 1860, but many were in debt and listed on the delinquent tax rolls; soon they would simply abandon their holdings. "You have no conception of the entire prostration of all kinds of business," wrote one landowner shortly after the war began. Nichols was better off than many of her neighbors; she still held $4,500 in assets, but the value of her property was declining rapidly and cash was in short supply.[4] More immediately threatening than these economic woes was the onset of a two-year drought. "The earth needs rain," Nichols had written Susan Wattles in June. "We have had just enough to keep alive the *hope* of crops!" After grasshoppers began feasting on the remaining crops in September, settlers piled into wagons in a slow exodus to avoid the ensuing famine. "All over Kansas were vacant homes, telling of an invader more terrible than 'border ruffians,'" Nichols explained. While the nation became fractured over the impending election of Abraham Lincoln, Kansans faced a "winter of despair, sickness and starvation."[5] By November 1860, they had organized a national relief campaign, and donations of food, clothing, and other goods arrived from nearby states.

Perhaps these conditions help explain why Nichols temporarily left the state in pursuit of lecture fees elsewhere until the next legislative session. She could hardly have expected to draw a large audience in starving Kansas. While Republicans in northern states championed Lincoln for president, Nichols took the train to Wisconsin, where she visited friends from the temperance campaign and gave several lectures. She no doubt celebrated the Republican triumph with them when Lincoln was elected, but optimism about the fate of the Union quickly soured. After seven states in the Deep South seceded, Northerners waited anxiously for Lincoln's response after he took office in March. Meanwhile, without southern obstructionists in the senate, Kansas was finally admitted to the Union on January 28, 1861, rewarding the state's long-suffering free-state leaders. Nichols was not even in the state that winter to applaud with compatriots, for she had accepted an offer to lecture in Ohio, where activists had launched a campaign to achieve full property rights for married women and joint custody.

Nichols was well known as one of the most effective speakers on these is-sues, and she was eager to reconnect with colleagues who were spreading the woman's rights movement westward. At its tenth anniversary, activists con-gratulated themselves on having achieved some progress on property rights, especially after New York enacted a comprehensive law providing wives with rights to their own earnings separate from their husbands, one of their chief goals. In Ohio, advocates had been petitioning for legal and political rights for nearly a decade, but legislators had only amended the rules of coverture to protect women from economic hardship and failed to enact either full property rights for married women or suffrage. By 1861, favorable commit-tee reports and sufficient public awareness suggested that the momentum for reform was shifting in their direction. Moreover, leaders Elizabeth Jones of Ohio and Hannah Tracy Cutler, who had moved to Illinois, had campaigned successfully in New York; and Cutler and Frances Gage, who had recently moved to Columbus, had orchestrated a similar campaign in Illinois the pre-vious winter. Jones solicited Nichols's help and paid her $12 a week plus ex-penses for nine weeks of lecturing. Local canvassers gathered thousands of signatures on petitions from all over the state, inundating lawmakers. At the same time, there was growing turmoil in the nation. "Women in goodly num-bers came out to hear, but men of all classes waited in the streets, or congre-gated in public places to hear the news and discuss the political situation," Nichols recalled.[6]

These veteran warriors in the woman's rights campaign were just the company Nichols needed to rejuvenate her spirits. All were of an age, class, and experience to command respect from both audiences and legislators. Af-ter observing Jones, Cutler, and Gage address the senate, one admirer noted, they came with "none of the charm of youth or beauty," but as mothers and grandmothers, "earnest, truthful, womanly, [and] richly cultivated by the ex-periences of practical life."[7] Like Nichols, Cutler and Gage had championed temperance and antislavery through the press; both had been columnists for the *Ohio Cultivator*, where they provided housekeepers with advice while enlightening them about woman's rights.[8] They also had experience in politics. During the campaign, Jones garnered support from the press, worked closely with lawyers who drafted legislation, and lobbied legislators as well. After meeting with one lawmaker, Nichols was assured that "something should be done," but she doubted that they would grant equal custody. None of her colleagues seemed to care as much about "the children" as she did.[9] Despite concern about the emerging threat posed by secession, lawmakers passed a bill granting married women separate property rights. Joint custody would have to wait until after the Civil War. On her way home to Kansas, Nichols gave several more lectures in Illinois, spreading her gospel in another western state, which enacted a separate property statute that winter.

Nichols was ready and eager to lobby at the new state legislature in Topeka, but her hopes were dashed as she confronted the reality of political wrangling. "O dear, men are not so good as I wish they were," she wrote Susan Wattles. The legislature had become a "deadly scramble for power" between the supporters and opponents of James Lane, a candidate for the U.S. Senate. A former Democrat and notorious free-state man from Indiana, Lane had earned fame for his dynamic oratory, his support of a free Kansas against Missourians, and his ability to command followers. But he was also volatile, vengeful, and racist, with little sympathy for New England abolitionists, and no friend of the new governor, Charles Robinson. Nichols was thoroughly disgusted with both sides in the political struggle, lamenting that men would put aside their religion, their "political creed," and "all their demands for freedom of the ballot box" to resort to vendettas.[10] Eventually, Lane was elected, but the turmoil among legislators destroyed Nichols's ability to get their attention. Moreover, wet weather had returned to Kansas. It soaked the walls of the legislative hall, resulting in peeling plaster and complaints of colds. Nichols fell ill herself, wished she were home tending to her leaking roof, but had no money to pay for the stage to Quindaro. Yet she assured Wattles "there are better prospects ahead while we are well & able to work out our salvation." With her customary optimism, she continued to lobby whomever she could find in her boardinghouse, including the head of the education committee, whom she confirmed "is for us." In fact, a law was eventually approved in May 1861 specifying that "white females" over the age of twenty-one could vote on school matters, which affirmed the racial exclusion that still existed in Kansas. Nichols doubted that a proposed constitutional amendment for full suffrage would be forthcoming, but she hoped their petitions would still prepare the way for a future, when Kansas was not "fettered . . . by her poverty."[11]

The specter of poverty would haunt Nichols herself as the nation entered the bloodiest conflict in its history. For the next two and one-half years, she remained anchored in Quindaro as the nation disintegrated. The war placed burdens on nearly all American women, but more so on southerners, who not only sacrificed their family members but also endured scenes of battle, plunder, food shortages, and Yankee occupation. Northern women spent months—sometimes years—struggling to manage finances alone and feed their families while they sought ways to support the Union effort as best they could. In the process, many undertook work such as managing farms and businesses, nursing, or government jobs, which they had never considered before.[12] As an abolitionist and widow with experience supporting herself, Nichols faced both the challenge of earning a living in difficult times and the urge to participate in what many abolitionists hoped would be the final battle to end slavery. The war placed a premium on local support networks and female patriotism, which subordinated the cause of woman's rights to saving the Union and abolishing slavery.

By the close of 1861 conditions in Quindaro had already begun to deteriorate, and Clarina's family gradually dispersed. After President Lincoln called for militiamen to end the rebellion, the war drained Quindaro of men, and some of their family members either returned east or relocated in nearby Wyandotte. Ever since Clarina had returned from Ohio, Birsha had longed to resume her studies at Eagleswood, and they finally saved enough to at least send her east to Vermont by the fall. Howard Carpenter enlisted in October 1861 and began training at Leavenworth; Clarina feared for her youngest son, George, who was only seventeen. She had anticipated sending him east as well to complete his education, but instead he accompanied Lucy Armstrong's son to a new Methodist college, Baker University in Baldwin City, about 45 miles away, leaving Clarina to manage on her own during the winter term. "I am all alone in my house & care for my cows, calves, pigs, etc.," she wrote Susan Wattles. Her daughter-in-law Sarah, who lived next door, provided female companionship, but Clarina worried about her two young grandchildren, who needed her "motherly care" as well.[13]

Concerns about how she would stretch her own limited savings reawak-ened Clarina's Yankee thriftiness. A box of "necessaries" from Vermont and sufficient food sustained her for a time, but cash, credit, and clothing were scarce. With a sense of shared sacrifice, she and other women helped knit the deserted community together with neighborly assistance. Priding themselves on making "something out of nothing," they remade old clothes by turning skirts inside out, patched the seats and knees of men's pants, and pooled their coins to assist friends, even though Clarina was reluctant to loan her remain-ing cash. In the absence of the local physician, she was called upon to assist with medical care and midwifery. Many of her neighbors were "too poor to send out of town & confident that I understood the cases & remedies," she told Wattles. After treating twenty patients successfully, she began to feel more competent in her healing abilities and proudly announced that she had helped a former slave birth her first free child.[14] Clarina felt just as satisfied with these domestic accomplishments, especially the aid and comfort she gave to new mothers, as she had after delivering a warmly received lecture. But birth-ing babies rather than legislation was a measure of how drastically her world had changed in one year.

Quindaro residents had more than money and health to worry about. Lo-cated just a ferry ride away from Missouri, where Confederate sympathizers vied for power, the townspeople feared for their safety. Most able-bodied men enlisted in the Union army, and residents had donated Quindaro's eight-pound cannon to the Tenth Kansas Infantry.[15] Missouri eventually remained in the Union but not until after a contest that pitted Union troops against secession forces in pitched battle during 1861. Clarina followed these local military actions closely, even composing a patriotic poem that championed the exploits of the pro-Union forces in Missouri over cowardly "Dixie boys." During the remainder of the war, border areas in Kansas were vulnerable to guerilla warfare as free-state "Jayhawkers" and Confederate bushwhackers from Missouri continued to wreak havoc in revenge-driven attacks. Notorious for its abolitionist activities, Quindaro was an easy target. After false alarms had called out the remaining men, including young George, Clarina kept her "Carpet sack & camp pail packed" in anticipation of a quick exit. By Octo-ber Union troops were driven out of Parkville across the river and the ferry-boat destroyed. Concern about what would happen when the river became frozen caused Clarina to lament, "If I am burned out or driven away I don't know which way I would go."[16] Her fears diminished when the Ninth Kansas

Volunteers arrived to protect the town, but this new level of security only hastened the demise of Quindaro. For three months during the winter of 1862 the troops helped fill a void in the town center and populated church services, but the commander also allowed the idle troops to expropriate the town's vacant buildings for their own purposes, to quarter horses in empty warehouses and ransack residences for firewood. "Doors, windows, casings, everything of its vacated tenements but their stone walls" disappeared from the bluffs of Quindaro, Clarina remembered. By the time the soldiers were restationed, the town had been gutted and the local Committee of Safety outraged. Meanwhile, the mix of population in Quindaro was shifting. An increasing number of impoverished escaped slaves and pro-Union Wyandots from Indian territory sought refuge in the town, adding new strains on its limited resources and its Underground Railroad network.[17]

As bounty hunters from Missouri continued to be a threat, abolitionists kept the secret pathways open to protect former slaves, and Nichols assisted when she could. On a beautiful fall evening shortly after the outbreak of the war, Fielding Johnson asked her to protect a fugitive from capture by a posse of fourteen slave hunters who were camped nearby. She quickly hid the woman, named Caroline, by lowering her into her cistern and covering it with a washtub, where the woman crouched "trembling and almost paralyzed with fear of discovery." Suffering from mental and physical trauma, Caroline required constant attention and words of reassurance, as her daughter had just been sold to a Texas slaveholder and her arm had recently been broken, perhaps in a struggle to save her daughter from the irons of the Deep South. To keep watch, Nichols pretended to sit up nursing George, who lay in an improvised "sickbed" close enough for her to monitor her charge without raising suspicion about her midnight movements back and forth to reassure Caroline. The evening passed without incident, and Caroline was secreted to another station in the network later that morning.[18]

While Nichols partook of these shared sacrifices, she chafed at her inability to take effective public action—to either assist the Union effort or pursue her political agenda. Sewing bandages and preparing lint for soldiers' relief were hardly enough to reassure Nichols that she was doing her part as bravely as her son Howard. Initially, she had considered joining Dorothea Dix's corps of army nurses, a patriotic impulse in light of the futility of political activism, but an appointment never materialized. She concluded that pursuit of the suffrage campaign was not only wasted time and money but might also appear selfish and unpatriotic when "men are struggling for the preservation of Govt." Moreover, she surmised that legislative reforms in Kansas had progressed as much as possible without "Constitutional equality." In her pragmatic fashion, she warned Susan Wattles that the cause would become "hackneyed" if they were not "careful to strike a hot iron."[19] Yet this assessment did not diminish her frustration that the war had interrupted their campaign. She was vulnerable to both poverty and bushwhacker pillaging, she felt increasingly isolated from both family and colleagues, and she was unable to express her patriotism more vigorously.

Susan Anthony and Elizabeth Cady Stanton echoed these sentiments in the spring of 1863 when they issued a call for the organization of the Woman's Loyal National League (WLNL), a new female-only political lobby formulated in conjunction with abolitionists and the Loyal or Union League movement. Both women had become frustrated with wartime politics, with their inability to find a role for themselves, and with Lincoln's limited Emancipation Act, which applied only to those slaves held in Confederate states, where he exercised no authority. Proclaiming that women were "equally interested and responsible" in a democracy, they hoped to steer Republican politicians toward freedom as a war aim and enlisted patriotic northern women into a massive national petition campaign urging Congress to abolish slavery forever. To avoid the taint of partisanship, the WLNL replicated the formation of Loyal National League clubs and Ladies Loyal Leagues to press for emancipation, which Stanton and Anthony believed would eventually lead to equal rights for all. By urging women to write, speak, and organize around a national issue of such importance, the pair hoped not only to end slavery but also to display the effectiveness of women's moral power in the nation's politics and their readiness for the franchise.[20]

Their appeal to a "grand idea, such as freedom or justice" resonated immediately with Nichols. In a letter to the WLNL convention in New York City, she proclaimed, *"No sacrifice of right, no conservation of wrong,* should be the rally-call of mothers whose sons must vindicate the one and expiate the other in blood!" Slavery was indeed a moral wrong that the nation could no longer tolerate, and she linked its continued existence to the "disfranchisement of the women of '76," who would have freed the slaves long ago if they had been "armed with ballots." As a result the Union was in a sorry state, Nichols concluded, "the national life is in peril, and woman is constitutionally disabled from rushing to her country's rescue." If given the vote, women could have checked the tide of disloyalty and "copperhead treason," she surmised, but instead the war was "adding a vast army of widows and orphans to this already large class of unrepresented humanity."[21]

Nichols's feminist plea was just the medicine Stanton and Anthony would have prescribed to stem female apathy, but it was out of step with the patriotic sentiments of most northern women at the time. By mid-1863 Stanton and Anthony reveled in renewed political action and their desire to support the presidential candidacy of John C. Frémont as an alternative Republican to the moderate Lincoln. But they also chafed at warnings about appearing either too feminist or too partisan in their organizing work. Appealing foremost to women's patriotism was a way to deflect attention from their former political work and their effort to influence presidential politics while broadening the base of the woman's rights movement. Most women who responded to the call were eager to show their loyalty to the Union, not enlist in a feminist cause that would have appeared selfish at the time. By February 1864, the WLNL had gathered 100,000 signatures to present to the Senate; it eventually garnered four times that many before final passage of the Thirteenth Amendment abolishing slavery on January 13, 1865.[22]

By that time Clarina Nichols had been in Washington, D.C., herself for over a year. It may have been her desperate need for money or the deteriorating situation in Kansas that finally spurred her to abandon her home and seek a way to make a living elsewhere for the duration of the war. The notorious bushwhacker William Quantrill with 700 men had raided Lawrence on August 20, 1863, burning buildings and killing 200 people, and residents in border towns panicked. In retaliation, the local Union commander ordered the evacuation of four Missouri counties in an effort to prevent future attacks, which created more chaos as Union sympathizers sought refuge in Kansas. Clarina's son George was nineteen, and she probably believed he could manage their home on his own. Howard had been disabled by an accident and transferred to the Veterans Reserve Corps for clerical duties; his wife Sarah joined him, working as a laundress to support the troops. More important, after teaching for a time at Eagleswood, Birsha had sought and received an appointment as a copyist in the Internal Revenue Office in Washington, and Clarina determined to join her and seek a clerkship for herself in December 1863.[23]

Both women would enjoy one of the more lucrative positions a woman could attain during the Civil War. Birsha secured her job through the patronage of Kansas Senator Samuel C. Pomeroy, whom Clarina knew from his role as general agent for NEEAC. Elected in 1861 during the tumultuous session of the first state legislature, Pomeroy was aligned with the abolitionist wing of the Republican Party with whom she had associated at the capitol. His office secretary endorsed Birsha as a woman of "Character" and intelligence, the daughter of "an earnest advocate and defender of the rights of the female race" and a party to the "great struggle for freedom" in Kansas.[24] Pomeroy was probably responsible for Clarina's appointment to a position in the Quartermaster General's Office as well. Hired as a copyist of government documents, she earned sufficient funds to remain in Washington, watch over her daughter, and satisfy her desire for patriotic service. The two women may have shared boardinghouse space, thereby reducing the high cost of living in the crowded city.[25]

Clarina and her daughter were beneficiaries of one of the federal government's first experiments in the employment of female clerks. Francis Spinner, head of the Treasury Department, had promoted the new policy as a cost-cutting and efficient means of expanding the workforce and freeing men for service during wartime. Birsha was the third woman hired in Internal Revenue, a division of the treasury, where she earned $600 a year at first and $720 by 1865, about half the wages of male clerks but considerably more than that of a teacher. Eventually the department hired nearly 450 "government girls," most of whom garnered appointments by proving both their middle-class respectability and their support for the Union cause.[26] Like Birsha, most of the newly employed clerks were young, single, and educated but also removed from family oversight and pioneering in a male workplace. As they took their places in government offices populated with young men, they were under considerable public scrutiny. Were they capable of doing the work efficiently? Would they distract the men with female "coquetries," or even worse, compromise their womanly virtue? Journalist Jane Grey Swisshelm, whom Clarina may have met because she also worked for the quartermaster general, cast her scornful eye on women who flirted and dressed inappropriately, but she also complained that the male clerks undermined the women's professional status as civil service workers with their polite but supercilious manners. A few months after Clarina arrived, rumors of "illicit relations" in the Treasury Department rocked the capital when improprieties practiced among three women and a treasury official reached the press. The ensuing congressional investigation tarnished the image of the female workforce until a House committee eventually dismissed the case as bogus, exonerated the official, and proclaimed the virtue of the "noble" female employees.[27] As a middle-aged widow with a son in patriotic service, Nichols was able to fulfill her duties without fear of compromising her respectability, but salaried employment per se placed her in a new and uncomfortable position.

As wartime employment drew increasing numbers of middle-class women into the workplace, they became objects of sympathy, perceived as needy and exploited. Perhaps that is why fellow copyist Jane Swisshelm sought to upgrade the professionalism of her colleagues. The image of the woman worker as a victim of misfortune rather than an independent, competent employee was enhanced in late 1864, when the female clerks mounted a joint effort to increase their salaries. The process of publicizing their plight highlighted the poverty of their living conditions and their meager salaries compared with those of men. "These are ladies of culture and refinement, reduced by misfortunes," who were doing the same work as men for less pay, reported one Washington correspondent. Birsha partook of the protest by writing two congressmen about the issue, one of her few efforts on behalf of women.[28] Yet Clarina was unaccustomed to this role; since the 1840s she had empathized with the plight of working-class women but hardly thought of herself as a member of the group.

While she endured the social ramifications of her new employment, Nichols confronted the equally challenging task of finding her way among the sea of white and black faces that had clamored into wartime Washington. "The city is like a beehive on swarming day," exclaimed Washington correspondent Lois Adams, "all bustle, activity and apparent confusion." Sprawling in all directions, its muddy streets were lined with a mix of magnificent but unfinished public buildings, "ungainly" townhouses, dilapidated shacks, and soldiers' makeshift quarters. Women traversed the walkways gingerly, hoping to avoid blackening their wide skirts in the dirty debris strewn in the gutters and sidewalks. They jostled amid columns of uniformed men, hustling merchants, lobbyists, and an expanding population of freed people. Seeking refuge and aid behind Union lines, these "contrabands," as they were called, arrived daily on foot or in wagons, finding shelter in makeshift government-run camps. Slavery had only recently been abolished in the District of Columbia, and congressmen found daunting the task of accommodating the overwhelming number of former slaves—over 20,000 by the end of the war—with food, clothing, and work. Many lived in shanties or slept in alleyways and roamed the streets looking for food or work.[29]

In this teeming and multiethnic crowd, Nichols found ways to associate with women who shared both her class and ardent patriotism, if not her more advanced views on woman's suffrage. Senator Pomeroy's wife, Lucy, whom she had known in Kansas, would have provided the perfect introduction, but Lucy had been a victim of typhoid after failing to leave the city during the hot summer months when disease spread rapidly.[30] Still, the senator may have introduced Nichols to the circle of active Washington ladies, including wives and daughters of politicians, army officers, journalists, and other northern women who had flocked to the city to work in hospitals or freedmen's aid. In May 1864 she witnessed the organization of the Ladies National Covenant, a patriotic group designed to unite northern women around a boycott of foreign-made cloth and apparel. The society appealed to women to follow the example of their Revolutionary foremothers, who boycotted British tea and consumer products in the interest of liberty, and to help stem the flow of gold out of the country during the crisis. Anna S. Stephens, a popular New York author, spearheaded the movement after critics suggested that northern women were far less patriotic than their southern counterparts and that wealthy women in particular were selfishly donning silks and ribbons and entertaining themselves at parties while men were dying in the field.[31] At the organizational meeting, Nichols became frustrated with the limited nature of the covenant pledge, which was to begin in two months' time and contained an obvious loophole in that women could continue to buy foreign goods if "absolutely necessary." Noting that "the country needs our help" now, Nichols roused the silent audience to a bustling rabble in a patriotic speech appealing to soldiers' hardships even as the presiding minister sought to keep order. Lurking in the wings was Elizabeth Cady Stanton, who seconded Nichols's motion to strike the offending language. In the end, their efforts resulted in the adoption of a more self-sacrificing pledge, hardly a radical move for two women who had been promoting woman's suffrage for fifteen years and seeking to end slavery through direct political action.[32]

Other northern women in the city were more attuned to Nichols's benevolent and abolitionist sensibilities and linked through the WLNL in a network of female associations. Many had migrated to Washington during the war as agents of northern antislavery societies, which became active in the freedmen's relief effort by sewing clothing, raising money, and distributing aid to former slaves. Both white and black women traveled south as teachers and aid workers; others, such as the renowned Sojourner Truth and Josephine Griffing of Ohio, came to Washington to work in the government camps and for private agencies like the National Freedman's Relief Association or under the auspices of the Freedmen's Bureau. For her part, Griffing was overwhelmed with the sight of decrepit old men, miserable mothers with babies, and feeble invalids who were without decent shelter, blankets, or food, and believed black families had been completely degraded by their former enslavement.[33]

Whether it was through these associations or Clarina's acquaintance with Senator Pomeroy, she also turned to aiding freed women and children. A little over a year after her arrival in Washington, she was hired as matron of the Home for Destitute Colored Women and Children in Georgetown. Lucy Pomeroy had helped organize the charity before her death, and with a keen interest in its success, perhaps the senator suggested Nichols to fill the matron position. Incorporated as the National Association for the Relief of Destitute Colored Women and Children by Congress in early 1863, the society succeeded in securing housing in a stately home resting upon a knoll in Georgetown and surrounded by eighty acres. From the beginning the project appealed to the wives of leading northern congressmen and officials as well as abolitionists from Boston and Philadelphia who funded the organization by becoming life members. They left the management of the home largely to the middle-class women of Washington, but the prominence of its supporters helped ensure the full cooperation of the War Department and later the Freedmen's Bureau. In fact, Secretary of War Edwin M. Stanton confiscated the Georgetown residence of Richard S. Cox, who had abandoned his home to join the Confederate army, and turned it over to Lucy Pomeroy, the first president of the association.[34]

When Nichols arrived on the scene in February 1865, however, the organization was recovering from a public scandal over mismanagement. During the intervening months the members had successfully raised funds from freedmen's aids groups and other benevolent organizations throughout the Northeast but had failed to find a satisfactory matron to cope with difficulties at the home. Housing, feeding, clothing, and educating thirty to forty orphan children and several old women posed considerable challenges in a mansion designed for a family residence. Freedmen's labor had been used to construct a dormitory, laundry, cookhouse, and schoolroom, and Maria Mann, niece of Massachusetts school reformer Horace Mann, was hired as teacher.[35] But when matron Lucy N. Colman, a former teacher and seasoned abolitionist from New York, began to work at the home, she found the children living

Clarina Howard Nichols, vignette, c. 1864–1866, when she lived in Washington, D.C. Courtesy of the Grace Hudson Museum and Sun House, City of Ukiah, California.

in crowded quarters, ill fed, unclean, and infested with lice, parasites, and various contagious diseases. Colman blamed Mann for ignoring the deplorable conditions and mistreating the children with cruel and inappropriate discipline. An investigating committee recommended firing both Mann and Colman, but the board failed to act. Colman promptly resigned anyway, convinced that the managers were reluctant to confront the situation for fear of losing their philanthropic support from well-known Boston reformers.[36] The controversy would have remained at the board level but for the intervention of Jane Swisshelm, who considered herself a champion of the oppressed and enemy of self-interest and political corruption. As a member who had contributed to the home, she appeared at the annual meeting to issue a scathing rebuke against Mann, the organization's board members, and the philanthropists from Boston who supported them. Swisshelm painted Mann as "rigid, severe, and even barbarous in the treatment of the children" and accused her of throwing several helpless, sick children outside to die after they had soiled their beds. Swisshelm blamed the board for sidestepping the issue to protect the teacher and their financial backing. Widely reported in Washington, the scandal cast a shadow over the organization. Mann eventually resigned, taking the desks and other school equipment she had secured with her.[37]

Clarina Nichols became the new matron a month later. Her willingness to assume this challenging position—which cut her wages to $300—reflected her commitment to both aiding freed slaves and performing the kind of benevolent work to which she was more accustomed. Not only was she confident in her housekeeping and management skills but she anticipated associating with like-minded women in a common endeavor. They sought to apply "Christian love and charity" to improving the prospects for "the colored race" by sheltering them and teaching them how to read and to support themselves.[38] This motherly attitude typified the approach of many northern white women, who perceived blacks as members of a dependent, racially inferior group rather than equals. Although white women organized and ran the home, it was also a focus for black women involved in racial uplift. Elizabeth Keckley, dressmaker to Mary Todd Lincoln and organizer of the Contraband Relief Society, had helped support the founding of the organization, and just prior to Nichols's appointment, the well-known former slave Harriet Tubman had agreed to help restore order, clean up the premises, and nurse sick children until a matron could be found.[39]

UNIVERSITY OF WINCHESTER
LIBRARY

Conditions at the home improved significantly during Nichols's tenure, causing the executive board to praise "our excellent Matron," whose "varied acquirements have rendered her peculiarly adapted to the position." Luckily for her, the home's notoriety had brought increased attention from General Oliver Otis Howard, head of the Freedmen's Bureau, who provided food rations, secured a fresh water supply, and reconstructed the outbuildings with freedmen's labor. Although six children died that winter, the home began to thrive under Nichols's management, an assistant, and new teachers furnished through northern charities. Crops were planted on the adjoining fields, and the children began to adapt under kinder discipline. Still, it was a new and daunting task. This was the first time Nichols had been in charge of a large institution or lived intimately among former slaves, most of whom were not accustomed to the standards of cleanliness and decorum demanded from middle-class women. When an inspector from the Freedmen's Bureau arrived to review the operation, he found it in sufficiently good order to begin placing more children under Nichols's care, which raised the number to sixty-nine. She enlisted help from Birsha, who showed great sympathy for the children and taught the girls to sew. With endless needs to be met, the board continued to raise funds and secure donations of clothing, toys, and food, which arrived monthly from northern aid societies. Nichols collected nearly $50; on a trip to Vermont in May she secured clothing and other donations through her sisters and other relatives in Townshend, Chester, and Meriden, Connecticut, as well as from her Quaker friend Hannah Darlington in Pennsylvania. Despite the difficulties of the project, the cause combined her need to be actively involved in a patriotic effort, her empathy for the poor, her antipathy to slavery, and her self-identity as a benevolent woman.[40]

While in Washington, Nichols witnessed both the heights of celebration as the long war came to a close and the depths of despair at the assassination of President Lincoln. After the fall of Richmond, the city was the scene of a marvelous "jubilee" marked by throngs of celebrants who crowded the streets to view fireworks, listen to marching bands, and enjoy the illuminated buildings draped with Union flags. The Treasury Department, where Birsha still worked, "glowed like an immense furnace." But only ten days later, the city was "shrouded in mourning" and unable to function as church bells tolled for the slain president.[41]

For the remainder of 1865 Nichols maintained her post at the home, but changing postwar conditions clouded its future. Amid the crowds of Union soldiers passing through the city, freedmen sought jobs and aid; anxious politicians hoped to procure favorable appointment in President Andrew Johnson's administration; and former Confederates returned to the capital offering loyalty oaths to the reborn nation. During the summer, rumors that Richard Cox would seek a pardon to regain his property and his subsequent offer of a thousand dollars for the association to vacate the premises prompted board members to petition the president to forestall his pardon. With the support of Stanton and Howard, nearly a hundred women appealed to Johnson in person, hoping to use their moral authority and status to persuade him not to restore the irresponsible and disloyal rebel on the site of their benevolent project. Although the issue remained unresolved through the remainder of Nichols's administration, Cox was eventually pardoned. He reoccupied his home even before the association was ready to move to new quarters and later sued for damages. In the meantime, Nichols had submitted her resignation in February 1866 and returned to Kansas.[42]

The war years had been a tumultuous and disruptive time for Clarina, who found greater use for her enviable domestic skills than her political acumen. Her family had been dispersed, but luckily all her children had survived largely unharmed. She had experienced both the privations of wartime living and some of the new opportunities it opened for women. She had worked in an office for the first time and lived in a multiracial home. Mostly, however, she had been frustrated, as national priorities obliterated her access to politics and she became debilitated by trying to avoid poverty. With the exception of a brief statement in her memoir about "saving the helpless waifs of slavery," Clarina never mentioned the two years she spent in Washington, which left her drained rather than triumphant. It was Kansas and her political work at home, not the chaotic scene at the nation's capital, that inspired Clarina and provided her with a unique identity. The war had "broken the chains of the slave," yet it was still unclear how either Kansas or the nation would treat its new citizens or the women who had lent their moral power to the cause.[43]

Visions of Universal Freedom

> The hour of universal freedom is coming for us without violence. Those
> who have . . . freed the slave and demand suffrage for him, will not
> forget the women who prayed and wept and wrought for them in the
> battlefield, in hospital and rebel prison. We have been on a political
> equality with the negro too long not to be lifted with him now.
> *C. I. H. Nichols, 1867*

Nearly a year after the Civil War ended Clarina Nichols mounted
the steep hillside above the Missouri River to her home in Quindaro,
where she sought refuge after her labors in Washington. In her late
fifties with a recurring wintertime cough, she was weary from the
experience, but she fully intended to resume her political work, believing the promise of "universal freedom" would finally become a
reality through the political process. The war had rearranged politics forever, insuring the predominance of the Republican Party, on
which Nichols had pinned her hopes for attaining woman suffrage.
Yet the party was deeply divided over how to restore the Union. In
Washington, she had already observed the way President Johnson
had pardoned Confederates and reinstated their property and the
split among congressional Republicans over how to readmit southern
states and redefine citizenship. Leaders of the woman's rights movement who had quieted their demands and proved their loyalty during
the war were now ready to hold the party accountable for guaranteeing the natural and civil rights of women along with those of blacks.
Kansas, where "Liberty fought her first victorious battles with Slavery" and where lawmakers had passed progressive legislation for

women, would become a central battleground in that struggle. It would represent Nichols's last opportunity "to fight a *big* fight."[1]

Nichols remained optimistic that her Republican friends in Kansas would honor their promise to support woman suffrage now that statehood had been attained, but postwar Kansas was not the same as the territory she had come to call her home. Republicans controlled state politics, but Yankee free-state leaders could no longer claim a dominant place in the legislature or in Quindaro as newcomers flocked to Kansas after the war. The state's population would triple by 1870, when 13 percent was foreign-born and nearly 5 percent African American. With the slavery question settled, eastern Kansans were building railroads and institutions while the new wave of settlers pushing into western frontier areas was causing conflict with the remaining Indian nations.

Quindaro had also become more diverse, but the town's commercial activity paled next to that of neighboring Wyandotte. Empty buildings and newly sprouted cottonwood trees in formerly bustling streets were visible reminders that the value of Nichols's property had shrunk markedly, though she had purchased more promising but undeveloped land in Wyandotte during the war. A few of Quindaro's original settlers persisted and small businesses survived, but some of Clarina's friends were gone, and the population mix was shifting. The town hosted the Wyandot Tribal Council, yet Wyandots were far less numerous than blacks. Reverend Eben Blachly and his wife had opened a school for black children, renamed it Freedman's University in 1865, and offered basic education and training. By 1870, nearly a third of the town's 2,100 residents were African American.[2]

Meanwhile, Clarina's family was becoming racially mixed as well. While she was in Washington, her son George had married Mary C. Warpole, a fifteen-year-old Wyandot whose family had originally migrated from Ohio. After her parents died, Mary had found shelter in the home of John and Mary Hicks, Wyandot farmers with seven children of their own. Son of the last hereditary chief, Hicks had chosen citizenship over further migration in 1855 when the tribe negotiated a treaty with the federal government providing allotments for their land in Wyandotte County. He served on the tribal council, performed official duties for the tribe, and became trustee for Mary's government annuity in 1859. As a member of the Wyandot community, Mary had no doubt been raised in the Methodist church and educated at one of two schools the tribe operated.[3] Clarina left no record of her initial reaction to her son's marriage, but she had a number of friends among the Wyandots and later expressed sympathy with her new daughter-in-law, whose health was frail. A year after Clarina returned home, Mary and George had a baby daughter. The infant was not the only youngster in the household, for Birsha had adopted a three-year-old black child, probably from the Georgetown home, whom she brought back to Quindaro. In her mid-thirties, Birsha "wanted a child to love & care for" and convinced her mother that Lucy Lincoln, who was named after the slain president, would remain her responsibility.[4] Two years later Mary and George had another daughter, and a son was born in 1871. They named him Birney, perhaps after George's friend at Eagleswood, son of abolitionist James G. Birney.

Just as the next generation was remaking Clarina's household, so too the woman's rights movement was reshaped during national Reconstruction. Passage of the Thirteenth Amendment abolishing slavery raised former slaves to the same legal status as women, and woman's rights leaders recognized a historic opportunity to secure universal rights as Congress attempted to redefine citizenship on a national basis. Elizabeth Cady Stanton and Susan B. Anthony were horrified, however, when radical Republicans proposed wording in the Fourteenth Amendment to guarantee black civil rights in a reconstructed South but specifically excluded women by inserting "male" as a qualification for suffrage. Leading abolitionists, black and white, were convinced that former slaves held a greater claim to the protection derived from suffrage than women. Rather than combining the issues, they began collaborating with radical Republicans to secure black suffrage while pacifying Stanton and Anthony with the notion that "this hour belongs to the negro," as Wendell Phillips famously remarked.

Seeking a new strategy, activists turned the 1866 national woman's rights meeting into a forum for organizing the American Equal Rights Association (AERA) with a goal of linking black rights and woman's rights through a campaign for universal suffrage. They still hoped to convince Republicans in Congress that their work for emancipation and their wartime loyalty proved their worthiness as voters, but their lobbying efforts proved fruitless. Frustrated with the Republican Party and with those abolitionists who resisted a joint campaign, Stanton, Anthony, Lucy Stone, and other leaders in AERA redirected their energies to the states, where voting rights had traditionally been defined and lawmakers were considering constitutional reform. In a provocative move targeting the failings of the Republican Party, Stanton even

ran for Congress, hoping to test whether women could hold office; she garnered twenty-five votes. By the close of 1866, woman's rights leaders were
preparing to launch a series of campaigns in New York, New Jersey, Massachusetts, and other states just as legislators in Kansas raised the prospects for
enfranchisement in one of the most progressive states in the nation.[5]

When the Kansas legislature convened in January 1867, Nichols was far
more confident in the Republicans than her eastern colleagues. With a clear
legislative majority, the Republicans were anxious to uphold the state's reputation for expanding human rights. Under the leadership of Charles H. Langston, a convention of "Colored Men" had promoted black suffrage as early as
1864, and after two more years of lobbying, they had extracted a promise
from incoming Governor Crawford to introduce the issue as a proposed referendum.[6] But divisions emerged quickly between radicals, who sought to
punish the South by disqualifying traitors from voting and advancing black
rights, versus a pro–President Johnson minority reluctant to grant any additional rights in Kansas. A smaller faction of liberal Republicans, men Nichols
had known from free-state days, was committed to universal suffrage, and she
and other local women from Wyandotte and Lawrence circulated petitions to
bolster that effort. After easily ratifying the Fourteenth Amendment, legislators deliberated for nearly two months over whether to remove "white" and
"male" from the suffrage clause in the state constitution. Though Nichols was
apparently ill and unable to lobby in person, other women attended the session. Woman suffrage had legislative champions in Speaker of the House Dr.
William W. Updegraff from Miami and especially in Senator Sam Wood, who
had originated the issue in Kansas at the Leavenworth constitutional convention in 1858. Both men were instrumental in securing passage of a compromise whereby the legislature offered three referenda for voter approval: one to
delete "white" from the suffrage clause, another to delete "male," and a third
to disqualify former Confederates from voting. Notwithstanding her misgivings about the Republican Party, Susan Anthony rejoiced and predicted that
"Kansas, the young and beautiful hero of the West, may be the first State in
the Union to realize a genuine Republic."[7]

Nichols's enthusiasm bubbled over as she anticipated that Republicans
would deliver on their promise of 1859. In a letter to the *Vermont Phoenix,*
she informed her eastern friends that she had "found a generous soil" in
Kansas after all because "those who have fought the oppressor, and freed the
slave and demand suffrage for him" would not forget the loyal women.[8] Her

assessment was premature, however, and overlooked the Republicans' partisan goals. They were willing to grant black suffrage not only because blacks deserved it but also to obtain their votes and ensure Republican dominance, whereas woman suffrage could potentially empower Democrats, for many believed that white women would simply vote with their husbands.

Nichols's hopes were quickly undermined when leading Republicans decided to target Sam Wood for having perpetrated "the shabbiest and most disgusting" of "tricks and shams" ever to defeat their Reconstruction goals. An enigmatic political operative, Wood was a free-state leader and forceful advocate of human rights but also notorious for having undercut black suffrage in 1864 when it served his political ends. To Henry Blackwell, the short, "slouchy" Wood was a hero, despite his "extremely careless" appearance. His blue eyes could "twinkle with the wickedest fun" and his "witty, sarcastic, and cutting" remarks could devastate opponents. To radical Republicans, especially Langston, he appeared to be blocking the black suffrage proposal unless it included women and manipulating Democrats into supporting woman suffrage on racial grounds. Opponents dubbed the session "Sam Wood's Circus," questioning his sincerity. Wood argued that it was inconsistent not to open the franchise to the women of Kansas, who clearly displayed their loyalty to the Union, unlike the rebels who deserved to be disfranchised. But fears that woman suffrage would ill serve the campaign to make Kansas a shining example of progressive reform and black freedom would prove to be well founded in the heated summer ahead.[9]

Believing in Wood's sincerity, Nichols followed his lead as he sought to outmaneuver the radicals into making woman suffrage a party issue. Shortly after the legislature adjourned, he organized an "Impartial Suffrage Convention" in Topeka, at which former governor Charles Robinson asked Nichols to speak. To give the campaign legitimacy, Wood convinced the group to elect the current governor and lieutenant governor as top officials, using their prestige without their tacit agreement. He appealed to the AERA for both money and effective speakers who could lend legitimacy to the joint effort from their association with abolition. In this way, Wood sought to build momentum for universal rights and position himself as the champion of an international movement. Lucy Stone and her husband, Henry Blackwell, arrived in Kansas in time to attend the convention, where she joined Nichols in the effort to persuade reluctant Republicans not to "drop the woman" from the meaning of "impartial." But Wood's strategy was a dangerous one, given the anger of

Samuel N. Wood, a staunch "woman's rights man," introduced equal suffrage at the constitutional convention in Leavenworth in 1858. Courtesy of the Kansas State Historical Society.

his opponents. These professional lecturers from the East, followed later by Olympia Brown, Elizabeth Cady Stanton, and Susan Anthony, attracted large audiences, but they also became easy targets for opponents, who labeled them as outside agitators and as "strong-minded women" largely interested in their own fees, not in the concerns of Kansas women.[10]

That was not true of Nichols, who was delighted to see Stone in Kansas and to witness that local women, lauded for their "strong-mindedness" during territorial days, were becoming active in the movement. Sara Robinson and others organized a vibrant wing of the Impartial Suffrage Association in Lawrence, and other local societies coalesced around the state. Casting themselves second only to "the pilgrim mothers of America, having endured more privations and taken a more active part in public affairs" than any women in the nation, they argued that the closing of "dram shops" and construction of schoolhouses proved that women were wielding their "power for good" in Kansas. Blackwell reported to Stanton that "all the old settlers" supported the issue, having seen the bravery and endurance of their pioneering wives, and Stone reiterated, "the women here are grand," concluding that "it is not possible for the husbands of such women to back out." Blackwell was giddy with their success at subduing Republican insurgents and prematurely counted black leaders, judges, ministers, and a majority of the state's newspaper editors as allies. Nor did the couple display any reservations about soliciting "utterly unscrupulous" Democrats even if Republicans peeled away. With great anticipation for their speaking tour around the state, Blackwell predicted that "the woman and the negro will rise or fall together."[11]

The optimism that infused the initial weeks of the campaign faded slowly during the summer. While Blackwell had ignored potential pitfalls, Stone had recognized the dangers in the political landscape. It was clear to her that Kansas politicians distrusted Sam Wood but regularly sacrificed party principles themselves and maintained a "terrible desire for office."[12] During the ensuing months, Wood not only faced the ire of radical leaders who saw woman suffrage as a political threat but also had difficulty organizing sponsors among small-town Republicans because he lacked the attention to detail required to schedule lecturers and distribute campaign literature effectively. Much to Anthony's distress, AERA was too lean to forward eastern money, nor could she secure money from the Hovey and Jackson funds. She eventually supplied five thousand woman's rights tracts for circulation, including Nichols's 1851 speech on "The Responsibilities of Woman." Wood contacted legislators in

rural areas, but he neglected to follow through with instructions for canvassing and sometimes failed to supply the lecturers he had promised. Inadequate
local organizing meant little advertising and disappointed audiences. Nonetheless, Olympia Brown, a graduate of Antioch College in Ohio and pastor of
a Universalist church in Massachusetts, proved to be a popular, effective, and
indefatigable speaker. She spent four months canvassing the state and educating receptive audiences in hundreds of lectures, yet she complained about her
grueling schedule; she gave two or three speeches and traveled up to forty or
fifty miles a day in a crude buggy over rugged dirt roads in the beating hot
July sun. In Mound City she met with "disaster misfortune & defeat" partly
because Wood had not supplied her with the itinerary. Despite assurances that
her traveling expenses were covered and an escort supplied, these services often devolved upon uninformed local people instead.[13]

Nichols encountered her own difficulties engaging in the campaign and
working with Sam Wood. Using her remaining funds from the Moneka Woman's Rights Association, she spent four weeks in the spring lecturing in nearby
counties where she could travel by horse while he was organizing the state
and offering to supply her services as a speaker. Yet the two had not agreed
about the schedule or compensation. Nichols had little money to cover distant
traveling expenses; canvassing had interrupted planting, and grasshoppers
had eaten the remainder of her crops. Moreover, Wood had rearranged the
schedule and promised her appearances while she found it necessary to operate a summer school at home to help meet expenses. In turn he accused her of
acting on her own in the vain hope of reaping all the rewards of a successful
campaign, rather than coordinating with him in a systematic approach to the
canvass. The two were clearly at odds over tactics and perhaps over political
style as well. They both appealed to Susan Anthony, who wrote to Wood: "We
must leave each to work in their own individual way," she advised, "for each
one's peculiarities meet some needs which the other's cannot."[14]

Nichols's presence in the 1867 campaign was unique because she represented the achievements of the past. On the one hand, she was the only well-
known suffragist in the state, the singular, outspoken, and homegrown mother
of Kansas. Thanks to Nichols, advocates could claim that women had voted in
school meetings with no adverse consequences and perhaps strengthened "the
cause of popular education." Yet even to Republicans, she was a reminder
that women in Kansas already possessed a considerable array of privileges.
With property rights, equal custody, access to education, and school suffrage

to their credit, what more did Kansas women need? Moreover, the legislature had recently passed a temperance measure that would allow women to vote on the issuance of local liquor licenses in most towns. Nichols's motherly style had highlighted this kind of feminine influence, not the universal rights that Wood was proclaiming. Her "Responsibilities" speech was fifteen years old and addressed the concerns of an earlier generation of women—access to education and property rights—not suffrage per se. Republican opponents such as John A. Martin, editor of the *Atchison Daily Champion* who had published her defense of woman's rights in 1860, turned her sentimental appeal to home virtues into a defense of the status quo. He suggested that far from protecting the home, woman suffrage would destroy the harmony of the home and marriage with it; the state's liberal legislation protecting the interests of women proved that they were adequately represented.[15]

If Wood found Nichols's approach outmoded, his concerns were somewhat misplaced. Not only was preservation of the home still a central concern to voters, but fifteen years of political activism and frontier experience had also reshaped Nichols and her rhetoric as much or perhaps more than any woman in the movement. Mothers' inequality under the law was still a prominent feature of her speeches, but now she articulated their need for the ballot as a measure of protection just like that of former slaves. She assured audiences that her remarks applied "equally to the Negro" and appealed to their pride in a progressive Kansas by warning that the state's advanced civil rights legislation for women could easily be reversed by "the prejudices of Eastern people coming into the State." In print she argued that Republican government rested upon the consent of the governed and forcefully defended the right of black women and men to the elective franchise as a measure of their equality. Reminding the white men of Kansas of their own history, she shamed them for violently resisting the "bogus" laws of 1855 and then creating a "bogus" government themselves, which unfairly subjected the "women and blacks of the state" to laws and taxation without their consent.[16]

Her reasoning, if not her righteous scolding, matched the dominant pro-suffrage rhetoric of the era. Civil rights activists insisted that the future of the republic depended upon the protection of every class of Americans through a government by consent of all adults. Kansas was just the place where that could happen. Even the British liberal John Stuart Mill, who was advocating for universal suffrage in Parliament, portrayed Kansas as "foremost in the struggle for the equal claims of all human beings." Though he refused to openly support the Kansas campaign, Theodore Tilton of the *New York Independent* went one step further to flatter Kansans, noting that it "is only a partial innovation" in Kansas "because women already vote ... on all questions relating to schools." Local proponents predicted the state would not only remain a beacon for enlightened citizens everywhere but also reap just rewards by enfranchising its "virtuous, intelligent, clear-headed and *sober*" women, who would "cleanse the stream of vice, intemperance and corruption" in the state and help attract a wave of intelligent newcomers.[17] This argument that women brought special capacities to the ballot box often accompanied the more predominant refrain for universal rights.

But the advocates of woman suffrage faced a rising tide of opposition within the Republican Party, and neither Nichols nor other activists were able to work collaboratively within the partisan environment. At the national level, Republicans renewed their focus on black suffrage as a means to implement Reconstruction policies; failure to achieve such a measure in Kansas would represent a major embarrassment to the state party and fuel the resurgence of Democrats. One by one, proposals for black suffrage had been defeated in other northern states, except Iowa and Minnesota, and the woman suffrage proposal threatened its survival in Kansas as well. By the end of June woman suffrage had been summarily dismissed elsewhere, most importantly in New York, where Stanton had lobbied the legislature intensely. Anti-Wood Republicans in Kansas dodged the issue at first and then adopted a platform without it, affirming that it was not a party issue and releasing party men from any obligation to vote for it. The formation of an Anti-Female Suffrage committee in September crowned the Republican effort to defeat the measure by pitting the two referenda against each other. Outwardly the state's congressional delegation remained committed to both proposals, but even Senator Pomeroy, a leader of the universal suffrage effort in Washington, campaigned too little and too late in Kansas to reverse the cleavage between the two measures.[18]

Black leaders were equally frustrated. Notwithstanding his initial fury at Wood, Langston had put aside his anger and planned to work cooperatively, but he noted that unless black suffrage was achieved, "striking the word male out will do me nor my race any good." By September he and other black leaders were just as disenchanted with the anti–female suffrage Republicans and affirmed their support for impartial suffrage while canvassing the state for the black vote. Democrats disavowed all three referenda, but a number of rebel Democrats signaled their willingness to entertain woman suffrage, perhaps only to insure its defeat. Republican newspaper editors remained outwardly neutral, but by summer's end a handful lashed out against the specter of women voters. Discredited by his party, Wood retreated to his home in Cottonwood Falls, where he continued to coordinate his faltering campaign and briefly issued his own paper espousing "progressive principles." In late September, his participation diminished inexplicably due either to illness or political calculation.[19]

Without sufficient funds for travel and frustrated with Wood's arrangements, Nichols abandoned plans to lecture in August and turned her attention to defending woman suffrage in the press. She responded vehemently when leaders of the Anti-Female Suffrage committee attacked her friend Lucy Stone. Long after Stone had left the state, Charles V. Eskridge, a leading Republican legislator, labeled her "the petticoat chief" with "free-love proclivities" in the pages of Isaac Kalloch's *Western Home Journal.* "She don't believe in marriage for life," he charged, "but wishes all to do like her and that seed-wart she carries around with her," referring to Henry Blackwell and the couple's egalitarian marriage. Irate, Nichols defended the absolute legality of Stone's marriage and her belief in the integrity of the institution, noting that Stone had issued a "scorching rebuke" to free-love advocates in the early 1850s. Nichols charged Eskridge with "gross slander" and reminded readers that women could reject men like him from public office if they had the ballot. No friend to woman suffrage either, editor Kalloch was a Baptist minister and a Republican operative. He ridiculed the issue by calling it a "joke" and insisted that the women of Kansas were uninterested in gaining the vote. Yet to fuel the debate he printed Nichols's retort, which represented a clear reproach to both men and her first open break with a Baptist and his political party.[20]

Nichols's challenge to clerical authority became more explicit three months later when she defended her own lectures against the claims of a Presbyterian minister, Eben Blachly of Quindaro. With the support of friendly editor Richard B. Taylor, who placed her articles entitled "Equal Rights" prominently on the front page of the *Wyandotte Commercial Gazette,* she confronted Blachly, president of Freedman's University and a hero to former slaves. Whereas some clerics supported the issue, he attacked woman suffrage by grounding male political authority, not in rule by consent but in God's plan as outlined in Scripture and delegated to men. Ultimately, he relied upon physiological sex differences to support his position; women could not enforce submission to their rule, he asserted, because they are weaker than men. Just as the wrath of a vengeful God was necessary to punish transgressors, so too manly physical power would enforce just government.[21]

In a lengthy refutation later entitled "The Bible Position of Woman, or Woman's Rights From a Bible Stand-Point," Nichols outlined her alternative reading of Scripture. Rather than male prowess, she rested her morality on Christ's teachings "to establish *love* as the rule of a regenerated world" and the apostles' practice of Christian forbearance. She had been developing her philosophy for some time and had given several well-received speeches on the topic even before the war. Like other woman's rights leaders, she sought to discredit the scriptural injunction that wives submit to their husbands because of Eve's original sin while also appealing to a higher law of God's creation. Returning to Genesis I: 27–28, she emphasized the marital partnership embedded in the creation story, highlighting the phrase "male and female created He them." By coupling simultaneous creation with God's command to "multiply and replenish the earth," antebellum feminists had established the co-sovereignty of women and men. To refute Blachly's rule by "brute force," she presented her own image of an intelligent and virtuous Eve, a paragon of nineteenth-century womanhood. As a co-sovereign with equal rights and responsibilities, Eve was a companion without whom Adam, an obvious sinner, would fail. The subjection of women arose from the tyranny of men and the application of Eve's predicament to all women, she avowed, not from God's law. As for wifely submission and silence, the apostles taught the same forbearance to "unjust rulers, oppressive masters and domineering husbands" as a necessity to insure the survival of the infant church and the spread of Gospel principles in the adverse political context of the first century. Moreover, the nation's men had already defied St. Paul by overthrowing a "monarchical government," employing "civil" rather than religious tribunals, and freeing "millions of slaves," and could therefore "hardly refuse to abolish the last relic of barbarous government by conferring on women the right of self government."[22]

Nichols's exegesis was an attempt to reconcile her life's work with the religious ideology that shaped her worldview and animated her sense of mission. For years she had simply ignored the contradictions between her political activism and biblical interdiction on women, preferring instead to highlight her Christian love of humanity. By the mid-1860s she had reached a level of maturity—and perhaps frustration—that spurred her to respond publicly to the kind of provocative attacks that she would have only fumed about privately in the past. Now she aligned with those feminists who had long ago rejected ecclesiastical authorities while retaining religious principle. In an expanded version of her position published in 1870 to influence Vermont's suffrage campaign, she buttressed her arguments with comments from respected theologians and dissected the Old Testament. Supplying example after example of women engaged in public affairs, the economy, and civil society, she refuted the notion that women were completely subject to male authority in biblical times and lauded their role as Christian teachers in the early church.[23] Reverend Olympia Brown, who delivered sermons while advocating woman suffrage on her lecture tour in Kansas, also highlighted the complementary gender roles in God's worldly scheme and connected the link between Christian love—rather than brute force—and the advancement of women. Even Elizabeth Cady Stanton, known for her religious skepticism, took this essential view of women at the time and reassured Kansans that women's moral worth as found in the Bible would elevate politics. Both women later abandoned their commitment to Christianity as the root of goodness in the world, and Stanton eventually became the leading proponent of the falsity of the Bible—indeed of all divinely inspired religious ideologies—as the source of women's bondage.[24] But Nichols continued to cling to Scripture as a moral and spiritual guide, even as she decoded the Bible as a historical text subject to misuse for political purposes.

Dispensing with religious sanctions on women was one way Nichols could continue to participate in the 1867 campaign, though it was Anthony and Stanton who dominated the headlines with rallies throughout the region. They arrived in Kansas in September with high hopes of rejuvenating the Impartial Suffrage Association, which by this time was competing with a parallel canvass sponsored by the Republican Party. In the larger cities, their speeches were gala affairs, often accompanied by a brass band or the popular Hutchinson Family Singers, who delivered four-part harmony in support of temperance, abolition, and woman's rights. The campaign in Kansas had garnered great significance for the future of the woman suffrage movement. If successful, it could prove to Republicans that woman suffrage and black suffrage were not antithetical, validating the approach of AERA. Stanton and Anthony remained frustrated that none of the leading male abolitionists or politicians would come to Kansas. Even though the New York abolitionist press and Republican radicals in Congress finally provided supporting statements in early October, they were thoroughly annoyed by the sluggish effort and infuriated by the influential editor of the *New York Tribune,* Horace Greeley. They held him accountable for having killed woman suffrage in New York; now he issued a begrudging statement agreeing to suffer the experiment in Kansas.[25]

Clarina must have been elated, however, when Anthony and Stanton finally arrived to work with her Republican friends, and she watched how warmly they were welcomed by large audiences in Wyandotte. Charles Robinson had agreed to shepherd Stanton on an exhaustive 1,500-mile tour. She bumped along with him in an open-air carriage on dusty roads, slept in log huts, and spoke in unfinished schoolhouses and churches even in Democratic strongholds. Enthused at first with the "charming weather" and feeling "like a new being" as she explored "the outskirts of civilization," Stanton was soon disabused of the notion that pioneering, much less canvassing, in Kansas was easy. Her speeches, however, were lauded throughout the state as she championed human rights for all, praised the people of Kansas as the "first to consecrate her own soil to liberty and equal rights with the precious blood of her citizens," and displayed a complete mastery of the topic. She reported that Kansas women, who had often withstood the "difficulties & dangers" of defending their homes alone, were clearly "ready for the new doctrine." Taking advantage of Nichols's legacy, they had come out in the dead of winter to carry the vote for a new schoolhouse in one district, and their refusal to endorse liquor licenses had kept the state from becoming a seat of "rum holes."[26]

By the time Stanton returned to Lawrence, however, Anthony had made a fatal shift in strategy. In their vexation with the Republican Party and sensing defeat, the eastern feminists decided to appeal to Democrats, only a quarter of the electorate in Kansas, hoping to convert their instincts for partisan revenge into a positive outcome for woman suffrage. At the suggestion of an activist from St. Louis, Anthony planned a lecture tour with the flamboyant Charles Francis Train, a Copperhead and notorious self-promoter who supported woman suffrage but also aimed to defeat the Republican Party. An accomplished performer, Train entertained his audiences dressed as a dandy by shattering their commonly held assumptions about politics with comic one-liners and epigrams ridiculing Republicans and belittling blacks, which drew record-breaking crowds. Mostly he promoted himself while paying lip service to the virtues of intelligent female voters over those who possessed only "Muscle and Color and Ignorance." The laughter he elicited was often coupled with disgust at his irreverent attacks on national leaders and racial slurs; advocates feared that he was ridiculing woman suffrage along with every other progressive notion he mocked. Nichols may have witnessed his saucy performance in Wyandotte; if not, she certainly read about his irreverence and his racist remarks. Yet Anthony and Stanton, who had been known to elevate the voting potential of educated womanhood over "the lower orders of black and white" men, appeared unaware of the partisan implications of their collaboration or that Train was a significant liability.[27]

In fact, it was not even clear to them after election day that they had misjudged his potential to destroy their credibility and undermine their high-minded efforts. Train's rhetoric trivialized both measures and aggravated Republicans, especially his transparent attempt to split the party along racist lines. They accused the eastern feminists of partisan tactics and lumped all the outsiders together, claiming that Kansans need not listen to "advice from strong minded women or copperhead gas-bags."[28] Although 9,091 men opted for woman suffrage on election day, a record number, they represented fewer than a third of voters, whereas 10,483 (one-third) voted for black suffrage. Only the referendum disfranchising rebels, the one measure that clearly met the Republican Party's goals for Reconstruction, passed. The Democratic vote probably boosted the total for woman suffrage in some counties—especially Leavenworth, where party men included the measure on ballots prepared for voters. But it was Republican slippage that worried Charles Robinson, who believed Train had done more harm than good and politely educated Stanton about the political fallout. Only the old "liberal thinking, antislavery men & women" remained committed to the movement, and he predicted, "not one of Train's democrats can be relied upon in the future." Where would the "true friends of female suffrage" find a party now, he lamented.[29]

In the end, it was clear that woman suffrage would benefit neither the Republican Party's goals nor a majority of male voters, who would not hesitate to honor the legendary free-state mothers of Kansas but feared the consequences of opening the franchise to women or to blacks. The appeal to Democrats reinforced the notion that outside advocates of woman suffrage were anti-Republican and seeking their own political gain, which undermined their central argument that equal justice required suffrage for all. Even without this mistake, radical Republicans no longer found the martyrdom of the state's "strong-minded" women useful to their partisan goals, and the moniker lost its positive application as the campaign became a stage for the national debate over Reconstruction policy. As much as Nichols and other local advocates sought to remind them that women had served the state well, most voters believed women were adequately represented through the family and the state's progressive legislation.

The defeat in Kansas proved to Republican leaders that woman suffrage was a lethal issue, but for Nichols it was evidence that male politicians were unlikely to act on principle. This was the second time her advocacy of woman suffrage had become embroiled with black civil rights and she had seen woman suffrage subordinated to party goals. Not only did she feel betrayed by Republicans who sacrificed their moral principles by poisoning the campaign with those "white male dragon's teeth," but the debacle also confirmed her fears that the constitutional rights she had secured for women were under threat. Even in light of these misgivings, however, Nichols did not reject future collaboration with the party, noting only that men would enact legislation favorable to women when their "*general interests* carried women's interest with them."[30]

Stanton and Anthony, to the contrary, were disgusted with partisanship and the Republican Party. They continued to associate temporarily with Train, who generously offered to fund a new weekly paper, the *Revolution*, devoted to woman's rights. But the alliance and Train's racism had infuriated Lucy Stone and other members of AERA who maintained ties with the party, and the bitterness that arose between these leaders eventually split the movement. Feeling betrayed by the abolitionists, Stanton and Anthony created the National Woman Suffrage Association (NWSA) and sought new allies in the labor movement, claiming that the Republicans were establishing "an aristocracy of sex on this continent," while Stone, Blackwell, and others formed the American Woman Suffrage Association (AWSA) in 1869. Caught between loyalty to race and sex, black feminists largely straddled these divisions, which persisted for twenty years as eastern leaders began a new crusade devoted solely to the advancement of women.[31]

If Kansas appeared to be losing its place as the beacon of universal rights in the West, Clarina Nichols and a few other stalwart men and women were still determined to prove otherwise. Iowa and Minnesota adopted black suffrage before passage of the Fifteenth Amendment, which enfranchised black men in 1870, but no western state opened the ballot to women. Even so, in 1869 the territory of Wyoming outdid Kansas by enfranchising women, a measure initiated not by Republicans but by a Democrat. With prompting from activist women, he employed a racially charged strategy lauding the potential of white women voters, who supposedly would help "civilize" the sparsely populated territory.[32] In Kansas, while Sam Wood and editor Richard Taylor of the *Wyandotte Commercial Gazette* persisted in a short-lived effort to maintain the Impartial Suffrage Association, Nichols met with her old friend Lucy Armstrong and other women in Wyandotte to organize a suffrage association. But lack of money plagued the effort of this and other local suffrage groups. Nichols complained, "I can't get to any of our conventions, even in Kansas—*expenses!*" Members of the Woman Suffrage Association of Topeka submitted petitions to both national and state legislators to eliminate "male" from the constitution, and Nichols offered to lecture if they would underwrite her. Lacking adequate funds, they declined. Nichols eventually delivered her favorite talk on the "Bible Position of Woman" to the group, but without sponsorship, plagued by fragile health, and lacking spare cash from her farm produce, her public speaking career was all but over.[33]

Yet one of Clarina's strengths was her ability to bounce back from adversity and to avoid holding grudges against opponents. With an abiding interest in politics, she sought to maintain a persistent voice for women. Rather than losing faith or harboring ill will against the Republican Party, she attended local Republican rallies and was quick to seek an opportunity to shake General Ulysses Grant's hand when he passed through Kansas during the presidential campaign of 1868. "As one of the mothers of Kansas," she greeted him, "if we could vote, we would vote for Grant," assuring him that "when we are enfranchised we will vote for just such men." Accustomed to avoiding confrontation, Nichols remained loyal to Susan Anthony and supplied her with material for the *Revolution* whenever she could, while sympathizing with the organization of the AWSA as well. "These petty struggles are hateful, belittleing,"[sic] she later wrote her friend, bolstering Anthony's last effort at maintaining unity as the eastern movement split. Hoping to preserve this vital friendship as her lifeline to former colleagues, Clarina reaffirmed her belief in Anthony's "whole-souled, unbroken" commitment and predicted that they "were strong enough to swarm." Anthony and Stanton had become outspokenly racist in protesting the Fifteenth Amendment, which rankled Stone and other abolitionists; in 1869 the two women proposed a Sixteenth Amendment to enfranchise women. Nichols noted only that the former amendment was "mean" in excluding women but a progressive step nonetheless and maintained faith in constitutional reform, either through the NWSA's national strategy or the state-by-state approach the AWSA's leaders pursued. Safely removed from the personal bitterness that characterized divisions among eastern leaders, she was freer to support any strategy to promote women's advancement.[34]

To keep her voice alive and earn a few dollars as well, Nichols resumed her role as a press correspondent. She reconnected with her roots in Brattleboro by sending columns to Addison Brown, her ally on school suffrage, who had become editor of the *Vermont Phoenix*. As a "daughter of Vermont," Nichols praised Brown for supplying readers with "soul food, good and digestible" and touted Kansas, where "provisions plenty," rising land prices, and bountiful fruit harvests awaited them. Far from radical at first, it was nearly a year before she complained that Vermont had made little progress in protecting the natural rights of married women compared with Kansas. Boldly asserting that "marriage to woman is legal death," she outlined why women needed the ballot, and made her final venture into Vermont politics with publication of the "Bible Position of Woman."[35] Just as Lucy Stone and other suffragists were touring the state in winter 1870 to advocate for a constitutional amendment enfranchising women, Nichols submitted her biblical exegesis. But neither her revisionist theology nor Stone's speeches made much headway against the rhetoric of the state's orthodox ministers or a barrage of press invective. At the constitutional convention in June, where Clarina's conservative brother Aurelius served as a delegate, only one man voted for the measure, and it was not Aurelius. It is tempting to conclude that she was still fighting old battles.[36]

Closer to home, Nichols pursued a defensive strategy to hold Kansas legislators to account for the reforms they had passed as the political climate became increasingly conservative. With little faith in the legislature, she insisted that only constitutional reform would safeguard woman's rights. After the editor of the official state journal, the *Kansas Daily Commonwealth*, solicited her commentary, she had an outlet to show why women's "speedy enfranchisement" was necessary to stem backsliding and to prevent newcomers with antiquated ideas from tampering with the constitution.[37] Her fears were not overstated. Much to Nichols's dismay, in 1868 legislators eliminated women's access to the vote on liquor licenses in cities, where half the population lived. Wyandotte and other cities were left to wallow in the "whiskey demon," she complained, because the city council rather than a majority of men and women opposed to licenses determined the outcome. Meanwhile, she urged women to exercise their right to vote for state and county school superintendent, a matter of interpretation under their equal constitutional right to participate in school affairs. After judges rejected ballots from several women in Topeka, Carrie Winans and the Topeka Woman Suffrage Association challenged the ruling, prompting the Kansas Supreme Court to deny that women could exercise this option. Irate, Nichols wrote a fierce defense of her constitutional clause, "the Supreme Court of Kansas to the contrary notwithstanding." By 1870 she concluded that "little by little," men were "chipping away the rights secured to women by our first Legislature."[38]

Much of Nichols's advocacy in the post-1867 political environment involved defending against what she called "class legislation," which favored men and disregarded women's interests and the precious homes they had created. Mothers' rights were still implicit in her commentary but she stressed the recognition of women as equal citizens within marriage. She complained that notwithstanding a wife's separate property, a husband could do whatever he wanted with the couple's common home and their stock of goods, livestock, and crops without her consent; widows, but not widowers, with children over the age of twenty-one were entitled to only half the estate and were often forced out of their homes during property divisions. Wives needed equal access and control over all marital property, Nichols argued, advocating in effect for an equitable community property system.[39] Although she continued to rely upon women's superior claim to home values, she was more forthright in demanding women's citizenship on a par with men's. When opponents accused her of fomenting unnecessary dissent between husbands and wives destructive to society, Nichols denied her ill intent and blamed unequal laws for any "antagonism between the sexes." Affirming that "our christian [sic] civilization is mainly responsible, both for woman's subjection and for the rights and privileges she now enjoys," she aimed only to harvest the fruits of "the practical unity of the sexes—as of the races—in the development and perfection of society and government."[40] Equal protection in marital law and enfranchisement would bring the full measure of women's special qualities to bear on social problems.

If this subtle shift in her philosophy signaled a more expansive role for women in society, it did not diminish Nichols's rhetorical skills. She was still seated cozily before an open fireplace on an October evening with a "cup of fragrant Japanese, a pumpkin sweet and a Yankee doughnut." She flattered lawmakers by appealing to "noble manhood," worthy of women's "respect and love," even if their wives were mortified by their "low jests" regarding womanhood. To those who accused her of "wearing the breeches," she proposed replacing the American eagle with this "emblematic of male government" to ensure the "perfect unity and fitness" of our symbols with our principles. But underlying her sarcastic quips, she was profoundly exasperated. "Again the sovereigns—white men folk—of Kansas are being represented in Legislative session at the Capital," she mused, "while the unenfranchised women of the State, thoughtful, often sorrowfully, and with little hope of any great good to the oppressed and suffering victims of legalized wrong, watch reports of their proceedings."[41]

This sense of fading hopes and lost opportunities reflected the turmoil and difficulties Clarina faced in her household as much as her frustration with the growing conservatism of Kansas politicians. Even before the 1867 campaign was over, her son Howard had begun the process of moving her house in Quindaro to property she had purchased during the war in neighboring Wyandotte. By the following winter she had settled into "one of the most beautiful and romantic situations in the State," according to editor Richard Taylor, a local booster. Far from "romantic," the new venture would require both money and labor to make it productive and cause her considerable frustration. She likened the move to having been "pulled up and, with rootlets torn and limbs barked and broken, set out again to recover the old growth and vigor."[42] She would miss the sympathetic group of men and women who had shaped Quindaro culture and suffered together during the war. In her mind the town had been a seat of radical abolition and liberal thinking, whereas Wyandotte, where proslavery Democrats had persecuted blacks and city fathers condoned drinking, was symbolically repugnant.

Yet the move to Wyandotte seemed a wise investment. In the postwar years, Wyandotte had experienced explosive population growth as new settlers flooded into the area, and unlike sleepy Quindaro, it was developing as a center of regional transport and commerce. In the six years since Clarina had purchased her new thirty-four-acre farm, she claimed that land prices had increased fourfold. She was still located in a rural, racially mixed neighborhood, but Wyandotte had swelled with nearly 4,800 residents. Situated at the juncture of the Kansas and Missouri Rivers, the city boasted new bridges that funneled traffic in all directions, facilitating its development as a railroad hub to the West and agricultural processing center for the county.[43] Clarina's son George helped her with her farming work, but for a while at least he and

Mary lived in Quindaro, where Mary's Wyandot connections remained strong, and she held allotment rights. Meanwhile, Howard bought an adjoining lot in Wyandotte and developed a mixed-produce farm with Sarah and their two adolescent children.[44]

In addition to help from her sons, Clarina had anticipated her daughter's companionship and financial contributions. Birsha had used some of her savings to continue her education after returning to Kansas, perhaps in anticipation of pursuing a teaching career or schooling children again in their home. But these plans were all put aside when Birsha agreed to marry widower George Franklin Davis, a former Civil War general from Vermont. At thirty-seven, she was a latecomer to marriage, but that did not inhibit Davis from pursuing her to Kansas in hopes that she could fill the empty place in his household. Despite a fifteen-year gap in their ages, Birsha's childhood friendship with Davis's deceased wife linked her to Vermont and the possibility that she could replace the mother of his two children. When they married on June 19, 1868, and subsequently left for Vermont with the children, Clarina lost her dearest companion. "Since Bertia [sic] left my sky is leaden," she bemoaned a year later. "I seem to have lost power to make sunshine."[45] She had not only relied upon her daughter for support and enjoyed her sunny disposition but also harbored a slim hope that Birsha would even become involved in women's politics. That was unlikely with her new husband. Notwithstanding his age, his ready-made family, and the demands of domestic management Birsha faced, it was his old-fashioned ideas and, ironically, his devotion to the orthodoxy of the Baptist Church that galled Clarina. She wished her daughter well and even wrote affectionate letters to her new step-grandchildren, but she held out little hope for Birsha's future.

To make matters worse, Birsha had left her five-year-old adopted daughter, Lucy Lincoln, behind with Clarina. Though Clarina had not welcomed the added burden Lucy posed, she cared for the child for nearly three years, struggling with her unruly behavior and nursing her through a difficult illness. Lucy was not only an irritating and recalcitrant child but also a sad reminder that Birsha was gone and had shirked her responsibility. Even Birsha had become frustrated with Lucy, who displayed a talent for lying and evasion at an early age though she had first appeared "so white & pretty," according to Clarina. In frustration, she claimed Lucy was a "natural born thief & liar" able to "beat any white woman or men" at the practice and eventually vowed to "get rid of her" as soon as she could. These racist remarks belied Clarina's

publicly expressed hope for racial mixing in America, but they were not unusual at the time. Many northerners and even other abolitionists held ste-
reotypical beliefs about the immorality, misbehavior, and laziness of blacks,
racial preconceptions that in this case inhibited Clarina from recognizing
Lucy's individuality. Instead, she dubbed her "my Topsy," after the young,
unruly slave child in Harriet Beecher Stowe's *Uncle Tom's Cabin,* a term she
also applied to another young black woman George "scared up" for household work. But unfortunately, Lucy could not be transformed by the power of
love like Stowe's Topsy, nor would Clarina fully grasp her own form of race
prejudice.[46]

By contrast, she expressed nothing but concern for her daughter-in-law
Mary and respect for her Wyandot relatives. Mary's health was so frail, especially during and after her pregnancies, that she could do little of the domestic
and farm labor most households required of women. She harbored common
symptoms of tuberculosis, a recurring cough and "weakness of the lungs"
with sporadic hemorrhaging.[47] But her deficiencies did not cause Clarina to
resent her presence. In fact, Clarina spent considerable effort investigating the
administration of the Wyandot tribal agency and why Mary failed to receive
either the total amount due her from sale of allotment lands or the annuity money set aside for minors from her former guardian. Having befriended
Christianized Wyandots for years, Clarina regarded Mary as a descendant of
a proud and intelligent people with admirable cultural traditions and fine
moral values. After witnessing the annual Green Corn Festival in Quindaro,
she praised former governor William Walker's informative address about
tribal history and marveled at the "home like, every day simplicity" of the
large kettles of free succotash for everyone. Less enthusiastic about the "mo-
notonous" drumming and "ungraceful" dance, she admired the "good order"
and absence of smoking. Yet she had little patience with corrupt Wyandot officials, who cheated Mary out of most of her allowance, and little faith in the
ability of the probate court to rectify the injustice.[48]

These financial worries only added to Clarina's household frustrations and
the sense of helplessness she felt stemming from her constant need for more
cash to meet expenses. While extolling the harvest of plentiful crops during
good seasons for her readers—including her own potatoes, oats, wheat, corn,
melons, tomatoes, onions, apples, and peaches—she suffered with the problems all farmers faced: unstable prices, high labor costs, unpredictable rain-
fall, and constant debt. Offsetting poor harvests with sales of eggs, chickens,

or butter became a last resort. It was not that Clarina lacked thrifty habits—mending a worn-out garment to make it look new still gratified her sense of Yankee pride. But she was older and her health more fragile. The high price and scarcity of labor sometimes forced her into the fields to mow clover, where on one occasion she fell, bruised her arm, and injured her hip. Barely able to "rake together" enough to pay expenses, she suffered under the burden of a $250 debt and constant worry about meeting her tax payments.[49]

Indeed, from the time she moved to Wyandotte, Nichols began complaining publicly about taxes as the source of her economic woes. "Taxes absorb the fruits of the economy and leave the larder bare," she bemoaned in 1869. To her dismay, the Wyandotte county clerk had failed to pay her an $11 refund due her on twelve acres of city land, and she chose to make him accountable. It was not unusual for Clarina to fuss about money in private, but this time she publicized her plight in Wyandotte's *Commercial Gazette,* thinly veiling her self-interest with remarks about the tight budgets of disfranchised widows forced to hire expensive male labor or plow the fields themselves. When the clerk defended his integrity, she refused to let the issue die and even submitted her tax receipts for publication to prove her case. Despite the politeness of her rebuttal, by airing personal grievances, Clarina undermined her credibility as an advocate and showed her proclivity to slip into a form of righteous public scolding. No longer reticent about her personal life, she appeared angry and frustrated rather than high-minded.[50]

Nichols's willingness to turn her monetary problems into public—even political—issues reflected both her stretched finances and her inability to be as politically active as she would like. Unable to make headway on woman suffrage, she projected her frustrations onto Wyandotte officials, whom she continually berated for allowing whiskey licenses. She even joined a legislative petition to return a section of the city, including her twelve acres, to its former status as part of the township, a political move putting her at odds with Republican editor and ally Richard Taylor. He supported the city council whereas Nichols blamed it for taxing her without improving the rural roads she and her neighbors relied upon.[51] In frustration, she resurrected her old pseudonym, Deborah Van Winkle, a reincarnated old farm woman from Jersey Forks, Wyandotte Turnpike. "Aunt Debby" had "mazin" things on her mind that would soon "give way" if she didn't "speek out." Over the next few months, Van Winkle issued her petty complaints mixed with occasional quips about the "clamor of the strong minded wimin for rights," as she ruminated in the folksy and sarcastic style that had served her well in the past. As an outlier in Wyandotte, she aimed her barbs at "City sportsmen" who shot her ducks and boys who snatched her ripe apples; the "shabby look" of her neighborhood was distressing, and irresponsible city officials had shut the office and gone to a "dog fight" between "two miserable, degraded men." Aunt Debby offered snide remarks about the new "evangelical horrorzen" arrayed against the "wimin's rights movement" and queried about the fate of ministers and churches if the women who populated them all "turn infidels," as some claimed they would.[52] Taylor seemed to enjoy Nichols's entertaining columns and even reprinted one of her signed essays on property rights in the same paper as a folksy column "From Aunt Debby." But after a less flattering columnist from Quindaro insinuated that Van Winkle was a self-promoter and all but exposed her identity, she politely retired her pen, ending Nichols's double life. In turn, he forgave her for "occasional exhibitions of crabbedness" as these effusions were emitted from a learned woman "on a farm made almost isolated from the world by bad roads, dangerous bridges, impenetrable forests, impassable ravines, and no good Mr. Van Winkle or 'any other man' to share her solitude."[53] To some extent, he was right. She was lonely and unhappy, yet his comments also revealed an appreciation for her witty retorts and superior intellect.

Returning to earlier forms of writing accompanied by vague memories from her past would become recurring themes for Clarina as she reached her sixties. Both her Van Winkle columns and her letters to the *Commonwealth* were filtered with brief glimpses from her childhood and former career that surfaced to enrich her prose. Family scenes reminded her of how much she still missed her daughter, and recollections of the early days in territorial Kansas evoked a life of vigor and public activism that she could no longer pursue. "Ah, Susan," she wrote Anthony, "you are a favored individual, to be allowed to fight a *big* fight." Gleaning small comfort from this private and public correspondence, she wanted to "cry out" against the circumstances that kept her "from joining the triumphant march of womanhood."[54] Yet during the next decade she would become even more isolated from her roots in Vermont and the site of her most significant triumphs. She had made her mark in frontier Kansas, when political opportunities had opened to advance woman's rights. But those conditions no longer existed, and she would soon be migrating to another American frontier.

10

The Last Frontier: California

> As isolated, historical facts, how very trivial all these "reminiscences"
> appear! . . . But to the social and political reformer . . . trifles teach the
> relations of things, and indicate the methods and course of action that
> result in world-wide good or evil.
>   *C. I. H. Nichols, 1881*

Age and nostalgia prompted Clarina Nichols to begin reminiscing
about her life as a reformer even before she left her adopted state of
Kansas, the place where she had hoped to create a western haven for
women and freed slaves. Despite frustrations with its politicians, she
believed the most conservative lawyers and ministers remained back
East, that she was still part of a vanguard of enlightened citizens
dedicated to liberalizing and civilizing the West, and that she could
inspire another generation of idealists. By 1870 women in the territories of Wyoming and Utah could vote, an apparent recognition of the
progressive nature of change west of the Mississippi River. Clarina
doubted that she would ever leave Kansas and continue further west,
even though two of her children had removed to opposite ends of
the nation. "My children wander from me," she lamented. "I am
now too old to follow. I never can make another home. The years are
few to look ahead: long, very long as I look back to girlhood."[1] Yet in
December 1871 Clarina sat somewhat uncomfortably in a Union Pacific railcar on a well-worn pathway to California, headed for another
adventure in frontier living. Resettlement in a new state dislodged
her sense of place on the prairies of Kansas but not her identification
with its founding or with the march of reformers across the nation.

She was familiar with the privations of pioneer existence, the spare living, the trials of farming, and isolation from dear friends, and she knew how to bridge that gap with her pen. Indeed, further migration had its benefits for the loquacious Mrs. Nichols, who felt more liberated than ever from the restraints of conformity and the imbroglio of politics that had circumscribed her public voice in the past. At sixty-one, her persistent desire to use and develop her intellect would help her to adapt once again. Disengaged from local affairs and no longer accountable to a network of extended family or friends, she could freely express her opinions about the hardships of the marriage system and proclaim the absolute necessity of women's citizenship. Assessing her career from a distance, Nichols would begin using her own past as a rhetorical tool to instruct her readers about the moral force of womanhood in America.

Clarina's new home in Potter Valley, where Relie had settled and where she would spend the remaining fourteen years of her life, represented a return to the relatively isolated, rural existence of her childhood and of early Kansas. Relie and Helen Carpenter had left Kansas by wagon train and settled in Potter Valley in 1859. They bought several parcels of land formerly inhabited by Pomo Indians, established a farm of 190 acres, and began raising four children. An enterprising man who sought a variety of jobs—from farming and teaming, to typesetting, editorial work, tax assessment, and, most notably, photography—Relie was not satisfied with rural existence. He ventured as far as San Francisco in search of opportunities, and in 1869 he and Helen moved eighteen miles southwest to Ukiah.[2] Relie had been urging his mother and stepbrother George to move west ever since, hoping George would take over the farm, which he believed held more promise for his stepbrother's young family than their struggling existence in Kansas.

Clarina felt torn by ties to her children, spread across the breadth of the nation. Relie's proposition offered a new start for George, who could put his knowledge of stock raising to good use, but venturing west would increase her distance from Birsha, whom she longed to see, and wrench her from son Howard and her adopted home. "It is hard to be pulled up by the roots and transplanted, after one has formed social relations with kindred spirits, and made a valiant fight with unsubdued nature for a home that begins to be a home in its best sense," she had mused on leaving Quindaro. By mid-1871 her home in Wyandotte was just "getting into fine trim." Yet she was also too "old and worn" to struggle with the "hoe & spade," her wintertime cough persisted, and her recurrent back pain had reemerged to make standing unpleasant.[3]

As her energy ebbed and her health declined, the difficulties of hiring help, repeated grasshopper devastations, and high taxes made California's mild climate and fertility seem ever more appealing. Consequently, after she and George had secured some of Mary Nichols's allotment money and Mary's health improved modestly, they sold much of their farm equipment, stock, and household goods, and leased Clarina's Wyandotte farm, hoping to use the proceeds to stock the California ranch. She anticipated a grand reunion with Relie and Helen, confident that Howard could manage her Kansas properties. He sold the acreage in the city in the late 1870s and the remainder in 1881—for half its value, according to Clarina.[4] Neither he nor Birsha would ever see their mother again.

The Nichols's journey west hardly matched Relie and Helen's pioneering experience by wagon train fifteen years earlier. To save money, the family booked passage in a third-class boxcar on the Union Pacific Railway for $62. The transcontinental route had sped migrants to Sacramento for two years, when Clarina, George, Mary, their two daughters and infant son, along with provisions, blankets, and mattresses, were loaded on board for the eight-day trip. With twelve other passengers—mainly French and Danish—the Nichols nestled into the boxcar, making their own tea to provide warmth during snowstorms. Accustomed to traveling in first class, Clarina found the first few days "crowded and dirty," but she made the best of the passage and later justified traveling on the "immigrant cars" by extolling the intellectual talents of her fellow passengers, who were studying English and "could discuss any topic of general interest with sense and feeling."[5]

The family's first few months in California rejuvenated Clarina's spirits as she became enthralled with the region's natural beauty. With a mix of canyon-like dales, gurgling streams, "forever green" mountains, and vibrant arrays of wildflowers, Potter Valley exhilarated her as much as the mild winters diminished her perennial cold-season cough. Surrounded by mountains again, she was comforted by the low foothills, where sheep and cattle grazing kept the grass green, leaving only "snow-crowned summits piercing the heavens."[6] A hundred and thirty miles north of San Francisco in Mendocino County, the inland valley had seen Anglo settlement since 1857 and now housed about 700 residents. There were several villages, small shops, two stores, and three schools but little in the way of established churches. The village of Pomo, where the Carpenters had settled, hosted a post office, store, hotel, and about twenty houses, comparable to the settlement in West Townshend, where

Clarina had grown up. Unlike her birthplace, however, there were few ministers, lawyers, doctors, or merchants and little cultural life.[7]

The Carpenters' farm, like Clarina's first homestead in Kansas, occupied land recently reclaimed from Native Americans. The Northern Pomo had lived in villages in the area until they came in conflict with Anglo settlers, whose cattle depleted the food supply. By the 1870s, most local Pomos had rejected resettlement at nearby Round Valley Reservation, preferring instead to indenture themselves to Anglo settlers as a means of subsistence. These "digger" Indians, as they were often called, lived in the mountains or under ranchers' protection throughout the valley and worked intermittently, a silent but crucial supply of labor during harvest or sheep shearing. Helen and Relie Carpenter, who maintained a benevolent but patronizing regard for the Pomo, acted as guardians and employed them at low wages when needed. Despite the Pomos' value as laborers, Anglo settlers generally considered them a simple and downtrodden but dying breed, not easily assimilated into the community, and their mixed-race children were unwelcome in local schools.[8]

Ensconced in her farmhouse, Clarina had little contact with the Pomo. Indeed, her world had shrunk markedly. Tight quarters and limited finances meant that she was unable to even furnish a room of her own, where she could read and write quietly. Access to Potter Valley was limited to one narrow, winding mountain road, making mail delivery unreliable; with farms widespread and Clarina's interest in organized religion flagging, the potential for developing friendships with like-minded residents was minimal. Luckily, neighbor Samuel Mcwhinney and his family, free-state Kansans who had migrated west with the Carpenters, were close enough to assure Clarina that she was not completely alone in a valley dominated by Democrats, whom she still referred to as Border Ruffians. Otherwise she relied upon her reading for intellectual stimulation, interspersed with occasional visits to former friends and relatives from Vermont who lived in San Francisco and coastal California. The latter provided rare converse with "thoughtful intelligent, unconventional women," which invariably rejuvenated her spirits and sparked her political instincts.[9]

For the most part, farm production, not politics, preoccupied the family, as the Nicholses sought to replicate Mcwhinney's wheat crop and his wife's chickens in another mixed farming operation. Clarina bought 27 hens, hatched 300 chicks the first winter, and sold nine dozen to wholesalers from San Francisco at $3.50 to $4.00 a dozen. The sale of eggs, hens, and ducks yielded ready cash

Relie and Helen Carpenter Ranch in Potter Valley, California, where Clarina lived from 1872 until her death in 1885. Courtesy of the Grace Hudson Museum and Sun House, City of Ukiah, California.

while George waited to harvest his fifteen acres of wheat and ten of corn. Eventually they would also raise sheep, hogs, and several acres of vegetable crops. A surplus of fruits, easily dried during the summer, kept Clarina busy as long as she was able. Only a year after their arrival, however, her farming ambitions were cut short when she fell from a wagon, catapulting her into months of pain in her chest, shoulder, and arm, and crimping her work habits and mobility.[10] Both George, who proved to be an industrious and doting son, and Relie expressed great devotion to their mother, but George was preoccupied with farmwork and Relie was developing his career in Ukiah. Clarina had a warm but distant relationship with her daughter-in-law Helen, but she was too far away to provide routine support. Sadly, Mary Nichols, who was probably suffering from tuberculosis, became increasingly weak and eventually died, in January 1873.

While Clarina maintained the household as best she could, she became preoccupied with the education of six-year-old Katie and younger sister Helen, her only female companions and domestic help. They baked bread, sewed, and tended their two-year-old brother, Birney, in between reading lessons. The scene resembled Clarina's youthful pleasures in the Howard household, where instruction in arts and sciences was interwoven with bread kneading

Relie and Helen Carpenter with their children, c. 1873 (from the left): Grant, Frank, May (above), and Grace, who became well known for her paintings of the local Pomo Indians. Courtesy of the Grace Hudson Museum and Sun House, City of Ukiah, California.

and hard labor over the washtub. Local schools were over two miles away and "poor" in Clarina's estimation. Inept teaching and political controversy had reigned during the 1860s, when parents set up two schools, one for southern sympathizers and the other for Republicans. Whether it was inconvenience or concern about prospects for her mixed-race granddaughters, Clarina's home-schooling became one of her great pleasures. The girls delighted her by reading her newspaper columns as early as eight and ten years old, and little Birney, who proved to be an endearing child, developed a "remarkable memory" and facility with language that she prized.[11]

Yet Clarina's health remained precarious, and severe illness periodically infected the rest of the family as well. In 1878 George was just recovering from a bout with pneumonia when seven-year-old Birney fell ill with a form of neuralgia that precipitated piercing pains throughout his body. When her precious grandson, who suffered without complaint, died shortly thereafter, Clarina collapsed immediately with a fever lasting three weeks. Overwhelmed with grief and depressed by her own frailty, she recovered, but sciatica continued to cripple her work style, limiting her hours on her feet and depleting her energy. Later that year, her teeth ached; George pulled several out, and she arranged for a new plate to be fitted in Ukiah. With little excess cash to hire consistent help, Clarina put aside the housekeeping standards that had framed much of her adult life and limited herself for the most part to sewing, writing, and reading.[12] The Nichols's home had been reduced to four, and Clarina sought solace in intellectual pursuit.

Given both her fragile health and her isolation in the hills of northern California, it is remarkable that Clarina maintained not only her interest in politics but also her desire to participate in the intellectual life of the nation. "The love of reading & writing has been my never failing resource from loneliness—my power of companionship and intellectual enjoyment thro[ughout] life," she wrote her brother-in-law.[13] Relying upon the mails and her former connections outside the valley to keep informed and to pursue her passion, she resumed her practice of reporting about her new venture in glowing terms. Readers back in Kansas learned about the lush Potter Valley, its beneficial climate, and the abundant agricultural production but not the hard work, loneliness, and physical difficulties she endured. An avid reader of the *Wyandotte Gazette* as soon as it arrived by mail, she ventured her opinion on activities

Clarina's granddaughters Katherine Howard Nichols, left, and Helen Clarina Nichols, right, c. 1876. Courtesy of the Wyandot Nation of Kansas Tribal Archives.

and legislative actions in Kansas as well. Her commitment to the Republican Party remained firm, though she largely avoided partisanship in public.

When Nichols focused her attention on women's status in California, she discovered that the state was far less progressive than Kansas. Mention of woman suffrage locally would bring only laughs and disbelief among Potter Valley folk, she surmised; they were hardly educated on the subject, even though gender-role boundaries were often transgressed in this rural backwater. Women and men commonly shared the hard labor of farming, and frontiersmen were accustomed to keeping themselves and the household in "apple-pie order" in the absence of womenfolk.[14] Yet after studying California's property laws and reports of legal cases, she concluded that wives out West were nearly as "*dead* in law" as women in the East, despite the state's progressive image. California's constitutional guarantees of separate property rights and common ownership of marital property had been eviscerated by legislative enactment and court rulings so that married women had little control over either their separate or common property. Though the courts displayed considerable "liberality" in providing for widows, wives lacked rights to their children and were unable to control their own earnings or operate businesses without legal certification that their husbands had failed as breadwinners.[15]

Too distant to make connections with politically active women in California, Clarina resumed her correspondence with Susan B. Anthony, hoping to maintain her link to progressive women. The *Revolution* was no longer under Anthony's supervision, but she and Stanton remained the leading lights of the National Woman Suffrage Association, and Clarina began sending letters regularly for yearly meetings. Her warm feelings for Susan formed the basis of her enduring link with the NWSA even after the association lost its momentum. Stanton's persistent claim that divorce was a woman's rights issue, that gaining freedom within marriage was as important as gaining political rights, and her association with the flamboyant Victoria Woodhull, who proclaimed her belief in free love over traditional marriage relations, had reignited public criticism. The mainstream press linked the NWSA to female sexual immorality, driving many suffrage advocates away from the association. Removed from much of the rancor surrounding the movement, Nichols valued her friendship with Anthony, and in turn her loyalty appeared to bolster the embattled leader under the strain of public criticism and internecine conflict. Nichols also maintained cordial relations with Lucy Stone and members of the American Woman Suffrage Association. They were outraged by Woodhull, yet the Boston-based association was thoroughly embroiled in the free-love controversy as well. Both groups suffered from Woodhull's efforts to connect the suffrage movement to a radical campaign for women's freedom to love and marry at will, and the association with immorality followed the leaders wherever they spoke.[16]

Just as the trumped-up link between woman suffrage and free love bedeviled Anthony and Stanton, so too it seriously infected the California movement. Both women had lectured in California in the spring of 1871 and ignited local critics who claimed that the movement would destroy marriage. Activists in San Francisco, who organized the California Woman Suffrage Association (CWSA) in 1870 and hosted the eastern leaders, were boldly defending Laura Fair, a woman imprisoned for killing her married lover, apparently in self-defense. Anthony linked the case to women's poverty and lack of real

Susan B. Anthony, 1879. Courtesy of the Nebraska Historical Society. RG2669 PH 0 5. Image contrast adjusted and slightly cropped.

protection, and local activists spoke out against the unfair trial, prompting mainstream California presses to condemn Anthony along with her hosts. Controversy over free love reached a crescendo during the November 1872 election campaign, when Woodhull ran for president and publicly revealed the adulterous affair between Henry Ward Beecher, former president of the AWSA, and Elizabeth Tilton, wife of another suffrage advocate.[17] Meanwhile, divisions among leaders of the CWSA over the defense of free love and disputes over whether to ally with the NWSA helped stifle the local movement for woman suffrage. Nichols followed the progress of their legislative petitions for equal rights; by 1874 activists had secured women's right to hold school offices and equal pay in schools but little else. With her customary optimism, Nichols praised those legislators who had also advocated women's right to vote in school meetings, concluding that "little by little, woman is getting her foot in."[18] Yet it would be more than thirty-five years before women in California were enfranchised in any elections.

If Nichols maintained her reassuring voice for followers back in Kansas, she also expressed her outrage that the movement had become linked to sexual impropriety. In a letter to Anthony for the NWSA convention in Washington, D.C., in 1873, she vigorously promoted the concept of "self-ownership" as part of "Bible Christianity" and insisted that current marital law denied women the "right of personal freedom." No longer fearing political repercussions, she turned the immorality charge onto men and chided them for tolerating licentious behavior, prostitution, and polygamy in territorial Utah, while subordinating their wives to willful oppression and marital rape. Nichols's condemnation of male sexual license reflected her habitual sense of female propriety, but it also displayed a new frankness absent from her previous political discourse. Comparing women's subjection within marriage to black slavery, she endorsed *"free marriage,"* a term reflective of Stanton's sentiments, and dismissed free love as a "misnomer." Still, Nichols was not ready to condone divorce as a remedy. Indeed, notwithstanding her support of divorce for abused wives, she maintained her optimism that equality within marriage was the answer; if legally instituted, husbands would respect their wives and couples could achieve the "divine idea of marriage."[19] By the time Nichols's outspoken letter appeared, however, Anthony and members of the NWSA were preoccupied with claiming national citizenship by defending their right to vote under the Fourteenth Amendment, a new strategy they believed would guarantee the "privileges and immunities" of American citizens against state-imposed voting restrictions. Having chosen to test her citizenship status by attempting to vote in the 1872 election, Anthony was defending her rights in court after her arrest and hoping questions regarding marriage would disappear from public scrutiny.

Taking her cue from the NWSA's strategy, Nichols framed her advocacy for woman's rights from a national perspective while continuing to channel her reform ideas through the prism of marriage. She kept abreast of both wings of the eastern movement through their publications, in which she routinely condemned the twin prongs of sex oppression: marriage law and the clergy. Yearly letters to the NWSA appeared in the *Ballot Box*, a journal of the Toledo, Ohio, suffrage organization, which subsequently became the *National Citizen and Ballot Box*, in which she applauded efforts to advance a Sixteenth

Amendment. Less regularly but with equal fervor, she expressed her viewpoint on marital equity and corrected minor inaccuracies in reporting on state legislation in the AWSA's widely circulated *Woman's Journal.*

The national strategy provided Nichols with opportunities to blame women's disenfranchisement on national rather than state leaders at a time when she lacked viable contacts to a statewide movement. When members of the NWSA launched a protest against their exclusion from the national centennial celebration in Philadelphia, Nichols signed their "Woman's Declaration of 1876," which listed articles of impeachment against their male rulers. They condemned the nation's "aristocracy of sex" that denied married women basic American freedoms, the double standard of morality, and the failure of inconsistent and transient state legislation to protect women's equality of rights.[20] Nichols reiterated these themes for the NWSA's subsequent celebration of the Seneca Falls Convention and asserted that the adoption of English common law coupled with disfranchisement had "convert[ed] the marriage altar into an executioner's block." With considerable hyperbole, she composed an epitaph for the nation's wives: "'Here lies the relict of American freedom—taxed to pauperism, loved to death!'" Conceding only that most men were "better than their laws," she demanded suffrage for the "mothers, wives, and daughters of freemen" who would stem the tide of corruption threatening the nation. The capacity of Yankee women to purify the nation became a common rhetorical plea in the post-Reconstruction era, when political spoils and urban electoral fraud appeared rampant.[21]

If Nichols's rhetoric continued to reflect her unswerving belief in virtuous womanhood, it also displayed her preoccupation with women's economic freedom. Applying her legal expertise to federal law, she outlined how men's "autocratic rights" within marriage were encoded in the nation's legal and political system. Wives were "incompetent, under the laws of Congress," she claimed, because federal land allocation statutes ignored the individual rights of married women and widows to homestead and preemption rights, even though single women could acquire such rights. Moreover, the national government sustained state laws that treated women as a "subject and servile class." Still insistent upon both state and national reform, Nichols advocated for jointly owned marital property to prevent husbands from alienating it without their wives' consent.[22]

Nichols condemned the inequality embedded within the American system of marital law, but she also castigated the established clergy who compounded the legal and political power of husbands over their wives. Her animosity was reawakened after hearing a Baptist minister preach while on a rare visit in San Francisco, and she was prompted to respond to an article in the *Woman's Journal* advocating female preaching. "Yes, they must preach, and preach they will," Nichols proclaimed. She expounded in the *Journal* and later to the NWSA about the way the male clergy had enforced the "despotic relation of the sexes" by sermonizing about the biblical injunction to wives and exercising their personal power with un-Christian behavior. Linking the legal system with these clerical teachings, Nichols revealed the inner workings of church and state and insisted that ministers and lawyers clung to theological and legal tenets largely to maintain their status. Given that men were responsible for interpreting the Bible and submerging "God's law of co-sovereignty and co-possession," she advocated women's assumption of the ministry as a means to redeem men from perpetrating injustice. Continuing to adhere to her version of "divine law," Nichols was hardly abandoning her faith but repeating arguments she had espoused ten years earlier in "The Bible Position of Woman." Freed from any connection to the Baptist Church, she remained firmly anchored to God's design for women, a higher law that superseded the male notion of female subordination.[23]

Indeed, Clarina eventually defined her political philosophy in a two-part essay linking her Christian millennialism with the progress of the American republic. In 1881 she published "Christian Civil Government" in the *Woman's Herald of Industry and Social Science Cooperator,* a new and "fearless" monthly in San Francisco. Its outspoken and iconoclastic editor, Marietta L. Stow, had been associated with the CWSA and recently launched a one-woman campaign to reform unjust state and national probate laws. Her paper was "devoted to the interest of *Woman*" and served as the organ of her new venture, the California Woman's Social Science Association (CWSSA), designed to promote women's education and advancement through cooperative agricultural and industrial development. One of Stow's pet projects was a silk-producing cooperative to demonstrate how work could be reorganized on a gender-neutral basis. Nichols may have learned about the CWSSA and Stow's paper, which lasted only three years, from friends in San Francisco or through association with the *Pacific Rural Press.* The journal's publisher, A. T. Dewey, had hired Relie for seasonal editorial work, printed a few of Nichols's articles, and advertised Stow's venture. Nichols appreciated Stow's lively editorials and relished her "righteous indignation." It is doubtful whether she formed any other ties with Stow or members of the CWSSA, although they staged a benefit partly to raise funds to pay her.[24]

In "Christian Civil Government" Nichols recapitulated her plea for women's inclusion in government and predicted the future of the nation under the cooperative rule of men and women devoted to creating God's just society on earth. Men could ill afford to exclude a class of virtuous and intelligent citizens, she argued, not only because it would be unjust to them but also because the nation would fail to achieve its divine purpose: to become a truly Christian society, one that followed God's golden rule to love thy neighbor. Just as God created human beings accountable to themselves and others through self-rule and "free agency," so too his divine wisdom instituted government as a means of cooperation and progress among peoples. Women's essential moral influence, heretofore excluded from government decisionmaking, was crucial to the efficiency and progress of the nation. Hope for the future lay in the principled stance and bravery of individual reformers who had proven that injustice could be reversed. The nation had "saved itself" by granting the claims of "four millions of slaves," Nichols reminded her readers, but it had "yet to acknowledge by constitutional law, the equal legal and political rights of twenty millions of women." Only then would the government reflect Nichols's basic faith in "Christ's teachings of love and duty as practical rules." The "mothers of the State" could make a special claim to representation in government because of their accountability for children, she asserted, an even greater claim than the property rights of men, yet all women offered an essential moral force missing from present government operation.[25]

Like many suffragists in the 1880s, Nichols came to regard woman's civilizing mission, not just mothers' obligations, as one of the chief rationales for enfranchisement, thereby linking religion and suffrage politics to the fate of the nation. Rooted in women's essential difference on the one hand and their equality with the white men who had created the nation on the other, it was a convenient way of reconciling her faith with her political activism. Christian belief had inspired her millennialism and her evangelical fervor, but it had taken her nearly a lifetime to fully resolve the contradiction between her religion and her desire to engage in politics. Now she no longer feared ostracism from family and friends or clerical rebukes, and her philosophy matched the conservative end of a spectrum of opinion among prominent female activists. They sought to defend their political activities in an era of religious turmoil, when the advance of science had sparked heightened evangelicalism and zealous biblical disputations. Whereas Julia Ward Howe and Frances Willard employed similar interpretations of the Bible to bolster the role of women in a Christian state, under the influence of Freethought, Elizabeth Cady Stanton and Matilda Joslyn Gage became convinced that the Bible was the root of women's oppression. Others, like Marietta Stow, directed their activism into the advancement of women through science. Ironically, Stow coupled Nichols's article with a treatise on "The Religion of Positivism," which proffered a similarly progressive and cooperative view of change based on natural laws, not Christian truths.[26] Regardless, in Nichols's mind, the "great social moral questions of the day" could never be settled "without the light of woman's intellect and the transfusing of her mother heart and her vote." In the end, she was comforted by the belief that "God's promise is to and through woman to all the nations of the earth."[27]

This form of nationalism with its international and racial implications was consistent with the trajectory of the suffrage movement after Reconstruction. In the 1880s suffragists shifted the emphasis of their arguments from justice for women—derived from natural, universal rights—to women's beneficial influence on the nation. Even as they sought to appear disinterested, they effectively narrowed the basis of their claims to a concept of womanhood grounded in female moral superiority and consistent with white middle-class gender identities. Isabella Beecher Hooker, younger sister of Catherine and Harriet, began echoing Nichols's early appeals for "political equality for mothers," and claims about women's purifying influence on politics multiplied. The NWSA's campaign for a federal amendment, founded upon the notion that suffrage was a right secured by the nation, not the states, enhanced the focus on white women's essential contributions to achieving national greatness. The racism of this appeal, which sprouted out of the conflicts over the Fourteenth and Fifteenth amendments, became explicit as suffragists became antagonistic to securing black suffrage, ignored black women's rights, and responded to nativist fears that foreign immigrants would undermine the progress of the American republic.[28]

Nichols partook of this ideological shift, yet her rhetoric continued to express a fundamentally benevolent worldview and sympathy with former slaves. Unlike Anthony, who became infuriated with the Republican Party for not endorsing woman suffrage, Nichols continued to affirm the importance of black suffrage and stood by the election of James Garfield in 1880 as a bulwark against the southern states and efforts to disenfranchise blacks. Though she doubted partisanship could advance the cause, she believed Republicans were the best alternative to "the northern saloon and the southern shot-gun." Targeting former slaveholders, saloonkeepers, and gamblers, who perpetuated crime and misery, she predicted that the ballot in the hands of women would destroy them. Not immune to racial and ethnic prejudice, however, Nichols believed that the enfranchisement of women would improve the nation more than that of "ignorant bondmen," and she occasionally expressed her disdain for the legions of foreign men who could potentially become "sovereigns over themselves and American womanhood." Her emphasis was decidedly on the woman voter as a moral force to redeem the nation, cleanse politics, and hold the evils perpetrated by corrupt men at bay.[29]

Despite her frail health and advanced age, Nichols was determined to spread this philosophy and was amazingly persistent in finding outlets for her intellectual production. It may have been Relie who put her in contact with the editor of the *Pacific Rural Press,* who published her last significant columns in which she attempted to educate California readers. Looking for a way to earn money, she wrote several articles about her Kansas experiences for the sixteen-page agricultural monthly in 1878, for which she earned $5 each, and began more regular correspondence for a section called the "Home Circle" in 1880.[30] Designed for rural middle-class readers, the *Pacific Rural Press* promised to advance farming and gardening methods in the state and carried polite commentary about a wide range of household and farm issues for women readers. The "Home Circle" became a favorite feature for readers who relished its moral and religious flavor. In a sign of the shift in cultural values, the editor tolerated talk of woman's rights as long as it did not undermine the primacy of women's domestic role.

Nichols had long practiced this form of discourse, notably in the *Windham County Democrat* but throughout her career in Kansas as well. Opening a column entitled "Good News," she situated her readers comfortably at her tea table—"neatly set, the tea fragrant, the biscuits light, the cream and butter sweet"—before gloating over passage of school suffrage in Vermont. The state had jumped aboard the "western train of modern civilization," she announced triumphantly, and then regaled them with the story of her legislative appearance in 1852 to prove how far women had advanced by 1880. With her trademark array of domestic and biblical metaphors, Nichols reincarnated herself as the thrifty housewife who championed the well-adorned home while politely and openly advocating for woman suffrage. Saving her

anticlericalism for more radical publications, Nichols equated woman suffrage with the progress of the nation and God's providential hand.[31]

Recounting the history of women's advancements proved to be a useful
tool to educate the public and to camouflage Nichols's radicalism as she engaged in a familiar repartee with other columnists and readers, frequently
injecting anecdotes from her past. Most of the disputants appeared to be elderly men and a few women, who often recounted the backbreaking household labor they performed on California's ranches. They debated the quality
of women's brain power, their work, dispositions, legal rights, and aptitude
for politics, until the editor would no longer tolerate such controversial topics.
Nichols's continual interest in property law led her to outline the inequities of
California's community property statute. She noted the benefits women had
brought to higher education and benevolent reform and used examples of
women's achievements to argue for their equal participation in all aspects of
public life.[32] Unlike her experience in Vermont or Territorial Kansas, Nichols
was not a singular female voice for women's advancement. Several correspondents agreed with her, others dodged the subject, and a few proffered familiar
arguments to challenge her position that "women were all paragons of virtue,
knowledge and refinement." Writing under the pseudonym Peter Pitkin, one
correspondent resurrected the biblical injunction against wives, belittled the
specter of women involved in dirty politics, and disparaged the nastiness of
intellectual women. In a "Rejoinder," Nichols responded by agreeing with
Pitkin's assertion that there was "'not one word in the Bible about woman suffrage.' Neither is there one word about apple dumplings. I don't believe they
had any in Paul's day; nor *man* suffrage either," she quipped. In closing, she
demanded that he reveal his name, rather than "firing at women in the open
field from behind a—a *Pipkin!*"[33] Ironically, Nichols had begun her career
shielded by a similar anonymity, but she felt no need to invoke Debra Van
Winkle at this stage in her life.

Just as Nichols's wit remained as quick as ever, so too did her delight when
her columns prompted men to action. Her influence probably reached a peak
in a polite exchange with Edward Berwick of Carmel Valley, a fruit grower
who participated in local Republican politics. A willing convert to equal property rights for married women, he was reluctant to countenance women at
the polls because he believed they lacked the appropriate qualities of intellect and ultimately physical force to represent their own interest. He could
not condone her call for a constitutional amendment recognizing "equality

of rights, irrespective of sex," but acknowledged the justice of her teachings on property law and child custody. As a result, he apparently promoted but failed to submit a resolution on women's equal marital rights to the party's county convention, and Nichols graciously acknowledged that he "deserved the thanks of every woman in the state."[34]

This political work and her wide-ranging reading kept Nichols's intellect sharp and her passion for social reform alive during the last years of her life. Even as she lay prostrate with acute bronchitis in early 1885, she penned a final strongly worded indictment against tobacco, claiming that smoking was even more "destructive" than alcohol abuse. In keeping with her lifelong concern for women and children, she appealed to her California readers to help preserve innocent babies from suffocation and nursing mothers from inhaling the deadly poisons that cigar-smoking men unwittingly injected into the atmosphere of homes and public places.[35] Whether she was projecting her own bout of lung disease onto the breathing public or prescient about the damaging effects of secondhand smoke, Nichols interpreted her experience through a lens that had shaped her vision of the world. Disregarding the male smokers who could take care of themselves, she sought first to save the innocent women and helpless children.

Long before Clarina Nichols had reached her deathbed, she had begun the process of assessing the meaning of her life. "I am more & more aware that only those who write out their acts and relations to historic events will escape misrepresentation or win just recognition," she wrote a correspondent from Kansas. She had written about her past experiences as early as 1870, when her readings activated childhood memories, and she recognized how she could use history to demonstrate the benefits of fifty years of progress in America. Yet Clarina continually regretted her inability to remember names or details of past events and bemoaned the fact that she had failed to keep a record of the past. "I would have written my life years ago from the beginning," she confessed in 1884, "but for the conviction that . . . ten years of my life . . . could not be given to the public." Though she had come to terms with her first marriage and was willing to reveal the details in private, she was still reluctant to cast a shadow on her family or her own past. "What a legacy of instructive and entertaining experiences my long and eventful life would be to the thoughtful student of human nature!" Nichols mused. As an acknowledged member of a pioneering generation of activists, she undoubtedly sought recognition for her

accomplishments but still feared that inaccuracy—or worse, misrepresentation—would discredit her account.[36]

When Stanton and Anthony launched their project to write a history of the
woman's rights movement, Nichols began a more systematic examination of
her career. Sparked by the enthusiasm generated at the centennial celebration
of 1876, the two friends, with the assistance of Matilda Joslyn Gage, sought
to document their work and define the movement on their own terms. Many
of the early advocates, whom they lovingly called the "old-guard," were dying, the chief editors were slowing down themselves, and the movement had
reached what appeared to be insurmountable divisions and political road-
blocks. The history would serve not only as a record of the past but also as
a vehicle to rejuvenate the movement, celebrate their progress, and advance
women's equality. To the consternation of some contributors, Anthony and
Stanton insisted upon full editorial control of the content, infuriating their
chief rival, Lucy Stone. She refused to cooperate with their request for material despite her crucial role in the early movement, which only heightened
the enmity between the leaders. The first three volumes of the *History of
Woman Suffrage* that the editors produced represented both their own perspective on the movement and a compendium of diverse personal accounts
and documents.[37]

As a member of the "noble band of women" who had fomented the cause,
Nichols was one of the first to comply with Anthony's call for personal accounts. Her memoir, which originally appeared in the *National Citizen &
Ballot Box* in summer 1879, would become both a model for Anthony and
the chief source shaping the historical memory of Nichols. Anthony was so
delighted with her "simply and beautifully told" story that she advised others
to follow Nichols's example and devoted a whole chapter with little editing to
her singular experiences as a forerunner.[38] Glorifying her as a "large-hearted,
brave, faithful woman," Anthony and Stanton showed their appreciation for
a fellow activist who had clung to the NWSA during difficult times. She was
a hero of the West, they proclaimed, whose autobiographical account represented the "history of all that was done" in Vermont, Wisconsin, Kansas,
and Missouri before the Civil War.[39] This somewhat exaggerated claim not
only reflected the way Nichols had constructed her legacy but also Anthony's
appreciation for her loyalty at a time when conflict dominated the woman's
rights movement. Yet it obscured the role of men and other women, particularly in Kansas.

In fact, Anthony expressed her annoyance with the younger generation of women in Kansas, who appeared to have forgotten Nichols's heroism. With a remnant of bitterness, she scolded them for being "too apathetic to exercise" the civil rights Nichols had secured for them two decades earlier. In an effort to fund the history, Anthony had solicited help from Franklin G. Adams, secretary of the Kansas Historical Society, who organized local women to memorialize Nichols by contributing to the cost of a steel plate engraving of her. Mary Tenney Gray, who had witnessed Nichols's performance at the Wyandotte Constitutional Convention, wrote a testimonial honoring Nichols, and a committee of women circulated it to stimulate contributions and fund-raising events throughout the state. Noting that few women remembered Nichols, Gray explained that "her labors have been unheralded and unrequited, but we enjoy their fruits." Yet even Gray was leery of attaching her name to the cause, and despite enthusiasm from Margaret Wood and a few others, they eventually raised only $75, far less than the $125 Anthony had requested. In the meantime, Anthony had produced the first volume in May 1881 with an engraving of Nichols that no one liked, including her son Howard, making it even more difficult to solicit contributions.[40]

Yet Nichols's account clearly revived her memory among women in Kansas. Filled with poignant and triumphant stories, it authenticated her experience and the progress of the movement at a time when its prospects appeared dim. She portrayed herself as a lady editor and reformer who "stood alone with her paper" or at the podium in a sea of male critics, from lawyers, to ministers, to legislators. Inspired by the "mother-love that shrinks neither from fire or flood, to rescue their loved ones," Nichols was seen ascending "every platform and pulpit in the land!" She told Anthony she wanted to appear "womanly" and "motherly" in her portrait, and indeed this was the image she had carefully constructed over a lifetime of activism. Posing as a mother to the women and children of the nation, Nichols told her tale of personal triumph over ignorance and oppression. In the course of her travels, she had enlightened naive women and unmasked the prejudices of gentlemen who adhered to a false chivalry by failing to protect the interests of women and children. "'Mrs. Nichols has made me ashamed of myself—ashamed of my sex!'" she quoted one male convert. A few courteous gentlemen tiptoe through her story, those who allowed her to speak or introduced legislation to remove women's legal disabilities. Even as she disclaimed her "egotistical" pen, Nichols shaped a heroic tale of a "true and loving woman" righteously defending her right to speak "before God and my own soul." With women's access to public spaces secured by the 1880s, she could clearly show that the woman's rights movement had effected change. "Latter-day laborers can have little idea of the trials of the early worker," she explained, "driven by the stress of right and duty against popular prejudices, to which her own training and early habits of thought have made her painfully sensitive."[41]

Nichols's real triumph, however, occurred in Kansas, the place she still identified with the freedom of the West. To prove that westerners were far in advance of the eastern establishment, she depicted Lawrence, Kansas, as an enlightened oasis where her reputation as a woman's rights advocate preceded her. She was greeted with "triumphant cheering" upon arrival, readily recognized by leading politicians, and promised that she could dedicate the new church building. Indeed, the settlers who prevailed in Kansas were more receptive of this woman who appeared to champion the domestic values prized on the frontier than the radical bloomer-wearing advocates of free love linked to the movement. Her story outlined her motherly advocacy but omitted the difficulties of frontier existence, her hopes and fears for her children, the problem of canvassing precarious settlements, and details of the failed 1867 campaign. Instead, she extolled the liberal attitudes and benefits of living in her adopted state compared with "conservative old Vermont" with its unjust laws and entrenched legal profession. Yet she named Republican Judge Samuel Kingman and his antiquated use of "'organic law'" as her leading opponent in the constitutional convention. Though she subsequently urged Anthony to purge this reference from her account—because Kingman had apparently "progressed" in his views—Anthony argued for accountability, and the reference remained to teach readers about the politics of woman's rights.[42]

There is little indication in Nichols's reminiscences that woman's rights had much to do with partisan politics, and indeed Nichols was sufficiently cynical about politicians by this time to distance herself from having engaged in what many considered a corrupt practice. Instead of Whigs or Democrats, it was mostly men who stood in her way, especially ministers and lawyers, but also slave owners and those who licensed the liquor traffic. To a considerable extent she was right; party men were largely dismissive of woman's rights before the Civil War. Nichols portrayed both Republicans and Democrats as seekers of partisan advantage, and though a few Republicans supported the cause in Kansas, their policy was to "'keep shady.'" Despite their opposition to her cause and their racism, Democrats often treated her with more courtesy. To disabuse readers of the notion that she had anything to do with partisanship, she characterized her lectures for Republicans in 1856 as "semi-political labors" in the interest of "suffering Kansas" and depicted women's political involvement as the work of "angels" troubling a "muddy pool."[43]

Nichols's narrative contributed to the dominant theme of volume one in the *History*, a story of trailblazers who had accomplished the impossible with little help or internal dissension. Notwithstanding their split with abolitionists and with Stone and Blackwell, the editors linked the "grand movement for woman's enfranchisement" with the successful and most significant reform in American history to end slavery.[44] With that goal accomplished, Nichols was outspoken about her own abolitionist views and recounted her success at lecturing to proslavery Missourians. Yet, unlike abolitionists, suffragists had not accomplished their goal, nor would the citizens be persuaded to adopt it for another forty years. They had made some progress, particularly on the legal rights of married women, and women's enfranchisement in the territories of Wyoming and Utah could be viewed as a harbinger of future success.

Ironically, Nichols had led the way on school suffrage, but Stanton and Anthony had largely ignored that issue. As Nichols had predicted, it became an "entering wedge," gathering momentum in the postwar years. By 1881, school voting rights had been enacted in seven more states, including New York and Massachusetts, and even Anthony noted that getting out the women's vote in school elections would counter the "cry of '*Women don't want to vote!*'" For the next two decades this form of partial suffrage would appeal to more female activists and legislators who believed women's connection with children was a viable rationale for women's participation in school affairs. Suffragists and temperance activists in Kansas built upon Nichols's strategy of pitting the benefits of women's moral influence against the current state of political corruption and convinced Republicans to expand women's franchise to municipal elections in 1887.[45] But it was not Nichols's leadership on school suffrage that convinced Anthony to give her story prominence in the *History of Woman Suffrage*. Instead, it was her enduring support of Susan during difficult times, her willingness to overlook the "petty grievances" that had infected the movement, and her loyalty to the NWSA.

For Clarina, the process of reconstructing her early career not only enriched her subsequent newspaper columns but also sparked deeper memories that bubbled to the surface. She found herself circling back in time to places and experiences in a random reverie filled with homespun sights and sounds. Seeking to record the harvest from deeper places in the recesses of her brain, she began a record of childhood recollections in 1880 but never completed the process. She did, however, draw some conclusions about the roots and direction of her career. She marveled that the trials, anxiety, and loss of friends she had experienced had not precluded days filled with "rational, solid enjoyment." Admitting privately that "the fearful looking for trouble has been the greatest trouble after all," Clarina finally found peace with herself.[46]

Writing her reminiscences for Susan Anthony had strengthened the bond between the two women over their shared early experiences. Despite their distance and limited previous contact, in the final years of Clarina's life their correspondence became increasingly confidential, each drawing strength from remembrances of their pioneering days in the movement. Susan confessed that "always with the 'old guard,' [she] had perfect confidence that the wise and the right thing would be said." Now she feared that "our younger sisters" would not be "equal to the emergency." Clarina affirmed, "I have loved & trusted you—for what I saw you were and would grow to." She assessed her lifework for Susan and in hindsight asserted that her "plan of work for humanity—for salvation of woman & thru & by her of the race" had been "pre-meditated every step from the first." Finding its roots in her failed marriage, she aligned her life in a strait trajectory of committed, sustained reform work.[47]

Despite her fears along the way, Clarina believed her sense of mission had held immense personal and social benefits. Not only had she accomplished more than expected, but she confessed to Susan: "I am a great deal better woman than I expected to be—more self-controlled, self-contained than I dared hope and I am so because I began determined to know nothing but woman (humanity) crucified—to count no sacrifice, indulge no regrets, and make no reprisals for offended dignity." Notwithstanding her outbursts of righteousness and occasional male scolding, reform work had been "the caustic, the balm, the pabulum" that fed her intellectual growth and personal strength, providing her with a sense of accomplishment and contentment. Unlike many activists who shrank from setbacks or who allowed their personal lives to interrupt their participation, Nichols had persisted and not retreated in the face of opposition or personal privations except when her health failed. To a considerable extent, she was sustained by her optimism about the future, a hopefulness that rested upon her faith in God's divine plan and her role as his agent on earth. A hallmark of nineteenth-century reform, this missionary zeal and her abiding "interest in the progress of affairs all over the world" kept Clarina's intellect vibrant in old age.[48]

During the last few years of her life, when she was largely confined to home and even to her bed, Nichols continued to write the columns and letters that sustained her despite failing health. In the third volume of the *History of Woman Suffrage*, published after Nichols's death, Anthony marveled that these articles were "written in such conditions of weakness and suffering, as only a hero could have overcome." Despite her "rather straightened circumstances," Nichols was "uniformly calm and cheerful, living in an atmosphere above the petty annoyances of everyday-life ... too much absorbed in the vital questions of the hour even to take note of her personal discomforts." Appreciative of her loyalty, Anthony eventually replaced the controversial engraving of Nichols with another the family supplied for a second printing of volume one and expressed her continued interest in the welfare of Clarina's granddaughters. Just a few days before Clarina died, she penned a note to Susan describing her ill health and protesting her impending death with a claim that she was not "utterly hopeless." Nor would she be as she sent her trusted friend a final message: "God is with us—there can be no failure, and no defeat outside ourselves that will not roll up the floodwood and rush away every obstruction."[49]

Clarina Nichols died at her California home with little fanfare two weeks before her seventy-fifth birthday in 1885. Content with herself and surrounded by her sons and grandchildren, this "mother of humanity" found a peaceful ending. Relie memorialized his mother by praising her intellectual power, her "persistent equanimity" in the face of obstacles, and her commitment to "her fellow beings." She was also a tender mother and sympathizing friend. Anthony and Stanton lauded Nichols as a "good writer, an effective speaker, and a preeminently brave woman." Clarina would have been pleased with a memorial poem that appeared in the *Pacific Rural Press* in the sentimental style she had frequently adopted for Brattleboro newspapers. The poet lauded her "brave words" and "proud deeds," which had "ennoble[d] her weak sex, and pointed them to higher possibilities." Other tributes were equally generous, noting her role as a pioneer mother of Kansas, her legal expertise, and her labor for married women's rights. By 1885 the promotion of married women's property and custody rights, which most states had granted, was a recognized accomplishment of the woman's rights movement, and Nichols's intrepid stand for victimized mothers and children rendered her one of its early heroes. In Kansas, Nichols's historic role at the Wyandotte Constitutional Convention helped to keep her memory alive. "Another founder of the State has passed away, another star has set," lamented the *Lawrence Weekly Herald-Tribune*, and subsequently she became known among Kansas women as a "real home defender" rather than a suffrage advocate.[50]

Nichols's burial site in the pristine Potter Valley is a fitting reminder that she cast her future in the West and with the progress of the nation. Her career as a champion of women's rights across America highlights the way the movement intersected with the migration of peoples and ideas in the nineteenth century. Although Nichols was drawn to the West by a combination of idealism and economic opportunism, like many of her fellow travelers, she also sought the freedom to express herself and the chance to participate in politics that would shape the nation. Early Kansas was fertile ground for such a reformer, who believed that it would be far easier to secure "just laws in the organization of a new State" than to repeal laws in "an old State." There were few women like Nichols at state constitutional conventions as the West was settled, yet a number of western states adopted liberal property laws for married women. By 1850 feminists had articulated the problem of dependent wives effectively, and the nation was expanding exponentially. Providing women with equal access to the economy in a mobile nation simply made sense for early settlers because it enhanced development and the image of the West as a place ripe with opportunity.[51]

But access to political power, as Nichols discovered, was another story. The fluidity of politics in Kansas and the intersection of her life with abolition and the Civil War opened windows of political opportunity and personal growth for Nichols and other feminists. They sought to exploit the opening in the interest of their own enfranchisement. Despite their failure to fully achieve that goal, Nichols's experiences in the West and her engagement in racial politics at midcentury broadened her social and political perspective. Although Nichols targeted black suffrage as the complicating factor impeding her agenda for women, universal suffrage had become her ultimate goal. It was the inability of suffragists to fully access partisan politics and entrenched ideas about gender that derailed women's campaigns for the ballot. Many western states would adopt woman suffrage before any in the East, but enactment was rarely spontaneous. Instead, activists campaigned for decades, eventually learned how to form political coalitions, and took advantage of shifting partisan loyalties before achieving their goals.[52]

To a considerable extent, Nichols's suffrage activism reveals the conundrum of feminism in the second half of the nineteenth century. Throughout her career Nichols placed more emphasis on women's essential femininity rather than their equality with men because she utilized a theory of natural rights grounded in women's reproductive role that meshed with contemporary cultural prescriptions for women. Her womanly style was a practical way to maintain her respectability and to open avenues for writing and speaking in public. Yet to point to women's difference was to risk that male opponents, and many women as well, would deny that equality of rights was applicable to the opposite sex. This paradox has underlain feminism throughout its history, but it became particularly salient after the Civil War. Like many of Nichols's colleagues, by the 1870s and 1880s her pleas for enfranchisement became more clearly derivative of "redemptive womanhood," the belief that women—particularly white women—were better than men and represented the hope of a corrupt nation. On the one hand, this notion could propel women out of private life and into politics; on the other, it smacked of racism and imperialism.[53] In Nichols's case, female moral authority became a way to reconcile her evangelical worldview with political action, to carve out a female voice in partisan debate, and finally to link her quest for justice for women with national citizenship. This conception drew many women into suffrage and reform work—and a minority to antisuffrage organizations—which enhanced women's influence in politics, but the rhetoric of woman as redeemer would not prove successful enough to achieve political power.

Nichols's legacy to the movement rested instead upon her willingness to risk a life of comfort and convenience for the dangers of the lecture circuit and the privations of frontier existence. She was a woman to be admired for her skill with words, her practical politics, her loyalty to others, and her sustained commitment to women's economic equality. Driven into public life by her personal grievances, Nichols made the most of her intellectual talents and developed the self-control and equanimity necessary to face obstacles that would have crushed many women of her day. Finally, she refused to be waylaid by the strategic differences and emotional retaliation that infected the relationships among many of her colleagues, choosing instead to stand apart, adhering to her own truth and her faith in her place in God's universe. In the words of her friend Susan B. Anthony, she was a "preeminently brave woman, gifted with that rarest of all virtues, common sense."[54]

NOTES

Abbreviations

CIHC	Clarina Irene Howard Carpenter
CIHN	Clarina Irene Howard Nichols
ECS	Elizabeth Cady Stanton
HWS	*History of Woman Suffrage*
KHQ	*Kansas Historical Quarterly*
KSHS	Library and Archives Division, Kansas State Historical Society, Topeka
MWRA	Moneka Women's Rights Association
Nichols Papers	Papers of Clarina I. H. Nichols, originally in the possession of Mrs. Patricia Rabinovitz, Ann Arbor, Michigan, microfilmed by KSHS in 1973; given to Schlesinger Library (SL) in 1980; letters and miscellaneous documents
PRP	*Pacific Rural Press*
SBA	Susan B. Anthony
SL	Schlesinger Library, Radcliffe Institute of Advanced Study, Harvard University, Cambridge, Massachusetts
THS	Townshend Historical Society, Townshend, Vermont
VHS	Leahy Library, Vermont Historical Society, Barre, Vermont
WCD	*Windham County Democrat*
WG/WCG	*Wyandotte Gazette/Wyandotte Commercial Gazette*

Introduction: Remembering a "Forgotten Feminist"

1. CIHN to SBA, 11 November 1880, cited in Joseph G. Gambone, ed., "The Forgotten Feminist of Kansas: The Papers of Clarina I. H. Nichols, 1854–1885," *KHQ* 40 (Spring 1974): 453; Elizabeth Cady Stanton, "Mrs. C. I. H. Nichols," in *Eminent Women of the Age: Being Narratives of the Lives and Deeds of the Most Prominent Women of the Present Generation* James Parton et al. (Hartford, Conn.: J. M. Betts, 1869), 396; Elizabeth Cady Stanton, Susan B. Anthony, and Matilda Joslyn Gage, eds., *HWS* (Rochester, N.Y.: Fowler & Wells, 1881; 2nd ed., 1887), 1:171.

2. Mary T. Gray, "Clarina I. Howard Nichols," *Woman's Tribune,* 5 May 1888.

3. Clara Bewick Colby, "Clarina I. Howard Nichols," *Woman's Tribune,* 5 October 1907.

4. Ellen Carol DuBois, *Feminism and Suffrage: The Emergence of an Independent Women's Movement in America, 1848–1869* (Ithaca, N.Y.: Cornell University Press, 1978), 84–85, quotation on 84; Eleanor Flexner, *Century of Struggle: The Woman's Rights Movement in the United States* (Cambridge,

Mass.: Harvard University Press, 1959; reprint, New York: Atheneum, 1971), 63, 92–93; Sylvia D. Hoffert, *When Hens Crow: The Woman's Rights Movement in Antebellum America* (Bloomington: Indiana University Press, 1995), 15, 43.

5. DuBois, *Feminism and Suffrage,* 21–52; Hoffert, *When Hens Crow,* 53–72; Aileen S. Kraditor, *The Ideas of the Woman Suffrage Movement, 1890–1920* (New York: Columbia University Press, 1965; reprint, Garden City, N.Y.: Anchor, 1971), 38–43.

6. Gambone, "Forgotten Feminist," 39 (Spring 1973): 12.

7. See, for example, Madeleine M. Kunin, "Clarina Howard Nichols: Green Mountain Suffragette," *Vermont Life* 28 (Winter 1973): 14–17; Deborah P. Clifford, *More than Petticoats: Remarkable Vermont Women* (Guilford, Conn.: Globe Pequot, 2009), 28–38; Florene Parsons, "Clarina Irene Howard Nichols and the Kansas Constitution," paper given to the Delta Kappa Gamma Society, typescript, 1959; Adrienne E. Christiansen, "Clarina Howard Nichols: A Rhetorical Criticism of Selected Speeches" (M.A. thesis, University of Kansas, 1987). For an exception, see T. D. S. Bassett, "Nichols, Clarina Irene Howard," in *Notable American Women, 1607–1950: A Biographical Dictionary,* ed. Edward T. James, Janet Wilson James, and Paul S. Boyer (Cambridge, Mass.: Belknap Press of Harvard University Press, 1971), 2:625–627.

8. Nancy Isenberg, *Sex and Citizenship in Antebellum America* (Chapel Hill: University of North Carolina Press, 1998), 38, 116, 119, 192, 195; Michael D. Pierson, *Free Hearts and Free Homes: Gender and American Antislavery Politics* (Chapel Hill: University of North Carolina Press, 2003), 57–58, 60–61, 71–73, 91–94.

9. Diane Eickhoff, *Revolutionary Heart: The Life of Clarina Nichols and the Pioneering Crusade for Women's Rights* (Kansas City, Kans.: Quindaro Press, 2006).

10. *Proceedings of the Woman's Rights Convention Held at the Broadway Tabernacle, in the City of New York, on Tuesday and Wednesday, September 6th and 7th, 1853* (New York: Fowlers & Wells, 1853), 57. For other woman's rights activists drawn into partisan politics before the Civil War, see Faye Dudden, "New York Strategy: The New York Woman's Movement and the Civil War," in *Votes for Women: The Struggle for Suffrage Revisited,* ed. Jean H. Baker (New York: Oxford University Press, 2002), 56–76.

11. CIHN, "Reminiscences," in Stanton et al., *HWS,* 1:175. For other epithets, see Hoffert, *When Hens Crow,* 91–115.

12. For the classic statement and highly debated theory about the American frontier and its closing, see Frederick Jackson Turner, "The Significance of the Frontier in American History," *Annual Report of the American Historical Association for the Year 1893* (Washington, D.C.: Government Printing Office, 1894), 199–227. For another journalist with womanly influence in the Midwest, see Carol Steinhagen, "The Two Lives of Frances Dana Gage," *Ohio History* 107 (Winter–Spring 1998): 22–38.

13. For the Kansas myth and gender, see Michael Lewis Goldberg, *An Army of Women: Gender and Politics in Gilded Age Kansas* (Baltimore: Johns Hopkins University Press, 1997), 9–14.

14. For Yankee culture in the West, see Susan E. Gray, *The Yankee West: Community Life on the Michigan Frontier* (Chapel Hill: University of North Carolina Press, 1996), 2–15. For settler women as colonizers, see Antonia I. Castañeda, "Women

of Color and the Rewriting of Western History: The Discourse, Politics, and De-colonization of History," in *Women and Gender in the American West: Jensen-Miller Prize Essays from the Coalition for Western Women's History*, ed. Mary Ann Irwin and James F. Brooks (Albuquerque: University of New Mexico Press, 2004), 66–88; and Glenda Riley, *Confronting Race: Women and Indians on the Frontier, 1815–1915* (Albuquerque: University of New Mexico Press, 2004). For imperial-ist dimensions of the suffrage movement, see Louise Michele Newman, *White Women's Rights: The Racial Origins of Feminism in the United States* (New York: Oxford University Press, 1999), 18–19.

15. Goldberg, *Army of Women*, 13–14, 57–85. For this shift in the national movement, see Ellen Carol DuBois, "Outgrowing the Compact of the Fathers: Equal Rights, Woman Suffrage, and the United States Constitution, 1820–1878," *Journal of American History* 74 (December 1987): 848–852; and Carolyn DeSwarte Gifford, "Frances Willard and the Woman's Christian Temperance Union's Conversion to Woman Suffrage," in *One Woman, One Vote: Rediscovering the Woman Suffrage Movement*, ed. Marjorie Spruill Wheeler (Troutdale, Ore.: New Sage Press, 1995), 117–133.

16. See, for example, Mari J. Matsuda, "The West and the Legal Status of Women: Explanations of Frontier Feminism," *Journal of the West* 24 (January 1985): 47–56; Beverly Beeton, *Women Vote in the West: The Woman Suffrage Movement, 1869–1896* (New York: Garland, 1986); Rebecca J. Mead, *How the Vote Was Won: Woman Suffrage in the Western United States, 1868–1914* (New York: New York University Press, 2004); Suzanne M. Marilley, *Woman Suffrage and the Origins of Liberal Feminism in the United States, 1820–1920* (Cambridge, Mass.: Harvard University Press, 1996), 83–98, 124–158; and Alexander Keyssar, *The Right to Vote: The Contested History of Democracy in the United States* (New York: Basic, 2000), 195–196. For gender in western political discourse, see especially Goldberg, *Army of Women*; for female moral authority in western development, see Peggy Pascoe, *Relations of Rescue: The Search for Moral Authority in the American West, 1874–1939* (New York: Oxford University Press, 1990), 7–10.

17. CIHN to Abby Hemenway [1881], in Gambone, "Forgotten Feminist," 40:524.

18. CIHN, "Early Reminiscences of My Life, Written in Her Invalid Hours by Clarina I. H. Nichols, 1880," in ibid., 40:455–456.

19. See especially Jo Burr Margadant, *The New Biography: Performing Femininity in Nineteenth-Century France* (Berkeley: University of California Press, 2000), 1–25. See also Carolyn G. Heilbrun, *Writing a Woman's Life* (New York: Ballantine, 1988); Estelle C. Jelinek, *The Tradition of Women's Autobiography: From Antiquity to the Present* (Boston: Twayne, 1986); and Sara Alpern, Joyce Antler, Elisabeth Israels Perry, and Ingrid Winther Scobie, eds., *The Challenge of Feminist Biog-raphy* (Urbana: University of Illinois Press, 1992). For an approach focusing on language, see Joan Wallach Scott, *Only Paradoxes to Offer: French Feminists and the Rights of Man* (Cambridge, Mass.: Harvard University Press, 1996), 15–16.

20. For the link between evangelical Protestantism and politics, see Robert H. Abzug, *Cosmos Crumbling: American Reform and the Religious Imagination* (New York: Oxford University Press, 1994); and Daniel Walker Howe, "The Evangelical Movement and Political Culture in the North during the Second Party System,"

UNIVERSITY OF WINCHESTER LIBRARY

Journal of American History 77 (March 1991): 1216–1239. For domesticity, see, for example, Nancy F. Cott, *The Bonds of Womanhood: "Woman's Sphere" in New England, 1780–1835* (New Haven, Conn.: Yale University Press, 1977), 63–100, 197–206.

21. Paula C. Baker, "The Domestication of Politics: Women and American Political Society, 1780–1920," *American Historical Review* 89 (June 1984): 620–647; Mary Kelley, *Learning to Stand and Speak: Women, Education, and Public Life in America's Republic* (Chapel Hill: University of North Carolina Press, 2006), esp. 5–15, 28–31; Lori D. Ginzberg, *Women and the Work of Benevolence: Morality, Politics, and Class in the Nineteenth-Century United States* (New Haven, Conn.: Yale University Press, 1990), 11–35; Kathryn Kish Sklar, *Catherine Beecher: A Study in American Domesticity* (New Haven, Conn.: Yale University Press, 1973). Daniel Scott Smith first used the term *domestic feminism* to refer to the increased authority and autonomy middle-class women achieved in the Victorian family. See Daniel Scott Smith, "Family Limitation, Sexual Control, and Domestic Feminism in Victorian America," *Feminist Studies* 1 (Winter-Spring 1973): 40–57. Michael Pierson applies the term broadly to women's engagement in civil society in the antebellum era; see Pierson, *Free Hearts and Free Homes,* 11–13.

22. For use of domestic feminism as political rhetoric, see Janet L. Coryell, "Superceding Gender: The Role of the Woman Politico in Antebellum Partisan Politics," in *Women and the Unstable State in Nineteenth-Century America,* ed. Alison M. Parker and Stephanie Cole (College Station: Texas A&M University Press, 2000), 84–112; and Pierson, *Free Hearts and Free Homes,* 11–13, 71–96.

23. Hoffert, *When Hens Crow,* 32–52; Isenberg, *Sex and Citizenship,* xi–xiv, 71–74, quotation on xviii; Judith Wellman, *The Road to Seneca Falls: Elizabeth Cady Stanton and the First Woman's Rights Convention* (Urbana: University of Illinois Press, 2004), 184–208; Lori D. Ginzberg, *Untidy Origins: A Story of Woman's Rights in Antebellum New York* (Chapel Hill: University of North Carolina Press, 2005), 36–44, 83–106. For the historical foundations of feminist theory, see Nancy F. Cott, *The Grounding of Modern Feminism* (New Haven, Conn.: Yale University Press, 1987), 3–7, 16-20; and Scott, *Only Paradoxes to Offer,* 3–13.

24. For examples of the reform ethos in western development, see Stewart H. Holbrook, *The Yankee Exodus: An Account of Migration from New England* (New York: Macmillan, 1950), esp. chaps. 4, 8, 13; and Lynne Marie Getz, "Partners in Motion: Gender, Migration, and Reform in Antebellum Ohio and Kansas," *Frontiers: A Journal of Women Studies* 27 (2006): 102–135.

Chapter 1. Frontier Legacies

1. *Kansas Daily Commonwealth,* 24 April 1870, in Joseph G. Gambone, ed., "The Forgotten Feminist of Kansas: The Papers of Clarina I. H. Nichols, 1854–1885," *KHQ* 40 (Summer 1974): 257; Elizabeth Cady Stanton, "Mrs. C. I. H. Nichols," in *Eminent Women of the Age: Being Narratives of the Lives and Deeds of the Most Prominent Women of the Present Generation,* James Parton et al. (Hartford, Conn.: J. M. Betts, 1869), 369.

2. C[larina]. I[rene]. H[oward]. C[arpenter]., "For the Phoenix," *Vermont Phoenix*, 13 March 1840.

3. For the early history of Townshend, see esp. James H. Phelps, *Collections Relating to the History and Inhabitants of the Town of Townshend, Vermont, in Three Parts* (Brattleboro, Vt.: George E. Selleck, 1877); and Townshend Historical Society, *A Stitch in Time: Townshend, Vermont, 1753–2003* (Townshend, Vt.: Townshend Historical Society, 2003), 9–46. For white settlement in the region, see Michael Sherman, Gene Sessions, and P. Jeffrey Potash, *Freedom and Unity: A History of Vermont* (Barre: Vermont Historical Society, 2004), 73–80.

4. *Kansas Daily Commonwealth*, 24 April 1870, in Gambone, "Forgotten Feminist," 40:258.

5. CIHN to SBA, 24 March 1852, Nichols Papers.

6. Adin Ballou, *History of the Town of Milford, Worcester County, Massachusetts, from Its First Settlement to 1881* (Boston: Rand, Avery, 1882), 55–58, 76–79, 100, 101–102, 791–796.

7. Revolutionary War Pension Records, Massachusetts, Series M805, roll 413, file S16141, accessed through Heritage Quest Online, http://persi.heritagequeston line.com; Townshend Historical Society, *Stitch in Time*, 110–111, 274; Phelps, *Collections*, 2:76–78, 129, 131.

8. Phelps, *Collections*, 2:77–88, 91, 101; Sherman et al., *Freedom and Unity*, 73–116.

9. Proprietors' Book, Townshend, Vermont, 1753–1782, Office of the Town Clerk, Townshend, Vermont, 91, 158; Townshend Historical Society, *Stitch in Time*, 27–29; Warren E. Booker, ed., *Historical Notes, Jamaica, Windham County, Vermont* (Brattleboro, Vt.: Hildreth, 1940), 5–8, 33.

10. *Kansas Daily Commonwealth*, 24 April 1870, in Gambone, "Forgotten Feminist," 40:257–259.

11. Revolutionary War Pension Records, Rhode Island, Series M805, roll 746, file S18600, http://persi.heritagequestonline.com.

12. Phelps, *Collections*, 2:129–181.

13. Ibid., 158–159, 163, 179.

14. *Kansas Daily Commonwealth*, 24 April 1870, in Gambone, "Forgotten Feminist," 40:258.

15. Phelps, *Collections*, 2:56, 130–149, 158–184; Townshend Historical Society, *Stitch in Time*, 18–22, 48–49, 61, 75.

16. Abby Maria Hemenway, *Vermont Historical Gazetteer* (Brandon, Vt.: Carrie E. H. Page, 1891), 5: pt. 2, 546.

17. CIHN, "Early Reminiscences of My Life, Written in Her Invalid Hours, 1880," in Gambone, "Forgotten Feminist," 40:457.

18. *Kansas Daily Commonwealth*, 6 October 1869, in Gambone, "Forgotten Feminist," 40:127.

19. CIHN, "Early Reminiscences," 457. For portraiture and social status, see David Jaffee, "One of the Primitive Sort: Portrait Makers of the Rural North, 1760–1860," in *The Countryside in the Age of Capitalist Transformation: Essays in the Social History of Rural America* (Chapel Hill: University of North Carolina Press, 1985), 104, 130.

20. The Howard household included one extra male and two extra females in 1820.

"Population Schedules of the Fourth Census of the United States, 1820," Vermont, Windham County, vol. 3, microcopy 33, roll 128, p. 125. For shifts in women's household production, see Catherine E. Kelly, *In the New England Fashion: Reshaping Women's Lives in the Nineteenth Century* (Ithaca, N.Y.: Cornell University Press, 1999), 23–35.

21. Birsha Carpenter to CIHN, 16 October 1848, Nichols Papers; "'The Union' and Mrs. Nichols in a New Dress," *Freedom's Champion*, 25 February 1860.

22. *Kansas Daily Commonwealth*, 6 October 1869, in Gambone, "Forgotten Feminist," 40:127. Memory of a childhood friend is in CIHC, "For the Daughter of a Deceased Friend," *WCD*, 9 June 1842.

23. *Kansas Daily Commonwealth*, 24 April 1870, in Gambone, "Forgotten Feminist," 40:258; CIHN, "Early Reminiscences," 456, 458.

24. Phelps, *Collections*, 2:177, 180–181; Townshend Historical Society, *Stitch in Time*, 112–115.

25. Townshend Town Records, vol. 1, 1786–1813; vols. 3–4, 1813–1844, Office of the Town Clerk, Townshend, Vermont.

26. Hamilton Child, comp., *Gazetteer and Business Directory of Windham County, Vermont, 1724–1884* (Syracuse, N.Y.: Hamilton Child, 1884), 304; Phelps, *Collections*, 2:159.

27. *Herald of Freedom*, 17 May 1856, in Gambone, "Forgotten Feminist," 39:249; Phelps, *Collections*, 2:227.

28. *Boston Evening Transcript*, 9 January 1855, in Gambone, "Forgotten Feminist," 39:38; Townshend Town Records, vol. 1. On Vermont's quasi-religious establishment, see David M. Ludlum, *Social Ferment in Vermont, 1791–1850* (New York: AMS, 1966), 46.

29. Phelps, *Collections*, 2:106, 193–205; Booker, *Historical Notes*, 33–34; Henry Crocker, *History of Baptists in Vermont* (Bellows Falls, Vt.: P. H. Gobie, 1913), 204–205.

30. Phelps, *Collections*, 2:189–190; William G. McLoughlin, *New England Dissent, 1630–1833: The Baptists and the Separation of Church and State* (Cambridge, Mass.: Harvard University Press, 1971), xviii–xxi; Ludlum, *Social Ferment*, 44–49; Randolph A. Roth, *The Democratic Dilemma: Religion, Reform, and the Social Order in the Connecticut River Valley of Vermont, 1791–1850* (Cambridge: Cambridge University Press, 1987), 26–27, 31–36, 55; T. D. Seymour Bassett, *The Gods of the Hills: Piety and Society in Nineteenth-Century Vermont* (Montpelier: Vermont Historical Society, 2000), 130.

31. Phelps, *Collections*, 2:193–195, 263–266; CIHN, "Early Reminiscences," 456–457.

32. CIHN, "Early Reminiscences," 456–457; *Proceedings of the Woman's Rights Convention, Held at Worcester, October 15th and 16th, 1851* (New York: Fowlers & Wells, 1852), 31.

33. Untitled poem, 1839, CIHN Journal, Nichols Papers; Record Book of the Baptist Church, West Townshend, 1810–1820, Windham County Historical Society, Newfane, Vermont; Phelps, *Collections*, 2:266, 261.

34. Phelps, *Collections*, 2:249–252, quotation on 250. For revivalism in Vermont, see Ludlum, *Social Ferment*, 92, 102–105, 163–166; P. Jeffrey Potash, *Vermont's Burned Over District: Patterns of Community Development and Religious Activity,*

1761–1850 (Brooklyn, N.Y.: Carlson, 1991), 147–152, 162–163; and Roth, *Democratic Dilemma*, 26–27.

35. Townshend Historical Society, *Stitch in Time*, 114; Crocker, *History of Baptists*, 435. For women's role in antebellum revivalism, see Mary P. Ryan, *Cradle of the Middle Class: The Family in Oneida County, New York, 1790–1865* (Cambridge: Cambridge University Press, 1981), 60–104; and Marilyn S. Blackwell, "Surrogate Ministers: Women, Revivalism, and Maternal Associations in Vermont," *Vermont History* 69 (Winter 2001): 68–72.

36. CIHN, "Early Reminiscences," 456.

37. Evidence of Chapin's equal treatment and his landholdings is found in Windham County Probate Records, 20:65–83, Westminister District Probate Court, Bellows Falls, Vermont.

38. CIHN, "Early Reminiscences," 458–459.

39. [Mary Palmer Tyler], *The Maternal Physician: A Treatise on the Nurture and Management of Infants from the Birth until Two Years Old. Being the Result of Sixteen Years' Experience in the Nursery. Illustrated by Extracts from the Most Approved Medical Authors. By an American Matron* (New York: Isaac Riley, 1811; reprint, New York: Arno Press, 1972), 273. For classic statements of Republican Motherhood, see Linda K. Kerber, *Women of the Republic: Intellect and Ideology in Revolutionary America* (Chapel Hill: University of North Carolina Press, 1980), 203–209; and Nancy F. Cott, *The Bonds of Womanhood: "Woman's Sphere" in New England, 1780–1835* (New Haven, Conn.: Yale University Press, 1977), 104–109.

40. *Kansas Daily Commonwealth*, 24 April 1870, in Gambone, "Forgotten Feminist," 40:258; *Vermont Phoenix*, 6 March 1868, in ibid., 39:541. For family reading, see William J. Gilmore, *Reading Becomes a Necessity of Life: Material and Cultural Life in Rural New England, 1780–1835* (Knoxville: University of Tennessee Press, 1989), 64–65, 254–282.

41. [CIHN], *The Responsibilities of Woman: A Speech by Mrs. C. I. H. Nichols, at the Woman's Rights Convention, Worcester, October 15, 1851* (Rochester, N.Y.: Steam Press of Curtis, Butts, & Co., 1854), 18.

42. Cott, *Bonds of Womanhood*, 104–125; Gilmore, *Reading Becomes a Necessity*, 45–49; Kelly, *In the New England Fashion*, 70–75; Mary Kelley, *Learning to Stand and Speak: Women, Education, and Public Life in America's Republic* (Chapel Hill: University of North Carolina Press, 2006), 67–84.

43. Phelps, *Collections*, 2:182–185.

44. Ibid.; [CIHN], *Responsibilities of Woman*, 17.

45. [CIHN], *Responsibilities of Woman*, 17; Cott, *Bonds of Womanhood*, 110–123; Kelley, *Learning to Stand and Speak*, 69–75, 86–92.

46. West Townshend Lyceum, Record Book, 1832–1836, VHS; *Proceedings of the Woman's Rights Convention, 1851*, 75.

47. Townshend Historical Society, *Stitch in Time*, 75–79, 114–119. Alphonso Taft became a U.S. diplomat and father of President William Howard Taft.

48. *Proceedings of the Woman's Rights Convention, 1851*, 75. Nichols's sciatica is mentioned in CIHN to Relie & Helen, 12 May 1871, Nichols Papers.

49. *Proceedings of the Woman's Rights Convention, 1851*, 31.

50. Kelley, *Learning to Stand and Speak*, 83–111.
51. [CIHN], *Responsibilities of Woman*, 17.
52. CIHN to SBA, 17 December 1880, in Gambone, "Forgotten Feminist," 40:453; *Proceedings of the Woman's Rights Convention, 1851,* 76.

Chapter 2. The "Wrongs of Woman"

1. Hamilton Child, comp., *Gazetteer and Business Directory of Windham County, Vermont, 1724–1884* (Syracuse, N.Y.: Hamilton Child, 1884), 204; Abby Maria Hemenway, *Vermont Historical Gazetteer* (Brandon, Vt.: Carrie E. H. Page, 1891), 5: pt. 3, 8; *Official History of Guilford, Vermont, 1678–1961. With Genealogies and Biographical Sketches* (Guilford, Vt.: Town of Guilford, 1961), 248–249, 261, 385; Amos B. Carpenter, *A Genealogical History of the Rehoboth Branch of the Carpenter Family in America Brought down from Their English Ancestor, John Carpenter, 1303, with Many Biographical Notes of Descendants and Allied Families* (Amherst, Mass.: Carpenter & Morehouse, 1898), 243, 405.
2. Henry Crocker, *History of Baptists in Vermont* (Bellows Falls, Vt.: P. H. Gobie, 1913), 187, 196–197; Child, *Gazetteer of Windham County*, 304; *Amherst College 1993 Biographical Record: A Record of Amherst College, 1821–1992: Alumni/ae, Trustees, Faculty, Officers, Undergraduates and Honorees* (White Plains, N.Y.: Bernard Harris, 1993), 8, 14.
3. William S. Tyler, *A History of Amherst College during the Administration of Its First Five Presidents from 1821 to 1891* (New York: Frederick H. Hitchcock, 1895), chaps. 3–5; *Amherst College 1993 Biographical Record*, 8, 14; *Union University Centennial Catalog, 1795–1895, of the Officers and Alumni of Union College in the City of Schenectady, N.Y.* (Troy, N.Y.: Troy, Times, 1895), 37; Union Alumni File.
4. James H. Phelps, *Collections Relating to the History and Inhabitants of the Town of Townshend, Vermont, in Three Parts* (Brattleboro, Vt.: George E. Selleck, 1877), 2:234; Windham County Probate Records, 20:80–82, Westminister District Court, Bellows Falls, Vermont. Chapin gave each child $1,500 at marriage, but Clarina actually received $1,814.89, probably to cover legal or other expenses after her separation.
5. See Nancy F. Cott, *The Bonds of Womanhood: "Woman's Sphere" in New England, 1780–1835* (New Haven, Conn.: Yale University Press, 1977), 76–84; Karen Lystra, *Searching the Heart: Women, Men, and Romantic Love in Nineteenth-Century America* (New York: Oxford University Press, 1989), 227–237; and Ellen K. Rothman, *Hands and Hearts: A History of Courtship in America* (New York: Basic Books, 1984), 26–44, 56–75.
6. "Album Dedicatory," 1827, CIHN Journal, Nichols Papers; see also Diane Eickhoff, *Revolutionary Heart: The Life of Clarina Nichols and the Pioneering Crusade for Women's Rights* (Kansas City, Kans.: Quindaro Press, 2006), 24–25.
7. [CIHN], *The Responsibilities of Woman: A Speech by Mrs. C. I. H. Nichols, at the Woman's Rights Convention, Worcester, October 15, 1851* (Rochester, N.Y.: Steam Press of Curtis, Butts, 1854), 17–18; Catherine E. Kelly, *In the New England Fashion: Reshaping Women's Lives in the Nineteenth Century* (Ithaca, N.Y.: Cornell University Press, 1999), 128–137.

8. *Proceedings of the Woman's Rights Convention, Held at Worcester, October 15th and 16th, 1851* (New York: Fowlers & Wells, 1852), 31.

9. *Proceedings of the Woman's Rights Convention, 1851,* 76; *WCD,* 2 November 1846; "The Bible Position of Woman, or Woman's Rights from a Bible Stand-Point," *Vermont Phoenix,* January–February 1870, in Joseph G. Gambone, ed., "The Forgotten Feminist of Kansas: The Papers of Clarina I. H. Nichols, 1854–1885," *KHQ* 40 (Summer 1974): 105; CIHN, "In reply to 'Amor te' written by J.C. on a News Paper," CIHN Journal, November 1837. For the religious meaning of marriage, see Kelley, *In the New England Fashion,* 137–145; and Lystra, *Searching the Heart,* 237–250.

10. *Woman's Journal,* 4 August 1877, in Gambone, "Forgotten Feminist," 40:426; Jonathan Pearson, Diary, 11 August 1833, accessed through Erie Canal website, http://www.eriecanal.org/UnionCollege/Bankwatch.html.

11. For local establishments, see *Brockport Free Press,* 1830–1832. For history, see Jonathan Mark Smith, "Brockport, New York: A Narrative of That Place (and the Place of This Narrative)" (Ph.D. diss., Syracuse University, 1991); [Charlotte Elizabeth Martin], *Story of Brockport for One-Hundred Years, 1829–1929, as Told by Charlotte Elizabeth Martin* (Brockport, N.Y.?, 1929), 3–25.

12. *Brockport Free Press,* 13 October 1830; Smith, "Brockport," 315–316.

13. *Brockport Free Press,* 19 January 1831, 26 January 1831, 9 February 1831, 16 February 1831, 23 February 1831, 2 March 1831, 16 March 1831, 30 March 1831, and 23 November 1831.

14. Ibid., 26 January 1831; 16 March 1831, 30 March 1831, and 21 September 1831.

15. Ibid., 20 October 1830; Paul E. Johnson, *A Shopkeeper's Millennium: Society and Revivals in Rochester, New York, 1815–1837* (New York: Hill & Wang, 1978), 109–110, 188; Nancy A. Hewitt, *Women's Activism and Social Change: Rochester, New York, 1822–1872* (Ithaca, N.Y.: Cornell University Press, 1984), 74–79; Mary P. Ryan, *Cradle of the Middle Class: The Family in Oneida County, New York, 1790–1865* (Cambridge: Cambridge University Press, 1981), 60, 92–94.

16. Johnson, *Shopkeepers' Millennium,* 114.

17. *Brockport Free Press,* 20 October 1830.

18. Ibid., 6 July 1831; Eickhoff, *Revolutionary Heart,* 29.

19. *Minutes of the Leyden Baptist Association, Held in the Baptist Meeting-House, in Guilford, Vt., on Wednesday and Thursday, October 14 and 15, 1829* (n.p., 1829?), 4; Constitution, Townshend Temperance Society Record Book, THS.

20. *Western Star, or Impartial Miscellany,* 7 December 1831; *Brockport Free Press,* 5 October 1831 and 14 March 1832; [CIHC] to Parents, 14 July 1833, Nichols Papers.

21. *Ukiah Press,* 16 January 1885; "'The Union' and Mrs. Nichols in a New Dress," *Freedom's Champion,* 25 February 1860. Clarina's affidavit in her grandfather David Smith's Revolutionary War Pension record placed the couple in New York City in May 1833. See Revolutionary War Pension Records, series M805, roll 746, file S18600, accessed through Heritage Quest Online, http://persi.heritage questonline.com.

22. *Union University Centennial Catalog, 1795–1895,* 37; Union Alumni File; Eickhoff, *Revolutionary Heart,* 30. For street life in lower Manhattan, see especially

Christine Stansell, *City of Women: Sex and Class in New York, 1789–1860* (New York: Knopf, 1986); and Patricia Cline Cohen, *The Murder of Helen Jewett: The Life and Death of a Prostitute in Nineteenth-Century New York* (New York: Knopf, 1998), 62–63, 68–69.

23. "'The Union' and Mrs. Nichols in a New Dress," *Freedom's Champion*, 25 February 1860; [CIHN], *Responsibilities of Woman*, 12–13.

24. CIHN to SBA, 24 March 1852, Nichols Papers.

25. CIHN Journal, 1836–1839. The journal is not in chronological order, and many poems are undated. Two marked "Pub. in Lady's Book" (i.e., *Godey's Lady's Book*) could not be found, and titles of other potential New York publishers are illegible.

26. "Female Influence," *Western Star*, 7 December 1831; CIHN to SBA, 24 March 1852, Nichols Papers; CIHN Journal; "'The Union' and Mrs. Nichols in a New Dress," *Freedom's Champion*, 25 February 1860. For domestic abuse, see Randolph A. Roth, "Spousal Murder in Northern New England, 1776–1865," in *Over the Threshold: Intimate Violence in Early America*, ed. Christine Daniels and Michael V. Kennedy (New York: Routledge, 1999), 65–86.

27. Mary Beth Sievens, *Stray Wives: Marital Conflict in Early National New England* (New York: New York University Press, 2005), 24–29, 60–64, 86–114; Norma Basch, *Framing American Divorce: From the Revolutionary Generation to the Victorians* (Berkeley: University of California Press, 1999), 99–120; *Acts and Resolves Passed by the Legislature of the State of Vermont, October Session, 1822* (Montpelier: State of Vermont, 1822), 17.

28. *Acts and Resolves, Vermont, 1840* (Burlington: State of Vermont, 1840), 18; CIHN to Franklin G. Adams, 25 March 1884, in Gambone, "Forgotten Feminist," 40:557–558.

29. "Carpenter, Clarina I. H., vs. Justin Carpenter, Petition for Divorce," 1843, Windham County Court Records, 4:317, Windham County Courthouse, Newfane, Vermont. The court dismissed Clarina's 1842 petition, perhaps because she still failed to meet the three-year residency requirement.

30. CIHN to Franklin G. Adams, 25 March 1884, in Gambone, "Forgotten Feminist," 40:558. Custody was awarded neither in the divorce decree nor in extant probate records; family tradition suggests Clarina was awarded custody. Fathers normally retained guardianship unless proven unfit, though their custody rights were eroding; see *Revised Statutes of the State of Vermont, Passed November 19, 1839* (Burlington, Vt.: Chauncy Goodrich, 1840), 331–335; and Michael Grossberg, *Governing the Hearth: Law and the Family in Nineteenth-Century America* (Chapel Hill: University of North Carolina Press, 1988), 238–253.

31. [CIHN] to SBA, 1883, in Gambone, "Forgotten Feminist," 40:551; CIHN to SBA, 24 March 1852, Nichols Papers.

32. *Vermont Phoenix*, 31 January 1840.

33. "Population Schedules of the Sixth Census of the United States 1840," Vermont, Windham County, vol. 5, microcopy 704, roll 547, p. 54; Townshend Historical Society, *A Stitch in Time: Townshend, Vermont, 1753–2003* (Townshend, Vt.: Townshend Historical Society, 2003), 111–112. For Chapin's mortgage lending, see

Townshend Land Records, vols. 7 and 8, Office of the Town Clerk, Townshend, Vermont.

34. Child, *Gazetteer of Windham County,* 304; Townshend, Vermont, Families, Book 2, Windham County Historical Society, Newfane, Vermont; Carpenter, *Genealogical History of the Carpenter Family,* 405–406.

35. *Vermont Phoenix,* 31 January 1840. For sciatica, see CIHN to Sara T. D. Robinson, 25 September 1882, in Gambone, "Forgotten Feminist," 40:533.

36. Townshend Historical Society, *Stitch in Time,* 77–78; *Catalogue of Townshend Academy,* 1838–1839, 1840, 1841, 1843, 1844, 1846, 1846–1847; *Catalogue of Leland Seminary,* 1848–1849, 1850–1851, THS; *WCD,* 22 August 1839.

37. C. I. H. Carpenter to Parents, 14 July 1833; CIHN Journal, "Aurelius, my son," Meriden, August 1839, Nichols Papers; Eickhoff, *Revolutionary Heart,* 33.

38. CIHN Journal, January 1838, Nichols Papers. See also CIHN to F. G. Adams, 25 March 1884, in Gambone, "Forgotten Feminist," 40:557–558.

39. *Quindaro Chindowan,* 6 June 1857.

40. T. D. Seymour Bassett, "Vermont Politics and the Press in the 1840s," *Vermont History* 47 (Summer 1979): 196–213; William J. Gilmore, *Reading Becomes a Necessity of Life: Material and Cultural Life in Rural New England, 1780–1835* (Knoxville: University of Tennessee Press, 1989), 26.

41. *Vermont Phoenix,* 31 January 1840, 7 February 1840, 21 February 1840, 6 March 1840, 13 March 1840, and 27 March 1840.

42. Mary Kelley, *Learning to Stand and Speak: Women, Education, and Public Life in America's Republic* (Chapel Hill: University of North Carolina Press, 2006), 8–10. Journalist Jane Storm, for example, received $2 per page in the late 1840s. See Linda S. Hudson, *Mistress of Manifest Destiny: A Biography of Jane McManus Storm Cazneau, 1807–1878* (Austin: Texas State Historical Association, 2001), 50.

43. For sentimentalism in regional culture, see Randolph A. Roth, *The Democratic Dilemma: Religion, Reform, and the Social Order in the Connecticut River Valley of Vermont, 1791–1850* (Cambridge: Cambridge University Press, 1987), 284–285; Cott, *Bonds of Womanhood,* 64–74.

44. *Vermont Phoenix,* 6 March 1840.

45. *WCD,* 9 June 1842; *Vermont Phoenix,* 21 February 1840 and 31 January 1840.

46. *Vermont Phoenix,* 13 March 1840.

47. For women's benevolent work, see, for example, Ryan, *Cradle of the Middle Class,* 105–127; Lori D. Ginzberg, *Women and the Work of Benevolence: Morality, Politics, and Class in the Nineteenth-Century United States* (New Haven, Conn.: Yale University Press, 1990), 2–35; Barbara Cutter, *Domestic Devils, Battlefield Angels: The Radicalism of American Womanhood, 1830–1865* (DeKalb: Northern Illinois University Press, 2003), 7–17; and Anne M. Boylan, *Origins of Woman's Activism: New York and Boston, 1797–1840* (Chapel Hill: University of North Carolina Press, 2002), 136–169.

48. Phelps, *Collections,* 2:255; Townshend Temperance Society, Record Book, THS.

49. Geo. W. Nichols to Mrs. C. I. H. Carpenter, 12 February [1841?], Nichols Papers.

50. Henry Burnham, *Brattleboro Windham County, Vermont: Early History with Biographical Sketches of Some of Its Citizens* (Brattleboro, Vt.: D. Leonard, 1880), 181;

Mary R. Cabot, *Annals of Brattleboro, 1681–1895* (Brattleboro, Vt.: Hildreth, 1921–1922), 1:338, 379–380, 419. Cabot lists Nichols's birth in 1782, but the 1850 census confirms his birth in 1785. See "Population Schedules of the Seventh Census of the United States 1850," Vermont, Windham County, microcopy 932, roll 929, pp. 351–352.

51. Geo. W. Nichols to Mrs. C. I. H. Carpenter, 12 February [1841?], Nichols Papers.
52. Ibid.; *WCD*, 2 November 1846.

Chapter 3. Pathway to Politics

1. *Vermont Phoenix*, 13 March 1840; *WCD*, 28 September 1853.
2. Edwin Allan Fessenden, *The Fessenden Family in America*, ed. Mary Elizabeth Fessenden Washburn (n.p.: Edwin Allan Fessenden, 1971), 657, 672; "Population Schedules of the Seventh Census of the United States 1850," Vermont, Windham County, microcopy 432, roll 929, pp. 351–352; CIHN to SBA, 21 August 1881, in Joseph G. Gambone, ed., "The Forgotten Feminist of Kansas: The Papers of Clarina I. H. Nichols, 1854–1885," *KHQ* 40 (Winter 1974): 514–515.
3. *Catalogue of Townshend Academy*, 1841, 1843–1844, 1846–1851.
4. *Vermont Phoenix*, 6 November 1835; Mary R. Cabot, *Annals of Brattleboro, 1681–1895* (Brattleboro, Vt.: Hildreth, 1921–1922), 1:366–372, 407–416, 437–442, 595–596; Randolph A. Roth, *The Democratic Dilemma: Religion, Reform, and the Social Order in the Connecticut River Valley of Vermont, 1791–1850* (Cambridge: Cambridge University Press, 1987), 16–22.
5. Cabot, *Annals of Brattleboro*, 441–442, 423–431, 595–596; Constance M. McGovern, "The Insane, the Asylum, and the State in Nineteenth-Century Vermont," *Vermont History* 52 (Fall 1984): 205–216.
6. *Vermont Phoenix*, 12 August 1847; Cabot, *Annals of Brattleboro*, 564–578.
7. *WCD*, 16 July 1851 and 3 July 1845; CIHN to Henry Wadsworth Longfellow, 28 November 1845, Henry Wadsworth Longfellow Letters, Houghton Library, Harvard College, Cambridge, Massachusetts. Clarina mentions Longfellow's poetry in *WCD*, 24 December 1846. For Gove Nichols, see Jean L. Silver-Isenstadt, *Shameless: The Visionary Life of Mary Gove Nichols* (Baltimore: Johns Hopkins University Press, 2002), 72–75.
8. "Memorial of Ladies of Brattleboro on the Subject of Temperance," 1837, Vermont State Archives, Montpelier, Vermont. For revivalism in the region, see Roth, *Democratic Dilemma*, 188–219, 223–229; for women's activities, see Marilyn S. Blackwell, "Surrogate Ministers: Women, Revivalism, and Maternal Associations in Vermont," *Vermont History* 69 (Winter 2001): 70–75.
9. Cabot, *Annals of Brattleboro*, 338; Frederick S. Knight, "A Century for Christ," *First Baptist Church of Brattleboro Organized April 2, 1840, 100th Anniversary, March 31 to April 4, 1940* (n.p., 1940), 8–11.
10. Cabot, *Annals of Brattleboro*, 463; *WCD*, 16 March 1843; Blackwell, "Surrogate Ministers," 69. For evangelical values, see Daniel Walker Howe, "The Evangelical Movement and Political Culture in the North during the Second Party System," *Journal of American History* 77 (March 1991): 1216–1239.

11. *Brattleboro Messenger*, 14 September 1827, 13 June 1828, 4 July 1828, 30 June 1832, and 1833–1834. For anti-Masonry and Vermont politics, see Michael Sherman, Gene Sessions, and P. Jeffrey Potash, *Freedom and Unity: A History of Vermont* (Barre: Vermont Historical Society, 2004), 183–187; and Roth, *Democratic Dilemma*, 152–158, 173–177, 246–250.

12. *Vermont Phoenix*, 10 July 1835; Cabot, *Annals of Brattleboro*, 379–380, 419, 422; T. D. Seymour Bassett, "Vermont Politics and the Press in the 1840s," *Vermont History* 47 (Summer 1979): 210–211.

13. *WCD*, 19 November 1840.

14. Ibid., 19 November 1840, 21 May 1841, 9 June 1842, 22 August 1839, and 7 November 1839. For northern Democratic ideology, see Jean H. Baker, *Affairs of Party: The Political Culture of Northern Democrats in the Mid-Nineteenth Century* (Ithaca, N.Y.: Cornell University Press, 1983), 109–130.

15. CIHN to SBA, 24 March 1852, Nichols Papers. See also "A Wife as Is a Wife," *Lily* 2 (January 1850): 5; and *WCD*, 16 July 1851.

16. Madelon Golden Schilpp and Sharon M. Murphy, *Great Women of the Press,* (Carbondale: Southern Illinois University Press, 1983); Patricia Okker, *Our Sister Editors: Sarah J. Hale and the Tradition of Nineteenth-Century American Women Editors* (Athens: University of Georgia Press, 1995), 6–37; Carolyn L. Karcher, *The First Woman in the Republic: A Cultural Biography of Lydia Maria Child* (Durham, N.C.: Duke University Press, 1994), 267–291.

17. Janet L. Coryell, "Superseding Gender: The Role of the Woman Politico in Antebellum Partisan Politics," in *Women and the Unstable State in Nineteenth-Century America*, ed. Alison M. Parker and Stephanie Cole (College Station: Texas A&M University Press, 2000), 84–87; Linda S. Hudson, *Mistress of Manifest Destiny: A Biography of Jane McManus Storm Cazneau, 1807–1878* (Austin: Texas State Historical Association, 2001), 45–68; Sylvia D. Hoffert, *Jane Grey Swisshelm: An Unconventional Life, 1815–1884* (Chapel Hill: University of North Carolina Press, 2004), 104–131.

18. See Catherine Allgor, *Parlor Politics: In Which the Ladies of Washington Help Build a City and a Government* (Charlottesville: University Press of Virginia, 2000); Elizabeth R. Varon, *We Mean to Be Counted: White Women and Politics in Antebellum Virginia* (Chapel Hill: University of North Carolina Press, 1998), 71–102; Rebecca Edwards, *Angels in the Machinery: Gender in American Party Politics from the Civil War to the Progressive Era* (New York: Oxford University Press, 1997), 13–18; Robert J. Dinkins, *Before Equal Suffrage: Women in Partisan Politics from Colonial Times to 1920* (Westport, Conn.: Greenwood, 1995), 30–50; and Christopher J. Olsen, "Respecting 'The Wise Allotment of Our Sphere': White Women and Politics in Mississippi, 1840–1860," *Journal of Women's History* 11 (Autumn 1999): 104–125.

19. *WCD*, 19 November 1840.

20. Ibid., 28 November 1849, 23 December 1847, and 2 October 1845; Danville *North Star*, 5 July 1847. For provincial values in the Connecticut River Valley, see Catherine E. Kelly, *In the New England Fashion: Reshaping Women's Lives in the Nineteenth Century* (Ithaca, N.Y.: Cornell University Press, 1999), 8–10.

21. *WCD*, 2 November 1846.
22. Ibid., 25 July 1844 and 28 November 1849.
23. Ibid., 2 October 1845 and 16 March 1843.
24. Ibid., 2 November 1846; 3 July 1850 and ? 1850, clippings in Nichols Papers.
25. *WCD*, 24 December 1846, 20 November 1845, and 23 November 1846.
26. Danville *North Star*, reprint from *WCD*, 5 July 1847; ibid., 13 December 1847. For contemporary female ideals, see especially Barbara Welter, "The Cult of True Womanhood, 1820–1860," *American Quarterly* 18 (Summer 1966): 151–175; Ruth H. Bloch, "American Feminine Ideals in Transition: The Rise of the Moral Mother, 1285–1815," *Feminist Studies* 4 (1978): 101–126; and Nancy Cott, *Bonds of Womanhood: "Woman's Sphere" in New England, 1780–1835* (New Haven, Conn.: Yale University Press, 1977), 63–100.
27. *WCD*, 24 December 1846; T. D. S. Bassett, "Nichols, Clarina Irene Howard," in *Notable American Women, 1607–1950: A Biographical Dictionary*, ed. Edward T. James, Janet Wilson James, and Paul S. Boyer (Cambridge: Oxford University Press, 1971), 2:625.
28. *WCD*, 19 November 1840, 25 July 1844, and 15 August 1844; see also 9 November 1846.
29. *WCD*, 14 November 1844. For Democratic ideology, see Baker, *Affairs of Party*, 109–114.
30. *WCD*, 20 November 1845 and 2 October 1845.
31. David M. Ludlum, *Social Ferment in Vermont, 1791–1850* (New York: AMS, 1966), 229–233; Horace Mann, "Eighth Annual Report of the Secretary of the Board of Education, December 10, 1844," in *Common School Journal* 7 (March 1845): 87.
32. *WCD*, 14 November 1844.
33. Ibid., 14 November 1844 and 6 June 1849; for news, see 9 November 1846.
34. For the Washingtonian movement, see Ian Tyrell, *Sobering Up: From Temperance to Prohibition in Antebellum America, 1800–1860* (Westport, Conn.: Greenwood, 1989), 159–190.
35. Brattleboro Town Meeting Records, Book 3, 135, Office of the Town Clerk, Brattleboro, Vermont. For temperance politics, see Samuel B. Hand, Jeffrey D. Marshall, and Gregory Sanford, "'Little Republics': The Structure of State Politics in Vermont, 1854–1920," *Vermont History* 53 (Summer 1985): 148–149; and Ludlum, *Social Ferment*, 79–81.
36. *WCD*, 21 November 1844 and 9 November 1846; *Vermont Mercury*, 4 April 1845.
37. *Vermont Phoenix*, 2 October 1835 and 7 July 1837; Cabot, *Annals of Brattleboro*, 365. For the Colonization movement in Vermont, see Ludlum, *Social Ferment*, 145–146; and Roth, *Democratic Dilemma*, 103–106, 178–183.
38. *WCD*, 9 June 1842 and 29 June 1843. For rural Democrats, see Bruce Laurie, *Beyond Garrison: Antislavery and Social Reform* (Cambridge: Cambridge University Press, 2005), 50–51, 135–152.
39. For Baptists, see Henry Crocker, *History of Baptists in Vermont* (Bellows Falls, Vt.: P. H. Gobie, 1913), 463–467; for Townshend, see Townshend Historical Society, *A Stitch in Time: Townshend, Vermont, 1753–2003* (Townshend, Vt.: Townshend Historical Society, 2003), 142–143; for Phelps, "Fifth Annual Meeting of the

Vermont Anti-Slavery Society," *Voice of Freedom*, 2 March 1839. For overviews of women's antislavery work, see especially Beth A. Salerno, *Sister Societies: Women's Antislavery Organizations in Antebellum America* (DeKalb: Northern Illinois University Press, 2005); and Susan Zaeske, *Signatures of Citizenship, Antislavery, and Women's Political Identity* (Chapel Hill: University of North Carolina Press, 2003).

40. *WCD*, 25 July 1844, 15 August 1844, 22 August 1844, 24 December 1846, and 31 December 1846, quotation from 20 November 1845. For northern Democrats, see Jonathan H. Earle, *Antislavery and the Politics of Free Soil, 1824–1854* (Chapel Hill: University of North Carolina Press, 2004), 62–72, 78–94.

41. *WCD*, 14 November 1844; Harley F. Smith to Cousin C., 15 August 1847, Warsaw [N.Y.], Nichols Papers.

42. *Vermont Phoenix*, 23 September 1847, 5 November 1847, and 13 October 1848; Harley F. Smith to Cousin C., 15 August 1847, Warsaw [N.Y.], Nichols Papers; George W. Nichols to Charles G. Eastman, 3 July 1848, Eastman Papers, VHS; Ludlum, *Social Ferment*, 183–197; Earle, *Antislavery and the Politics of Free Soil*, 129–143, 177.

43. *WCD*, 30 December 1847. For female journalists' style, see Coryell, "Superseding Gender," 96–102.

44. *Vermont Phoenix*, 29 October 1847; *WCD*, 6 June 1849.

45. *Semi-Weekly Eagle*, 23 August 1849.

46. *WCD*, 28 November 1849; Edward P. Brynn, "Vermont's Political Vacuum of 1845–1856 and the Emergence of the Republican Party," *Vermont History* 38 (Spring 1970): 113–123; Reinhard O. Johnson, "The Liberty Party in Vermont, 1840–1848: The Forgotten Abolitionists," *Vermont History* 47 (Fall 1979): 258–275; Earle, *Jacksonian Antislavery*, 169–197.

47. Michael D. Pierson, *Free Hearts and Free Homes: Gender and American Antislavery Politics* (Chapel Hill: University of North Carolina Press, 2003), 57–58.

48. CIHN, "Reminiscences," in Elizabeth Cady Stanton, Susan B. Anthony, and Matilda Joslyn Gage, eds., *HWS* (Rochester, N.Y.: Fowler & Wells, 1881; 2nd ed., 1887), 1:172.

49. Hudson, *Mistress of Manifest Destiny*, 49, 58; "The Legal Wrongs of Women," *Democratic Review* 14 (May 1844): 483; see also *Democratic Review* 18 (April 1846): 250.

50. Richard H. Chused, "Married Women's Property Law, 1800–1850," *Georgetown Law Journal* 71 (1983): 1359–1425; Norma Basch, *In the Eyes of the Law: Women, Marriage, and Property in Nineteenth-Century New York* (Ithaca, N.Y.: Cornell University Press, 1982), 136–161; Peggy A. Rabkin, *Fathers to Daughters: The Legal Foundations of Female Emancipation* (Westport, Conn.: Greenwood, 1980), 85–98, 110–111; Judith Wellman, *The Road to Seneca Falls: Elizabeth Cady Stanton and the First Woman's Rights Convention* (Urbana: University of Illinois Press, 2004), 145–148.

51. *Middlebury Register*, 9 July 1850.

52. For women's political rhetoric, see Zaeske, *Signatures of Citizenship*, 54–68, 83–90.

53. CIHN, "Reminiscences," 172. Whigs in the Senate voted overwhelmingly for separate estates, but they split over the issue in the House. Democrats were opposed to separate estates. See *Journal of the Senate of the State of Vermont, October Session, 1847* (Montpelier: Vermont State Senate, 1848), 16, 37, 48, 51, 62, 67; *Journal of the House of the State of Vermont, October Session, 1847* (Montpelier: Vermont House, 1848), 203, 206–207. For the bipartisan nature of debate over the issue in New York, see Basch, *In the Eyes of the Law*, 150–155. For Whigs' desire to protect the family, see Edwards, *Angels in the Machinery*, 19–20.

54. *Bellows Falls Gazette*, 5 November 1847; *Caledonian*, 20 November 1852.

55. See Gambone, "Forgotten Feminist," 40:452; *Journal of the House of the State of Vermont, 1847*, 206–207.

56. *Vermont Phoenix*, 26 November 1847; *WCD*, 24 July 1850, clipping in Nichols Papers.

57. Wellman, *Road to Seneca Falls*, 135–153, 172–177, 207–210; Lori D. Ginzberg, *Untidy Origins: A Story of Woman's Rights in Antebellum New York* (Chapel Hill: University of North Carolina Press, 2005), 131–152.

58. Wellman, *Road to Seneca Falls*, 207–210; Pierson, *Free Hearts and Free Homes*, 33–74; Hoffert, *Jane Grey Swisshelm*, 68–69, 104–111, 147.

59. *WCD*, 6 June 1849.

60. For Republican Motherhood, see especially Linda K. Kerber, *Women of the Republic: Intellect and Ideology in Revolutionary America* (Chapel Hill: University of North Carolina Press, 1980), 209–231, 227–231, 283–288.

61. *Acts and Resolves Passed by the Legislature of the State of Vermont at Their October Session, 1849* (Montpelier: State of Vermont, 1849), 14–18; ibid., *1850* (Montpelier: State of Vermont, 1850), 8–9; CIHN, "Reminiscences," 172; *WCD*, 1849, clipping in Nichols Papers. For the connection between homestead exemptions and married women's property laws, see Paul Goodman, "The Emergence of Homestead Exemption in the United States: Accommodation and Resistance to the Market Revolution, 1840–1880," *Journal of American History* 80 (September 1993): 488–489.

62. *Middlebury Register*, 18 June 1850. For other states, see Chused, "Married Women's Property Law," 1359–1425; and Basch, *In the Eyes of the Law*, 115–126, 136–161.

63. *Middlebury Register*, 9 July 1850, 16 July 1850, 18 June 1850, and 6 August 1850.

64. *WCD*, 24 July 1850, clipping in Nichols Papers; [CIHN], "Notes by the Wayside," *WCD*, 7 July 1852. For journalistic style, see Coryell, "Superseding Gender," 96–102.

65. *Lily* 2 (January 1850): 5; *WCD*, 16 July 1851.

66. *WCD*, 28 November 1849.

67. [CIHN], *The Responsibilities of Woman: A Speech by Mrs. C. I. H. Nichols, at the Woman's Rights Convention, Worcester, October 15, 1851* (Rochester, N.Y.: Steam Press of Curtis, Butts & Co., 1854), 11; *WCD*, 16 July 1851. For religion and women's citizenship, see Ginzberg, *Untidy Origins*, 36–44; and Nancy Isenberg, *Sex and Citizenship in Antebellum America* (Chapel Hill: University of North Carolina Press, 1998), 75–78. For women's use of female moral authority in reform politics, see Barbara Cutter, *Domestic Devils, Battlefield Angels: The Radicalism of American Womanhood, 1830–1865* (DeKalb: Northern Illinois University Press, 2003),

101–112. For evangelicalism, see Robert H. Abzug, *Cosmos Crumbling: American Reform and the Religious Imagination* (New York: Oxford University Press, 1994), 5–8.

68. Birsha Carpenter to CIHN, 16 October 1848 and undated, c. 1848; Birsha Howard, frag., n.d., Nichols Papers.

69. "Lady Editors," *Lily* 2 (March 1850): 23; *WCD*, 16 July 1851.

Chapter 4. The Politics of Motherhood

1. CIHN to Abbey Hemenway, [1881]; to SBA, [1883], both in Joseph G. Gambone, ed., "The Forgotten Feminist of Kansas: The Papers of Clarina I. H. Nichols, 1854–1885," *KHQ* 40 (Winter 1974): 524, 551.

2. For the political line between women's writing and public speaking, see Nancy Isenberg, *Sex and Citizenship in Antebellum America* (Chapel Hill: University of North Carolina Press, 1998), 64–69.

3. "Lady Editors," *Lily* 2 (March 1850): 23. For sisterly relations among editors, see Patricia Okker, *Our Sister Editors: Sarah J. Hale and the Tradition of Nineteenth-Century American Women Editors* (Athens: University of Georgia Press, 1995), 18–25.

4. "Lady Writers," *Lily* 2 (June 1850): 43; 2 (September 1850): 71. For editors, see Sylvia D. Hoffert, *When Hens Crow: The Woman's Rights Movement in Antebellum America* (Bloomington: Indiana University Press, 1995), 85–88; and Martha M. Solomon, "The Role of the Suffrage Press in the Woman's Rights Movement," in *A Voice of Their Own: The Woman Suffrage Press, 1849–1910* (Tuscaloosa: University of Alabama Press, 1991), 15. Pierson became assistant editor of Anne Elizabeth McDowell's *Woman's Advocate* (1855–1860); see Okker, *Our Sister Editors*, 204. For the significance of sewing and knitting, see Catherine E. Kelly, *In the New England Fashion: Reshaping Women's Lives in the Nineteenth Century* (Ithaca, N.Y.: Cornell University Press, 1999), 47–51. Later Nichols criticized Swisshelm for subordinating woman's rights to other reforms. See CIHN, "Women and Temperance," *Lily* 4 (April 1852): 30–31; and *WCD*, 20 April 1853.

5. "Lady Editors" and "Woman's Rights," *Lily* 2 (March 1850): 22–23.

6. For women in civil society, see, for example, Anne Boylan, *Origins of Woman's Activism: New York and Boston, 1797–1840* (Chapel Hill: University of North Carolina Press, 2002), 136–169; Barbara Cutter, *Domestic Devils, Battlefield Angels: The Radicalism of American Womanhood, 1830–1865* (DeKalb: Northern Illinois University Press, 2003), 8–17; and Mary Kelley, *Learning to Stand and Speak: Women, Education, and Public Life in America's Republic* (Chapel Hill: University of North Carolina Press, 2006).

7. "Lady Editors," *Lily* 2 (March 1850): 23; see also June 1849, 46; August 1849, 61–62; and April 1850, 29. For Nichols on voting, see Elizabeth Cady Stanton, Susan B. Anthony, and Joslyn Gage, eds., *HWS* (Rochester, N.Y.: Fowler & Wells, 1881; 2nd ed., 1887), 1:355. For Swisshelm, see Sylvia D. Hoffert, *Jane Grey Swisshelm: An Unconventional Life, 1815–1884* (Chapel Hill: University of North Carolina Press, 2004), 143–148.

8. "From Lucretia Mott," *Anti-Slavery Bugle*, 27 April 1850; "From Mrs. C. I .H. Nichols," *Anti-Slavery Bugle*, 4 May 1850.

9. Elizabeth Cady Stanton, "Why Must Women Vote," *Lily* 2 (May 1850): 38; "Should Women Vote?" *Lily* 2 (July 1850): 55. For Stanton's role at the Seneca Falls Convention, see Judith Wellman, *The Road to Seneca Falls: Elizabeth Cady Stanton and the First Woman's Rights Convention* (Urbana: University of Illinois Press, 2004), 192–203.

10. CIHN, "Women Voting and Holding Office," *Lily* 2 (August 1850): 60; *WCD*, reprinted in *Lily* 3 (February 1851): 10.

11. Nancy Isenberg, *Sex and Citizenship in Antebellum America* (Chapel Hill: University of North Carolina Press, 1998), 28–32, 69–74; Wellman, *Road to Seneca Falls*, 190–203; Julie Roy Jeffrey, "Permeable Boundaries: Abolitionist Women and Separate Spheres," *Journal of the Early Republic* 21 (Spring 2001): 79–93.

12. Lori D. Ginzberg, "'The Hearts of Your Readers Will Shudder': Fanny Wright, Infidelity, and American Free Thought," *American Quarterly* 46 (June 1994): 195–226; Cutter, *Domestic Devils*, 100–125; Jean Fagan Yellin and John C. Van Horne, eds., *The Abolitionist Sisterhood: Women's Political Culture in Antebellum America* (Ithaca, N.Y.: Cornell University Press, 1994).

13. For the political nature of women's benevolence, see Paula Baker, "The Domestication of Politics: Women and American Political Society," *American Historical Review* 89 (June 1984): 620–647; and Lori D. Ginzberg, *Women and the Work of Benevolence: Morality, Politics, and Class in the Nineteenth-Century United States* (New Haven, Conn.: Yale University Press, 1990). For political rallies, see Elizabeth R. Varon, *We Mean to Be Counted: White Women and Politics in Antebellum Virginia* (Chapel Hill: University of North Carolina Press, 1998), 71–102.

14. Hoffert, *When Hens Crow*, 97–107; Ginzberg, "'The Hearts of Your Readers Will Shudder,'" 195–226.

15. "'Public' Women," [Vermont] *Union Whig*, reprinted in *Middlebury Register*, 7 May 1850; CIHN to SBA, 24 March 1852, Nichols Papers. For Nichols's anxieties about public speaking, see *Burlington Courier*, 25 November 1852.

16. "From Mrs. C. I. H. Nichols," *Anti-Slavery Bugle*, 4 May 1850; Mary R. Cabot, *Annals of Brattleboro, 1681–1895* (Brattleboro, Vt.: Hildreth, 1921–1922), 1:613–614, 395–398.

17. *Proceedings of the Woman's Rights Convention, held at Worcester, October 23rd and 24th, 1850* (Boston: Prentiss & Sawyer, 1851).

18. Ibid., 51–54, quotation on 7; Isenberg, *Sex and Citizenship*, 29–37; Linda K. Kerber, "A Constitutional Right to Be Treated Like American Ladies: Women and the Obligations of Citizenship," in *U.S. History as Women's History: New Feminist Essays*, ed. Linda K. Kerber, Alice Kessler-Harris, and Kathryn Kish Sklar (Chapel Hill: University of North Carolina Press, 1995), 23–27.

19. *Proceedings of the Woman's Rights Convention, 1850*, 72–73; quotation from Elizabeth Wilson, *A Scriptural View of Woman's Rights and Duties, in All the Important Relations of Life* (Philadelphia: William S. Young, 1849), 254; Isenberg, *Sex and Citizenship*, 71.

20. *Proceedings of the Woman's Rights Convention, 1850*, 20, 48; Isenberg, *Sex and*

Citizenship, 71–72; [CIHN], "Worcester Convention," Susan B. Anthony Papers, Folder 17, SL.

21. For activists and religious dissent, see Isenberg, *Sex and Citizenship,* 75–101, quotation on 77; and Anna M. Speicher, *The Religious World of Antislavery Women: Spirituality in the Lives of Five Abolitionist Lecturers* (Syracuse, N.Y.: Syracuse University Press, 2000), 61–73. For social analysis of the leadership and emphasis on natural law, see Hoffert, *When Hens Crow,* 10–22; and Judith Wellman, "The Seneca Falls Women's Rights Convention: A Study of Social Networks," *Journal of Women's History* 3 (Spring 1991): 9–37. For "moral crusaders," see Alice S. Rossi, ed., *The Feminist Papers: From Adams to de Beauvoir* (Boston: Northeastern University Press, 1973), 246–278.

22. CIHN, "Reminiscences," in Stanton et al., *HWS,* 1:172; *WCD,* [1850], clipping in Nichols Papers; *Middlebury Register,* 16 July 1850; *Acts and Resolves Passed by the Legislature of the State of Vermont at Their October Session, 1850* (Burlington: State of Vermont, 1850), 8–9.

23. *Proceedings of the Woman's Rights Convention Held at Akron, Ohio, May 28 and 29, 1851* (Cincinnati: B. Franklin Book & Job Office, 1851), 42–43.

24. *WCD,* 16 July 1851.

25. *New York Herald,* 25 October 1850. For newspaper coverage, see the U.S. Women's History Workshop website, http://www.1assumption.edu/whw/old/newspaper %20accounts_1850.html; and Hoffert, *When Hens Crow,* 76–78, 91–115.

26. *Proceedings of the Woman's Rights Convention, held at Worcester, October 15th and 16th, 1851* (New York: Fowlers & Wells, 1852), 7–13; Stanton et al., *HWS,* 1:356.

27. [CIHN], *The Responsibilities of Woman. A Speech by Mrs. C. I. H. Nichols, at the Woman's Rights Convention, Worcester, October 15, 1851* (Rochester, N.Y.: Curtis, Butts, & Co., 1854), 1; CIHN to SBA, 24 March 1852, Nichols Papers.

28. CIHN, "Dear Friends," to the National Woman Suffrage Association Convention, 25 February 1884, in Gambone, "Forgotten Feminist," 40:556; [CIHN], *Responsibilities of Woman,* 2.

29. CIHN to SBA, 24 March 1852; *New York Daily Tribune,* 3 September 1853. For Nichols's height, see *WCD,* 16 July 1851. For a structural analysis of Nichols's rhetoric, see Adrienne Christiansen, "Clarina Howard Nichols: A Rhetorical Criticism of Selected Speeches" (M.A. thesis, University of Kansas, 1987), 64–88.

30. [CIHN], *Responsibilities of Woman,* 1, 7, 12–13.

31. Ibid., 3, 10, 15, 18; *Proceedings of the Woman's Rights Convention, 1851,* 69.

32. [CIHN], *Responsibilities of Woman,* 4, 16. For women's economic claims, see Reva Siegel, "Home as Work: The First Woman's Rights Claims Concerning Wives' Household Labor, 1850–1880," *Yale Law Journal* 103 (March 1994): 1117–1118.

33. For Republican Motherhood, see Linda K. Kerber, *Women of the Republic: Intellect and Ideology in Revolutionary America* (Chapel Hill: University of North Carolina Press, 1980), 283–288. For its extension through the conversion of obligations to rights claims, see Kerber, "Constitutional Right to Be Treated Like American Ladies," 20–27; and Rosemarie Zagarri, "The Rights of Man and Woman in Post-Revolutionary America," *William and Mary Quarterly* 55 (April 1998): 203–230.

34. *Proceedings of the Woman's Rights Convention, 1851,* 33, 50.

35. Stanton et al., *HWS*, 1:606; Paulina Wright Davis, comp., *A History of the National Woman's Rights Movement, for Twenty Years, with the Proceedings of the Decade Meeting Held at Apollo Hall, October 20, 1870, from 1850 to 1870. With an Appendix Containing the History of the Movement during the Winter of 1871, in the National Capitol* (New York: Journeymen Printers' Co-Operative Association, 1871), 14.

36. Stanton et al., *HWS*, 1:522; *Proceedings of the Woman's Rights Convention Held at West Chester, Pa., June 2nd and 3rd, 1852* (Philadelphia: Merrihew & Thompson, 1852), 7. For contradictions in feminist theory, see Joan Wallach Scott, *Only Paradoxes to Offer: French Feminists and the Rights of Man* (Cambridge, Mass.: Harvard University Press, 1996), 3–13.

37. *WCD*, 23 February 1853.

38. CIHN to SBA, 24 March 1852, Nichols Papers.

39. "Mrs. Kemble and Her New Costume," *Lily* 1 (December 1849): 94; "Our Dress," 3 (April 1851): 30; see also 3 (September 1851); Isenberg, *Sex and Citizenship*, 48–53.

40. *Anti-Slavery Bugle*, 21 June 1851; see also "A Puzzle," *Lily* 3 (August 1851): 60; and *WCD*, 16 July 1851. For Swisshelm, see Hoffert, *Jane Grey Swisshelm*, 29–30, 141–142.

41. Elizabeth Cady Stanton, "To Women's Temperance Meeting, Albany," 28 January 1852, in *The Selected Papers of Elizabeth Cady Stanton and Susan B. Anthony*, ed. Ann D. Gordon (New Brunswick, N.J.: Rutgers University Press, 1997), 1:191–193, quotation on 192; see also Stanton et al., *HWS*, 1:482–488. For Bloomer, see "The Duty of Drunkard's Wives—Divorce," *Lily* 4 (August 1852): 69.

42. CIHN to SBA, 24 March 1852, Nichols Papers. See also Nichols's letter to the New York Temperance Convention, 18 April 1852, in Stanton et al., *HWS*, 1:847–848; and *Lily* 5 (June 1853): 3. For the divorce debate in the 1850s, see Norma Basch, *Framing American Divorce: From the Revolutionary Generation to the Victorians* (Berkeley: University of California Press, 1999), 72–79.

43. CIHN to SBA, 24 March 1852, Nichols Papers; [CIHN], *Responsibilities of Woman*, 18.

44. For Bloomer, see *Lily* 4 (November 1852): 94. Nichols's pamphlet was advertised in *Lily* 6 (15 March 1854): 46, but no copies have been found: C. I. H. Nichols, *Intemperance and Divorce; or the Duty of the Drunkard's Wife* (New York: Fowlers & Wells, 1854).

45. Francoise Basch, "Women's Rights and the Wrongs of Marriage in Mid-Nineteenth-Century America," *History Workshop Journal* 22 (Autumn 1986): 35–37; Andrea Moore Kerr, *Lucy Stone: Speaking Out for Equality* (New Brunswick, N.J.: Rutgers University Press, 1992), 72, 111–112; Elizabeth Cazden, *Antoinette Brown Blackwell: A Biography* (Old Westbury, N.Y.: Feminist Press, 1983), 67–70.

46. Stanton et al., *HWS*, 1:355; "Notes by the Wayside, *WCD*, 7 July 1852.

47. "National Woman's Rights Convention," *New York Tribune*, 10 September 1852, 11 September 1852, and 14 September 1852; quotations from 10 and 14 September.

48. *WCD*, 27 October 1852. For Anthony and morality, see Kathleen Barry, *Susan B.*

Anthony: A Biography of a Singular Feminist (New York: New York University Press, 1988), 9, 27–53.

49. *WCD*, 13 April 1853.

50. *Herald of Freedom*, 17 May 1856, in Gambone, "Forgotten Feminist," 39:249; George B. Nichols to Mother and Father, 26 February 1854, Nichols Papers.

51. "A. O. Carpenter," in [Lyman L. Palmer], *History of Mendocino County, California* (San Francisco: Alley, Bowen, 1880), 633; *Catalogue of Townshend Academy, 1846–1847, Catalogue of Leland Seminary*, 1848–1849, 1850–1857.

52. Birsha Carpenter to CIHN, 16 October 1848, Nichols Papers; CIHN to SBA, August 1853? Miscellaneous letter, A/N617, SL.

53. "The Cricket's Song," *Lily* 2 (December 1850), 92.

54. "Notes by the Wayside," *WCD*, 7 July 1852.

55. CIHN to SBA, 24 March 1852, Nichols Papers.

56. "The Paupers' Removal," *WCD*, 2 March 1853.

57. "Treatment of Paupers, Criminals, etc.," *WCD*, 18 February 1852.

58. *WCD*, 20 April 1853; "The Birds," reprinted in *Lily* 4 (June 1852): 50–51.

59. *WCD*, 6 June 1849; for Vermont politics, see Edward P. Brynn, "Vermont's Political Vacuum of 1845–1856 and the Emergence of the Republican Party," *Vermont History* 38 (Spring 1970): 117–120; Jonathan H. Earle, *Jacksonian Antislavery and the Politics of Free Soil, 1824–1854* (Chapel Hill: University of North Carolina Press, 2004), 177; and *Burlington Sentinel*, 16 May 1851 and 11 July 1851. For other editors in the Connecticut River Valley, see Bruce Laurie, *Beyond Garrison: Antislavery and Social Reform* (Cambridge: Cambridge University Press, 2005), 160–163.

60. *WCD*, 16 July 1851, 27 August 1851.

61. Ibid., 27 August 1851, 7 July 1852; Michael D. Pierson, *Free Hearts and Free Homes: Gender and American Antislavery Politics* (Chapel Hill: University of North Carolina Press, 2003), 57–61. For critiques, see *Semi-Weekly Eagle*, 1 September 1851 and 20 May 1852.

62. *WCD*, 27 October 1852; *Frederick Douglass' Paper*, 25 February 1853, quoted in Pierson, *Free Hearts and Free Homes*, 57. Pierson asserts that Nichols, Harriet Beecher Stowe, and Jane Grey Swisshelm linked political antislavery with "domestic feminism" and bolstered party unity through moralistic rhetoric.

63. Lori D. Ginzberg, "Moral Suasion Is Moral Balderdash: Women, Politics, and Social Activism in the 1850s," *Journal of American History* 73 (December 1986), 601–610; Alice Taylor, "From Petitions to Partyism: Antislavery and the Domestication of Maine Politics in the 1840s and 1850s," *New England Quarterly* 77 (March 2004): 70–84. For abolitionists' engagement in politics, see Laurie, *Beyond Garrison*, chap. 5.

64. Antoinette L. Brown, "A Woman Politician," *Lily* 4 (November 1852), 100; "National Woman's Rights Convention," *New York Tribune*, 14 September 1852; *WCD*, 27 October 1852.

65. *Caledonian*, 6 November 1852; *Semi-Weekly Eagle*, 5 January 1852; CIHN to SBA, 24 March 1852, Nichols Papers. Nichols also spoke at a ladies "Tea Party," a nonalcoholic event nearby on the Fourth of July; see *WCD*, 7 July 1852.

66. Harriet Kesia Hunt, *Glances and Glimpses; or Fifty Years Social, Including Twenty Years Professional Life* (Boston: J. P. Jewett, 1856), 293–300; *Lily* 3 (February 1851): 10; *Anti-Slavery Bugle*, 12 June 1852; Claudia Knott, "The Woman Suffrage Movement in Kentucky, 1879–1920" (Ph.D. diss., University of Kentucky, 1989), 197.

67. CIHN, "Reminiscences," 172. For local school reform, see *Semi-Weekly Eagle*, 4 March 1852 and 15 March 1852.

68. The petition is no longer extant, but Barrett quoted from it in his report to the House Education Committee; see *Journal of the House of the State of Vermont, October Session, 1852* (Burlington, Vt.: Goodrich, 1852), 353. Nichols partly explained her rationale in 1856; see *Herald of Freedom*, 8 March 1856, in Gambone, "Forgotten Feminist," 39:240.

69. *WCD*, 12 October 1853.

70. CIHN, "Reminiscences," 173.

71. *PRP*, 29 January 1881, in Gambone, "Forgotten Feminist," 40:505.

72. CIHN, "Reminiscences," 173; *Semi-Weekly Eagle*, 25 October 1852 and 1 November 1852. Whigs dominated the Senate but held only a slim majority over Democrats, Free Democrats, and Free Soilers in the House of Representatives. For Nichols's reputation as a Free Soil journalist and the connection between Free Soil politics and women's rights, see Pierson, *Free Hearts and Free Homes*, 57–58.

73. *PRP*, 29 January 1881, in Gambone, "Forgotten Feminist," 40:505; CIHN, "Reminiscences," 173.

74. *Burlington Courier*, 25 November 1852; *Green Mountain Freeman*, 4 November 1852; *New York Tribune*, 3 December 1852. None of these papers included additional remarks about school suffrage.

75. CIHN, "Reminiscences," 173.

76. Ibid., 174; *Journal of the House, 1852*, 105, 167, 186, 191, 210, 235–237, 259–260, quotation on 353.

77. *Burlington Courier*, 25 November 1852; *Caledonian*, 6 November 1852 and 20 November 1852; CIHN, "Reminiscences," 174.

78. CIHN to SBA, 16 January 1853, Nichols Papers; *WCD*, 27 August 1851 and 26 January 1853; *Semi-Weekly Eagle*, 1 September 1852; "Next Step for the Freemen of the County," *WCD*, 23 February 1853; CIHN, "Operation of the Liquor Law," *Weekly Eagle*, 21 April 1854 and 28 April 1854.

79. CIHN, "Reminiscences," 174; "The Paupers' Removal," *WCD*, 2 March 1853; see also *WCD*, 13 April 1853.

Chapter 5. Lady Orator

1. *WCD*, 26 January 1853, 2 March 1853, and 13 April 1853.

2. CIHN to SBA, 17 December 1880, in Joseph G. Gambone, ed., "The Forgotten Feminist of Kansas: The Papers of Clarina Howard Nichols, 1854–1885," *KHQ* 40 (Autumn 1974): 453; *WCD*, 6 July 1853. For Stone in Brattleboro, see *WCD*, 26 January 1853; Joelle Million, *Women's Voice, Women's Place: Lucy Stone and the Birth of the Women's Rights Movement* (Westport, Conn.: Praeger, 2003), 131–133;

Alice Stone Blackwell, *Lucy Stone: Pioneer of Woman's Rights* (Boston: Little, Brown, 1930), 83–84; and *Liberator*, 26 August 1853 and 2 September 1853.

3. CIHN to SBA, 16 January 1853, Nichols Papers.

4. CIHN, "Reminiscences," in Elizabeth Cady Stanton, Susan B. Anthony, and Matilda Joslyn Gage, eds., *HWS* (Rochester, N.Y.: Fowler & Wells, 1881; 2nd ed., 1887), 1:175–178, 183–184. Quotations from *Vergennes Vermonter* quoted in *Lily* 5 (April 1853): 4; *Weekly Eagle*, 10 March 1854; CIHN to SBA, 16 January 1853, Nichols Papers. Nichols recalled that she received less than $20 per lecture, but in 1860 she told a colleague in Kansas that $25 was one-quarter of what she had received in the East; see CIHN to SBA, [1883], in Gambone, "Forgotten Feminist," 40:551; and CIHN to Susan Wattles, 21 April 1860, Augustus Wattles Papers, KSHS.

5. *WCD*, 23 February 1853.

6. "Mrs. Nichols' Lecture," *Daily Free Press*, 13 April 1853.

7. CIHN, "Letter from Mrs. Nichols," *Milwaukee Daily Free Democrat*, 8 February 1854; *Weekly Eagle*, 24 February 1854; CIHN, "Reminiscences," 175–178.

8. *Weekly Eagle*, 24 February 1854; CIHN, "Reminiscences," 175–178. For railroad stories, see Amy G. Richter, *Home on the Rails: Women, the Railroad, and the Rise of Public Domesticity* (Chapel Hill: University of North Carolina Press, 2005), 28–39.

9. CIHN to Bertia C. C. Davis, 26 February 1880, Nichols Papers; CIHN to SBA, [1883], in Gambone, "Forgotten Feminist," 40:551–552.

10. For the Welds, see Gerda Lerner, *The Grimké Sisters from South Carolina: Pioneers for Woman's Rights and Abolition* (New York: Schoken, 1967), 315–318, 327–330; Benjamin P. Thomas, *Theodore Weld: Crusader for Freedom* (New Brunswick, N.J.: Rutgers University Press, 1950), 176–177; and Ann D. Gordon, ed., *The Selected Papers of Elizabeth Cady Stanton and Susan B. Anthony* (New Brunswick, N.J.: Rutgers University Press, 1997), 1:174–176, 181–182.

11. [George B. Nichols] to Mother and Father, 26 February 1854 and 16 June 1854, Nichols Family Collection, Grace Hudson Museum, Ukiah, California; to Mother, January 1853; Bertia to Mother, 1 February [1853?], Nichols Papers.

12. George Nichols to Mother, 29 January 1855, Nichols Papers. For Eagleswood, see Lerner, *Grimké Sisters*, 316–318, 327–339; "Raritan Bay Union School," *Una* 2 (August 1854): 311; Thomas, *Theodore Weld*, 225–237; Jayme A. Sokolow, "Culture and Utopia: The Raritan Bay Union," *New Jersey History* 94 (Summer–Autumn 1976): 89–100; and Marie Marmo Mullaney, "Feminism, Utopianism, and Domesticity: The Career of Rebecca Buffum Spring, 1811–1911," in *A New Jersey Anthology*, ed. Maxine N. Lurie (New Brunswick, N.J.: Rutgers University Press, 2002), 161–186. Tuition at Eagleswood was approximately $60 per quarter, but it was also dependent upon ability to pay.

13. SBA to Elizabeth Cady Stanton, 11 November 1853, in Gordon, *Selected Papers of ECS and SBA*, 1:231; *Lily* 6 (June 1853): 4, 6; Stanton et al., *HWS*, 1:490–500; Ian R. Tyrell, "Women and Temperance in Antebellum America, 1830–1860," *Civil War History* 28 (June 1982): 146–152.

14. CIHN to SBA, August 1853?, Miscellaneous letter, A/N617, SL.

15. CIHN to SBA, 11 November 1880 and 21 August 1881, in Gambone, "Forgotten Feminist," 39:452, 513.

16. Hannah Darlington to CIHN, 5 March 1854, Nichols Papers; for Darlington, see Stanton et al., *HWS*, 1:344–350.

17. Stanton et al., *HWS*, 1:499–509.

18. *New York Daily Tribune*, 5 September 1853, 4–5; for vegetarianism, see Diane Eickhoff, *Revolutionary Heart: The Life of Clarina Nichols and the Pioneering Crusade for Women's Rights* (Kansas City, Kans.: Quindaro Press, 2006), 42.

19. *Proceedings of the Whole World's Temperance Convention Held at Metropolitan Hall, in the City of New York, on Thursday and Friday, September 1st and 2nd, 1853* (New York: Fowlers & Wells, 1853), available on the E Pluribus Unum Project website, http://www.assumption.edu/ahc/1853TemperanceConvention.html; *New York Daily Tribune*, 3 September 1853 and 5 September 1853.

20. *Proceedings of the Whole World's Temperance Convention, 1853*.

21. *Proceedings of the Woman's Rights Convention Held at the Broadway Tabernacle, in the City of New York, on Tuesday and Wednesday, September 6th and 7th, 1853* (New York: Fowlers & Wells, 1853); Stanton et al., *HWS*, 1:546–575.

22. *Proceedings of the Woman's Rights Convention, 1853*, 57–60, quotations on 58 and 59.

23. Ibid., 60–96, quotations on 96; Stanton et al., *HWS*, 1:556–575; Sylvia D. Hoffert, *When Hens Crow: The Woman's Rights Movement in Antebellum America* (Bloomington: Indiana University Press, 1995), 93–94.

24. Stanton et al., *HWS*, 1:548–575; *Liberator*, 30 September 1853; Tyrell, "Women and Temperance in Antebellum America," 150–151.

25. *Liberator*, 24 February 1854 and 26 May 1854.

26. CIHN, "Reminiscences," 178–179; *Daily Free Democrat*, 13 September 1853, 23 September 1853, and 26 September 1853.

27. *WCD*, 5 October 1853; CIHN, "Reminiscences," 178; John B. Blake, "Fowler, Lydia Folger," in *Notable American Women, 1607–1950: A Biographical Dictionary*, ed. Edward T. James, Janet Wilson James, and Paul S. Boyer (Cambridge, Mass.: Belknap Press of Harvard University Press, 1971), 1:654–655. For Booth, see Genevieve G. McBride, *On Wisconsin Women: Working for Their Rights from Settlement to Suffrage* (Madison: University of Wisconsin Press, 1993), 11–18; and Diane S. Butler, "The Public Life and Private Affairs of Sherman Miller Booth," *Wisconsin Magazine of History* 82 (Spring 1999): 167–175.

28. *WCD*, 5 October 1853.

29. *Daily Free Democrat*, 30 September 1853, 1 October 1853, and 7 October 1853; McBride, *On Wisconsin Women*, 18–19.

30. *Daily Free Democrat*, 3 October 1853 and 4 October 1853.

31. CIHN, "Reminiscences," 181–183; *Daily Free Democrat*, 3 October 1853.

32. *Daily Free Democrat*, 30 September 1853, 4 October 1853, 19 October 1853, 20 October 1853, 22 October 1853, and 1 November 1853; *WCD*, 12 October 1853. See also Michael J. McManus, *Political Abolitionism in Wisconsin, 1840–1861* (Kent, Ohio: Kent State University Press, 1998), 80–84.

33. Nichols later claimed credit for passage of a bill allowing wives of drunkards the right to their own earnings and custody of children. Wisconsin had passed

a married women's property rights act in 1850 excluding earnings. See CIHN, "Reminiscences," 184; McBride, *On Wisconsin Women*, 19–21; and McManus, *Political Abolitionism*, 86–88.

34. *WCD*, 12 October 1853; *Daily Free Democrat*, 26 October 1853 and 31 December 1853.

35. "All Honor to the Women of Michigan," *Lily* 5 (July 1853): 14; "The Women and the Groggeries," *Lily* 6 (April 1854): 60; Anne C. Coon, *Hear Me Patiently: The Reform Speeches of Amelia Jenks Bloomer* (Westport, Conn.: Greenwood, 1994), 17–24; Andrea Moore Kerr, *Lucy Stone: Speaking Out for Equality* (New Brunswick, N.J.: Rutgers University Press, 1992), 71–74; "What They Think and How They Talk 'out West,'" *WCD*, 6 July 1853; Nichols to Lucy Stone, 1 June 1854, printed in *Una* 2 (July 1854): 300–301.

36. *Syracuse Journal*, 19 November 1853; Darlington to CIHN, 5 March 1854, Nichols Papers; CIHN to Mr. Otis, 19 December 1853, VHS; CIHN to SBA, 16 January 1853, Nichols Papers. For Nichols in Boston, see *Liberator*, 17 March 1854.

37. CIHN to Bertia C. C. Davis, 26 February 1880, Nichols Papers; "Vermont Correspondence," *Daily Free Democrat*, 12 April 1854.

38. *Vermont Phoenix*, 8 March 1867, in Gambone, "Forgotten Feminist," 39:515; "Vermont Correspondence," *Daily Free Democrat*, 31 December 1853, 12 April 1854; CIHN, "Reminiscences," 193. For the petition on custody, see *WCD*, 12 October 1853.

Chapter 6. "This New Oasis of Freedom"

1. CIHN, "Reminiscences," in Elizabeth Cady Stanton, Susan B. Anthony, and Matilda Joslyn Gage, eds., *HWS* (Rochester, N.Y.: Fowler & Wells, 1881; 2nd ed., 1887), 1:193.

2. *Springfield Daily Republican*, 15 November 1854, in Joseph G. Gambone, ed., "The Forgotten Feminist of Kansas: The Papers of Clarina I. H. Nichols, 1854–1885," *KHQ* 39 (Spring 1973): 34; CIHN, "Reminiscences," 1:193; Charles Robinson to SBA (copy to CIHN), 5 August 1876, in Gambone, "Forgotten Feminist," 39:28n70.

3. Chapin Howard's divisible estate was valued in 1860 at approximately $56,723. In addition to $1,815 he had given Clarina during his life, she received an advance of $1,423 in June 1855, $2,280 in July 1860, and subsequent minor distributions after her mother died. See Windham County Probate Records, 20:65–83; 22:415–416; and 24:173–174, Westminister District Probate Court, Bellows Falls, Vermont.

4. Eric Foner, *Free Soil, Free Labor, Free Men: The Ideology of the Republican Party before the Civil War* (New York: Oxford University Press, 1970), 11–39, 93–95, 156–168; Sean Wilentz, *The Rise of American Democracy: Jefferson to Lincoln* (New York: W. W. Norton, 2005), 671–675.

5. The Massachusetts Emigrant Aid Company was rechartered as the New England Emigrant Aid Company in 1855. See Louise Barry, "The Emigrant Aid Company Parties of 1855," *KHQ* 12 (August 1943): 227–268.

6. For reaction to the Kansas-Nebraska Act, see Michael Morrison, *Slavery and the American West: The Eclipse of Manifest Destiny and the Coming of the Civil War* (Chapel Hill: University of North Carolina Press, 1997), 126–187; James McPherson, *Battle Cry of Freedom* (New York: Oxford University Press, 1989), 125–130; and William H. Freehling, *The Road to Disunion* (New York: Oxford University Press, 1990), 1:550–567. For the border conflict, see Nicole Etcheson, *Bleeding Kansas: Contested Liberty in the Civil War Era* (Lawrence: University Press of Kansas, 2004). On the New England Emigrant Aid Company, see Gunja SenGupta, *For God and Mammon: Evangelicals and Entrepreneurs, Masters and Slaves in Territorial Kansas, 1854–1860* (Athens: University of Georgia Press, 1996); and Samuel A. Johnson, *The Battle Cry of Freedom: The New England Emigrant Aid Company in the Kansas Crusade* (Lawrence: University of Kansas Press, 1954).

7. *Daily Free Democrat*, 14 November 1854, in Gambone, "Forgotten Feminist," 39:35; *Report of the Committee of the Massachusetts Emigrant Aid Company* (Boston: Massachusetts Emigrant Aid Company, 1854), KSHS. See also Eli Thayer, *The New England Emigrant Aid Company, and Its Influence, through the Kansas Contest, upon National History* (Worcester, Mass.: Franklin P. Rice, 1887).

8. Massachusetts Emigrant Aid Company, "Purpose," unknown author, c. 1854, New England Emigrant Aid Collection, 624, KSHS; SenGupta, *For God and Mammon*, 1–4, 24–27, 80–87.

9. *Daily Free Democrat*, 25 January, 5 April 1854; "Dear Lucy," *Una* 2 (July 1854): 301; *Lily* 6 (November 1854): 158, and *Worcester (Mass.) Daily Transcript*, 26 October 1854, both in Gambone, "Forgotten Feminist," 39:20n36, 29n74.

10. Barry, "Emigrant Aid Company Parties," *KHQ* 12 (May 1943): 115–155; *Vermont Phoenix*, 24 February 1855.

11. *Springfield Daily Republican*, 15 November 1854, in Gambone, "Forgotten Feminist," 39:33–34; A. O. Carpenter, "Letter from Kansas," *Weekly Eagle*, 29 December 1854. For white women and colonization in the West, see Antonia I. Castañeda, "Women of Color and the Rewriting of Western History: The Discourse, Politics, and Decolonization of History," in *Women and Gender in the American West: Jensen-Miller Prize Essays from the Coalition for Western Women's History*, ed. Mary Ann Irwin and James F. Brooks (Albuquerque: University of New Mexico Press, 2004), 66–88.

12. *Boston Evening Telegraph*, 31 October 1854, in Gambone, "Forgotten Feminist," 39:30–31.

13. *Springfield Daily Republican*, 15 November 1854, in ibid., 32, 34.

14. *Boston Evening Telegraph*, 31 October 1854, in ibid., 29–30; *Springfield Daily Republican*, 15 November 1854, in ibid., 32–34, quotations on 33, 34.

15. Sara T. L. Robinson, *Kansas, Its Interior and Exterior Life, including a Full View of Its Settlement, Political History, Social Life, Climate, Soil, Productions, Scenery, etc.* (Boston: Crosby & Nichols, 1856), 42. For Margaret Wood, see *Herald of Freedom*, 13 January 1855; and Kristen Tegtmeier Oertel, *Bleeding Borders: Race, Gender, and Violence in Pre–Civil War Kansas* (Baton Rouge: Louisiana State University, 2009), 60–64. For other free-state women, see Oertel, *Bleeding Borders*, 58–84; and Nichole Etcheson, "'Labouring for the Freedom of This Territory': Free State

Kansas Women in the 1850s," *Kansas History* 21 (Summer 1998): 71–87. For pioneering women and gender norms, see Joan E. Cashin, *A Family Venture: Men and Women on the Southern Frontier* (New York: Oxford University Press, 1991); Julie Roy Jeffrey, *Frontier Women: The Trans-Mississippi West, 1840–1880* (New York: Hill & Wang, 1979); John Mack Faragher, *Women and Men on the Overland Trail* (New Haven, Conn.: Yale University Press, 1979); and Glenda Riley, *The Female Frontier: A Comparative View of Women on the Prairie and the Plains* (Lawrence: University Press of Kansas, 1988).

16. *Boston Evening Telegraph*, 9 January 1855, in Gambone, "Forgotten Feminist," 39:40. For women's moral influence in the West, see Robert L. Griswold, "Anglo Women and Domestic Ideology in the American West in the Nineteenth and Early Twentieth Centuries," in *Western Women: Their Land, Their Lives*, ed. Lillian Schlissel et al. (Albuquerque: University of New Mexico Press, 1988), 18–29, quotation on 22.

17. CIHN, "Reminiscences," 185–186. A Congregational minister from the American Home Mission Society had organized the church a few weeks earlier, but he was apparently not available. See SenGupta, *For God and Mammon*, 67.

18. *Daily Free Democrat*, 14 November 1854, in Gambone, "Forgotten Feminist," 39:36–37.

19. CIHN, "Reminiscences," 186.

20. *Boston Evening Telegraph*, 9 January 1855, in Gambone, "Forgotten Feminist," 39:37–40.

21. *Vermont Phoenix*, 24 February 1855 and 9 June 1855; *Weekly Eagle*, 29 December 1854. For Lawrence, see Frank W. Blackmar, *The Life of Charles Robinson, The First State Governor of Kansas* (Topeka: Crane, 1902), 116–117.

22. B. F. Stringfellow, "Kansas–Slavery," *New York Daily Tribune*, 27 January 1855.

23. *New York Daily Tribune*, 5 February 1855, in Gambone, "Forgotten Feminist," 39:44–50, quotations on 48–49.

24. For the gendered nature of Republican ideology, see Michael D. Pierson, *Free Hearts and Free Homes: Gender and American Antislavery Politics* (Chapel Hill: University of North Carolina Press, 2004); for women and party politics, see Melanie Gustafson, *Women and the Republican Party* (Urbana: University of Illinois Press, 2001), 11–21.

25. *New York Daily Tribune*, 5 February 1855, in Gambone, "Forgotten Feminist," 39:49–50; Stringfellow, "Kansas–Slavery," *New York Daily Tribune*, 27 January 1855. For the conflicting understandings of liberty, see Etcheson, *Bleeding Kansas*, 2–5.

26. CIHN, "Reminiscences," 198–199; Gambone, "Forgotten Feminist," 39:41n94.

27. Barry, "Emigrant Aid Company Parties," 227–268; CIHN to Samuel Woodward, 5 April 1855 and 7 April 1855, both in Gambone, "Forgotten Feminist," 39:50–56, quotation on 51; CIHN, "Reminiscences,"185. Nichols confused the details of her first and second trips up the Missouri. Captain Chouteau commanded the steamboat when she lectured on board.

28. CIHN to Samuel Woodward, 5 April 1855 and 7 April 1855, both in Gambone, "Forgotten Feminist," 39:50–56, quotations on 54, 52, 56.

29. *Vermont Phoenix*, 5 May 1855 and 9 June 1855; CIHN to Samuel Woodward, 21

April 1855, in Gambone, "Forgotten Feminist," 39:221–223. Under preemption laws, a 160-acre claim could be registered and acquired for $1.25 an acre if settlers lived on it.

30. CIHN to Samuel Woodward, 21 April 1855, in Gambone, "Forgotten Feminist," 39:220, 224; *Kansas Tribune*, cited in *Lily* 8 (June 1855), in ibid., 228 and 228n17.

31. CIHN to Samuel Woodward, 21 April 1855 and 14 May 1855, both in ibid., 39:220–227, quotation on 224; see also 228n17.

32. Julia Louisa Lovejoy, "Letters from Kanzas," *KHQ* 11 (February 1942): 34, 44.

33. Wilcomb E. Washburn, *The American Indian and the United States: A Documentary History* (New York: Random House, 1973) 1:62. For the impact of the conflict on relations with Native Americans, see Oertel, *Bleeding Borders*, 9–32, 109–119.

34. Charles M. Chase to the Illinois *True Republican and Sentinel*, 19 August 1863, in miscellaneous Chase file, KSHS.

35. CIHN to Samuel Woodward, 7 April 1855, in Gambone, "Forgotten Feminist," 39:54; Amelia Bloomer, *Lily* (November 1855), cited in Louise Noun, "Amelia Bloomer, A Biography: Part II, the Suffragist of Council Bluffs," *Annals of Iowa* 47 (Spring 1985): 578. For Nichols's sympathetic view of Christian missionaries, see *Springfield Daily Republican*, 8 January 1855, in Gambone, "Forgotten Feminist," 39:42–43.

36. Gambone, "Forgotten Feminist," 39:221n4; John Brown, "Speech," March 1857, John Brown Collection, no. 299, KSHS.

37. John T. Jones to Gov. James W. Denver, 16 January 1858, James W. Denver Collection, no. 328, KSHS; CIHN to Samuel Woodward, 21 April 1855, in Gambone, "Forgotten Feminist," 39:221–224.

38. CIHN to Samuel Woodward, 14 June 1855, in Gambone, "Forgotten Feminist," 39:229.

39. *Herald of Freedom*, 17 May 1856; CIHN to Samuel Woodward, 6 October 1855, both in ibid., 39:246–247, 230–231; Bertia C. Carpenter to CIHN, 21 September [1855], ms. copy in T. D. S. Bassett Papers, in author's possession.

40. CIHN to Samuel Woodward, 6 October 1855, in Gambone, "Forgotten Feminist," 39:230–231; Diane Eickhoff, *Revolutionary Heart: The Life of Clarina Howard Nichols and the Pioneering Crusade for Women's Rights* (Kansas City, Kans.: Quindaro Press, 2006), 115–116.

41. Blackmar, *Life of Charles Robinson*, 130–135, quotations on 402, 404, 405; John McCool, "Conventional Wisdom," KansasHistoryOnline, ed. Henry J. Fortunato, 2006, http://www.kansashistoryonline/ksh/articlepage.asp?artid=285.

42. *Herald of Freedom*, 11 August 1855.

43. Ibid., 25 August 1855 and 8 September 1855.

44. Ibid., 6 October 1855 and 10 November 1855.

45. "Affairs in Kansas," Message, the President of the United States (Washington, D.C.: 1856), KSHS; CIHN, "Reminiscences," 186; Charles Robinson, *The Kansas Conflict* (New York: Harper, 1892), 176–177.

46. On sectional tensions and the Wakarusa War, see Etcheson, *Bleeding Kansas*, 70–88.

47. Oertel, *Bleeding Borders,* 76–84; *Vermont Phoenix,* 16 February 1856; Ansel Phelps, editor of the *Greenfield (Mass.) Gazette and Courier,* praised Nichols's sacrifice. See Gambone, "Forgotten Feminist," 39:236n33.

48. CIHN to Samuel Woodward, 6 October 1855, in Gambone, "Forgotten Feminist," 39:232.

49. See Jacob Merritt Anthony to "Dear Parents," *Rochester Daily Democrat,* 15 May 1856, in ibid., 39:256n71. See also Oertel, *Bleeding Borders,* 101–108.

50. *Herald of Freedom,* 8 March 1856, in Gambone, "Forgotten Feminist," 39:237–238.

51. Franklin Pierce, "Special Message to Congress," 24 January 1856; "Proclamation," 11 February 1856, cited in William E. Connelley, *A Standard History of Kansas and Kansans* (Chicago, Lewis Publishing, 1918), 1:270.

52. *Herald of Freedom,* 8 March 1856, in Gambone, "Forgotten Feminist," 39:238.

53. Clarina received $200, representing her dower right to a third of George's estate. Marlboro District Probate Records, 21:335, 338, 353, 394, 398–399, 411, Brattleboro District Court House, Brattleboro, Vermont.

54. *Herald of Freedom,* 8 March 1856, in Gambone, "Forgotten Feminist," 39:240 and n42.

55. *Herald of Freedom,* 8 March 1856, and 17 May 1856, in Gambone, "Forgotten Feminist," 39:239–240, 247.

56. *Herald of Freedom,* 8 March 1856, 26 April 1856, 17 May 1856, in Gambone, "Forgotten Feminist," quotations on 39:240, 241–242, 248, 250. Only taxpaying widows could vote in Kentucky school meetings. For women's property rights in the West, see Mari J. Matsuda, "The West and the Legal Status of Women: Explanations of Frontier Feminism," *Journal of the West* 24 (1985): 47–56.

57. G. W. Brown to Eli Thayer, 4 June 1856, Eli Thayer Collection, no. 519, KSHS.

58. CIHN to Emma, 24 May 1856, in Gambone, "Forgotten Feminist," 39:253. On Relie and the Battle of Black Jack, see Marvin A. Schenck, Karen Holmes, and Sherrie Smith-Ferri, *Aurelius O. Carpenter: Photographer of the Mendocino Frontier* (Ukiah, Calif.: Grace Hudson Museum and Sun House, 2006), 21–23; and William L. Cutler, *History of the State of Kansas* (Chicago: A. T. Andreas, 1883), part 34, part 1, Kansas Collection website, http://www.kancoll.org/books/cutler/terr hist/terrhist-p34.html; see also Etcheson, *Bleeding Kansas,* 114.

59. CIHN to Samuel Woodward, 8 July 1856, in Gambone, "Forgotten Feminist," 39:254.

60. Pierson, *Free Hearts and Free Homes,* 117–133; Gustafson, *Women and the Republican Party,* 18–20. See also Sally Denton, *Passion and Principle: John and Jessie Frémont, the Couple Whose Power, Politics, and Love Shaped Nineteenth-Century America* (New York: Bloomsbury, 2007).

61. Michael D. Pierson, "'A War of Extermination': A Newly Uncovered Letter by Julia Louisa Lovejoy, 1856," *Kansas History* 16 (Summer 1993): 120–123; "Letters of Julia Louisa Lovejoy, 1856–1864," *KHQ* 14 (May 1947): 136–137; Pierson, *Free Hearts and Free Homes,* 149.

62. Pierson, *Free Hearts and Free Homes,* 148–163; Robinson, *Kansas; Its Interior and Exterior Life;* Lydia Maria Child, "The Kansas Emigrants," *New York Daily*

Tribune, 23 October 1856. See also Carolyn L. Karcher, "From Pacifism to Armed Struggle: L. M. Child's 'The Kansas Emigrants' and Antislavery Ideology in the 1850s," *ESQ: A Journal of the American Renaissance* 34, no. 3 (1988): 140–158; Karcher, *The First Woman in the Republic: A Cultural Biography of Lydia Maria Child* (Durham, N.C.: Duke University Press, 1994), 392–397; and Margaret Kellow, "'For the Sake of Suffering Kansas': Lydia Maria Child, Gender and the Politics of the 1850s," *Journal of Women's History* 5 (Fall 1993): 32–49.

63. CIHN to Thaddeus Hyatt, 4 October 1856, in Gambone, "Forgotten Feminist," 39:257.

64. SBA to CIHN, September 1856, in ibid., 256n69; CIHN to Thaddeus Hyatt, 4 October 1856, Thaddeus Hyatt Collection, no. 401, KSHS.

65. CIHN, "Reminiscences," 187–189; *New York Daily Tribune*, 27 September 1856; O. M. Clauherty to CIHN, Havana, 20 September 1856, Nichols Papers.

66. *New York Daily Tribune*, 1 November 1856; "To the Women of the State of New York," November 1856, in Gambone, "Forgotten Feminist," 39:258–260. For women at Republican events, see Pierson, *Free Hearts and Free Homes*, 140–150; and Gustafson, *Women and the Republican Party*, 8–20.

67. "Petition of Citizens of Kansas Territory," 8 January 1857; A. O. Carpenter to Mr. Hyatt, 22 November [1856]; [Thaddeus] Hyatt to My Dear Friend [Horace White] (No. 26), Telegraphic dispatch, 19 August 1856, Thaddeus Hyatt Collection, no. 401, box 2, KSHS.

68. *Lily* 8 (15 December 1856): 150–155; Stanton et al., eds., *HWS*, 1:651–652. Nichols appears as a vice president in the report in the *Lily* but not in *HWS*.

Chapter 7. Strong-Minded Woman

1. *WG*, 31 March 1882, in Joseph G. Gambone, ed., "The Forgotten Feminist of Kansas: The Papers of Clarina I. H. Nichols, 1854–1885," *KHQ* 40 (Winter 1974): 527–528.

2. *Herald of Freedom*, 8 March 1856, in Gambone, "Forgotten Feminist," 39:240.

3. Marvin A. Schenck, Karen Holmes, and Sherrie Smith-Ferri, *Aurelius O. Carpenter: Photographer of the Mendocino Frontier* (Ukiah, Calif.: Grace Hudson Museum and Sun House, 2006), 23.

4. Jeff R. Bremer, "'A Species of Town-Building Madness': Quindaro and Kansas Territory, 1856–1862," *Kansas History: A Journal of the Central Plains* 26 (Autumn 2003): 158–160.

5. Abelard Guthrie Journal, 9 April 1858 and 16 December 1858, KSHS; William Connelley, "Biographical Sketch of Abelard Guthrie," 1898, in Abelard Guthrie Journal file, KSHS. See also Bremer, "A Species of Town-Building Madness," 158–161; Alan W. Farley, "Annals of Quindaro: A Kansas Ghost Town," *KHQ* 22 (Winter 1956): 304–311; and Steve Collins, "The Underground Railroad in Quindaro, K.T.," typescript, n.d., in the authors' possession.

6. Schenck et al., *Aurelius O. Carpenter*, 23; Sandra L. Myres, ed., *Ho for California!* (San Marino, Calif.: Henry Huntington Library and Art Gallery, 1980), 95–96; Diane Eickhoff, *Revolutionary Heart: The Life of Clarina Nichols and the*

Pioneering Crusade for Women's Rights (Kansas City, Kans.: Quindaro Press, 2006), 135.

7. *WG*, 16 June 1882, in Gambone, "Forgotten Feminist," 40:530; *Quindaro Chindowan*, 20 June 1857, 22 August 1857, and 23 January 1858; Bremer, "A Species of Town-Building Madness," 161.

8. *Quindaro Chindowan*, 20 June 1857 and 13 May 1857; Bremer, "A Species of Town-Building Madness," 169.

9. *Quindaro Chindowan*, 23 January 1858 and 13 May 1857.

10. Ibid., 13 May 1857.

11. Ibid., 23 May 1857 and 4 July 1857, in Gambone, "Forgotten Feminist," 39:392–394, 407.

12. Ibid., 13 June 1857, in Gambone, "Forgotten Feminist," 39:397–398; see also 397nn6–7.

13. *Quindaro Chindowan*, 30 May 1857.

14. Ibid., 13 June 1857 and 27 June 1857.

15. Ibid., 13 June 1857; Michael Morrison, *Slavery and the American West: The Eclipse of Manifest Destiny and the Coming of the Civil War* (Chapel Hill: University of North Carolina Press, 1997), 110.

16. *Quindaro Chindowan*, 4 July 1857, in Gambone, "Forgotten Feminist," 39:406–408.

17. Ibid., 20 June 1857, in Gambone, "Forgotten Feminist," 39:401.

18. CIHN to Susan Wattles, 2 May 1859, in Augustus Wattles Papers, KSHS (hereafter cited as Wattles Papers).

19. Ibid., 27 March 1859; Gunja SenGupta, *For God and Mammon: Evangelicals and Entrepreneurs, Masters and Slaves in Territorial Kansas, 1854–1860* (Athens: University of Georgia Press, 1996), 70; Collins, "Underground Railroad," 23; *Quindaro Chindowan*, 17 April 1858.

20. *WG*, 22 December 1882 and 29 December 1882, in Gambone, "Forgotten Feminist," 40:540; *Quindaro Chindowan*, 20 June 1857.

21. William Hutchinson, "Sketches of Kansas Pioneer Experience," *Transactions of the Kansas State Historical Society, 1901–1902* (Topeka, Kans.: KSHS, 1902), 7:405. For women's use of hatchets, see also Richard D. Cordley, *A History of Lawrence, Kansas* (Lawrence, Kans.: Lawrence Journal Press, 1895), 169.

22. *Quindaro Chindowan*, 27 June 1857, in Gambone, "Forgotten Feminist," 39:404.

23. *Quindaro Chindowan*, 27 June 1857, 3 October 1857, 23 January 1858, and 17 April 1858.

24. Ibid., 8 August 1857, 15 August 1857, and 5 September 1857. After the debate Howard became president, and the debating rules were changed to ensure that no one had to argue against his or her own principles.

25. Ibid., 1 August 1857 and 23 January 1858. For Nichols's troubles with Walden, see Susan Wattles to CIHN, 4 May 1858, Nichols Papers; see also Eickhoff, *Revolutionary Heart*, 142, 258n142.

26. *WG*, 22 December 1882 and 29 December 1882, in Gambone, "Forgotten Feminist," 40:541; Samuel F. Tappan to Thomas Wentworth Higginson, 24 January 1858, cited in Collins, "Underground Railroad," 15; *Quindaro Chindowan*, 8

August 1857. Nichols described hooting in CIHN to SBA, n.d., in Gambone, "Forgotten Feminist," 39:430.

27. *WG*, 22 December 1882 and 29 December 1882, in Gambone, "Forgotten Feminist," 40:541–542. For the slave manacles, see CIHN to Bertia Carpenter Davis, 26 February 1880, Nichols Papers.

28. CIHN to Susan Wattles, 27 March 1859, Wattles Papers; Susan Wattles to CIHN, 14 April 1859, Nichols Papers.

29. Nichole Etcheson, *Bleeding Kansas: Contested Liberty in the Civil War Era* (Lawrence: University Press of Kansas, 2004), 143–165.

30. CIHN, "Reminiscences," in Elizabeth Cady Stanton, Susan B. Anthony, and Matilda Joslyn Gage, eds., *HWS* (Rochester, N.Y.: Fowler & Wells, 1881; 2nd ed., 1887), 1:196. For constitutional provisions regarding married women's property rights, see Article XV, Section 5, Topeka Constitution, 1855, and Article XV, Section 6, Lecompton Constitution, September 1857, in Daniel W. Wilder, *Annals of Kansas* (Topeka, Kans.: George W. Martin, 1875), 100, 186. For the southern practice of protecting wives' personal property, see Suzanne Lebsock, *The Free Women of Petersburg: Status and Culture in a Southern Town* (New York: Norton, 1985), 57–86.

31. Lynne Marie Getz, "Partners in Motion: Gender, Migration, and Reform in Antebellum Ohio and Kansas," *Frontiers* 27 (2006): 123–124; John Brown to Mary Brown, 16 November 1859, John Brown Collection, KSHS.

32. Getz, "Partners in Motion," 125; MWRA, Secretary's Book, KSHS.

33. MWRA, Secretary's Book, 5, 10; Getz, "Partners in Motion," 125; *Wyandotte Weekly Western Argus*, 4 June 1859.

34. MWRA, Secretary's Book, 13.

35. Samuel F. Tappan to Thomas Higginson, 7 April 1858, Thomas W. Higginson Collection, KSHS (cited hereafter as Higginson Papers); Susan Wattles to CIHN, 4 May 1858, Nichols Papers.

36. Tappan Journal, Leavenworth Constitutional Convention, 31 March 1858 and 2 April 1858, History, Constitutions, no. 570, KSHS; Samuel F. Tappan to Thomas Higginson, 7 April 1858, Higginson Papers.

37. Stanton et al., *HWS*, 1:929. For codification of property and custody rights, see *General Laws of the Territory of Kansas Passed at the Fifth Session of the Legislative Assembly Begun at the City of Lecompton on the 1st Monday of Jan'y, 1859, and Held and Concluded at the City of Lawrence* (Lawrence, Kans., 1859), 564–566, 576–577. Under this legislation, fathers retained guardianship of minors until death or incapacity.

38. Lucy Stone to Susan B. Anthony, September/October 1856, and Elizabeth Cady Stanton to Susan B. Anthony, 20 July 1857, both cited in *Women's Suffrage in America: An Eyewitness History*, ed. Elizabeth Frost and Kathryn Cullen-DuPont (New York: Facts on File, 1992), 136–137.

39. *Herald of Freedom*, 30 March 1856, in Gambone, "Forgotten Feminist," 39:242.

40. See Ellen Carol DuBois and Richard Candida Smith, eds., *Elizabeth Cady Stanton, Feminist as Thinker: A Reader in Documents and Essays* (New York: New

York University Press, 2007), 155–178; and Stanton et al., *HWS*, 1:674–77. For legal rights in New York, see Norma Basch, *In the Eyes of the Law: Women, Marriage, and Property in Nineteenth-Century New York* (Ithaca, N.Y.: Cornell University Press, 1982), 162–199.

41. Mari J. Matsuda, "The West and the Legal Status of Women: Explanations of Frontier Feminism," *Journal of the West* 24 (January 1985): 50.

42. CIHN to Susan Wattles, 29 March 1859, Wattles Papers. See also MWRA, Secretary's Book, 19–24.

43. CIHN to Susan Wattles, 27 March 1859 and 2 May 1859, Wattles Papers.

44. Ibid., 2 May 1859 and 29 March 1859. For the debate over slavery at the Wyandotte convention see Gary L. Cheatham, "'Slavery All the Time or Not at All': The Wyandotte Constitution Debate, 1859–1861," *Kansas History: A Journal of the Central Plains* 21 (Autumn 1998): 168–187.

45. *Freedom's Champion*, 18 June 1859; *Weekly Western Argus*, 4 June 1859. For Wood, see "The Republican Party in Kansas," *Liberator*, 8 July 1859.

46. *Herald of Freedom*, 2 July 1859; CIHN to Susan Wattles, 29 March 1859, Wattles Papers.

47. CIHN to Susan Wattles, 29 March 1859, Wattles Papers; CIHN to SBA, 18 June 1859, in Gambone, "Forgotten Feminist," 39:413–414. See also CIHN, "Reminiscences," in Stanton et al., *HWS*, 1:190.

48. CIHN, "To the Constitutional Convention of Kansas," in Gambone, "Forgotten Feminist," 39:416; see also MWRA, Secretary's Book, 20.

49. Daniel R. Anthony to SBA, 10 June 1859, in Ann D. Gordon, ed., *The Selected Papers of Elizabeth Cady Stanton and Susan B. Anthony* (New Brunswick, N.J.: Rutgers University Press, 1997), 1:388. In addition to the Francis Jackson legacy, Charles F. Hovey left $50,000 in his will to Wendell Phillips and others for disbursement in antislavery, woman's rights, and other reforms. For information on the Woman's Rights fund see Stanton et al., *HWS*, 1:667.

50. *Lawrence Republican*, 23 June 1859; CIHN to Susan B. Anthony, 18 June 1859, in Gambone, "Forgotten Feminist," 39:414.

51. *Lawrence Republican*, 23 June 1859; *Herald of Freedom*, 25 June 1859; *Topeka Tribune*, 30 June 1859.

52. *Topeka Tribune*, 30 June 1859; *Leavenworth Ledger*, [June 1859], in Gambone, "Forgotten Feminist," 39:422n73; "To the Constitutional Convention of Kansas," Legislature, 1859, Kansas Territorial Papers, KSHS; Abelard Guthrie Journal, 4 July 1859.

53. CIHN, "Reminiscences," in Stanton et al., *HWS*, 1:190; Mary T. Gray, "Clarina I. Howard Nichols," *Woman's Tribune*, 5 May 1888; "Read before the Wyandotte County Historical Society at Chelsea Park, June 13, 1896," Biographical Scrapbook 5:59–61, KSHS.

54. *New York Times*, 27 July 1859; CIHN to Susan Wattles, 14 July 1859, Wattles Papers; *New York Evening Post*, 25 July 1859, cited in Gambone, "Forgotten Feminist," 39:417n61. See also Eickhoff, *Revolutionary Heart*, 147–152, for conditions at the convention.

55. *Woman's Journal,* 16 August 1879, in Gambone, "Forgotten Feminist," 40:437; CIHN to Susan B. Anthony, 21 July 1859, in ibid., 39:421, 423; Hutchinson, "Sketches of Kansas Pioneer Experience," 390–408.

56. *Woman's Journal,* 16 August 1879, in Gambone, "Forgotten Feminist," 40:438. For Armstrong, see L. Dodge to Lucy Armstrong, 10 January 1855; Silas Armstrong to Lucy Armstrong, 2 December 1856; and "Affidavit of Wyandotte Chiefs regarding Munsee Payments," 5 January 1858, in Lucy Bigelow Armstrong Papers, 1846–1858, Wyandotte, box 7, XXV B, in Indian History, Collection no. 590, KSHS; William Cutler, *History of the State of Kansas* (Chicago: A. T. Andreas, 1883), "Wyandotte County, Pt. 2: The Wyandot Nation, Pt. 1."

57. CIHN, "Reminiscences," in Stanton et al., *HWS,* 1:191.

58. *Kansas Constitutional Convention: A Report of the Proceedings and Debates of the Convention which Framed the Constitution of Kansas at Wyandotte in July, 1859. Also the Constitution Annotated to Date, Historical Sketches, etc.* (Topeka, 1920), 72–75, quotation on 73; *New York Evening Post,* 25 July 1859, in Gambone, "Forgotten Feminist," 39:417n61; CIHN to Susan B. Anthony, 16 July 1859, in Gambone, "Forgotten Feminist," 39:417–418; CIHN to Susan Wattles, 14 July 1859, Wattles Papers. See also G. Raymond Gaeddert, *The Birth of Kansas* (Lawrence: University of Kansas, 1940), 49–51.

59. CIHN to Susan Wattles, 14 July 1859, Wattles Papers; *Kansas Constitutional Convention,* 136–137. See also CIHN to Susan B. Anthony, 16 July 1859, in Gambone, "Forgotten Feminist," 39:417–418. For the school provision see *Constitution of the State of Kansas,* Art. 2, Sec. 23.

60. *Kansas Constitutional Convention,* 169, 188, 324, 335; CIHN to Susan B. Anthony, 16 July 1859 and 21 July 1859, in Gambone, "Forgotten Feminist," 39:417–421; CIHN to Susan Wattles, 25 July 1859, Wattles Papers. See *Constitution of the State of Kansas,* Art. 15, Sec. 6, "The Legislature shall provide for the protection of the rights of women, in acquiring and possessing property, real, personal and mixed, separate and apart from the husband; and shall also provide for their equal rights in the possession of their children."

61. *Kansas Constitutional Convention,* 315; Gaeddert, *Birth of Kansas,* 54–55. See also Matsuda, "The West and the Legal Status of Women," 52–53.

62. CIHN to SBA, 16 July 1859, in Gambone, "Forgotten Feminist," 39:417; *Philadelphia Evening Bulletin,* 15 July 1859, in ibid., 39:417n59; CIHN to Susan Wattles, 25 July 1859, Wattles Papers.

63. *New York Times,* 22 July 1859.

64. Gaeddert, *Birth of Kansas,* 55–57; quotation from James Hanway, 18 July 1859, James Hanway Collection, no. 372, KSHS; CIHN to Susan Wattles, 25 July 1859, Wattles Papers. See also Cheatham, "'Slavery All the Time, or Not at All,'" 172–175.

65. CIHN to SBA, 21 July 1859, in Gambone, "Forgotten Feminist," 39:421; *Kansas Constitutional Convention,* 300.

66. *Herald of Freedom,* 16 July 1859.

67. *Kansas Constitutional Convention,* 188, 324; *Herald of Freedom,* 16 July 1859; CIHN, "Reminiscences," in Stanton et al., *HWS,* 1:192–193.

68. *Cottonwood Falls Kansas Press,* 1 August 1859. For eastern activists, see Gordon, *Selected Papers of ECS and SBA,* 1:381–382, 389–391, 396–397; and Stanton et al., *HWS,* 1:258, 674–677. See also Marilyn Schultz Blackwell, "The Politics of Motherhood: Clarina Howard Nichols and School Suffrage," *New England Quarterly* 78 (December 2005): 570–598.

69. *Kansas Constitutional Convention,* 135–137; *Herald of Freedom,* 20 August 1859; *Lecompton Kansas National Democrat,* 11 August 1859.

70. Gaeddert, *Birth of Kansas,* 72–75; *Herald of Freedom,* 13 August 1859, 20 August 1859; CIHN, "Reminiscences," in Stanton et al., *HWS,* 1:191; *Freedom's Champion,* 1 October 1859.

71. *WCG,* 29 July 1859.

72. CIHN to Susan Wattles, 12 October 1859, Wattles Papers; MWRA, Secretary's Book; John Martin to J. M. Winchell, 7 September 1859, Wyandotte Correspondence no. 570, KSHS.

73. CIHN, "Reminiscences," in Stanton et al., *HWS,* 1:191–192.

74. *Lawrence Republican,* 29 September 1859; Nichols note on fragment, Susan Wattles to Susan B. Anthony, 29 [? 1859], Susan B. Anthony Papers, microcopy 142, reel 2, F. 21, SL.

75. CIHN, "Reminiscences," in Stanton et al., *HWS,* 1:197–198.

76. Grand Jury Indictment of Daniel Read Anthony, 27 September 1859, Records of the U.S. District Courts, National Archives and Records Administration (Kansas City).

77. CIHN to SBA, n.d., in Gambone, "Forgotten Feminist," 39:422–429. See also "Quindaro," *Lawrence Republican,* 22 March 1860, 29 March 1860, and 28 June 1860; *PRP* 16 (7 September 1878): 150, (7 December 1878): 358. The story appears with minor variation in Eickhoff, *Revolutionary Heart,* 3–8.

78. For the divorce statute, see *General Laws . . . 1859,* 564–566.

79. CIHN to SBA, n.d., in Gambone, "Forgotten Feminist," 39:422–429. See also "Quindaro," *Lawrence Republican,* 22 March 1860 and 29 March, 1860; *PRP* 16 (7 September 1878): 150, (7 December 1878): 358.

80. See citations in note 79 above.

81. "Quindaro," *Lawrence Republican,* 22 March 1860, 29 March 1860; CIHN to SBA, n.d., in Gambone, "Forgotten Feminist," 39:429; Eickhoff, *Revolutionary Heart,* 8–9.

82. For Susan Anthony's involvement in a similar case in 1860, see Kathleen Barry, *Susan B. Anthony: A Biography of a Singular Feminist* (New York: New York University Press, 1988), 142–145; and Gordon, *Selected Papers of ECS and SBA,* 1:456–458.

83. MWRA Secretary's Book, December 1859; CIHN to Susan and Esther Wattles, 6 November 1859, Wattles Papers.

84. *WCD,* 12 October 1853.

85. See Gambone, "Forgotten Feminist," 39:430n104; and *General Laws . . . 1859,* 576. New York passed the first equal custody law in 1860. For changes in custody law, see Michael Grossberg, *Governing the Hearth: Law and the Family in Nineteenth-Century America* (Chapel Hill: University of North Carolina Press, 1985), 238–253.

86. CIHN to Susan B. Anthony, n.d., in Gambone, "Forgotten Feminist," 39:424. CIHN was paid $55 for serving as assistant clerk for the territorial council.

87. *Lawrence Republican,* 1 March 1860; CIHN to Susan B. Anthony, n.d. [August 1853], fl. A/N617, SL; *General Laws of the State of Kansas, in Force at the Close of the Session of the Legislature Ending March 6th, 1862* (Topeka: J. H. Bennet, 1862), 472–477; Gambone, "Forgotten Feminist," 39:430n104, 431nn105, 107; *General Statutes of the State of Kansas: Revised by John M. Price, Samuel A. Riggs, and James McCahon, Commissioners Appointed by the Governor, under an Act Approved February 18, 1867, Reported to, and Amended and Adopted by, the Legislature, at Its Regular Session in 1868* (Lawrence, Kans.: John Speer, 1868), 512.

88. *Lawrence Republican,* 2 February 1860, in Gambone, "Forgotten Feminist," 39:430–431.

89. Ibid.; "'The Union' and Mrs. Nichols in a New Dress," *Freedom's Champion,* 25 February 1860.

90. "'The Union' and Mrs. Nichols in a New Dress," *Freedom's Champion,* 25 February 1860.

91. Stanton et al., *HWS,* 3:704; CIHN to Susan B. Anthony, 14 April 1868, in Gambone, "Forgotten Feminist," 39:547.

Chapter 8. The Price of Patriotism

1. Daniel W. Wilder, *Annals of Kansas, 1541–1885* (Topeka, Kans.: T. Dwight Thacher, 1886), 304.

2. Nichols estimated that she needed to earn at least $25 (a quarter of her eastern pay per lecture) plus expenses of $50 a month to pay for a servant at home and clothes. See CIHN to Susan Wattles, 21 April 1860, Augustus Wattles Papers, KSHS (hereafter cited as Wattles Papers). For Howard's accident see *Quindaro Chindowan,* 23 January 1858.

3. CIHN to Susan Wattles, 21 April 1860, 3 June 1860, 21 August 1861, Wattles Papers. For Susannah's capture, see also "Atrocious Kidnapping in Quindaro," *Lawrence Republican,* 5 April 1860.

4. Alfred Gray quoted in Alan W. Farley, "Annals of Quindaro: A Kansas Ghost Town," *KHQ* 22 (Winter 1956): 316; Jeff R. Bremer, "'A Species of Town-Building Madness': Quindaro and Kansas Territory, 1856–1863," *Kansas History: A Journal of the Central Plains* 26 (Autumn 2003): 165–171. For Nichols's assets, see "Population Schedules of the Eighth Census of the United States 1860," Kansas Territory, Wyandotte County, microcopy no. 653, roll no. 352, p. 923.

5. CIHN to Susan Wattles, 3 June 1860, Wattles Papers; CIHN, "Testimony to the Memory of Lucy Gaylord Pomeroy," in Joseph G. Gambone, ed., "The Forgotten Feminist of Kansas: The Papers of Clarina I. H. Nichols, 1854–1885," *KHQ* 39 (Autumn 1973): 441.

6. Elizabeth Cady Stanton, Susan B. Anthony, and Matilda Joslyn Gage, eds., *HWS* (Rochester, N.Y.: Fowler & Wells, 1881; 2nd ed., 1887), 1:167–170, quotation on 199; CIHN to Susan Wattles, March 1861, Wattles Papers.

7. Stanton et al., *HWS,* 1:169.

8. Elizabeth B. Warbasse, "Hannah Maria Conant Tracy Cutler," *Notable American Women: 1607–1950: A Biographical Dictionary*, ed. Edward T. James, Janet Wilson James, and Paul S. Boyer (Cambridge, Mass.: Harvard University Press, 1971), 1:426–427; Eugene H. Roseboom, "Frances Dana Barker Gage," in ibid., 2:2–4.

9. CIHN to Susan Wattles, March 1861, Wattles Papers.

10. CIHN to Susan Wattles, 30 March 1861, Wattles Papers.

11. Ibid., 30 March 1861 and 10 April 1861; *General Laws of the State of Kansas, in Force at the Close of the Session of the Legislature Ending March 6th, 1862* (Topeka: J. H. Bennet, 1862), 808.

12. See, for example, Nina Silber, *Daughters of the Union: Northern Women Fight the Civil War* (Cambridge, Mass.: Harvard University Press, 2005), 41–86.

13. CIHN to Susan Wattles, 21 October 1861, Wattles Papers.

14. Ibid.; CIHN, *WG*, 22 December 1882, in Gambone, "Forgotten Feminist," 40:537–539.

15. Steve Collins, "The Underground Railroad in Quindaro, K.T.," typescript, 1984, 18.

16. CIHN to Susan Wattles, 21 October 1861, Wattles Papers; "Come all you jolly Union Boys . . . ," in Gambone, "Forgotten Feminist," 39:438–439.

17. CIHN, *WG*, 22 December 1882, in Gambone, "Forgotten Feminist," 40:530; Collins, "Underground Railroad," 18–19; Farley, "Annals of Quindaro," 316.

18. CIHN, *WG*, 22 December 1882 and 29 December 1882, in Gambone, "Forgotten Feminist," 40:542.

19. CIHN to Susan Wattles, 21 October 1861, Wattles Papers; for Nichols's application for nursing, see Gambone, "Forgotten Feminist," 39:26n62.

20. Stanton et al., *HWS*, 2:53; Wendy Hamand Venet, *Neither Ballots nor Bullets: Women Abolitionists and the Civil War* (Charlottesville: University Press of Virginia, 1991), 101–122; Faye Dudden, "New York Strategy: The New York Woman's Movement and the Civil War," in *Votes for Women: The Struggle for Suffrage Revisited*, ed. Jean H. Baker (New York: Oxford University Press, 2002), 64–70.

21. CIHN to SBA, 4 May 1863, in Gambone, "Forgotten Feminist," 39:442–443.

22. Venet, *Neither Ballots nor Bullets*, 116–122, 134–148; Dudden, "New York Strategy," 66–70; Silber, *Daughters of the Union*, 153–156.

23. *Report of the Adjutant General of the State of Kansas* (Leavenworth, Kans., 1867), 1:734; Diane Eickhoff, *Revolutionary Heart: The Life of Clarina Nichols and the Pioneering Crusade for Women's Rights* (Kansas City, Kans.: Quindaro Press, 2006), 165; Register of Female Clerks, 1861–1868, p. 285, Records of the Division of Appointments, Record Group 56, National Archives, Washington, D.C.

24. W. F. Downs to G. W. Boutwell, 29 December 1862, box 87, Applications and Recommendations for Positions in Washington, D.C., Records of the Division of Appointments, Record Group 56, National Archives, Washington, D.C.

25. William H. Boyd, comp., *Boyd's Washington and Georgetown Directory, . . . 1865* (Washington, D.C.: Boyd & Waite, 1865), 288; T. D. S. Bassett MS research notes, in author's possession.

26. United States, *Register of Officers and Agents, Civil, Military, and Naval, in the Service of the United States on the Thirtieth September, 1865* (Washington, D.C.:

Government Printing Office, 1866), 53; Mary Elizabeth Massey, *Bonnet Brigades* (New York: Knopf, 1966), 132–133; Cindy Sondik Aron, *Ladies and Gentlemen of the Civil Service: Middle-Class Workers in Victorian America* (New York: Oxford University Press, 1987), 70–73, 84.

27. Sylvia D. Hoffert, *Jane Grey Swisshelm: An Unconventional Life, 1815–1884* (Chapel Hill: University of North Carolina Press, 2004), 94–95; Massey, *Bonnet Brigades,* 134–138.

28. Lois Bryan Adams, *Letter from Washington, 1863–1865,* ed. Evelyn Leasher (Detroit: Wayne State University Press, 1999), 217–220, 339–341, quotation on 219; T. D. S. Bassett, MS research notes.

29. For descriptions of wartime Washington from a northern woman's perspective, see Adams, *Letter from Washington,* 33–51, quotation on 33; and Carol Faulkner, *Women's Radical Reconstruction: The Freedmen's Aid Movement* (Philadelphia: University of Pennsylvania Press, 2004), 87, 104–105.

30. CIHN, "Testimony to the Memory of Lucy Gaylord Pomeroy," in Gambone, "Forgotten Feminist," 39:440–442; [Ruth P. Bascom], *Memoir of Mrs. Lucy Gaylord Pomeroy* (New York: John W. Amerman, 1865), 162–165, 173–176.

31. Silber, *Daughters of the Union,* 156–158.

32. Adams, *Letter from Washington,* 134–141; "The Ladies National Covenant," *New York Times,* 4 May 1864.

33. Faulkner, *Women's Radical Reconstruction,* 83–99.

34. Charles Moore, comp., *Report of the Joint Select Committee to Investigate the Charities and Reformatory Institutions in the District of Columbia,* pt. 3 (Washington, D.C.: Government Printing Office, 1898), 126–127; [Bascom], *Memoir of Lucy Pomeroy,* 167–173.

35. *Special Report of the Commissioner of Education on the Condition and Improvement of Public Schools in the District of Columbia, Submitted to the Senate June, 1868, and to the House, with Additions, June 13, 1870* (Washington, D.C.: Government Printing Office, 1871), 233–237.

36. Lucy N. Colman, *Reminiscences* (Buffalo, N.Y.: H. L. Green, 1891), 60–63; Hoffert, *Jane Grey Swisshelm,* 156–157.

37. Hoffert, *Jane Grey Swisshelm,* 155–159; *Washington Star,* 11 January 1865 and 17 January 1865, quotation from 11 January.

38. *Annual Report of the National Association for the Relief of Destitute Colored Women and Children, 1866* (Washington, D.C.: Chronicle Steam, 1866), 6–10.

39. Colman, *Reminiscences,* 63; Faulkner, *Women's Radical Reconstruction,* 80–81.

40. *Annual Report of the National Association for the Relief of Destitute Colored Women and Children, 1866,* 6, 8, 13–14; "National Association for the Relief of Colored Women and Children," *Washington Star,* 9 January 1866.

41. *Washington Star,* 5 April 1865; Adams, *Letter from Washington,* 256.

42. *Annual Report of the National Association for the Relief of Destitute Colored Women and Children, 1866,* 6–7; *Special Report . . . on . . . Public Schools,* 235–236.

43. CIHN, "Reminiscences," Stanton et al., *HWS,* 1:200; CIHN to SBA, 4 May 1863, in Gambone, "Forgotten Feminist," 39:443.

Chapter 9. Visions of Universal Freedom

1. Elizabeth Cady Stanton, Susan B. Anthony, and Matilda Joslyn Gage, eds., *HWS* (Rochester, N.Y.: Fowler & Wells, 1881; 2nd ed., 1887), 2:229; CIHN to SBA, in the *Revolution*, 3 February 1870, in Joseph G. Gambone, ed., "The Forgotten Feminist of Kansas: The Papers of Clarina I. H. Nichols, 1854–1885," *KHQ* 40 (Summer 1974): 244. For women's relationship with the Republican Party, see Melanie Susan Gustafson, *Women and the Republican Party, 1854–1924* (Urbana: University of Illinois Press, 2001), 32–37.

2. Jeff R. Bremer, "'A Species of Town-Building Madness': Quindaro and Kansas Territory, 1856–1862," *Kansas History: A Journal of the Central Plains* 26 (Autumn 2003): 170–171; Steve Collins, "The Underground Railroad in Quindaro, K.T.," typescript, 1984, 19–20.

3. Record of the Executive Council, 155, 158, Wyandott Indian Council Records, 1855–1871, KSHS; "Population Schedules of the Eighth Census of the United States 1860," Kansas Territory, Wyandotte County, microcopy M653, roll 352, p. 931; Perl W. Morgan, ed. and comp., *History of Wyandotte County Kansas and Its People* (Chicago: Lewis, 1911), 1:68–78.

4. CIHN to Helen Carpenter, 21 March 1871, Nichols Papers.

5. Ellen Carol DuBois, *Feminism and Suffrage: The Emergence of an Independent Women's Movement in America, 1848–1869* (Ithaca, N.Y.: Cornell University Press, 1978), 51–67, quotation on 59; Gustafson, *Women and the Republican Party,* 35–36.

6. Richard B. Sheridan, "Charles Henry Langston and the African American Struggle in Kansas," *Kansas History* 22 (Winter 1999–2000): 274–276; Eugene H. Berwanger, "Hardin and Langston: Western Black Spokesmen of the Reconstruction Era," *Journal of Negro History* 64 (Spring 1979): 105.

7. CIHN to Samuel N. Wood, 19 June 1867, in Gambone, "Forgotten Feminist," 39:526–527; Lucy Stone to Elizabeth Cady Stanton, 10 April 1867, in Stanton et al., *HWS*, 2:235; Helen Ekin Starrett, "Reminiscences," in ibid., 2:250–251; *House Journal of the Legislative Assembly of the State of Kansas, Begun and Held at Topeka, on Tuesday, January 8th, A.D. 1867* (Leavenworth, Kans.: Clarke, Emery, 1867), 125–126, 339, 574, 629, 635–637; *Senate Journal of the Legislative Assembly of the State of Kansas, Begun and Held at Topeka on Tuesday, January 8th, A.D. 1867* (Leavenworth, Kans.: Clarke, Emery, 1867), 13, 412. For Anthony's remark, see *Proceedings of the First Anniversary of the American Equal Rights Association, Held at the Church of the Puritans, New York, May 9 and 10, 1867* (New York: R. J. Johnston, 1867), 5–7, in Ann D. Gordon, ed., *The Selected Papers of Elizabeth Cady Stanton and Susan B. Anthony* (New Brunswick, N.J.: Rutgers University Press, 2000), 2:62.

8. *Vermont Phoenix*, 8 March 1867, in Gambone, "Forgotten Feminist," 39:515–517.

9. Henry B. Blackwell to E. C. Stanton and SBA, 21 April 1867, in Stanton et al., *HWS*, 2:236; *Atchison Daily Champion*, 5 April 1867, quoted in Sandra A. Madsen, "1867 Campaign for Woman Suffrage" (Ph.D. diss., University of Kansas, 1975), 46; Sister Jeanne McKenna, "With the Help of God and Lucy Stone," *KHQ* 36 (Spring 1970): 13–26; Sheridan, "Charles Henry Langston," 274–277.

10. McKenna, "With the Help of God and Lucy Stone," 14–15; DuBois, *Feminism and Suffrage,* 81–83; Madsen, "1867 Campaign," 120–125; Lucy Stone to Elizabeth

Cady Stanton, 10 April 1867, and Henry Blackwell to Elizabeth Cady Stanton, 5 April 1867, both in Stanton et al., *HWS*, 2:232–235.

11. "Address by the Women's Impartial Suffrage Association of Lawrence, Kansas," in Stanton et al., *HWS*, 2:932–933; Lucy Stone to Elizabeth Cady Stanton, 10 April 1867, and Henry Blackwell to Elizabeth Cady Stanton, 5 April 1867, in ibid., 2:232–235.

12. Lucy Stone to Elizabeth Cady Stanton, 10 April 1867, in ibid., 2:234–235.

13. Madsen, "1867 Campaign," 60–62; McKenna, "With the Help of God and Lucy Stone," 21–24; Olympia Brown to SBA, 16 March 1882, in Stanton et al., *HWS*, 2:260.

14. CIHN to S. N. Wood, 19 June 1867 and 18 July 1867, in Gambone, "Forgotten Feminist," 39:524–529; SBA to S. N. Wood, 9 August 1867, Woman Suffrage History Collection, box 1, KSHS.

15. *WCG*, 20 July 1867; Madsen, "1867 Campaign," 40–45.

16. *WCG*, 4 May 1867 and 1 June 1867; *Vermont Phoenix*, 8 March 1867; *Kansas Farmer*, April 1867, all in Gambone, "Forgotten Feminist," 39:515–519, 527n32, quotations on 527n32, 519.

17. J. Stuart Mill to S. N. Wood, 2 June 1867, in Stanton et al., *HWS*, 2:252; "Right and Wrong in Kansas," *New York Independent*, 3 October 1867; "Woman Suffrage," *WCG*, 10 August 1867.

18. Madsen, "1867 Campaign," 63–78, 98, 106–108, 119; DuBois, *Feminism and Suffrage*, 86–92.

19. C. H. Langston to S. N. Wood, 20 June 1867, Woman Suffrage History Collection, KSHS; Berwanger, "Hardin and Langston," 105–107, 110–111; Sheridan, "Charles Henry Langston," 278; Madsen, "1867 Campaign," 63–78. McKenna, "With the Help of God and Lucy Stone," 24–25.

20. *Western Home Journal*, 27 June 1867, in Gambone, "Forgotten Feminist," 39:522–524. Kollach helped organize the Anti-Female Suffrage State Committee and subsequently lectured against the measure. See Gordon, *Selected Papers of ECS and SBA*, 2:209n3.

21. *WCG*, 17 August 1867. Congregational minister Reverend Lewis Bodwell, by contrast, had planned to lecture with Nichols. See Gordon, *Selected Papers of ECS and SBA*, 2:98n6.

22. *WCG*, 28 September 1867, 19 October 1867, and 26 October 1867, all in Gambone, "Forgotten Feminist," 39:529–541, quotations on 534, 538–539; Madsen, "1867 Campaign," 86–87.

23. CIHN, "The Bible Position of Woman, or Woman's Rights from a Bible Stand-Point," *Vermont Phoenix*, 14 January 1870, 21 January 1870, 28 January 1870, 11 February 1870, 18 February 1870, and 25 February 1870, all in Gambone, "Forgotten Feminist," 40:88–113. For religion and early feminists, see Anna M. Speicher, *The Religious World of Antislavery Women: Spirituality in the Lives of Five Abolitionist Lecturers* (Syracuse, N.Y.: Syracuse University Press, 2000), 61–73, 110–115.

24. Dana Greene, ed., *Suffrage and Religious Principle: Speeches and Writings of Olympia Brown* (Metuchen, N.J.: Scarecrow Press, 1983), 70–78; Kathi Kern,

Mrs. Stanton's Bible (Ithaca, N.Y.: Cornell University Press, 2001), 58–59; Elizabeth Cady Stanton, *The Woman's Bible* (New York: New York European, 1895–1898; reprint, Boston: Northeastern University Press, 1993).

25. DuBois, *Feminism and Suffrage,* 79–91.

26. Elizabeth Cady Stanton, *Eighty Years and More: Reminiscences, 1815–1897* (n.p.: Unwin, 1898; 2nd ed., Boston: Northeastern University Press, 1993), 246–253; Stanton to Henry B. Stanton, 9 October 1867, in Gordon, *Selected Papers of ECS and SBA,* 2:96; "Speech by ECS in Burlington, Kansas," 12 October 1867, in ibid., 99; Stanton to Theodore Tilton, 15 September 1867, in ibid., 89–90; Madsen, "1867 Campaign," 80–84.

27. Gordon, *Selected Papers of ECS and SBA,* 2:95–112; George Francis Train, *The Great Epigram Campaign in Kansas: Championship of Women* (Leavenworth, Kans.: Prescott & Hume, 1867), 7; DuBois, *Feminism and Suffrage,* 92–96. For Stanton's prejudicial remarks, see "Female Suffrage Committee," *New York Tribune,* 19 June 1867, in Gordon, *Selected Papers of ECS and SBA,* 2:72.

28. *Atchison Daily Capital,* 17 November 1867, in Madsen, "1867 Campaign," 113.

29. Charles Robinson to Elizabeth Cady Stanton, 20 November 1867, in Gordon, *Selected Papers of ECS and SBA,* 2:102, election results on 643–644; DuBois, *Feminism and Suffrage,* 95–99; Madsen, "1867 Campaign," 106–108, 113, 116–117, 120–142.

30. CIHN to *SBA,* in *Revolution,* 30 April 1868, in Gambone, "Forgotten Feminist," 39:547; *WCG,* 7 March 1868, in ibid., 543.

31. DuBois, *Feminism and Suffrage,* 98–103; quotation from Stanton et al., *HWS,* 2:320, quoted in Gustafson, *Women and the Republican Party,* 38.

32. Alexander Keyssar, *The Right to Vote: The Contested History of Democracy in the United States* (New York: Basic Books, 2000), 89–93; Virginia Scharff, *Twenty Thousand Roads: Women, Movement, and the West* (Berkeley: University of California Press, 2003), 84–88.

33. *WCG,* 16 November 1867, 4 April 1868, and 14 November 1868; Constitution, Bylaws and Minutes, Woman Suffrage Association of Topeka, 1867–1875, 10 December 1868, 25 December 1868, and 8 January 1869, Woman Suffrage Collection, KSHS.

34. *WCG,* 1 August 1868, in Gambone, "Forgotten Feminist," 39:550; CIHN to SBA, in *Revolution,* 3 February 1870, in ibid., 40:244–245.

35. *Vermont Phoenix,* 6 March 1868, 18 September 1868, 16 October 1868, 14 January 1870, 21 January 1870, 28 January 1870, 11 February 1870, 18 February 1870, and 25 February 1870, all in Gambone, "Forgotten Feminist," 39:541–542, 556–563; 40:88–113.

36. See Deborah P. Clifford, "An Invasion of Strong-Minded Women: The Newspapers and the Woman Suffrage Campaign in Vermont in 1870," *Vermont History* 43 (Winter 1975): 1–19; T. D. Seymour Bassett, "The 1870 Campaign for Woman Suffrage in Vermont," *Vermont Quarterly* 14 (April 1946): 56–57.

37. CIHN to Aurelius and Helen Carpenter, 16 March 1869, in Gambone, "Forgotten Feminist," 40:79–80; *Kansas Daily Commonwealth,* 3 June 1869, in ibid., 84.

38. *Kansas Daily Commonwealth,* 9 December 1869, in ibid., 134; *WCG,* 12 September

1868, in ibid., 39:556; "Women Voting," *WCG*, 7 November 1868; Minutes, Woman's Suffrage Association of Topeka, 27 November 1868, Woman Suffrage Collection, KSHS; *Kansas Daily Commonwealth*, 2 November 1869, in Gambone, "Forgotten Feminist," 40:132; *Revolution*, 28 July 1870, in ibid., 40:270.

39. *Kansas Daily Commonwealth*, 3 June 1869, 24 June 1869, and 23 July 1869, all in Gambone, "Forgotten Feminist," 40:82–84, 88, 114–116, quotation on 115.

40. *Kansas Daily Commonwealth*, 10 September 1869, in ibid., 40:122–123.

41. *Kansas Daily Commonwealth*, 6 October 1869, 7 October 1869, and 26 January 1870, in ibid., 40:127, 129, 241.

42. *WCG*, 29 February 1868 and 22 August 1868, in ibid., 39:542n49, 552.

43. For Nichols's land dealings, see Gambone, "Forgotten Feminist," 39:542–547. For Quindaro and Wyandotte, see Bremer, "A Species of Town-Building Madness," 169–171; William G. Cutler, *History of the State of Kansas, Wyandotte County*, pt. 4 (Chicago: A.T. Andreas, 1883); and Morgan, *History of Wyandotte County*, 1:102–107, 271–283, 441–459.

44. "Population Schedules of the Ninth Census of the United States 1870," Kansas, Wyandotte County, microcopy 593, roll 443, pp. 537–538, 586; *Map of Wyandotte County, Kansas, Compiled from Official Records and Surveys and Published by Heisler and McGee, 1870* (Chicago: Ed. Mendel, 1870).

45. CIHN to ?, 30 September 1869, in Gambone, "Forgotten Feminist," 40:126.

46. CIHN to Helen Carpenter, 26 March 1871, Nichols Papers.

47. CIHN to Relie Carpenter, 1871?, Nichols Papers.

48. *WCG*, 22 August 1868, in Gambone, "Forgotten Feminist," 39:554; CIHN to Helen Carpenter, 26 March 1871 and 12 May 1871, Nichols Papers.

49. *WCG*, 1 August 1868, in Gambone, "Forgotten Feminist," 39:549; *Kansas Daily Commonwealth*, 9 December 1869, in ibid., 40:133; CIHN to Helen and Aurelius Carpenter, 18 July 1869, in ibid., 40:116; CIHN to SBA, in *Revolution*, 3 February 1870, in ibid., 40:244.

50. *Kansas Daily Commonwealth*, 9 December 1869, in ibid., 40:134; *WCG*, 7 March 1868 and 21 March 1868, in ibid., 39:543, 545.

51. *WCG*, 6 March 1869 and 20 March 1869, in ibid., 40:74–78; [R. B. Taylor], "Senate Bill Seventy Six Strangled," *WCG*, 13 February 1869; "Senator Cobb," ibid., 27 February 1869.

52. *WCG*, 24 April 1869, 8 May 1869, and 3 July 1869.

53. Ibid., 17 July 1869, 24 July 1869, 31 July 1869, 7 August 1869, and 14 August 1869, quotations from 14 August.

54. CIHN to SBA, in *Revolution*, 3 February 1870 and 3 March 1870, in Gambone, "Forgotten Feminist," 40:244, 250.

Chapter 10. The Last Frontier: California

1. CIHN to Helen and Aurelius Carpenter, 18 July 1869, in Joseph G. Gambone, ed., "The Forgotten Feminist of Kansas: The Papers of Clarina I. H. Nichols, 1854–1885," *KHQ* 40 (Spring 1974): 117.

2. Marvin A. Schenck, Karen Holmes, and Sherrie Smith-Ferri, *Aurelius O.*

Carpenter: Photographer of the Mendocino Frontier (Ukiah, Calif.: Grace Hudson Museum and Sun House, 2006), 25–26.

3. *WCG*, 22 August 1868, in Gambone, "Forgotten Feminist," 39:552; CIHN to Relie and Helen Carpenter, 12 May 1871, Nichols Papers.

4. [CIHN] to Relie, 26 December 1870, in Gambone, "Forgotten Feminist," 40:274; CIHN to SBA, 21 August 1881, in ibid., 40:514. Nichols left no record of the placement of Lucy Lincoln, whom she left in Kansas, though she was still caring for her in early 1871. See CIHN to Helen Carpenter, 26 March 1871, Nichols Papers.

5. *WG*, 30 May 1872, in Gambone, "Forgotten Feminist," 40:276.

6. Ibid., 277.

7. [Lyman L. Palmer], *History of Mendocino County, California: Comprising Its Geography, Geology, Topography, Climatography, Springs, and Timber* (San Francisco: Alley, Bowen, 1880), 445.

8. Ibid., 167–173; Helen M[cCowan] Carpenter, "Among the Diggers of Thirty Years Ago," *Overland Monthly* 21 (February and April 1893): 146–155, 389–399; Schenck et al., *Aurelius O. Carpenter*, 97–102.

9. *WG*, 30 May 1872, in Gambone, "Forgotten Feminist," 40:280; CIHN to Birsha Carpenter Davis, 11 February 187?, 28 April 1878, and 10 February 1876, Nichols Papers, KSHS.

10. *WG*, 15 August 1872, in Gambone, "Forgotten Feminist," 40:282–286; CIHN to Birsha, 5 November 1872, in ibid., 40:287–288.

11. CIHN to Birsha Carpenter Davis, 5 November 1872, 24 April 1876, and 28 April 1878, Nichols Papers; CIHN, "An Old Friend Returns," *PRP* 19 (8 May 1880): 314. For the school controversy, see Helen McCowen Carpenter Papers, micro, reel 3, 21138b, 21138c, Grace Hudson Museum and Sun House, Ukiah, California.

12. CIHN to Birsha Carpenter Davis, 28 April 1878; to Aurelius O. Carpenter, 8 August 1876, Nichols Papers.

13. CIHN to Mark Carpenter, 7 February 1877, Nichols Papers.

14. *WG*, 15 August 1872, in Gambone, "Forgotten Feminist," 40:285.

15. *WG*, 5 February 1875, in ibid., 40:416–418, quotation on 417. For married women and legal rights in California, see Donna C. Schuele, "'None Could Deny the Eloquence of this Lady': Women, Law, and Government in California, 1850–1890," *California History* 81 (Winter 2003): 169–198.

16. Andrea Moore Kerr, "White Women's Rights, Black Men's Wrongs: Free Love, Blackmail, and the Formation of the American Woman Suffrage Association," in Marjorie Spruill Wheeler, ed., *One Woman, One Vote: Rediscovering the Woman Suffrage Movement* (Troutdale, Ore.: New Sage Press, 1995), 71–77; Eleanor Flexner, *Century of Struggle: The Woman's Rights Movement in the United States* (Cambridge, Mass.: Harvard University Press, 1959; 2nd ed., New York: Atheneum, 1971), 151–155.

17. Ann D. Gordon, ed., *The Selected Papers of Elizabeth Cady Stanton and Susan B. Anthony* (New Brunswick, N.J.: Rutgers University Press, 2000), 2:433–435; Kathleen Barry, *Susan B. Anthony: A Biography of a Singular Feminist* (New York: New York University Press, 1988), 3–4, 237–242.

18. *WG*, 5 February 1875, in Gambone, "Forgotten Feminist," 40:418. For controversy

in the California suffrage movement, see Gayle Gullet, *Becoming Citizens: The Emergence and Development of the California Women's Movement, 1880–1911* (Urbana: University of Illinois Press, 2000), 13–17; Anne M. Breedlove, "'Inspired and Possessed': San Francisco Women Newspaper Publishers," *California History* 80 (Spring 2001): 48–63; and Sherilyn Cox Bennion, *Equal to the Occasion: Women Editors of the Nineteenth-Century West* (Reno: University of Nevada Press, 1990), 59–60. For the standard account, see Elizabeth Cady Stanton, Susan B. Anthony, and Matilda Joslyn Gage, eds., *HWS* (Rochester, N.Y.: Fowler & Wells, 1881; 2nd ed., 1887), 3:750–766.

19. CIHN to SBA, 27 December 1872, in Gambone, "Forgotten Feminist," 40:289–290. For Stanton on marriage, see Stanton, "Speech by ECS on Free Love," in Gordon, *Selected Papers of ECS and SBA*, 2:392–397.

20. Stanton et al., *HWS*, 3:27–34, quotation on 33.

21. Ibid., 44–50; CIHN to SBA, 26 June 1876, in Gambone, "Forgotten Feminist," 40:418–421, quotation on 419.

22. *National Citizen and Ballot Box*, July 1877, June 1880, and July 1881, all in Gambone, "Forgotten Feminist," 40:422–423, 439–442, 515–517, quotations on 517, 439, and 422.

23. *Woman's Journal*, 4 August 1877 and 7 August 1880; "Dear Mrs. Minor," *National Citizen and Ballot Box*, July 1879, both in Gambone, "Forgotten Feminist," 40:424–433, 443–444, quotations on 425 and 429.

24. *Woman's Herald of Industry and Social Science Cooperator* 1 (September 1881): 1 (October 1881): 3, and (January 1882) 1; Bennion, *Equal to the Occasion*, 98–103; Mrs. J. W. Stow, "Women's Social Science Associations," *PRP* 20 (30 October 1880): 278. Relie Carpenter was hired to produce the *Daily Fair Press*, a circular for the Mechanics' Institute Fair held in San Francisco during August and September. See [Palmer], *History of Mendocino County*, 633–634. Nichols's Vermont friend, "Mrs. Judge Shafter," wife of Oscar L. Shafter, was present at early meetings of the CWSA, as was Stow. See Stanton et al., *HWS*, 3:752.

25. CIHN, "Christian Civil Government," *Woman's Herald of Industry and Social Science Cooperator*, vol. 1 (September 1881 and October 1881), in Gambone, "Forgotten Feminist," 40:518–521.

26. George W. Lewis, "The Religion of Science," *Woman's Herald of Industry and Social Science Cooperator* 1 (October 1881): 3. For religion and activists, see Kathi Kern, *Mrs. Stanton's Bible* (Ithaca, N.Y.: Cornell University Press, 2001), 86–91.

27. CIHN, "Dear Friends," *National Woman Suffrage Association: Report of the Sixteenth Annual Washington Convention* (Rochester, N.Y.: Charles Mann, 1884), 129–131, in Gambone, "Forgotten Feminist," 40:554.

28. Ellen Carol DuBois, "Outgrowing the Compact of the Fathers: Equal Rights, Woman Suffrage, and the United States Constitution, 1820–1878," *Journal of American History* 74 (December 1989): 847–853, quotation on 851; Philip N. Cohen, "Nationalism and Suffrage: Gender Struggle in Nation-Building America," *Signs: Journal of Women in Culture and Society* 21 (Spring 1996): 707–717.

29. CIHN to SBA, 30 October 1880, in Gambone, "Forgotten Feminist," 40:448; "Eds. *Woman's Journal*," 8 November 1884, in ibid., 40:561; CIHN, "Christian Civil

Government," in ibid., 40:520; "Editors Press," *PRP* 24 (16 June 1883), in ibid., 40:545–548, quotation on 548.

30. CIHN to Birsha Carpenter Davis, 28 April 1878, Nichols Papers; Diane Eickhoff, *Revolutionary Heart: The Life of Clarina Howard Nichols and the Pioneering Crusade for Women's Rights* (Kansas City, Kans.: Quindaro Press, 2006), 204–205; CIHN, "An Old Friend Returns," *PRP* 19 (8 May 1880): 314.

31. CIHN, "Good News," *PRP* 21 (12 January 1881): 70.

32. See "Home Circle," *PRP* 20 (18 December 1880): 398; 21 (29 January 1881): 70; 21 (18 February 1881): 118; 21 (5 March 1881): 158; 21 (12 March 1881): 178; 21 (2 April 1881): 236; 21 (4 June 1881): 398; 23 (14 January 1882): 22; 23 (22 April 1882): 310; 23 (10 June 1882): 466; 24 (16 September 1882): 202; 24 (11 November 1882): 366; 24 (25 November 1882): 402–403; 24 (9 December 1882): 442.

33. Edward Berwick, "Editors Press," *PRP*, 24 (25 November 1882): 403; CIHN, "Men and Women and the Law," ibid., 24 (11 November 1882) 366; Peter Pitkin, "Editors Press," ibid., 21 (12 March 1881): 178; CIHN, "The Rejoinder," ibid., 21 (9 April 1881), in Gambone, "Forgotten Feminist," 40:509–510.

34. CIHN, "Woman's Rights and Wrongs—Suffrage," *PRP* 24 (16 September 1882): 202; "Men and Women and the Law," ibid., 24 (11 November 1882): 366; Edward Berwick, "Women and the Law," ibid., 24 (25 November 1882): 402–403.

35. CIHN, "The Tobacco Fiend," *PRP* 27 (10 January 1885): 26; Eickhoff, *Revolutionary Heart*, 211.

36. CIHN to Franklin G. Adams, 25 March 1884, in Gambone, "Forgotten Feminist," 40:557; CIHN, "Early Reminiscences of My Life, Written in Her Invalid Hours," in ibid., 40:455–456.

37. Lori D. Ginzberg, *Elizabeth Cady Stanton: An American Life* (New York: Hill & Wang, 2009), 153–156.

38. CIHN, "Reminiscences," in Stanton et al., *HWS*, 1:171; SBA to Harriet Robinson, 12 August 1879, in Gordon, *Selected Papers of ECS and SBA*, 3:469–470.

39. CIHN, "Reminiscences," 1:171.

40. Ibid.; Mary Tenney Gray, "Nichols Memorial to the Women of Kansas;" Mary Tenney Gray to Franklin G. Adams, 8 February 1881 and 22 June 1881, in "Correspondence about Portrait of Mrs. C. I. H. Nichols," History of Woman Suffrage Collection, KSHS; Ida Husted Harper, *Life and Work of Susan B. Anthony including Public Addresses, Her Own Letters, and Many from Her Contemporaries during Fifty Years: A Story of the Evolution of Woman* (Indianapolis: Hollenbeck, 1898–1908), 1:530.

41. CIHN, "Reminiscences," 172–184, quotations from 182, 183, 184; CIHN to SBA, 17 December 1880, in Gambone, "Forgotten Feminist," 40:453.

42. CIHN, "Reminiscences," 186, 193; Nichols to Anthony, 22 December 1880, in Gambone, "Forgotten Feminist," 40:454; Harper, *Life and Work of Susan B. Anthony*, 1:529–530.

43. CIHN, "Reminiscences," 190–191.

44. Ibid., 171.

45. CIHN to SBA, 14 April 1868, *Revolution*, 30 April 1868, in Gambone, "Forgotten Feminist," 39:547; SBA to Harriet Hanson Robinson, 12 August 1879, in Gordon,

Selected Papers of ECS and SBA, 3:470. See also Marilyn Schultz Blackwell, "The Politics of Motherhood: Clarina Howard Nichols and School Suffrage," *New England Quarterly* 78 (December 2005): 592–595. For a chronological list of state enactments, see Alexander Keyssar, *The Right to Vote: The Contested History of Democracy in the United States* (New York: Basic Books, 2000), 399–400. For municipal suffrage in Kansas, see Michael Lewis Goldberg, *An Army of Women: Gender and Politics in Gilded Age Kansas* (Baltimore: Johns Hopkins University Press, 1997), 57–85.

46. CIHN, [Diary], and "Early Reminiscences," in Gambone, "Forgotten Feminist," 40:455.

47. SBA to CIHN, September 1882, in Harper, *Life and Work of Susan B. Anthony*, 2:544; CIHN to SBA, 25 June [1884], in Gambone, "Forgotten Feminist," 40:560; CIHN to SBA, c. 1883, in ibid., 455, 551.

48. CIHN to SBA, c. 1883, and CIHN to Franklin G. Adams, 12 June 1884, both in Gambone, "Forgotten Feminist," 40:551, 559.

49. Stanton et al., *HWS*, 3:764–765; SBA to George B. Nichols, 22 March 1887 and 22 February 1888, in *Papers of Elizabeth Cady Stanton and Susan B. Anthony*, ed. Patricia G. Holland and Ann D. Gordon (Wilmington, Del.: Scholarly Resources, 1991), microfilm, reels 25 and 26; CIHN to SBA, 7 January 1885, in Gambone, "Forgotten Feminist," 40:562.

50. "In Memoriam," *Ukiah Press*, 16 January 1885; Stanton et al., *HWS*, 3:765; Mallie Stafford, "Into the Higher Life," *PRP* 29 (14 February 1885): 146; "In Memoriam," *Weekly Herald-Tribune*, 20 February 1885; Florene Parsons, "Clarina Irene Howard Nichols and the Kansas Constitution," typescript, [1959], 16. In 1933 the Women's Kansas Day Club honored Nichols with a plaque inscribed with "a real home defender."

51. CIHN, "Reminiscences," 193. Married women's property rights were included in the constitutions of Texas, California, and Oregon before Kansas. See Mari J. Matsuda, "The West and the Legal Status of Women: Explanations of Frontier Feminism," *Journal of the West* 24 (January 1985):50–51.

52. See, for example, Beverly Beeton, *Women Vote in the West: The Woman Suffrage Movement, 1869–1896* (New York: Garland, 1986); Gullet, *Becoming Citizens*; and Rebecca J. Mead, *How the Vote Was Won: Woman Suffrage in the Western United States, 1868–1914* (New York: New York University Press, 2004).

53. Barbara Cutter, *Domestic Devils, Battlefield Angels: The Radicalism of American Womanhood, 1830–1865* (DeKalb: Northern Illinois University Press, 2003), 7–13; Louise Michele Newman, *White Women's Rights: the Racial Origins of Feminism in the United States* (New York: Oxford University Press, 1999), 52–55.

54. Stanton et al., *HWS*, 3:765.

SELECTED BIBLIOGRAPHY

This listing includes major sources consulted. Genealogical and minor references can be found in the notes.

Manuscript Collections

Grace Hudson Museum, Ukiah, California
    Helen McCowan Carpenter Papers
    Nichols Family Collection
Kansas State Historical Society, Topeka, Kansas
    Lucy Bigelow Armstrong Papers
    George W. Brown Collection
    James W. Denver Collection
    Alfred Gray Correspondence
    Abelard Guthrie Journal
    Thomas W. Higginson Collection
    Thaddeus Hyatt Collection
    Charles and Julia Lovejoy Collection
    Samuel E. Martin Collection
    Moneka Woman's Rights Association Records
    Clarina I. H. Nichols Papers, microfilm; Letters and Miscellaneous
        Documents
    Charles and Sara T. D. Robinson Papers
    Eli Thayer Collection
    Augustus Wattles Papers
    Woman Suffrage History Collection
    Samuel and Margaret Wood Papers
    Wyandot Indian Council Records
Schlesinger Library, Radcliffe Institute for Advanced Study, Harvard
        University, Cambridge, Massachusetts
    Susan B. Anthony Papers
    Clarina Irene (Howard) Nichols Papers
Townshend Historical Society, Townshend, Vermont
    Townshend Academy Records
    Townshend Temperance Society, Record Book
Vermont Historical Society, Leahy Library, Barre, Vermont
    Eastman Papers
    Clarina Howard Nichols, Miscellaneous Letters
    West Townshend Lyceum Record Book

Newspapers and Periodicals

Anti-Slavery Bugle (Ohio)
Brattleboro (Vt.) Messenger
Brockport (N.Y.) Free Press
Burlington (Vt.) Courier
Caledonian (Vt.)
Daily Free Democrat (Wis.)
Freedom's Champion (Kans.)
Green Mountain Freeman (Vt.)
Herald of Freedom (Kans.)
Liberator (Mass.)
Lily (N.Y.)
Kansas Daily Commonwealth
Kansas Free State
Kansas National Democrat
Kansas Press
Middlebury (Vt.) Register
National Citizen and Ballot Box (Ohio)
New York (Daily) Tribune
New York Times
Pacific Rural Press (Calif.)
Prairie Star (Kans.)
Quindaro Chindowan (Kans.)
Semi-Weekly (Weekly) Eagle (Vt.)
Topeka Tribune (Kans.)
Una (R.I.)
United States Magazine and Democratic Review (N.Y.)
Vermont Phoenix
Washington (D.C.) Star
Weekly Western Argus (Kans.)
Windham County (Vt.) Democrat
Woman's Herald of Industry and Social Science Cooperator (Calif.)
Woman's Journal (Mass.)
Woman's Tribune (Neb.)
Wyandotte (Commercial) Gazette (Kans.)

Published Primary Sources

Acts and Resolves Passed by the Legislature of the State of Vermont at Their October Session, 1847; 1849; 1850. Burlington: State of Vermont, 1847, 1849, 1850.

Adams, Lois Bryan. *Letter from Washington, 1863-1865*, ed. Evelyn Leasher. Detroit: Wayne State University Press, 1999.

[Bascom, Ruth P.] *Memoir of Mrs. Lucy Gaylord Pomeroy.* New York, 1865.

Davis, Paulina W., comp. *A History of the National Woman's Rights Movement, for Twenty Years, with the Proceedings of the Decade Meeting Held at Apollo Hall,*

October 20, 1870, from 1850 to 1870. With an Appendix Containing the History of the Movement during the Winter of 1871, in the National Capitol. New York: Journeymen Printers' Co-Operative Association, 1871.

Gambone, Joseph G., ed. "The Forgotten Feminist of Kansas: The Papers of Clarina I. H. Nichols, 1854–1885." *Kansas Historical Quarterly,* 39 (Spring 1973): 12–57; 39 (Summer 1973): 220–261; 39 (Autumn 1973): 392–444; 39 (Winter 1973): 515–563; 40 (Spring 1974): 72–135; 40 (Summer 1974): 241–292; 40 (Autumn 1974): 410–459; and 40 (Winter 1974): 503–562.

General Laws of the State of Kansas, in Force at the Close of the Session of the Legislature Ending March 6th, 1862. Topeka: J. H. Bennet, 1862.

General Laws of the Territory of Kansas Passed at the Fifth Session of the Legislative Assembly Begun at the City of Lecompton on the 1st Monday of Jan'y, 1859, and Held and Concluded at the City of Lawrence. Lawrence, Kans., 1859.

Gordon, Ann D., ed. *The Selected Papers of Elizabeth Cady Stanton and Susan B. Anthony.* 3 vols. New Brunswick, N.J.: Rutgers University Press, 1997.

Harper, Ida Husted. *Life and Work of Susan B. Anthony Including Public Addresses, Her Own Letters and Many from Her Contemporaries during Fifty Years: A Story of the Evolution of Woman,* vol. 1. Indianapolis: Bowen-Merrill, 1899.

Holland, Patricia G., and Ann D. Gordon. *Papers of Elizabeth Cady Stanton and Susan B. Anthony.* Wilmington, Del.: Scholarly Resources, 1991, microfilm.

House [and Senate] Journal of the Legislative Assembly of the State of Kansas, Begun and Held at Topeka, on Tuesday, January 8th, A.D. 1867. Leavenworth, Kans.: Clarke, Emery, 1867.

Hunt, Kesia. *Glances and Glimpses; or Fifty Years Social, Including Twenty Years Professional Life.* Boston: J. P. Jewett, 1856.

Journal of the House of the State of Vermont: October Session, 1847; 1852. Montpelier, 1848; Burlington, Vt., 1852.

Journal of the Senate of the State of Vermont: October Session, 1847; 1852. Montpelier, 1848, 1852.

Kansas Constitutional Convention: A Report of the Proceedings and Debates of the Convention which Framed the Constitution of Kansas at Wyandotte in July, 1859. Also the Constitution Annotated to Date, Historical Sketches, etc. Topeka, Kans., 1920.

National Association for the Relief of Destitute Colored Women and Children. *Annual Report, 1866.* Washington, D.C.: Chronicle Steam, 1866.

Nichols, C[larina] I. H. *The Responsibilities of Woman: A Speech by Mrs. C. I. H. Nichols, at the Woman's Rights Convention, Worcester, October 15, 1851.* Rochester, N.Y.: Steam Press of Curtis, Butts & Co., 1854.

Parton, James, et al., eds. *Eminent Women of the Age: Being Narratives of the Lives and Deeds of the Most Prominent Women of the Present Generation.* Hartford, Conn., 1868.

Proceedings of the Whole World's Temperance Convention Held at Metropolitan Hall, in the City of New York, on Thursday and Friday, September 1st and 2nd, 1853. New York: Fowlers & Wells, 1853.

Proceedings of the Woman's Rights Convention Held at Akron, Ohio, May 28 and 29, 1851. Cincinnati, 1851.

Proceedings of the Woman's Rights Convention Held at the Broadway Tabernacle, in the City of New York, on Tuesday and Wednesday, September 6th and 7th, 1853. New York: Fowlers & Wells, 1853.

Proceedings of the Woman's Rights Convention Held at West Chester, Pa., June 2nd and 3rd, 1852. Philadelphia, 1852.

Proceedings of the Woman's Rights Convention Held at Worcester, October 15th and 16th, 1851. New York: Fowlers & Wells, 1852.

Proceedings of the Woman's Rights Convention, Held at Worcester, October 23rd and 24th, 1850. Boston: Prentiss & Sawyer, 1851.

Robinson, Sara T. L. *Kansas, Its Interior and Exterior Life, Including a Full View of Its Settlement, Political History, Social Life, Climate, Soil, Productions, Scenery, etc.* Boston: Crosby & Nichols, 1856.

Special Report of the Commissioner of Education on the Condition and Improvement of Public Schools in the District of Columbia, Submitted to the Senate June 1868, and to the House, with Additions, June 13, 1870. Washington, D.C.: Government Printing Office, 1871.

Stanton, Elizabeth Cady, Susan B. Anthony, and Matilda Joslyn Gage, eds. *Eighty Years and More: Reminiscences, 1815–1897.* N.p.: Unwin, 1898; 2nd ed. Boston: Northeastern University Press, 1993.

———. *History of Woman Suffrage.* 3 vols. Rochester, N.Y.: Fowler & Wells, 1881; 2nd ed., 1887.

Thayer, Eli. *The New England Emigrant Aid Company: And Its Influence, through the Kansas Contest, upon National History.* Worcester, Mass., 1887.

Train, George Francis. *The Great Epigram Campaign in Kansas: Championship of Women.* Leavenworth, Kans.: Prescott & Hume, 1867.

U.S. Bureau of the Census, Manuscript Population Schedules, 1820–1870. Microfilm. Washington, D.C.: National Archives, 1950–1964.

Wilson, Elizabeth. *A Scriptural View of Woman's Rights and Duties, in All the Important Relations of Life.* Philadelphia: William S. Young, 1849.

Secondary Sources

Abzug, Robert H. *Cosmos Crumbling: American Reform and the Religious Imagination.* New York: Oxford University Press, 1994.

Allgor, Catherine. *Parlor Politics: In Which the Ladies of Washington Help Build a City and a Government.* Charlottesville: University Press of Virginia, 2000.

Alpern, Sara, Joyce Antler, Elisabeth I. Perry, and Ingrid W. Scobie, eds. *The Challenge of Feminist Biography.* Urbana: University of Illinois Press, 1992.

Anderson, Bonnie S. *Joyous Greetings: The First International Women's Movement, 1830–1860.* New York: Oxford University Press, 2000.

Aron, Cindy Sondik. *Ladies and Gentlemen of the Civil Service: Middle-Class Workers in Victorian America.* New York: Oxford University Press, 1987.

Baker, Jean H. *Affairs of Party: The Political Culture of Northern Democrats in the Mid-Nineteenth Century.* Ithaca, N.Y.: Cornell University Press, 1983.

Baker, Paula C. "The Domestication of Politics: Women and American Political Society, 1780–1920." *American Historical Review* 89 (June 1984): 620–647.

Barry, Kathleen. *Susan B. Anthony: A Biography of a Singular Feminist.* New York: New York University Press, 1988.

Barry, Louise. "Emigrant Aid Company Parties of 1854; . . .1855." *Kansas Historical Quarterly* 12 (May and August 1943): 115–155, 227–268.

Basch, Francoise. "Women's Rights and the Wrongs of Marriage in Mid-Nineteenth-Century America." *History Workshop Journal* 22 (Autumn 1986): 26–47.

Basch, Norma. *Framing American Divorce: From the Revolutionary Generation to the Victorians.* Berkeley: University of California Press, 1999.

———. *In the Eyes of the Law: Women, Marriage, and Property in Nineteenth-Century New York.* Ithaca, N.Y.: Cornell University Press, 1982.

Bassett, T. D. Seymour. "The 1870 Campaign for Woman Suffrage in Vermont." *Vermont Quarterly* 14 (April 1946): 47–61.

———. *The Gods of the Hills: Piety and Society in Nineteenth-Century Vermont.* Montpelier: Vermont Historical Society, 2000.

———. "Nichols, Clarina Irene Howard." In *Notable American Women, 1607–1950: A Biographical Dictionary,* ed. Edward T. James, Janet Wilson James, and Paul S. Boyer. Cambridge: Oxford University Press, 1971.

———. "Vermont Politics and the Press in the 1840s." *Vermont History* 47 (Summer 1979): 196–213.

Beeton, Beverly. *Women Vote in the West: The Woman Suffrage Movement, 1869–1896.* New York: Garland, 1986.

Bennion, Sherilyn Cox. *Equal to the Occasion: Women Editors of the Nineteenth-Century West.* Reno: University of Nevada Press, 1990.

Blackmar, Frank W. *The Life of Charles Robinson, the First State Governor of Kansas.* Topeka: Crane, 1902.

Blackwell, Alice Stone. *Lucy Stone: Pioneer of Woman's Rights.* Boston: Little, Brown, 1930.

Blackwell, Marilyn Schultz. "Meddling in Politics: Clarina Howard Nichols and Antebellum Political Culture." *Journal of the Early Republic* 24 (Spring 2004): 27–41.

———. "'The Paupers' Removal': The Politics of Clarina Howard Nichols." *Vermont History* 75 (Winter/Spring 2007): 13–33.

———. "The Politics of Motherhood: Clarina Howard Nichols and School Suffrage." *New England Quarterly* 78 (December 2005): 570–598.

———. "Surrogate Ministers: Women, Revivalism, and Maternal Associations in Vermont." *Vermont History* 69 (Winter 2001): 66–89.

Bloch, Ruth H. "American Feminine Ideals in Transition: The Rise of the Moral Mother, 1285–1815." *Feminist Studies* 4 (1978): 101–126.

Boylan, Anne M. *Origins of Woman's Activism: New York and Boston, 1797–1840.* Chapel Hill: University of North Carolina Press, 2002.

Breedlove, Anne M. "'Inspired and Possessed': San Francisco Women Newspaper Publishers." *California History* 80 (Spring 2001): 48–63.

Bremer, Jeff R. "'A Species of Town-Building Madness': Quindaro and Kansas Territory, 1856–1862." *Kansas History: A Journal of the Central Plains* 26 (Autumn 2003): 156–171.

Brynn, Edward P. "Vermont's Political Vacuum of 1845–1856 and the Emergence of the Republican Party." *Vermont History* 38 (Spring 1970): 113–123.

Burnham, Henry. *Brattleboro Windham County, Vermont: Early History with Biographical Sketches of Some of Its Citizens.* Brattleboro, Vt.: D. Leonard, 1880.

Butler, Diane S. "The Public Life and Private Affairs of Sherman Miller Booth." *Wisconsin Magazine of History* 82 (Spring 1999): 167–197.

Cabot, Mary R. *Annals of Brattleboro, 1681–1895.* 2 vols. Brattleboro, Vt.: Hildreth, 1921–1922.

Carpenter, Helen M[cCowan]. "Among the Diggers of Thirty Years Ago." *Overland Monthly* 21 (February and April 1893): 146–155, 389–399.

Cashin, Joan E. *A Family Venture: Men and Women on the Southern Frontier.* New York: Oxford University Press, 1991.

Castañeda, Antonia I. "Women of Color and the Rewriting of Western History: The Discourse, Politics, and Decolonization of History." In *Women and Gender in the American West: Jensen-Miller Prize Essays from the Coalition for Western Women's History,* ed. Mary Ann Irwin and James F. Brooks, 66–88. Albuquerque: University of New Mexico Press, 2004.

Cazden, Elizabeth. *Antoinette Brown Blackwell: A Biography.* Old Westbury, N.Y.: Feminist Press, 1983.

Cheatham, Gary L. "'Slavery All the Time or Not at All': The Wyandotte Constitution Debate, 1859–1861." *Kansas History: A Journal of the Central Plains* 21 (Autumn 1998): 168–187.

Child, Hamilton, comp. *Gazetteer and Business Directory of Windham County, Vermont, 1724–1884.* Syracuse, N.Y.: Hamilton Child, 1884.

Christiansen, Adrienne E. "Clarina Howard Nichols: A Rhetorical Criticism of Selected Speeches." M.A. thesis, University of Kansas, 1987.

Chused, Richard H. "Married Women's Property Law, 1800–1850." *Georgetown Law Journal* 71 (1983): 1359–1425.

Clifford, Deborah P. "An Invasion of Strong-Minded Women: The Newspapers and the Woman Suffrage Campaign in Vermont in 1870." *Vermont History* 43 (Winter 1975): 1–19.

———. *More Than Petticoats: Remarkable Vermont Women.* Guilford, Conn.: Globe Pequot, 2009.

Cohen, Patricia C. *The Murder of Helen Jewett: The Life and Death of a Prostitute in Nineteenth-Century New York.* New York: Knopf, 1998.

Cohen, Philip N. "Nationalism and Suffrage: Gender Struggle in Nation-Building America." *Signs: Journal of Women in Culture and Society* 21 (Spring 1996): 707–717.

Collins, Steve. "The Underground Railroad in Quindaro, K.T." Typescript, n.d.

Connelley, William E. *A Standard History of Kansas and Kansans,* vol. 1. Chicago: Lewis, 1918.

Coon, Anne C. *Hear Me Patiently: The Reform Speeches of Amelia Jenks Bloomer.* Westport, Conn.: Greenwood, 1994.

Cordley, Richard D. *A History of Lawrence, Kansas.* Lawrence, Kans.: Lawrence Journal Press, 1895.

Coryell, Janet L. "Superceding Gender: The Role of the Woman Politico in Antebellum Partisan Politics." In *Women and the Unstable State in Nineteenth-Century*

America, ed. Alison M. Parker and Stephanie Cole, 84–112. College Station: Texas A&M University Press, 2000.

Cott, Nancy F. *The Bonds of Womanhood: "Woman's Sphere" in New England, 1780–1835.* New Haven, Conn.: Yale University Press, 1977.

Crocker, Henry. *History of Baptists in Vermont.* Bellows Falls, Vt.: P. H. Gobie, 1913.

Cullen-DuPont, Kathryn., ed. *Women's Suffrage in America: An Eyewitness History.* New York: Facts on File, 1992.

Cutler, William. *History of Kansas.* Chicago: A. T. Andreas, 1883.

Cutter, Barbara. *Domestic Devils, Battlefield Angels: The Radicalism of American Womanhood, 1830–1865.* DeKalb: Northern Illinois University Press, 2003.

Daniels, Christine, and Michael V. Kennedy. *Over the Threshold: Intimate Violence in Early America.* New York: Routledge, 1999.

Denton, Sally. *Passion and Principle: John and Jessie Frémont, the Couple Whose Power, Politics, and Love Shaped Nineteenth-Century America.* New York: Bloomsbury, 2007.

Dinkins, Robert J. *Before Equal Suffrage: Women in Partisan Politics from Colonial Times to 1920.* Westport, Conn.: Greenwood, 1995.

DuBois, Ellen C. *Feminism and Suffrage: The Emergence of an Independent Women's Movement in America, 1848–1869.* Ithaca, N.Y.: Cornell University Press, 1978.

———. "Outgrowing the Compact of the Fathers: Equal Rights, Woman Suffrage, and the United States Constitution, 1820–1878." *Journal of American History* 74 (December 1987): 836–862.

——— and Richard Candida Smith, eds. *Elizabeth Cady Stanton, Feminist as Thinker: A Reader in Documents and Essays.* New York: New York University Press, 2007.

Dudden, Faye. "New York Strategy: The New York Woman's Movement and the Civil War." In *Votes for Women: The Struggle for Suffrage Revisited,* ed. Jean H. Baker, 56–76. New York: Oxford University Press, 2002.

Earle, Jonathan H. *Jacksonian Antislavery and the Politics of Free Soil, 1824–1854.* Chapel Hill: University of North Carolina Press, 2004.

Edwards, Rebecca. *Angels in the Machinery: Gender in American Party Politics from the Civil War to the Progressive Era.* New York: Oxford University Press, 1997.

Eickhoff, Diane. *Revolutionary Heart: The Life of Clarina Nichols and the Pioneering Crusade for Women's Rights.* Kansas City, Kans.: Quindaro Press, 2006.

Etcheson, Nicole. *Bleeding Kansas: Contested Liberty in the Civil War Era.* Lawrence: University Press of Kansas, 2004.

———. "Labouring for the Freedom of This Territory: Free State Kansas Women in the 1850s." *Kansas History: A Journal of the Central Plains* 21 (Summer 1998): 71–87.

Faragher, John Mack. *Women and Men on the Overland Trail.* New Haven, Conn.: Yale University Press, 1979.

Farley, Alan W. "Annals of Quindaro: A Kansas Ghost Town." *Kansas Historical Quarterly* 22 (Winter 1956): 305–316.

Faulkner, Carol. *Women's Radical Reconstruction: The Freedmen's Aid Movement.* Philadelphia: University of Pennsylvania Press, 2004.

Flexner, Eleanor. *Century of Struggle: The Woman's Rights Movement in the United States.* Cambridge, Mass.: Harvard University Press, 1959; repr., New York: Atheneum, 1971.

Foner, Eric. *Free Soil, Free Labor, Free Men: The Ideology of the Republican Party before the Civil War.* New York: Oxford University Press, 1970.

Freehling, William H. *The Road to Disunion.* New York: Oxford University Press, 1990.

Gaeddert, G. Raymond. *The Birth of Kansas.* Lawrence: University of Kansas, 1940.

Getz, Lynne Marie. "Partners in Motion: Gender, Migration, and Reform in Antebellum Ohio and Kansas." *Frontiers: A Journal of Women's Studies* 27 (2006): 102–135.

Gilmore, William J. *Reading Becomes a Necessity of Life: Material and Cultural Life in Rural New England, 1780–1835.* Knoxville: University of Tennessee Press, 1989.

Ginzberg, Lori D. *Elizabeth Cady Stanton: An American Life.* New York: Hill & Wang, 2009.

———. "'The Hearts of Your Readers Will Shudder': Fanny Wright, Infidelity, and American Free Thought." *American Quarterly* 46 (June 1994): 195–226.

———. "Moral Suasion Is Moral Balderdash: Women, Politics, and Social Activism in the 1850s." *Journal of American History* 73 (December 1986): 601–622.

———. *Untidy Origins: A Story of Woman's Rights in Antebellum New York.* Chapel Hill: University of North Carolina Press, 2005.

———. *Women and the Work of Benevolence: Morality, Politics, and Class in the Nineteenth-Century United States.* New Haven, Conn.: Yale University Press, 1990.

Goldberg, Michael L. *An Army of Women: Gender and Politics in Gilded Age Kansas.* Baltimore: Johns Hopkins University Press, 1997.

Greene, Dana, ed. *Suffrage and Religious Principle: Speeches and Writings of Olympia Brown.* Metuchen, N.J.: Scarecrow Press, 1983.

Griswold, Robert L. "Anglo Women and Domestic Ideology in the American West in the Nineteenth and Early Twentieth Centuries." In *Western Women: Their Land, Their Lives,* ed. Lillian Schlissel, Vicki Ruiz, and Janice Monk. Albuquerque: University of New Mexico Press, 1988.

Grossberg, Michael. *Governing the Hearth: Law and the Family in Nineteenth-Century America.* Chapel Hill: University of North Carolina Press, 1988.

Gullet, Gayle. *Becoming Citizens: The Emergence and Development of the California Women's Movement, 1880–1911.* Urbana: University of Illinois Press, 2000.

Gustafson, Melanie. *Women and the Republican Party.* Urbana: University of Illinois Press, 2001.

Heilbrun, Carolyn G. *Writing a Woman's Life.* New York: Ballantine, 1988.

Hemenway, Abby M. *Vermont Historical Gazetteer,* vol. 5. Brandon, Vt.: Carrie E. H. Page, 1891.

Hewitt, Nancy A. *Women's Activism and Social Change: Rochester, New York, 1822–1872.* Ithaca, N.Y.: Cornell University Press, 1984.

Hoffert, Sylvia D. *Jane Grey Swisshelm: An Unconventional Life, 1815–1884.* Chapel Hill: University of North Carolina Press, 2004.

———. *When Hens Crow: The Woman's Rights Movement in Antebellum America.* Bloomington: Indiana University Press, 1995.

Howe, Daniel W. "The Evangelical Movement and Political Culture in the North during the Second Party System." *Journal of American History* 77 (March 1991): 1216–1239.

Hudson, Linda S. *Mistress of Manifest Destiny: A Biography of Jane McManus Storm Cazneau, 1807–1878.* Austin: Texas State Historical Association, 2001.

Hutchinson, William. "Sketches of Kansas Pioneer Experience." *Transactions of the Kansas State Historical Society, 1901–1902,* vol. 7. Topeka: KSHS, 1902.

Isenberg, Nancy. *Sex and Citizenship in Antebellum America.* Chapel Hill: University of North Carolina Press, 1998.

James, Edward T., Janet Wilson James, and Paul S. Boyer, eds. *Notable American Women, 1607–1950: A Biographical Dictionary,* 3 vols. Cambridge: Oxford University Press, 1971.

Jeffrey, Julie Roy. *Frontier Women: The Trans-Mississippi West, 1840–1880.* New York: Hill & Wang, 1979.

———. "Permeable Boundaries: Abolitionist Women and Separate Spheres." *Journal of the Early Republic* 21 (Spring 2001): 79–93.

Jelinek, Estelle C. *The Tradition of Women's Autobiography: From Antiquity to the Present.* Boston: Twayne, 1986.

Johnson, Paul E. *A Shopkeeper's Millennium: Society and Revivals in Rochester, New York, 1815–1837.* New York: Hill & Wang, 1978.

Johnson, Reinhard O. "The Liberty Party in Vermont, 1840–1848: The Forgotten Abolitionists." *Vermont History* 47 (Fall 1979): 258–275.

Johnson, Samuel A. *The Battle Cry of Freedom: The New England Emigrant Aid Company in the Kansas Crusade.* Lawrence: University of Kansas Press, 1954.

Karcher, Carolyn L. *The First Woman in the Republic: A Cultural Biography of Lydia Maria Child.* Durham, N.C.: Duke University Press, 1994.

———."From Pacifism to Armed Struggle: L. M. Child's 'The Kansas Emigrants' and Antislavery Ideology in the 1850s." *ESQ: Journal of the American Renaissance* 34, no. 3 (1988): 140–158.

Kelley, Mary. *Learning to Stand and Speak: Women, Education, and Public Life in America's Republic.* Chapel Hill: University of North Carolina Press, 2006.

Kellow, Margaret. "'For the Sake of Suffering Kansas': Lydia Maria Child, Gender, and the Politics of the 1850s." *Journal of Women's History* 5 (Fall 1993): 32–49.

Kelly, Catherine E. *In the New England Fashion: Reshaping Women's Lives in the Nineteenth Century.* Ithaca, N.Y.: Cornell University Press, 1999.

Kerber, Linda K. "A Constitutional Right to Be Treated Like American Ladies: Women and the Obligations of Citizenship." In *U.S. History as Women's History: New Feminist Essays.* ed. Linda K. Kerber, Alice Kessler-Harris, and Kathryn Kish Sklar. Chapel Hill: University of North Carolina Press, 1995.

———. *Women of the Republic: Intellect and Ideology in Revolutionary America.* Chapel Hill: University of North Carolina Press, 1980.

Kern, Kathi. *Mrs. Stanton's Bible.* Ithaca, N.Y.: Cornell University Press, 2001.

Kerr, Andrea M. *Lucy Stone: Speaking Out for Equality.* New Brunswick, N.J.: Rutgers University Press, 1992.

Keyssar, Alexander. *The Right to Vote: The Contested History of Democracy in the United States.* New York: Basic, 2000.

Knott, Claudia. "The Woman Suffrage Movement in Kentucky, 1879–1920." Ph.D. diss., University of Kentucky, 1989.

Kraditor, Aileen S. *The Ideas of the Woman Suffrage Movement, 1890–1920.* New York: Columbia University Press, 1965; reprint, Garden City, N.Y.: Anchor, 1971.

Kunin, Madeleine M. "Clarina Howard Nichols: Green Mountain Suffragette." *Vermont Life* 28 (Winter 1973): 14–17.

Lasser, Carol, and Marlene Deahl Merrill. *Friends and Sisters: Letters between Lucy Stone and Antoinette Brown Blackwell, 1846–1893.* Urbana: University of Illinois Press, 1987.

Laurie, Bruce. *Beyond Garrison: Antislavery and Social Reform.* Cambridge: Cambridge University Press, 2005.

Lebsock, Suzanne. *The Free Women of Petersburg: Status and Culture in a Southern Town.* New York: Norton, 1985.

Lerner, Gerda. *The Grimké Sisters from South Carolina: Pioneers for Woman's Rights and Abolition.* New York: Schoken, 1967.

Ludlum, David M. *Social Ferment in Vermont, 1791–1850.* New York: AMS, 1966.

Lovejoy, Julia Louisa. "Letters from Kanzas." *Kansas Historical Quarterly* 11 (February 1942): 29–44.

Lystra, Karen. *Searching the Heart: Women, Men, and Romantic Love in Nineteenth-Century America.* New York: Oxford University Press, 1989.

Madsen, Sandra A. "1867 Campaign for Woman Suffrage." Ph.D. diss., University of Kansas, 1975.

Margadant, Jo Burr. *The New Biography: Performing Femininity in Nineteenth-Century France.* Berkeley: University of California Press, 2000.

Marilley, Suzanne M. *Woman Suffrage and the Origins of Liberal Feminism in the United States, 1820–1920.* Cambridge, Mass.: Harvard University Press, 1996.

Matsuda, Mari J. "The West and the Legal Status of Women: Explanations of Frontier Feminism." *Journal of the West* 24 (January 1985): 47–56.

Mattingly, Carol. *Well-Tempered Women: Nineteenth-Century Temperance Rhetoric.* Carbondale: Southern Illinois University Press, 1998.

McBride, Genevieve G. *On Wisconsin Women: Working for Their Rights from Settlement to Suffrage.* Madison: University of Wisconsin Press, 1993.

McCool, John. "Conventional Wisdom." *KansasHistoryOnline,* ed. Henry J. Fortunato. Kansas Historical Society, 2006. http://www.kansashistoryonline/ksh/article page.asp?artid=285.

McKenna, Sister Jeanne, "With the Help of God and Lucy Stone." *Kansas Historical Quarterly* 36 (Spring 1970): 13–26.

McLoughlin, William G. *New England Dissent, 1630–1833: The Baptists and the Separation of Church and State.* Cambridge, Mass.: Harvard University Press, 1971.

McManus, Michael J. *Political Abolitionism in Wisconsin, 1840–1861.* Kent, Ohio: Kent State University Press, 1998.

McPherson, James. *Battle Cry of Freedom.* New York: Oxford University Press, 1989.

Mead, Rebecca J. *How the Vote Was Won: Woman Suffrage in the Western United States, 1868–1914.* New York: New York University Press, 2004.

Million, Joelle. *Women's Voice, Women's Place: Lucy Stone and the Birth of the Women's Rights Movement.* Westport, Conn.: Praeger, 2003.

Morgan, Perl W., ed. *History of Wyandotte County Kansas and Its People*. Chicago: Lewis, 1911.

Morrison, Michael. *Slavery and the American West: The Eclipse of Manifest Destiny and the Coming of the Civil War*. Chapel Hill: University of North Carolina Press, 1997.

Mullaney, Marie Marmo. "Feminism, Utopianism, and Domesticity: The Career of Rebecca Buffum Spring, 1811–1911." In *A New Jersey Anthology*, ed. Maxine N. Lurie. New Brunswick, N.J.: Rutgers University Press, 2002.

Myres, Sandra L., ed. *Ho for California!* San Marino, Calif.: Henry Huntington Library & Art Gallery, 1980.

Newman, Louise M. *White Women's Rights: The Racial Origins of Feminism in the United States*. New York: Oxford University Press, 1999.

Noun, Louise. "Amelia Bloomer, a Biography: Part I, The Lily of Seneca Falls; Part II, The Suffragist of Council Bluffs." *Annals of Iowa* 47 (Winter and Spring 1985): 575–621.

———. *Strong-Minded Women: The Emergence of the Woman Suffrage Movement in Iowa*. Ames: Iowa State University Press, 1969.

Oertel, Kristen Tegtmeier. *Bleeding Borders: Race, Gender, and Violence in Pre–Civil War Kansas*. Baton Rouge: Louisiana State University Press, 2009.

———. "Clarina Irene Howard Nichols: 'A Large-Hearted, Brave, Faithful Woman.'" In *John Brown to Bob Dole: Movers and Shakers in Kansas History*, ed. Virgil W. Dean, 56–67. Lawrence: University Press of Kansas, 2006.

Okker, Patricia. *Our Sister Editors: Sarah J. Hale and the Tradition of Nineteenth-Century American Women Editors*. Athens: University of Georgia Press, 1995.

Olsen, Christopher J. "Respecting 'The Wise Allotment of Our Sphere': White Women and Politics in Mississippi, 1840–1860." *Journal of Women's History* 11 (Autumn 1999): 104–125.

[Palmer, Lyman L.] *History of Mendocino County, California. Comprising Its Geography, Geology, Topography, Climatography, Springs, and Timber*. San Francisco: Alley, Bowen, 1880.

Parsons, Florene. "Clarina Irene Howard Nichols and the Kansas Constitution." Typescript, [1959].

Pascoe, Peggy. *Relations of Rescue: The Search for Moral Authority in the American West, 1874–1939*. New York: Oxford University Press, 1990.

Phelps, James H. *Collections Relating to the History and Inhabitants of the Town of Townshend, Vermont, in Three Parts*. Brattleboro, Vt.: George E. Selleck, 1877.

Pierson, Michael D. *Free Hearts and Free Homes: Gender and American Antislavery Politics*. Chapel Hill: University of North Carolina Press, 2003.

———. "'A War of Extermination': A Newly Uncovered Letter by Julia Louisa Lovejoy, 1856." *Kansas History: A Journal of the Central Plains* 16 (Summer 1993): 120–123.

Rabkin, Peggy A. *Fathers to Daughters: The Legal Foundations of Female Emancipation*. Westport, Conn.: Greenwood, 1980.

Richter, Amy G. *Home on the Rails: Women, the Railroad, and the Rise of Public Domesticity*. Chapel Hill: University of North Carolina Press, 2005.

Riley, Glenda. *Confronting Race: Women and Indians on the Frontier, 1815–1915.* Albuquerque: University of New Mexico Press, 2004.

———. *The Female Frontier: A Comparative View of Women on the Prairie and the Plains.* Lawrence: University Press of Kansas, 1988.

Robbins, Sarah. "'The Future Good and Great of Our Land': Republican Mothers, Female Authors, and Domesticated Literacy in Antebellum New England." *New England Quarterly* 75 (December 2002): 562–591.

Rossi, Alice S., ed. *The Feminist Papers: From Adams to de Beauvoir.* Boston: Northeastern University Press, 1973.

Roth, Randolph A. *The Democratic Dilemma: Religion, Reform, and the Social Order in the Connecticut River Valley of Vermont, 1791–1850.* Cambridge: Cambridge University Press, 1987.

Rothman, Ellen K. *Hands and Hearts: A History of Courtship in America.* New York: Basic, 1984.

Ryan, Mary P. *Cradle of the Middle Class: The Family in Oneida County, New York, 1790–1865.* Cambridge: Cambridge University Press, 1981.

Salerno, Beth A. *Sister Societies: Women's Antislavery Organizations in Antebellum America.* DeKalb: Northern Illinois University Press, 2005.

Saxton, Alexander. *The Rise and Fall of the White Republic.* New York: Verso, 1990.

Scharff, Virginia. *Twenty Thousand Roads: Women, Movement, and the West.* Berkeley: University of California Press, 2003.

Schenck, Marvin A., Karen Holmes, and Sherrie Smith-Ferri. *Aurelius O. Carpenter: Photographer of the Mendocino Frontier.* Ukiah, Calif.: Grace Hudson Museum and Sun House, 2006.

Schilpp, Madelon Golden, and Sharon M. Murphy. *Great Women of the Press.* Carbondale: Southern Illinois University Press, 1983.

Schuele, Donna C. "'None Could Deny the Eloquence of This Lady': Women, Law, and Government in California, 1850–1890." *California History* 81 (Winter 2003): 169–198.

Scott, Joan W. *Only Paradoxes to Offer: French Feminists and the Rights of Man.* Cambridge, Mass.: Harvard University Press, 1996.

SenGupta, Gunja. *For God and Mammon: Evangelicals and Entrepreneurs, Masters and Slaves in Territorial Kansas, 1854–1860.* Athens: University of Georgia Press, 1996.

Sheridan, Richard B. "Charles Henry Langston and the African American Struggle in Kansas." *Kansas History: A Journal of the Central Plains* 22 (Winter 1999–2000): 269–283.

Sherman, Michael, Gene Sessions, and P. Jeffrey Potash. *Freedom and Unity: A History of Vermont.* Barre, Vt.: Vermont Historical Society, 2004.

Siegel, Reva. "Home as Work: The First Woman's Rights Claims Concerning Wives' Household Labor, 1850–1880." *Yale Law Journal* 103 (March 1994): 1073–1217.

Sievens, Mary B. *Stray Wives: Marital Conflict in Early National New England.* New York: New York University Press, 2005.

Silber, Nina. *Daughters of the Union: Northern Women Fight the Civil War.* Cambridge, Mass.: Harvard University Press, 2005.

Silver-Isenstadt, Jean L. *Shameless: The Visionary Life of Mary Gove Nichols.* Baltimore: Johns Hopkins University Press, 2002.

Sklar, Kathryn K. *Catherine Beecher: A Study in American Domesticity.* New Haven, Conn.: Yale University Press, 1973.

Smith, Daniel S. "Family Limitation, Sexual Control, and Domestic Feminism in Victorian America." *Feminist Studies* 1 (Winter-Spring 1973): 40–57.

Sokolow, Jayme A. "Culture and Utopia: The Raritan Bay Union." *New Jersey History* 94 (Summer-Autumn 1976): 89–100.

Solomon, Martha M. "The Role of the Suffrage Press in the Woman's Rights Movement." In *A Voice of Their Own: The Woman Suffrage Press, 1849–1910.* Tuscaloosa: University of Alabama Press, 1991.

Speicher, Anna M. *The Religious World of Antislavery Women: Spirituality in the Lives of Five Abolitionist Lecturers.* Syracuse, N.Y.: Syracuse University Press, 2000.

Stansell, Christine. *City of Women: Sex and Class in New York, 1789–1860.* New York: Knopf, 1986.

Steinhagen, Carol. "The Two Lives of Frances Dana Gage." *Ohio History* 107 (Winter–Spring 1998): 22–38.

Taylor, Alice. "From Petitions to Partyism: Antislavery and the Domestication of Maine Politics in the 1840s and 1850s." *New England Quarterly* 77 (March 2004): 70–84.

Thomas, Benjamin P. *Theodore Weld: Crusader for Freedom.* New Brunswick, N.J.: Rutgers University Press, 1950.

Townshend Historical Society. *A Stitch in Time: Townshend, Vermont, 1753–2003.* Townshend, Vt.: Townsend Historical Society, 2003.

Tyrell, Ian R. *Sobering Up: From Temperance to Prohibition in Antebellum America, 1800–1860.* Westport, Conn.: Greenwood, 1989.

———. "Women and Temperance in Antebellum America, 1830–1860." *Civil War History* 28 (June 1982): 128–152.

Varon, Elizabeth R. *We Mean to Be Counted: White Women and Politics in Antebellum Virginia.* Chapel Hill: University of North Carolina Press, 1998.

Venet, Wendy Hamand. *Neither Ballots nor Bullets: Women Abolitionists and the Civil War.* Charlottesville: University Press of Virginia, 1991.

Washburn, Wilcomb E. *The American Indian and the United States: A Documentary History,* vol. 1. New York: Random House, 1973.

Wellman, Judith. *The Road to Seneca Falls: Elizabeth Cady Stanton and the First Woman's Rights Convention.* Urbana: University of Illinois Press, 2004.

———. "The Seneca Falls Women's Rights Convention: A Study of Social Networks." *Journal of Women's History* 3 (Spring 1991): 9–37.

Welter, Barbara. "The Cult of True Womanhood, 1820–1860." *American Quarterly* 18 (Summer 1966): 151–175.

Wheeler, Marjorie Spruill, ed. *One Woman, One Vote: Rediscovering the Woman Suffrage Movement.* Troutdale, Ore.: New Sage Press, 1995.

Wilder, Daniel W. *Annals of Kansas.* Topeka: George W. Martin, 1875.

Wilentz, Sean. *The Rise of American Democracy: Jefferson to Lincoln.* New York: Norton, 2005.

UNIVERSITY OF WINCHESTER
LIBRARY

Yellin, Jean Fagan, and John C. Van Horne, eds. *The Abolitionist Sisterhood: Women's Political Culture in Antebellum America.* Ithaca, N.Y.: Cornell University Press, 1994.

Zaeske, Susan. *Signatures of Citizenship, Antislavery, and Women's Political Identity.* Chapel Hill: University of North Carolina Press, 2003.

Zagarri, Rosemarie. "The Rights of Man and Woman in Post-Revolutionary America." *William and Mary Quarterly* 55 (April 1998): 203–230.

INDEX

76 (*see also under* Free Soil
movement)
Free-state movement and, 4, 143, 145,
148–49, 151, 156, 158, 159, 160–61, 165,
167, 170, 174–75, 180, 202
government job of, 211–13
health of, 27, 46, 155, 156, 206, 223, 245–
46, 248, 250, 259, 261, 267
literary writing of, 48–49, 50–51, 52
marriage to George Nichols of, 50–53,
103, 105
marriage to Justin Carpenter of, 30–44, 76
as medical practitioner, 208
motherly image of, 1–2, 3, 4, 46–47, 80,
119, 122, 166, 263
Native Americans and, 7, 150, 153–54,
221–22
political style of, 3–4, 5, 67, 82–83, 110–
11, 121, 128, 186, 201
portraits of, 14, 28, 40, 95, 187, 216
public speaking of, 89, 90, 94, 96, 113–15,
118, 119–20, 121, 125, 131, 133, 136–37,
145–46, 149, 165–66, 187, 195, 203,
204–5, 236
on racial equality, 157–58, 160–61, 170,
173, 174, 175–76, 179–80, 184–86, 192,
228, 240–41, 258
Republicans and, 166, 167, 175, 178, 179–
80, 186, 187–88, 195, 199–200, 220–21,
223–24, 227, 251, 258–59, 264–65
self-assessment by, 1, 259, 262, 263,
265–66
on slavery, 70–71, 72, 74, 75, 109, 141, 156,
162, 163, 174, 179–80, 210, 265
temperance movement and, 1, 4, 36–37,
50, 60–61, 69–70, 102, 114, 116,
125–26, 127, 128, 130–32, 133, 134,
144, 177, 237
on universal suffrage, 220–21, 223–24,
235–37
Whigs and, 109–10, 112, 113–14, 116, 118,
121, 131
on woman's role in family, 75, 77, 79–80,
82, 92, 97–99, 108–9, 112–13, 130, 175
on woman's sphere, 6, 28, 50, 62–63, 77,

80, 96, 98–99, 116–17, 118–19, 144–45,
175, 177
on woman suffrage (political), 79, 88–89,
103–4, 111, 129–30, 185, 198, 210–11,
220–21, 223–24, 228, 230, 239, 255,
258–59, 260, 268–69
on woman suffrage (school), 2, 5, 111–13,
114, 129–30, 161, 186, 190, 193, 198,
201, 206–7, 227, 238, 255, 259, 265
on women's custody rights, 42, 76, 97–98,
113, 114, 121–22, 125, 137, 191, 196,
197–99, 201
on women's economic and property rights,
2, 41, 75–76, 78, 80–81, 93, 96–98, 106,
108–9, 112, 114, 130, 135, 160–61, 180,
186, 191, 201, 238, 251–52, 255, 260
Nichols, Eliza Ann, 56
Nichols, George Bainbridge (son)
birth of, 56
in California, 245, 246, 248, 250
childhood of, 60, 105, 122, 123, 124–25,
139, 148–49, 170
education of, 122, 123, 124–25, 139, 207
in Kansas, 148–49, 154, 169, 170, 172, 203,
207, 208, 211, 221–22, 239–40, 241, 245
marriage of, 221–22
on parents' relationship, 105
photo of, 57
Nichols, George W. (husband), 83, 113, 132
character of, 52–53
children of, 56–57
death of, 154–55
Democrats and, 52, 62, 64, 70
as editor, 48, 50–51
on education reform, 68
on female editors, 87
in Kansas, 139, 148–49
marriage to Clarina of, 50–53, 103, 105
photo of, 57
religion and, 51–52, 60, 61
on slavery, 70, 72–73
on suffrage, 62
on temperance, 69
Windham County Democrat and, 48,
50–51, 52, 61–62, 64, 105, 136

UNIVERSITY OF WINCHESTER
LIBRARY